OBAMA

BRIAN ABRAMS

OBAMA

AN ORAL HISTORY 2009-2017

Little
a

Published by Little A, New York

www.apub.com

Amazon, the Amazon logo, and Little A are trademarks of Amazon.com, Inc., or its affiliates.

ISBN-13: 9781503951662 (hardcover)
ISBN-10: 1503951669 (hardcover)
ISBN-13: 9781503951655 (paperback)
ISBN-10: 1503951650 (paperback)

Cover design by Faceout Studio, Derek Thornton

Printed in the United States of America

First edition

That's what America understands, that we don't just inherit the world from our parents, but we also borrow it from our children. And that is why, tonight, as we stand here, we have to understand that we have another journey ahead, and it is going to be a journey even more challenging than the one we have already embarked on. There are people today, right now, who are as skeptical about the future as they were at the outset of this campaign . . .

And for those skeptics who believe that we can't accomplish what we set out to accomplish, if our minds are clear and our heart is pure and we believe in a just and merciful God, I say to them: look at this crowd tonight, look at this election today. And I have three words for them. The same three words that we started the campaign, the same three words that we finished the primary, the same three words that are going to carry us, because as Dr. King said, 'The arc of the moral universe is long, but it bends toward justice,' as long as we help bend it that way. I have three words for them. What are those words? Yes, we can.

—Senator-Elect Barack Obama's victory speech, Chicago, November 2, 2004.

PARTICIPANTS

Yohannes Abraham
- Deputy National Political Director, Obama-Biden 2012
- Chief of Staff, Office of Public Engagement and Intergovernmental Affairs, White House (2013–2017)

Rob Andrews
- D-New Jersey, First District, US House of Representatives (1990–2014)

Roy Austin Jr.
- Deputy Assistant Attorney General, Civil Rights Division, US Department of Justice (2010–2014)
- Deputy Assistant to the President for the Office of Urban Affairs, Justice, and Opportunity, Domestic Policy Council, White House (2014–2017)

David Axelrod
- Chief Strategist, Obama for America (2007–2008)
- Senior Advisor to the President, White House (2009–2011)
- Senior Strategist, Obama for America (2011–2012)

Melody Barnes
- Counsel to Senator Edward Kennedy, US Senate Judiciary Committee (1995–2003)
- Director, Domestic Policy Council, White House (2009–2012)

Joel Benenson
- Pollster, Obama-Biden 2008 and Obama-Biden 2012
- Chief Strategist, Clinton-Kaine 2016

Jared Bernstein
- Chief Economist and Economic Policy Advisor, Office of the Vice President (2009–2011)

Jeremy Bird
- Deputy National Director, Organizing for America (2009–2011)
- National Field Director, Obama for America (2011–2012)

Jeffrey Bleich
- Special Counsel to the President, White House (2009)
- Ambassador to Australia, US Department of State (2009–2013)

David Bowen
- Staff Director, US Senate Committee on Health, Education, Labor, and Pensions (HELP) (1999–2010)

Mary Bono
- R-California, Forty-Fourth District, US House of Representatives (1997–2003)
- R-California, Forty-Fifth District, US House of Representatives (2003–2013)

Barbara Boxer
- D-California, US Senate (1993–2017)

Scott Brown
- R-Massachusetts, US Senate (2010–2013)

Carol Browner
- Administrator, Environmental Protection Agency (1993–2001)
- Director, Office of Energy and Climate Change Policy, White House (2009–2011)

Jon Carson
- National Field Director, Obama for America (2007–2008)
- Chief of Staff, Council on Environmental Quality, White House (2009–2011)
- Director, Office of Public Engagement, White House (2011–2013)

Saxby Chambliss
- R-Georgia, Eighth District, US House of Representatives (1995–2003)
- R-Georgia, US Senate (2003–2015)

Arun Chaudhary
- Official White House Videographer (2009–2011)

Ted Chiodo

- Deputy White House Staff Secretary (2009–2014)

Dr. Steven Chu

- US Secretary of Energy (2009–2013)

Martha Coakley

- Attorney General of Massachusetts (D) (2007–2015)

Danielle Crutchfield

- Director of Scheduling, White House (2009–2014)

David Cusack

- Director of Advance, White House (2009–2011)
- Executive Director, Presidential Inaugural Committee (2012–2014)
- Director of Operations, White House (2015–2017)

Kareem Dale

- Associate Director, Office of Public Engagement, White House (2009–2013)

Bill Daley

- US Secretary of Commerce (1997–2000)
- White House Chief of Staff (2011–2012)

Tom Daschle

- D-South Dakota, US Senate (1987–2005)
- Senate Majority Leader (2001–2003); Senate Minority Leader (2003–2005)

Bill Dauster

- Deputy Staff Director and General Counsel, US Senate Finance Committee (2003–2011)
- Deputy Chief of Staff, US Senate Democratic Leader Harry Reid (2011–2017)

Ron Davis

- Police Chief, City of East Palo Alto (2005–2013)
- Director, Community Oriented Policing Services (COPS), US Department of Justice (2013–2017)
- Executive Director, President's Task Force on 21st Century Policing (2014–2017)

Brian Deese
- Special Assistant to the President, National Economic Council, White House (2009–2011)
- Deputy Director, National Economic Council, White House (2011–2013)
- Deputy Director, Office of Management and Budget, White House (2013–2015)
- Senior Advisor to the President, White House (2015–2017)

Tad Devine
- Chief Strategist, Bernie Sanders for President, 2016

John Dingell
- D-Michigan, Sixteenth District, US House of Representatives (1965–2003)
- D-Michigan, Fifteenth District, US House of Representatives (2003–2013)
- D-Michigan, Twelfth District, US House of Representatives (2013–2015)
- Dean, US House of Representatives (1995–2015)

Chris Dodd
- D-Connecticut, Second District, US House of Representatives (1975–1981)
- D-Connecticut, US Senate (1981–2011)
- Chair, US Senate Committee on Banking, Housing, and Urban Affairs (2007–2011)

Jim Douglas
- Governor of Vermont (R) (2003–2011)
- Chair, National Governors Association (2009–2010)

Arne Duncan
- Chief Executive Officer, Chicago Public Schools (2001–2008)
- US Secretary of Education (2009–2015)

Shomik Dutta
- Mid-Atlantic Finance Director, Obama for America (2006–2008)
- Special Assistant to White House Counsel (2009–2010)
- National Finance Consultant, Obama-Biden 2012

Rahm Emanuel
- Senior Advisor to the President, White House (1993–1998)
- D-Illinois, Fifth District, US House of Representatives (2003–2009)
- White House Chief of Staff (2009–2010)
- Mayor of Chicago (2011–)

Jon Favreau

- Director of Speechwriting, White House (2009–2013)

Jonathan Finer

- Special Advisor for Middle East Affairs, Office of the Vice President (2011–2012)
- Deputy Chief of Staff for Policy, Office of the Secretary of State (2013–2014)
- Chief of Staff and Director of Policy Planning, Office of the Secretary of State (2015–2017)

Heather Foster

- Advisor, Office of Public Engagement, White House (2011–2015)

Barney Frank

- D-Massachusetts, Fourth District, US House of Representatives (1981–2013)
- Chair, House Financial Services Committee (2007–2011)

Michael Froman

- Deputy National Security Advisor for International Economic Affairs, National Security Council and National Economic Council, White House (2009–2013)
- US Trade Representative, White House (2013–2017)

Jason Furman

- Deputy Director, National Economic Council, White House (2009–2013)
- Chair, Council of Economic Advisers, White House (2013–2017)

Teddy Goff

- Director of New Media for Battleground States, Obama for America (2007–2008)
- Digital Director, Obama for America (2011–2012)

Scott Goodstein

- External Online Director, Obama for America (2007–2008)

Austan Goolsbee

- Member, Council of Economic Advisers, White House (2009–2010)
- Chair, Council of Economic Advisers, White House (2010–2011)

Ferial Govashiri

- Senior Advisor to the Deputy National Security Advisor, White House (2009–2014)

- Personal Aide to the President of the United States, White House (2014–2017)

Jennifer Granholm
- Governor of Michigan (D) (2003–2011)

Vanita Gupta
- Principal Deputy Assistant Attorney General, Civil Rights Division, US Department of Justice (2014–2017)

Luis Gutiérrez
- D-Illinois, Fourth District, US House of Representatives (1993–)

Seth Harris
- Acting Secretary and Deputy Secretary, US Department of Labor (2009–2014)

Adam Hitchcock
- Special Assistant, Office of the Chief of Staff, White House (2009–2010)
- Chief of Staff, Council of Economic Advisers, White House (2010–2011)

Pete Hoekstra
- R-Michigan, Second District, US House of Representatives (1993–2011)

Brandon Hurlbut
- Deputy Director of Cabinet Affairs, White House (2009)
- Deputy Chief of Staff and Chief of Staff, US Department of Energy (2009–2013)

Valerie Jarrett
- Senior Advisor to the President, White House (2009–2017)
- Director, Office of Public Engagement, White House (2009–2017)

Brad Jenkins
- Associate Director, Office of Public Engagement, White House (2011–2015)

Van Jones
- Special Advisor, Council on Environmental Quality, White House (2009)

Christopher Kang
- Special Assistant to the President for Legislative Affairs, White House (2009–2011)

- Senior Counsel and Special Assistant to the President, White House (2011–2014)
- Deputy Counsel and Deputy Assistant to the President, White House (2014–2015)

Ted Kaufman
- D-Delaware, US Senate (2009–2010)

Cody Keenan
- Presidential Speechwriter, White House (2009–2011)
- Deputy Director of Speechwriting, White House (2011–2013)
- Director of Speechwriting, White House (2013–2017)

Dr. Harold Koh
- Legal Advisor, US Department of State (2009–2013)

James Kvaal
- Special Assistant to the President for Economic Policy, White House (2009–2010)
- Policy Director, Obama for America (2011–2012)
- Deputy Director of Domestic Policy, Domestic Policy Council, White House (2013–2016)

Ben LaBolt
- Deputy Press Secretary, Obama for America (2007–2008)
- Assistant Press Secretary, White House (2009–2010)
- National Press Secretary, Obama for America (2011–2012)

Barbara Lee
- D-California, Ninth District, US House of Representatives (1998–2013)
- D-California, Thirteenth District, US House of Representatives (2013–)

Eric Lesser
- Special Assistant to the Senior Advisor, White House (2009–2011)
- D-Massachusetts, State Senate (2015–)

Jake Levine
- National Advance Staff, Obama for America (2007–2008)
- Policy Analyst, Office of Energy and Climate Change, White House (2009–2010)

Jack Lew
- Director, Office of Management and Budget, White House (2010–2012)
- White House Chief of Staff (2012–2013)
- US Secretary of the Treasury (2013–2017)

Joe Lieberman
- D-Connecticut, US Senate (1989–2006)
- I-Connecticut, US Senate (2006–2013)

Mark Lippert
- Chief of Staff, National Security Council, White House (2009)
- Assistant Secretary of Defense for Asia and Pacific Security Affairs, US Department of Defense (2012–2013)
- Chief of Staff, Office of the Secretary of Defense (2013–2014)
- Ambassador to Republic of Korea, US Department of State (2014–2017)

Josh Lipsky
- Staff Assistant and Associate Director of Press Advance, White House (2009–2011)
- Special Advisor to the Under Secretary of State, US Department of State (2015–2017)

Joe Lockhart
- White House Press Secretary (1998–2000)

Reggie Love
- Special Assistant and Personal Aide to the President, White House (2009–2011)

Nate Lubin
- Writer/Producer, Obama for America (2008)
- Director of Digital Marketing, Obama for America (2011–2012)
- Director, Office of Digital Strategy, White House (2013–2015)

Carolyn Maloney
- D-New York, Fourteenth District, US House of Representatives (1993–2013)
- D-New York, Twelfth District, US House of Representatives (2013–)

Jim Messina
- National Chief of Staff, Obama for America (2007–2008)
- Deputy Chief of Staff for Operations, White House (2009–2011)

- Campaign Manager, Obama for America (2011–2012)

Matthew Miller

- Director, Office of Public Affairs, US Department of Justice (2009–2011)

Tyler Moran

- Policy Director, National Immigration Law Center (2001–2012)
- Deputy Policy Director, Domestic Policy Council, White House (2012–2014)
- Senior Policy Advisor, US Senate Democratic Leader Harry Reid (2014–2017)

Cecilia Muñoz

- Director of Intergovernmental Affairs, White House (2009–2012)
- Director, Domestic Policy Council, White House (2012–2017)

Ben Nelson

- Governor of Nebraska (D) (1991–1999)
- D-Nebraska, US Senate (2001–2013)

Richard Nephew

- Director, National Security Council, White House (2011–2013)
- Principal Deputy Coordinator for Sanctions Policy, US Department of State (2013–2015)

Jackie Norris

- Iowa State Director, Obama for America (2007–2008)
- Chief of Staff to the First Lady, White House (2009)

Glenn Nye

- D-Virginia, Second District, US House of Representatives (2009–2011)

David Ogden

- Deputy Attorney General, US Department of Justice (2009–2010)

Rob O'Donnell

- Press Assistant, Office of Public Affairs, US Department of Justice (2011)
- Director of Broadcast Media, White House (2015–2017)

Darienne Page

- West Wing Receptionist, White House (2009–2010)
- Director, Veterans, Wounded Warriors, and Military Families Outreach, Office of Public Engagement, White House (2010–2013)

Jennifer Palmieri
- Director of Communications, White House (2013–2015)
- Director of Communications, Hillary for America (2015–2016)

Leon Panetta
- Director, Central Intelligence Agency (2009–2011)
- US Secretary of Defense (2011–2013)

Jonathan Pershing
- Deputy Special Envoy for Climate Change, US Department of State (2009–2012)
- Senior Climate Advisor and Principal Deputy Director of the Office of Energy Policy and Systems Analysis, US Department of Energy (2013–2016)
- Special Envoy for Climate Change, US Department of State (2016–2017)

David Plouffe
- Campaign Manager, Obama for America (2007–2008)
- Senior Advisor to the President, White House (2011–2013)

Jen Psaki
- Deputy Communications Director, White House (2009–2011)
- Traveling Press Secretary and Senior Advisor, Obama for America (2012)
- Spokesperson, US Department of State (2013–2015)
- Communications Director, White House (2015–2017)

Steven Rattner
- Lead Advisor, Presidential Task Force on the Auto Industry (2009)

Margaret Richardson
- Counselor to the Attorney General, US Department of Justice (2009–2011)
- Deputy Chief of Staff to the Attorney General, US Department of Justice (2011–2012)
- Chief of Staff to the Attorney General, US Department of Justice (2012–2015)

Dennis Ross
- Senior Director for the Central Region, National Security Council, White House (2009–2011)

Kori Schulman
- Deputy Chief Digital Officer, Office of Digital Strategy, White House (2009–2017)

Allyson Schwartz

- D-Pennsylvania, Thirteenth District, US House of Representatives (2005–2015)

Dan Shapiro

- Senior Director for the Middle East and North Africa, National Security Council, White House (2009)
- Ambassador to Israel, US Department of State (2011–2017)

Nick Shapiro

- Assistant Press Secretary, White House (2009–2011)
- Senior Advisor to the Assistant to the President for Homeland Security and Counterterrorism, White House (2011–2013)
- Deputy Chief of Staff, Central Intelligence Agency (2013–2015)

Wendy Sherman

- Under Secretary of State for Political Affairs, US Department of State (2011–2015)
- Acting Deputy Secretary of State, US Department of State (2014–2015)

Ed Silverman

- Staff Director, US Senate Committee on Banking, Housing, and Urban Affairs (2009–2011)

Pete Souza

- Chief Official White House Photographer (2009–2017)

Gene Sperling

- Director, National Economic Council, White House (1996–2001)
- Counselor to the US Secretary of the Treasury (2009–2010)
- Director, National Economic Council, White House (2011–2014)

Michael Steel

- Press Secretary, House Republican Leader John Boehner (2008–2009)
- Press Secretary, Speaker of the House John Boehner (2011–2015)
- Press Secretary, Vice-Presidential Candidate Paul Ryan (2012)

Stuart Stevens

- Chief Strategist, Romney-Ryan 2012

Todd Stern

- Special Envoy for Climate Change, US Department of State (2009–2016)

Michael Strautmanis
- Chief Counsel and Deputy Chief of Staff, US Senator Barack Obama (2005–2008)
- Office of Governmental Affairs and Public Engagement, White House (2009–2011)
- Counselor for Strategic Engagement, White House (2010–2013)

Mona Sutphen
- Member, National Security Council, White House (1991–2000)
- Deputy Chief of Staff for Policy, White House (2009–2011)

Terry Szuplat
- Presidential Speechwriter, White House (2009–2017)

John Tanner
- D-Tennessee, Eighth District, US House of Representatives (1989–2011)

Trevor Timm
- Executive Director, Freedom of the Press Foundation (2012–)

Chris Van Hollen
- D-Maryland, Eighth District, US House of Representatives (2003–2017)
- D-Maryland, US Senate (2017–)

Tom Vilsack
- Governor of Iowa (D) (1999–2007)
- US Secretary of Agriculture (2009–2017)

Jeff Weaver
- Campaign Manager, Bernie Sanders for President, 2016

Frank Wolf
- R-Virginia, Tenth District, US House of Representatives (1981–2015)

Herbie Ziskend
- Policy Advisor, Office of the Vice President (2009–2011)

2004–2007

As an Illinois state senator serving at the turn of the millennium, Barack Obama gave speeches to the types of crowds one would imagine turning out to watch their state senators. "I invited him to come down and speak," recalled Kareem Dale, who extended his invitation via a student association at the University of Illinois law school. "We probably had about five or ten people in this big, two-hundred-person auditorium. Nobody came. They didn't know him at all."

Yet improbably, one of the state senator's public appearances helped set the table for a successful US Senate bid and, of course, the presidency. Only thirteen seconds of known footage exists of Obama's remarks during a lunchtime rally at Chicago's Federal Plaza. It was October 2002, and George W. Bush was ramping up his ill-fated Iraq War; in Washington, leaders from both parties were largely supportive, but in cities across the country, voices of opposition were rising. At the Chicago rally, signage read "War Is Not An Option" and "Don't Get Bush . No Blank Check." The headliner was the elder Jesse Jackson, the famed civil rights leader and a Chicago fixture.

Obama, then forty-one, was in the early stages of a two-year campaign to reach Capitol Hill. Already he had racked up $10,000 in debt from a failed primary race for US Congress two years prior, to say nothing of the student loans from Harvard Law School that he and his wife, Michelle, carried. His 1995 memoir, *Dreams from My Father*, was greeted with encouraging reviews and discouraging sales—the fate of many a gifted writer. The couple also had two daughters, aged one and four. Political consultant David Axelrod, who was then counseling Obama in an unofficial capacity, once wrote about a conversation around that time in which the candidate feared that if this campaign failed, he would "have to go out and make a living."

On a conference call three days before the Iraq rally, an advisor had warned Obama to soften his criticisms—after all, the majority of Washington supported Bush's hawkish agenda. Obama was unswayed. Transcripts from crude audio show Obama targeting "the armchair weekend warriors" who were devising "a dumb war" and "a rash war" in the Middle East, "a war based not on reason but on passion, not on principle but on politics." While "under no illusions" about the Iraqi president's slaughtering of his own people, Obama affirmed his belief that working with the United Nations to contain Saddam Hussein would result in sending him "the way of all petty dictators"—directly "into the dustbin of history."

After his speech, Obama retreated to his campaign office on South Michigan Avenue. (TV crews swarmed around Jesse Jackson.) Of course, Washington's elite did not exactly follow the wisdom of the young state senator—soon the war buildup began in earnest, with approval from Congress, the media, and big swaths of a bloodthirsty public. The local *Daily Herald* managed to squeeze the "dumb war" line from the speech into its coverage of the Chicago event. It was attributed to "Barak Obama."

Two years later, after the 2004 Democratic National Convention in Boston, newspapers would begin to spell his name correctly.

REGGIE LOVE

Special Assistant and Personal Aide to the President, White House (2009–2011)

I had read *Dreams from My Father* and obviously seen the speech he had given at the convention in '04. I think he was more concerned with the idea of trying to make our country a better place for as many people as possible than the idea of just becoming a US senator.

JOSH LIPSKY

Staff Assistant and Associate Director of Press Advance, White House (2009–2011)
Special Advisor to the Under Secretary of State, US Department of State (2015–2017)

I was a credentials checker at the convention, which was like one of those people who stood outside the door making sure people had the right badges. It was a great gig, because then I got to sneak into the hall myself. I had a friend who told me, "You should watch out for this state senator, he's gonna keynote at the convention, and if you could get his autograph for me, that'd be awesome."

REGGIE LOVE

Issues that were really important to me were also important to him around equality of rights and the ability for people to have access to health care and education. A fifth-grade education in Alabama was significantly different than a fifth-grade education in New York. He saw that and understood that.

JOSH LIPSKY

I saw him backstage and went up to him. "Senator, my friend's a big fan of yours. Could I get your autograph?" And he said, "Sure." Then he asked, "Do you want one, too?" And I ruefully remember saying, "Oh, no. I'm good. Thanks." He just wasn't on my radar at that time. There were so many other things at that convention, and then of course the speech . . . You know the whole history from there.

ERIC LESSER

Special Assistant to the Senior Advisor, White House (2009–2011)
D-Massachusetts, State Senate (2015–)

I was an unpaid intern for CNN that summer and went with the CNN team as a runner, to work at the convention in Boston. I was from Massachusetts, so it was easy. I just stayed with friends and made it work. And I remember I was in the hall when he gave the speech, and I was really kind of mesmerized by it.

DARIENNE PAGE

West Wing Receptionist, White House (2009–2010)
Director, Veterans, Wounded Warriors, and Military Families Outreach,
Office of Public Engagement, White House (2010–2013)

That convention speech pulled together everything I believed in. That you don't have to be a Democrat to be a patriot, or a Republican to be a patriot. We're all Americans. We all love this country. That's what I saw in my military service. It wasn't "everybody's a Republican" or "everybody's black or white." It was this melting pot.

ERIC LESSER

Every night, at the end of the convention, we'd pick up all the trash and grab all the excess banners to get ready for the next morning. You know how everyone raises their rally banners in the crowd with the names of the people? "Kerry-Edwards '04" signs would go up. "Max Cleland" signs would go up or whatever.

Usually they'd all get thrown on the ground, and everyone would go home. But when I ran out to do the nightly cleanup after Obama's speech, not a single Obama sign could be found anywhere. Everybody knew they had just seen something historic.

TOM DASCHLE

D-South Dakota, US Senate (1987–2005)
Senate Majority Leader (2001–2003); Senate Minority Leader (2003–2005)

I got to know Barack in the 2002, 2003 timeframe. As [Senate Democratic] leader, I had to go to Chicago frequently and made it a point to get to know Barack. I was impressed with his oratory. We bonded very early on, and I encouraged him to run [for Senate], and he came out of it very well. I lost and he won. I had a lot of unemployed former staff, including Pete Rouse [and] Denis McDonough. Probably about a dozen members of my staff went to work for him. And so as a result of having so many of my staff there, I felt even more invested in his early years in the Senate.

JOE LIEBERMAN

D-Connecticut, US Senate (1989–2006)
I-Connecticut, US Senate (2006–2013)

There was a program in the Senate to try and encourage, would you believe, more bipartisanship, and one of the ways that somebody could conceive to do that was to ask each incoming senator to choose two mentors, one Republican and one Democrat. Senator Obama chose George Voinovich, Republican of Ohio, and me to be his mentors. And I must say I was both fascinated and, in some sense, flattered. George and I invited Senator Obama to lunch in the Senate Dining Room. We had a really good talk—just about what it's like to be in the Senate and why it's important to try to work across party lines. And I said to George as we walked away, "I don't think this new senator is going to need a lot of mentoring."

TOM DASCHLE

So when he was deciding to run for president, at one point I counseled him. If I'm any indication, sometimes the windows of opportunity open unexpectedly, and I also have long felt that the longer you're in Washington, the less valuable you are nationally, because of people's frustration and cynicism about politics generally. And so I encouraged him to run early in his career rather than run later, because I thought he would be more viable as a candidate without a long record. And he chose to take that advice. I'm sure many people gave it to him.

JOE LIEBERMAN

At the end of '06, Senator Obama said he'd like to come to the office to talk to me. "I'm thinking of running for president for the Democratic nomination and wanted to get your advice." I said that I thought it was wide open. I thought that the odds were probably against him, but who knew? Sometimes, fate and opportunity strike. It was already evident that Hillary was going to run, but I said, "I've done things like this in my own career. I ran for the Senate thinking I had a chance to win. Otherwise I wouldn't have done it." Obviously, I'm not the reason he ran, but that was a fascinating discussion.

LUIS GUTIÉRREZ
D-Illinois, Fourth District, US House of Representatives (1993–)

December of 2006, he called me up: "Can you come down to the office, Luis?" And basically the gist of the conversation was *I'm going to Hawaii, and when I come back I will have decided whether I'm running for president.* He didn't really let me say much. He said, "And I know what you want." Just like that. "You want immigration reform," he said. "We're gonna do it right away. It's going to be a top priority, and you're going to lead on it." That was maybe a twenty-five-minute conversation, but what-the-fuck did I think he was going to become president? He was just, like, my favorite senator, right?

JACKIE NORRIS

Iowa State Director, Obama for America (2007–2008)
Chief of Staff to the First Lady, White House (2009)

I was invited to meet with Mrs. Obama, and I was pretty honest in saying, "Look, I've got three kids." At that point they all were under three, I think. "I'm happy to talk to her about the Iowa caucuses and share my experiences, but I am not doing this long term. I'm teaching." And I had a fabulous meeting. We hit it off. I really appreciated her intellectual grasp and desire to know about the Iowa process, and I came back and I was recalling this story to my classroom. One of my students said to me, "You're always telling us to stand up and fight for what you believe in. What the heck are you doing?" So I turned around the next day and said, "Okay, I'll do it." And that's how I came on as a senior advisor to the campaign, well before announcement time.

REGGIE LOVE

Aside from being the only African American in the Senate, he was, especially when he was running for president, promoted as . . . the one who would help bridge the divide between the Right and the Left. Racial tensions weren't in the headlines back then, so that wasn't the focus. It was antiwar.

HERBIE ZISKEND

Policy Advisor, Office of the Vice President (2009–2011)

I was sitting in my apartment in Ithaca in February of '07 when I watched the announcement from Springfield. I was captivated. I wanted to get involved. I didn't know anybody. My mom and dad didn't work in politics [or] know anyone in politics, so I drove my twenty-year-old car to New Hampshire, a six-hour ride. I basically just showed up. They gave me spreadsheets to enter people's names into, and I was just sitting in the corner of a mostly empty office in Manchester. I ended up skipping a bunch of school my senior year, traveling across New Hampshire, and helping set up events for Obama.

TEDDY GOFF

Director of New Media for Battleground States, Obama for America (2007–2008)
Digital Director, Obama for America (2011–2012)

He started running on February 10. I started on the campaign not long after and had a story that was fairly typical of the kids who graduated college in '06 and '07. I had been volunteering from my dorm room for the second semester of my senior year. Then I graduated and moved directly to Chicago.

JOEL BENENSON

Pollster, Obama-Biden 2008 and Obama-Biden 2012
Chief Strategist, Clinton-Kaine 2016

I started polling for him in 2007 in the primaries. I was one of the first people Axelrod called and asked to be part of the team. He said he wanted people with an "insurgent mentality." I thought it was such a great descriptor. He said because, you know, Senator Obama, at that point, was obviously going to be the insurgent candidate, even within the Democratic Party.

JEREMY BIRD

Deputy National Director, Organizing for America (2009–2011)
National Field Director, Obama for America (2011–2012)

I had come into politics through community organizing and building grassroots support at the local level. I'd worked on '04 for Howard Dean and then John Kerry and had basically disavowed presidential campaigns. But when I read *Dreams from My Father*, about being an organizer on the South Side, it really struck me that that's the kind of person I wanted in the White House— somebody who understood what it was like to live the American dream, but also understood what it was like to sit down with people who were trying to get asbestos out of their housing projects. So I thought I'd work for him.

SHOMIK DUTTA

Mid-Atlantic Finance Director, Obama for America (2006–2008)
Special Assistant to White House Counsel (2009–2010)
National Finance Consultant, Obama-Biden 2012

My pitch to the Obama campaign was, "The Clinton network is going to take all the establishment [donors]. What you need is someone who really understands the mid-Atlantic—the less established donors, the real-estate-developer folks who are not national donors and whom you can build a network from. I'm the guy to do that." I said that if I raised $5 million in the first month they had to make me a mid-Atlantic finance director. I ended up raising the $5 million and became the shithead twenty-three-year-old who ran the mid-Atlantic, which was pretty exciting.

HERBIE ZISKEND

Hillary was a big favorite to win, and I ended up getting to know Obama and the senior team well because I was just driving around with them in vans across New Hampshire. I'd walk into a coffee shop. I'd scan the room. I'd walk back out and say, "Hey, Senator, you're going to see the mayor of Keene on the left. You're gonna see this woman in the corner on the right—that's his niece." I got to know the team well. If Axelrod spilled ketchup on his shirt in Indiana, I'd run to the store and grab him a new shirt at Target. I picked up sandwiches and stocked the vans with candy. When they needed an extra person on the basketball court, I would play. I would run in to the events before Obama and hang the "Hope" or the "Change" signs on the podium, and I was in heaven.

ERIC LESSER

There was a crew of us from Cambridge that basically went up every weekend to help out. I just kind of moved to New Hampshire and [worked on the scheduling and] advance [team] for a while. I took a few trips to Iowa and eventually settled as one of the permanent advance staffers.

HERBIE ZISKEND

I met Eric on a connecting flight to Des Moines. He had just graduated from Harvard, and I had just graduated from Cornell. We were both so idealistic and drawn to Obama and the message that he was conveying and what he represented, but this was early on. He was behind in the polls. We were in Iowa in, like, middle-school gyms or at farms in Independence with eighty people.

SHOMIK DUTTA

I couldn't tell you the number of lawyers and folks I reached out to who would say, "You know, you're a good kid. I will make sure there's a job for you in the Clinton administration." There was this air of expectancy that never went away on them, which I found, of course, appalling.

BRANDON HURLBUT
Deputy Director of Cabinet Affairs, White House (2009)
Deputy Chief of Staff and Chief of Staff, US Department of Energy (2009–2013)

Bill Clinton was a legend in New Hampshire. That's where the "Comeback Kid" story happened. We would always bump up against that. We were always down in the polls in New Hampshire. We started working weekends very early in the process. If you were not in the campaign office on Sunday, April of 2007, or May, when you're thirty points down in the polls, people were asking questions.

ERIC LESSER

At this stage of the campaign, the events were small. There's very little security. There's very little hoopla. We were literally planning house parties in living rooms and stops at ice-cream parlors—visits to VFW halls.

HERBIE ZISKEND

Campaigning is hard. You're not really sleeping much. You're eating terrible food. But you're seeing towns across the country that you'd normally never go to. You wouldn't go to Kokomo, Indiana, or Toledo, Ohio, or Butte, Montana. And so this incredible bond was created, especially because Obama was an underdog, and to be part of that team from the beginning and watch it grow, extraordinary relationships were formed.

DAVID AXELROD

Chief Strategist, Obama for America (2007–2008)
Senior Advisor to the President, White House (2009–2011)
Senior Strategist, Obama for America (2011–2012)

Obama was, by his own admission, not a very good candidate for the first months of the campaign, and, you know, at one point actually said, "I'm not a good candidate now, but I will learn to be a good candidate. Just give me a little time here." You know, the enthusiasm that was out there for him, and the resources that we were able to raise—grassroots contributions, propelling a lot of it—gave him the time.

JEREMY BIRD

I was the field director down in South Carolina. No one knew how to pronounce his name. We were down massively with African American voters. We were losing with African American women by like forty points, and as people started to learn who we were, there was a feeling: *Well, he can't win. Even if I like what I'm hearing, I'm not sure I'm going to get behind him.*

JIM MESSINA

National Chief of Staff, Obama for America (2007–2008)
Deputy Chief of Staff for Operations, White House (2009–2011)
Campaign Manager, Obama for America (2011–2012)

Between her and her husband, Clinton had been organizing the early states for forever. The traditional Democratic machine was completely sewn up. It forced Senator Obama to develop this new model and find new people. At the beginning, the traditional establishments in places like Ohio, Iowa, and New Hampshire, and, like, DC operatives, they all had gone to Clinton.

JEREMY BIRD

We didn't have the political establishment with us. We had almost no elected officials supporting us from the beginning. We didn't have the ministers on board. So we built something that was incredibly ambitious. We ran a real community-organizing plan. The people who were with us were *really* with us. On the staff side they were young and really committed to him. Then the volunteers signed up on the website, had come to our rallies, and we're recognizing pretty early on that these people were ready for this guy. I didn't see that kind of energy in other campaigns.

JON CARSON

National Field Director, Obama for America (2007–2008)
Chief of Staff, Council on Environmental Quality, White House (2009–2011)
Director, Office of Public Engagement, White House (2011–2013)

We had a level of empowerment and responsibility to these supervolunteers, the likes of which I'd never done before. We gave them access to the voter files. We gave them login accounts. This was met with all sorts of worries that people would corrupt the data. We never really saw that at scale, and taking that leap of faith was the only real way to tap into the true energy that was out there.

JEREMY BIRD

We hired a lot of people who had never worked on any campaign. The people I had the most trouble with were the people who had worked on campaigns before. They expected something different, but we flipped that model. We were saying, "It's not going to be about how many voters that *you* as an organizer called today. It's going to be about how many people we can recruit to be volunteer leaders." The only way we were going to get to scale was if [our message] came from people that [the voters] knew, trusted, and respected. If it got in the barbershops, the beauty salons, the churches, and the schools, that's actually how we'd build this thing.

SETH HARRIS

Acting Secretary and Deputy Secretary, US Department of Labor (2009–2014)

Empowerment, that's exactly what the labor movement's all about. He talked about that all the time. "Yes we can" was the punch line, but there were paragraphs leading up to that about how *The power is in you, it's not in me.* That distinguished him from the top-down, longtime establishment, well-connected-at-the-elite-and-opinion-leader-level that then Senator Clinton had, and that would *really* distinguish him from George Bush and John McCain. They would never have used that kind of rhetoric and language.

JACKIE NORRIS

I was a huge believer in the role that our organizers played. These were typically kids, eighteen to twenty-three years old, getting paid next to nothing. It's door-to-door salesmanship. And they all ran the same circuit—Clinton, Edwards, Obama. Every candidate had their field organizer at every soup supper and wingding. They really were all in the same boat doing the same thing . . . The tension, I think it's fair to say, was more around the Edwards folks, because we saw them as a competitor for caucus voters.

TEDDY GOFF

I had much more distaste for John Edwards than I did for Clinton. I kind of liked the Clintons. That was how it was for the longest time, and then it started to get ugly as the [Iowa] caucus happened and as the South Carolina primary, in particular, happened. It was really fairly friendly for all of 2007, but it got worse.

DAVID PLOUFFE

Campaign Manager, Obama for America (2007–2008)
Senior Advisor to the President, White House (2011–2013)

Every quarter, candidates had to release how much money they raised, and we had an amazingly strong first quarter. Our suspicion was we either outraised Clinton or it would be close, and we knew that would be seen as a big moment.

And so we decided not to [immediately] put our numbers out. Generally if you have a good number you wanna rush it out there to prove your viability, and we thought that what would be really interesting [would be] to let the Clinton people go first. They'd announce their money, and then we'd come in over top of it and completely drown them out.

SHOMIK DUTTA

Those days were my favorite. We ended up beating Hillary Clinton in the first [six months] of fundraising 2007, which really put us on the map.

JIM MESSINA

Everyone expected Clinton to have a huge fundraising number. All of Washington was going, *Oh my God, he might be for real.*

DAVID PLOUFFE

More often than not, when we showed discretion and played the chess game out a little bit, as opposed to the traditional checkers game, we were better off for it.

ADAM HITCHCOCK
Special Assistant, Office of the Chief of Staff, White House (2009–2010)
Chief of Staff, Council of Economic Advisers, White House (2010–2011)

We knew that if we lost Iowa, it was over. And we knew that if we won Iowa, that just meant this thing would be drawn out and could possibly go all the way through all the primaries . . . At that point we were down in Iowa. The polling showed us way behind Hillary, and people started to say, "Oh, the strategy isn't working."

SHOMIK DUTTA

You remember Punjab-gate? We dropped an opposition-research memo on Hillary for being too close with an Indian donor, and someone in the research shop had put "Clinton (D-Punjab)" instead of "(D-NY)." The senator was in the air at the time. He hadn't seen or approved the memo, but it became an uproar, of course, because a *New York Times* reporter leaked the memo, which he was given on background. I think it was Patrick Healy. So the president landed, heard about this, was furious—canceled meetings. I was in the fundraising office across the street from the Hart Senate Building and got a call: "Senator's coming in two minutes." He was not on the schedule. I thought I was going to get fired because I was a superaggressive fundraiser . . . I had sort of an impression in mind of what I needed to be. I would hang up on donors, yell and curse, do whatever I had to do to raise money.

BRAD JENKINS
Associate Director, Office of Public Engagement, White House (2011–2015)

This was early '07 when Hillary was up like thirty points.

SHOMIK DUTTA

I was nervous as hell. I went downstairs to open the office. The senator looked at me. "Upstairs, right now." And he said, "Bring Ravi Gupta, too." Ravi was my assistant at the time, another Indian guy who had taken off a couple years of Yale Law School to work on the campaign. I was like, *Shit. He's gonna clean house.* And so we went up there and he said, "Guys, I just wanted to stop by to apologize to the two of you for this memo that came out. I know that you have families and friends in the community, and I don't want them to think any less of you or what this campaign stands for because of something like this." Ravi and I looked at each other like, *What? You never have to apologize to us for anything.*

VALERIE JARRETT
Senior Advisor to the President, White House (2009–2017)
Director, Office of Public Engagement, White House (2009–2017)

He had been spending a lot of time out on the campaign trail and I think was feeling a bit disconnected. He wanted to make sure the team was running the kind of campaign that he wanted them to run, and they weren't making big decisions without him being in the loop. In retrospect, [it was] very natural that the folks at headquarters were working 24/7 and cranking out events, fundraisers, and rallies. They just had their heads down, and I think the purpose of the [July 17] dinner [senior meeting at my Chicago town house] was for him to say, *This has to be my campaign and I have to own it if I'm going to enjoy it. And if I'm not enjoying it, then that's going to show.*

MICHAEL STRAUTMANIS
Chief Counsel and Deputy Chief of Staff, US Senator Barack Obama (2005–2008)
Office of Governmental Affairs and Public Engagement, White House (2009–2011)
Counselor for Strategic Engagement, White House (2010–2013)

Valerie was somebody who was Michelle and Barack Obama's mentor, and they were mine. Valerie was kind of one level above, when we were in Chicago, and wasn't somebody I had dealt with that much. But . . . as the campaign began, we both found that we really had the same mind-set. We wanted to see them be successful.

VALERIE JARRETT

The dinner began his seizing control of the tempo, and the momentum turned around. I also think it gave him an opportunity to encourage the team to bring more people into the tent. That's hard to do when you're going 180 miles an hour. So it was kind of a "Pause" button, and going forward from there he felt like it was his campaign. I'm not sure he owned it as much as he wanted to, or needed to, before that dinner.

DAVID AXELROD

There was a swing through Iowa in the summer of 2007 where I really felt like he was hitting his stride.

SHOMIK DUTTA

One of the things that made the senator unique was he was so normal, that he would still engage in normal, sort of lowbrow things. There was this early organizer in Iowa. He came from Texas, and the [senator pulled] him aside. "I love you. I know you're doing a great job. Thank you for all these volunteer pull-asides. You're introducing all these supervolunteers to me. It's important." And the [senator] said, "But are you sure that every volunteer from Texas is a twenty-two-year-old blonde girl named Ashley?"

DAVID AXELROD

What distinguished him from the others became more central to his presentation. You know, campaigns are exercises in market differentiation, and the clearer and more distinct your message is, the better you're going to do.

SETH HARRIS

The war was one of the means by which Senator Obama distinguished himself from then Senator Clinton. She voted for the war. He had spoken out against the war. It was a very important distinguishing characteristic.

ARUN CHAUDHARY
Official White House Videographer (2009–2011)

On foreign policy, they had an absolutely binary difference. You had someone who was, from the beginning, very much opposed to the Iraq War, and another candidate who had voted for it and who had been somewhat unwilling to even publicly commit to its having been a mistake. The idea that we could have a president who was going to come into office being antiwar, especially being anti this stupid war that we got ourselves involved in, meant that I was 100 percent behind him from the beginning.

JOE LIEBERMAN

I felt we did the right thing going into Iraq. It wasn't a 100 percent easy call. We totally messed it up after we overthrew Saddam, but now that we were there and the place was bleeding, if we just walked away, it would have diminished our strength in the world and made the world more dangerous for us and everybody else.

DAVID AXELROD

There were moments that seemed, to the conventional scorekeepers, [to be] setbacks, that actually helped propel him forward, both in his own mind and in the larger contest. One was this YouTube-sponsored debate in South Carolina in which he got a question about whether he would sit down with hostile leaders—Castro, Ahmadinejad, and so on—and he said he would, to advance America's agenda. His opponents jumped on him for being naive, for coddling dictators and so on, and he felt very strongly about this.

MARK LIPPERT
Chief of Staff, National Security Council, White House (2009)
Assistant Secretary of Defense for Asia and Pacific Security
Affairs, US Department of Defense (2012–2013)
Chief of Staff, Office of the Secretary of Defense (2013–2014)
Ambassador to Republic of Korea, US Department of State (2014–2017)

He went more off the script than anybody anticipated, but he believed it and delivered on it. It wasn't as though you had a candidate who tried to simply recall talking points. It was someone clearly comfortable with the subject matter, and I think that came through. This was a guy who was very comfortable and, therefore, combined with his analytics skills and strong intellect, was well suited to have a strong grasp of foreign policy.

DAVID AXELROD

It was very rare for him to get on our morning strategy calls. The next morning, after the debate, I was in a car with him and he said, "I wanna get on this call." And he got on the call, and he said, "I don't want anybody backing off one inch from what I said. I meant what I said." And he said, "I think this notion that, you know, we're somehow punishing these people by not being willing to talk to them is not what I believe. I don't think it's smart."

DAN SHAPIRO
Senior Director for the Middle East and North Africa,
National Security Council, White House (2009)
Ambassador to Israel, US Department of State (2011–2017)

It's true that he didn't have years of deep experience dealing with foreign policy, although he had spent a few years on the [Senate] Foreign Relations Committee. He obviously had an interest in the Middle East, including Israeli-Palestinian peace and issues surrounding the Iraq War, how it started, and how it should end.

DAVID AXELROD

This debate continued through the summer. It came up several times. He was steadfast in his belief, and it gave him a chance to say, you know, *The same people who are saying this are the people who thought invading Iraq was a good idea.* I remember him saying, "This helps me. It's crystallized in my mind what my place in this campaign is, why I'm doing this."

DAN SHAPIRO

I always found that I was dealing with a person whose judgment and analytical abilities were superior to anybody else's in the room. I always felt I had to be at the top of my game, because there was a good chance that he'd already thought of the arguments—and maybe the counterarguments—that we needed to be thinking about. He'd have a theory of the case for what he was trying to do.

BEN LABOLT

Deputy Press Secretary, Obama for America (2007–2008)
Assistant Press Secretary, White House (2009–2010)
National Press Secretary, Obama for America (2011–2012)

I dealt with a lot of the biographical stories, because then Senator Obama would sit down for these long pieces in the Senate office with reporters from the *Chicago Tribune* and magazines, but I wasn't really in a rapid-response capacity until I was spokesman on the campaign in August. That's where I worked closely with the self-research team to bat down false rumors and fight smears. These false email chains had been going around—the original "fake news."

DAN SHAPIRO

Every day there was some new crazy false rumor, and every day we were out there playing Whack-a-Mole. At some point you said, "We'll convince those who want to be convinced," and at some point people didn't need to be convinced because they started to see through the silliness, and you'd never convince the people who didn't want to be convinced.

BEN LABOLT

Some of this started in crazy corners of the internet. It wasn't necessarily well organized. A whole right-wing publishing world leaned into it. So we mounted a full-scale effort to fight back. Everybody on the campaign had learned the lessons of 2004—not responding to the Swift Boat attacks because the view at the time was that [responding] would elevate [the story] to a level that it didn't deserve. We knew this could be damaging and we had a team to fight back every day.

LUIS GUTIÉRREZ

It was nothing but blatant racism in America.

BEN LABOLT

In some ways the biggest threat to Obama's candidacy was because he was undefined, the candidacy was a whiteboard. So voters could fill in their aspirations on the whiteboard, but it also meant that if somebody's worst fears took hold, there was just as much of a chance for that to stick because he hadn't been on the national stage for a particularly long time . . . It wasn't only the madrassa allegation.[1] The front page of the *New York Times* claimed that he exaggerated his drug use in *Dreams from My Father* for political gain, which I thought was one of the craziest stories of the entire campaign.

BRANDON HURLBUT

A brick was thrown through one of our campaign-office windows with the N-word on it, and in central Pennsylvania, our field staff was hearing some ugly things. There was always this fear in the back of our minds that people could tell the pollsters one thing, but what would they do when no one's watching in that voting booth?

BEN LABOLT

It's all about convincing people that Obama represented the Other, that he wasn't truly American, that he didn't believe in American exceptionalism. You know, there was really a subterranean campaign to try and discredit him and raise doubts about his biography, and so we needed to mount a significant effort to make sure that people understood what his values were, who he was, where he came from, and, therefore, why he could lead the country. Campaigns are just as much about values as they are about policy.

---

1   Erroneous stories about Obama's identity date as far back as 2004, when a crackpot gained traction with the claim that the senator was "a Muslim who has concealed his religion." More falsehoods sprung from the presidential primary when the conservative *Insight* magazine suggested the candidate was indoctrinated in Islamic fundamentalism as a child at an Indonesian school.

DAVID AXELROD

Most people would agree that the real sort of watershed moment was the [Iowa] Jefferson-Jackson dinner in the fall of 2007. He really laid out his rationale, and it was an assault on the status quo. It was an assault on the politics of Washington, and he really differentiated himself from Hillary, and he did it on the most dramatic stage. The J-J dinner is, you know, part party fundraiser, part Roman Colosseum. It's held in a big arena, and the donors are at tables on the floor, and then supporters are in the stands of this arena. It is a happening, and it is a widely watched and covered event, and each candidate got, I think, eleven minutes to speak. No notes. No teleprompter.

JACKIE NORRIS

The Jefferson-Jackson political dinner . . . you knew that meant something. It meant they're going to show up on caucus night. When you started seeing such enthusiasm, acceptance, and excitement, you just knew that the state seemed ready for him.

DAVID AXELROD

He would spend each night in his room internalizing the speech, because he knew he wouldn't have any notes. And he was the last speaker of the night. All the other candidates had spoken. Hillary spoke right before him, and when he spoke, you could just feel the electricity in the room. And you could see how deflated her forces were after the speech. It was clear that he really laid down a rationale and distinguished himself.

SCOTT GOODSTEIN
External Online Director, Obama for America (2007–2008)

Mark Penn, Clinton's pollster, famously said Obama's campaign supporters "look like Facebook," that they're all young kids and Facebook was not going to show up and vote, and Facebook kids came out of the woodwork. They organized in Iowa and were getting new kids to volunteer, putting real efforts and energy in.

BRANDON HURLBUT

There always was this sort of romance and magic to Iowa, a connection that we didn't have in New Hampshire. I went to a labor event in Portsmouth with the candidate, maybe a couple months out from the [Iowa] caucus, and I remember him saying to me, "I'm going to win Iowa." He was so confident, and at the time, he wasn't leading in the polls. Edwards was going strong. Hillary was going strong. So this was not backed up by data. "I just know I'm going to win Iowa. I can feel it happening on the ground, and you guys need to get it done in New Hampshire, because I'm coming to New Hampshire with a victory."

JOE LIEBERMAN

I was really friendly with Obama and had been friendly with the Clintons forever, going back to their days at Yale Law School. Neither of them asked for my support, and so McCain called me somewhere before Thanksgiving in 2007. His basic pitch was, "I'm going to ask you a question, and if you can't do it, don't worry about it. It's never going to affect our friendship. We're going to be friends forever." He said, for him, his fate would be decided in New Hampshire. If he could surprise in New Hampshire, he had a chance to win the [Republican] nomination. And he said, "You know, in New Hampshire, independents can vote, and you're Mr. Independent. You could really help if you would endorse me publicly." And I thought, *What the hell? McCain is my buddy. I got reelected as an independent. To that extent, I'm a little free of party-loyalty concerns. The two Democrats are not asking for my support. I know that McCain can be a good president, and I'm going to do it.*

2008

On January 3, 2008, Iowa caucus voters cast their ballots for the Democratic and Republican nominees. Meanwhile, in New Hampshire, advance staffer Herbie Ziskend had been prepping inside the gymnasium of Nashua High School North, the venue for Barack Obama's Saturday rally, while watching the returns on a small TV. "It was this *Oh my goodness, he may actually become president* moment," Ziskend said. "Suddenly the meaning of my work in that gym in Nashua changed."

In Iowa, Obama had clinched a resounding victory. His 37.6 percent delegate margin bested his contenders'—with John Edwards at 29.8 percent and Hillary Clinton at 29.5 percent—likely on account of his campaign's months-long commitment to winning over independents and young voters in one of the whitest flyover states, which resulted in something north of 239,000 voters turning out for an election that in 2004 had produced somewhere around 124,000. "I just always knew," Jackie Norris recalled. "I just knew that young people, if they opened their minds and heard him, something would ignite." For comparison, among the approximately 108,000 Republican voters who walked into Iowa precincts that Thursday, 34 percent voted for former Arkansas governor Mike Huckabee, while former Massachusetts governor Mitt Romney trailed with 25 percent of the vote. Senator John McCain came in fourth behind Fred D. Thompson—a former Tennessee senator probably best known for his acting work in *Die Hard 2* and *Law & Order*—with 13 percent of the vote. Which is to say, as far as turnout went, Obama was already blowing the other side out of the water.

Former Iowa governor Tom Vilsack, a Clinton supporter, recalled "seeing people [he] had never seen before" at his own precinct, Ward One in Mount

Pleasant, a town with a population of around 8,700. "Under normal circumstances the number of people who showed up for [Clinton] would have been sufficient," he said. "But it was a year in which [Obama] basically encouraged people who had never been involved in politics before to get involved. They came in droves."

At his victory speech, Senator Obama congratulated his supporters at Des Moines's Hy-Vee Hall for achieving "what the cynics said we couldn't," bolstering this comparative outsider, who had been criticized for a lack of government experience and refusing to pay credence to Washington's power structure. Senator Edward Kennedy recognized that these characteristics should not be perceived as liabilities. He had spent months being courted by both the Obama and Clinton camps. As First Lady, Clinton had assisted Kennedy in passing the 1997 State Children's Health Insurance Program; he was a longtime ally of hers. But the Lion of the Senate, who had assumed his Massachusetts seat after his brother moved into the White House four decades prior, eventually joined his brother's daughter, Caroline, in endorsing Obama.

"There was another time, when another young candidate was running for president and challenging America to cross a new frontier," Senator Kennedy reminded the students of American University. "He faced public criticism from the preceding Democratic president, who was widely respected in the party. Harry Truman said we needed 'someone with greater experience' . . . and John Kennedy replied, 'The world is changing. The old ways will not do . . . It is time for a new generation of leadership.'"

TOM VILSACK
Governor of Iowa (D) (1999–2007)
US Secretary of Agriculture (2009–2017)

I often said that Hillary didn't lose that caucus—Obama won it. There's a difference. He understood that he had to reach beyond the traditional Democratic base to be successful. He invested his time and developed an almost-personal relationship with these folks, where they felt an obligation to show up for him. So he and his team did a tremendous job, and they deserved to win.

SCOTT GOODSTEIN

Thousands of kids showed up, [and] Mark Penn had to eat some of his words. Obama killed it.

BRANDON HURLBUT

It was a sprint, like five days until the New Hampshire primary, and he was campaigning across the state. You had these rallies where there was so much energy, this injection of enthusiasm, and it quickly unraveled. The voters were [of] a different breed. They felt like their jobs were to kick the tires on these candidates and meet them up close—really vet them for the country. I think many of them went into the voting booth and thought, *You know what? We're not going to hand it to this guy. We need to see him get tested a little bit more and make sure he earns it.* So there was a backlash. It was a shocking defeat.

HERBIE ZISKEND

Obama had won Iowa. Hillary had won New Hampshire. They split in Nevada,[2] and we went across these core towns and cities in South Carolina in the week leading up to the primary, and it was like the Messiah had come. South Carolina was the first state to secede from the Union, and here we are with this African American candidate, and there was such buzz and such excitement. People were holding up their babies on the street as the motorcade went by.

JEREMY BIRD

People saw the difference. Governor Hodges and Joe Erwin, a businessman from Greenville, as they recognized that we were getting grassroots volunteers and picking up steam, they started to come on board. It was Joe Erwin and Governor Hodges who said, *This is a campaign that is uniting the Democratic Party in ways that hadn't been the case in the past.*

HERBIE ZISKEND

And Obama ended up winning South Carolina by twenty-eight points.

BRANDON HURLBUT

Two days before Super Tuesday,[3] he came to Wilmington [Delaware] and did a rally in Rodney Square. It was cold, February on the East Coast. And we jammed that place. It was like twenty-five thousand people, and he delivered an amazing speech. And we won Delaware by eleven points. It was a twenty-two-point swing in one month.

---

2   Clinton technically won the Nevada caucuses, beating Senator Obama in the popular vote 51 percent to 45 percent. However, Obama picked up more delegates—thirteen to Clinton's twelve.

3   February 5, 2008.

JOEL BENENSON

I don't remember any discussions about Delaware being important.

DAVID PLOUFFE

Super Tuesday was the day we always feared. The more the numbers came in, and the states got called, Clinton was viewed to have been the victor by many in the media because she won the marquee states—the Californias and the New Yorks—but it was clear deep into the morning that we were actually going to come out on top in terms of the delegate distribution.

JOEL BENENSON

The currency of winning the nomination was delegates. It didn't matter how many states you won. It mattered if you won a majority of the delegates. Our whole campaign was designed around that. If you go back and look at Super Tuesday, by the way, we actually split the states pretty evenly.

DAVID PLOUFFE

And we knew we had a good ten or eleven states to come in the rest of February—the Virginias and the Wisconsins and the Marylands. So that was really the first time, I think, I certainly felt comfortable. And I told Senator Obama that morning—meaning like two in the morning—that, all things being equal, the nomination was ours. We were no longer the plucky underdog. Now, obviously, we endured a lot of pain during that period.

VALERIE JARRETT

We all thought that Reverend Wright was an existential threat to the campaign, and a lot of tried-and-true supporters didn't understand how someone as committed to an inclusive big tent as Barack Obama could have this man as his pastor. They were really hurt and worried. Some were angry and were looking for a better understanding.

DAVID PLOUFFE

[ABC News] started airing [Wright's sermons] and then they were basically everywhere. I mean, Jeremiah Wright's name ID within forty-eight hours of that incident was probably close to 80 or 90 percent. You couldn't turn on a computer, TV, [or] open a newspaper without seeing Reverend Wright. It was one of those moments that went from zero to a hundred in a second. It was an existential crisis. Because if we didn't come out the other side whole, superdelegates, in particular, would have had questions about us.

DAVID AXELROD

By then we were en route to the nomination and the question was: Would we be knocked off that path?

MICHAEL STRAUTMANIS

I watched the Jeremiah Wright thing with horror in my Senate office. [Obama] needed to explain it to people. He was new on the national scene. They saw what they thought was really authentic about the [senator], and then they saw these videos from his pastor.[4] It didn't really add up.

DAVID PLOUFFE

[The Clinton campaign] always denied it. We always assumed it was them. I don't think we ever verified that, but you can't really navel-gaze about why something happened to you. You just have to figure out how to deal with it.

---

4   Arguably the most notorious excerpt was during the forty-minute sermon "Confusing God and Government," recorded on April 13, 2003. Delivered inside Chicago's Trinity United Church of Christ, Wright admonished the United States for its systemic oppression of the African American community. "The government gives them the drugs, builds bigger prisons, passes a three-strike law, and then wants us to sing 'God Bless America.' No, no, no—not 'God Bless America.' God damn America! That's in the Bible—for killing innocent people! God damn America for treating her citizens as less than human! God damn America as long as she tries to act like she is God and she is supreme!"

JON FAVREAU

Director of Speechwriting, White House (2009–2013)

I learned on a Saturday-morning call with senior advisors that Obama wanted to give a speech that Tuesday . . . That was also the day that we moved into our big group house in Chicago in Lincoln Park, and I was the first one to move in. So I was in this large house by myself Saturday night. I didn't even know that we had all the electricity on, but I was sitting there by myself and Barack Obama called at ten o'clock. He'd been on the campaign trail all day, and I remember just first asking how he was doing. Because he had been going through this hell for the last couple days with Reverend Wright, and he said, "You know, this is what you have to do when you run for president. People deserve an explanation, and I want to make this a moment where I can talk about something bigger."

VALERIE JARRETT

When President Obama spoke from his heart, people trusted him. And I thought that he was going to be very able to explain, in human, authentic terms, the broader context of the black church, the black experience, and he took that issue and he turned it, I think, into a very optimistic and inclusive conversation about race and himself and the lives of his family members.

JON FAVREAU

He said, "I'm going to give you stream-of-consciousness thoughts and then hopefully you can turn them into a draft." And he gave me the most detailed outline of a speech that I could have imagined. "One, this. One-A, this. Two, this. Two-B, this." He just kind of went through the whole thing, [and before] I got off the phone, he said, "Why don't you go work on a draft and get me something tomorrow night before I put the girls to bed, and I'll work on it from there." I was pretty freaked out by the timeline. It was Saint Paddy's Day, so the first thing I did was meet everyone and have a beer to calm myself down. Then I went home early and went to bed. I woke up at six a.m., went to the Starbucks in Chicago, and wrote all day long.

VALERIE JARRETT

You have to meet people where they are, and you have to take 'em by the hand and lead them to where you are. In order to do that, they have to believe that you are authentic, and for leaders who are expecting to galvanize a state or a country, that trust, that covenant, means that they believe you have their best interests at heart. That's not always the case with politicians.

JON FAVREAU

I sent it to him that night, and at like four a.m. Monday morning, he emailed me back a draft that was all Track Changes. You couldn't see too much of mine. The stuff I wrote were the lines that almost any politician could have delivered about race. The historical stuff at the beginning and the flowery stuff, I had all that. But the stuff that he wrote were lines like "I can no more disown him than I can my white grandmother." Like, that's not a line that any speechwriter would give their boss.

MICHAEL STRAUTMANIS

It's gonna sound cliché, but one of the things that I always admired about Barack was he believed in the fundamental wisdom and goodness of people. There're people who're very cynical about politics. There're people who have been really hurt and damaged, whether it be through race relations, or economic policies, or through foreign policy, who maybe see that as naive, but he believed in it. I think he decided he was going to bet on himself.

JON FAVREAU

All day Monday I worked on his edits, and by that I mean not so much with the content, but shaping it, cutting it—making sure that it was a tight speech. And then I gave it back to him Monday night, and then, again, I got a draft from him at four in the morning that Tuesday—the morning he was giving the speech—and that draft was emailed to me, Plouffe, Axe, and Valerie. "No one's allowed to touch the content. Favs is allowed to edit it for style, tone, grammar. Maybe do some cuts, but other than that, this is what I want to say."

LUIS GUTIÉRREZ

He threw his grandma under the bus! Remember he said something like [how his] grandma would walk across the street and if she saw a black person, would use derogatory language to describe them.[5] Basically use the N-word, right? That's what he said about his grandmother. So, listen. I know all about racism, and I gotta tell you, man, as a grandfather, raising my grandson, you wanna stab me in the heart? Have my grandson tell you some mean, nasty things about Grandma. How're you gonna throw Grandma under the bus? But that's what Obama did, because that's the place Obama felt he was in. That he had to describe the situation as such—that he had white grandparents and he had a white mother.

VALERIE JARRETT

That speech was a good example of where he just opened himself up and said, *Here I am. Here's what I stand for. Here's my life experience. This was why I chose that church. This was what brought Reverend Wright into my life and this was why I'm now moving in a different direction.* There was no spin on the ball. It was all heart.

JON FAVREAU

I remember he delivered the speech and he called me right after: "Um, I don't know if I can be elected president saying the things I did about race today, but

---

5   "I can no more disown him than I can disown the black community. I can no more disown him than I can disown my white grandmother—a woman who helped raise me, a woman who sacrificed again and again for me, a woman who loves me as much as she loves anything in this world, but a woman who once confessed her fear of black men who passed her by on the street, and who, on more than one occasion, has uttered racial or ethnic stereotypes that made me cringe. These people are part of me. And they are part of America, this country that I love."

I also know that I don't deserve to be elected if I was too afraid to say them in the first place."

DAVID AXELROD

I think of presidential races as essentially very long auditions for the hardest job on the planet, and part of what you measure is how people do under pressure, and under enormous pressure he wrote and delivered one of the most meaningful speeches that has ever been delivered in any campaign, and he did it with grace, and he did it with wisdom. Those moments give people an insight into what kind of president someone will be, and so what looked to be a moment of peril for him turned into a moment of triumph.

Senator Obama's "A More Perfect Union" speech. The National Constitution Center, Philadelphia. March 18, 2008. William Thomas Cain, Getty

TOM DASCHLE

He always had a self-confidence about himself, which I think is so critical to be a good president. You have to really believe in yourself, but you also have to be empathetic.

CHRIS DODD
D-Connecticut, Second District, US House of Representatives (1975–1981)
D-Connecticut, US Senate (1981–2011)
Chair, US Senate Committee on Banking, Housing, and Urban Affairs (2007–2011)

I got a call from Vicki Kennedy in late May, a tearful call. I knew something was immediately wrong. She could hardly speak. My best friend in the Senate had brain cancer, and the question of how long was a matter of days. He managed to survive for over a year.

MELODY BARNES
Counsel to Senator Edward Kennedy, US Senate Judiciary Committee (1995–2003)
Director, Domestic Policy Council, White House (2009–2012)

For Senator Kennedy, one of the great causes of his life was trying to achieve universal health-care coverage. He described that in very personal terms, based on his familial experience and then as the experiences he had as a policymaker and the people that he met over the course of his forty-plus-year career.

DAVID BOWEN
Staff Director, US Senate Committee on Health, Education,
Labor, and Pensions (HELP) (1999–2010)

I was chief health-policy director for the Senate Committee on Health, Education, Labor, and Pensions, which Senator Kennedy chaired at the time of the consideration of the Affordable Care Act. My involvement in it began approximately the week before May 21 of 2008. The reason I know that date with precision was that it happened to be a few days before my birthday, but it was [also] a few days before Senator Kennedy got sick. We were in his hideaway, which was his office in the Capitol, and on a rare occasion that there was actually some downtime, we started talking about comprehensive health reform, which was very obviously on the docket for early 2009, regardless of who won in 2008.

MELODY BARNES

He saw Senator Obama as the one who could carry the torch, as someone who very specifically had the ability and desire to pass a comprehensive health-care bill.

CHRIS DODD

I never asked him this, but I often thought that a major factor in Teddy's endorsement of candidate Obama was the commitment to [Kennedy] that health care would be a major legislative item. I didn't know that to be the case, but knowing Teddy well enough, I suspect it was.

JEREMY BIRD

We were within one hundred delegates for a long time. So it was actually very close, and particularly around [losing] Pennsylvania, after the Jeremiah Wright stuff came out, there was a real chance, pretty late in the game, that we were going to lose, after we had strung together all those victories.

CODY KEENAN
Presidential Speechwriter, White House (2009–2011)
Deputy Director of Speechwriting, White House (2011–2013)
Director of Speechwriting, White House (2013–2017)

He made it a mathematical impossibility on June 3. Even then, it was *Be gracious. Don't demand any concession here. The most we'll do in the Saint Paul speech is not even claim the Democratic nomination but let her come around to endorsing on her own time.* Losing is hard, and the worst thing you could do was to tell someone "Get over it."

JEREMY BIRD

We couldn't have beaten Hillary, much less any other candidate, had we run a traditional campaign. We were not going to let that political pressure determine our strategy. We were going to do it in a way that's unique to a candidate and based on his bio and background.

ALLYSON SCHWARTZ

D-Pennsylvania, Thirteenth District, US House of Representatives (2005–2015)

I was a strong Hillary supporter and stayed with her until the very end, and it was difficult. Members of Congress and others asked, "Why aren't you coming over? Why aren't you for Obama yet?" I said, "When she's no longer a candidate, I will be for President Obama." I didn't pause for a moment to make that transition, but I supported Hillary all the way through.

JEREMY BIRD

We had some Clinton loyalists that we still needed to bring into the fold. I hired Jackie Bray, who had worked on the Clinton campaign. We hired Greg Schultz. We hired Aaron Pickrell, who was on the Clinton campaign, to start that healing process. It didn't take a long time, because we were in general [election] mode pretty quickly. It was much more about speaking to our base to get them to become the army that we could mobilize, and talk to people who were persuadable.

HERBIE ZISKEND

The general campaign created the vice-presidential nominee's team before there was a nominee, and I became the traveling staff assistant to whoever they would pick.

JIM MESSINA

I was in the room when they picked Biden, and he really was about adding foreign-policy credentials to the ticket. People forget: Barack Obama had been in the Senate for three years before he started running for president. And so, when I went to work for him, my [former] boss Max Baucus[6] said, "You don't really know him very well." They all knew Biden, and President Obama did really want to be "change." He brought in all the outside people, and Biden was much more comfortable with the inside game. And I thought together they were a powerful duo.

HERBIE ZISKEND

Biden had been chairman of the Senate Foreign Relations Committee.

LUIS GUTIÉRREZ

David Axelrod was blowing me off during the campaign. I called up and asked, "Where the fuck is immigration on your website?" Then, when we went to the convention, they didn't want to talk about it. Now, some of this could be personal, but here I was, the first Hispanic congressman to endorse him, and they put me at four o'clock! Speaking into some camera. That was supposed to be my speech at the Denver convention. You could tell they just didn't want to . . . there was never a connection in the campaign.

JOE LIEBERMAN

I spent a fair amount of time on the trail for the McCain campaign. There was a decision—in full disclosure, that was not an easy one—but it created more anger toward me. I think there would have been anger anyway among Democrats, but McCain asked if I would speak at the [Republican] convention on his behalf.

---

6   The Democratic US senator served Montana from 1978 to 2014 and chaired the Senate Finance Committee from 2007 to 2014.

And there again, I thought, *I'm supporting him, so why am I suddenly going to say no?*

JOEL BENENSON

The Friday right after our convention, we were all still bleary-eyed in Denver because we were partying pretty late that night. And we woke up ridiculously early, like at about four a.m. Colorado time—six a.m. Eastern time—with the news that he's picking Sarah Palin for vice president.

JENNIFER GRANHOLM
Governor of Michigan (D) (2003–2011)

She revved up their base with her convention speech. It was the first view the nation had of her. But shortly after that, it started to wilt. I think, in part, people generally know this is a big job. You are literally one step away from the presidency.

BRANDON HURLBUT

Remember, when she first came out she was the "mama bear." She was on a roll in the beginning, but when she started taking questions from the press, she revealed her true self.

JOEL BENENSON

Most of the folks thought this was a play for the base. He picked someone who seemed void of the qualifications to be vice president, let alone president. It was the kind of pick that, rather than strengthen the ticket, could actually stymie it long term. It undercut a core theme of his. Here was a guy, Senator McCain, a war hero, a veteran, [with] a well-known story about his time as a POW, who was running on "Country First."

HERBIE ZISKEND

There was a moment when this election was about foreign policy—Georgia was invaded by Russia in the summer of '08—and that certainly was relevant when Obama was thinking about his pick for vice president, but the day that Lehman collapsed and the financial crisis was under way, it became about the economy. Really from September on, we knew that we were dealing with an emergency that required a response.

NATE LUBIN
Writer/Producer, Obama for America (2008)
Director of Digital Marketing, Obama for America (2011–2012)
Director of the Office of Digital Strategy, White House (2013–2015)

I was in the office the day the Dow dropped, and sitting there, watching the world implode, we were all like, *Well, I guess we gotta keep doing our jobs.*

JOSH LIPSKY

The senator was supposed to do *Saturday Night Live*. We had walked through the studio to figure out what was gonna happen, and then plans changed. Both candidates got called to Washington, and then Senator McCain suspended his campaign. That whole week felt completely surreal. I remember being in the student union at Ole Miss to advance the debate, and I just thought, *Oh my God, what is happening?* Were they even going to debate? There was so much anxiety and confusion over what was going to happen next, not just for the election but for the country.

NATE LUBIN

Watching McCain shut down his campaign—it backfired. Whether it was a bad move going in, I don't even know. Clearly it was, but he was losing.

JAKE LEVINE

National Advance Staff, Obama for America (2007–2008)
Policy Analyst, Office of Energy and Climate Change, White House (2009–2010)

The release that the campaign put out was that it was because of the recession, but the scuttlebutt—and who knows how much of this was true—was that it was because of Palin's Katie Couric interview. Word from the reporters was that Palin didn't know anything. She didn't know how to answer questions like "What newspapers do you read?" and basics about foreign policy and US history. So there was some rumor that the recession was a pretense and that canceling the debates was really about changing the story from the Couric interview, which was a nightmare for the McCain campaign.

JOSH LIPSKY

I remember, within a few hours of that, we got the word from Axe and the rest of leadership like, *This debate's happening.* Like, *We're showing up. Obama's showing up. What McCain does is up to him.* So we just kept planning.

ERIC LESSER

There was all this mishegas about John McCain suspending his campaign. Then they were trying to get the TARP bill passed in Congress.[7] Bush called a meeting—actually, all of this has been recounted numerous times, about how Obama, Pelosi, and Reid went in synced up about what they were going to do. Pelosi and Reid, to their credit, deferred to Obama to speak for them as their party's nominee, as a united front of the Democratic mission, and McCain, McConnell, and Boehner were not on the same page.

---

7 The Troubled Asset Relief Program was part of the Emergency Economic Stabilization Act, signed into law by President George W. Bush on October 3, 2008, in response to the subprime-mortgage crisis. It authorized the Treasury to spend up to $700 billion to rescue the financial system from collapse; expenditures ranged from purchasing equity shares in the nation's eight largest banks to extending loans to the auto industry.

CHRIS DODD

People had been talking about reorganizing the architecture of the financial-services sector for decades, but Congress typically doesn't react to things unless there's a crisis. We never would have gotten to this, and you had the one window, in the wake of the crisis of the fall of 2008, [when it] came to a head with the AIG issue, Lehman Brothers, mortgages, and that mess. That created an opportunity for us to do something we'd been talking about doing for a long time, to try to set up an architecture not to stop all crises, but to make it possible to manage them in such a way that [we wouldn't] have the kind of metastasizing that could occur [due to] the lack of sharing information. That's really all the bill tried to do: set up mechanisms to make it possible for regulators to look over institutions.

AUSTAN GOOLSBEE

Member, Council of Economic Advisers, White House (2009–2010)
Chair, Council of Economic Advisers, White House (2010–2011)

The Bush administration, particularly Paulson, kept both presidential candidates completely apprised of what he was doing.[8] Paulson was doing that not out of kindness, but as a matter of survival. He was basically begging all the political figures not to publicly attack the TARP, specifically the rescue effort in general. He was nervous. Everyone was nervous. The system was about to collapse, and if we condemned the TARP and didn't rescue the financial system, we're looking at a depression. So he was basically calling all along to Obama and to McCain . . . they came to a loose agreement, which was to make the TARP spending in two halves. To oversimplify it, the Bush people could spend the first half however they saw fit, and then there would be a second half that the next president— whoever that would be—could use.

---

8   Hank Paulson, former chair and CEO of Goldman Sachs, who served as President Bush's Secretary of the Treasury from 2006 to 2009.

JAKE LEVINE

The Katie Couric interview blew over. There was no unbelievable bombshell that came out of it other than what people already knew, which was Palin was sort of a lightweight . . . Part of what was interesting for me about the first debate—and this was not really substantive in terms of whether Obama beat McCain or McCain beat Obama—was that it was in Mississippi and that it was at Ole Miss,[9] which were places that had a real palpable feeling around issues of race and some of the broader social and historical themes that I thought Obama had been able to tease out along the campaign trail.

JOSH LIPSKY

The debate is honestly a bit of a blur to me. In the spin room, I tried to watch the reporters as they reacted to what was going on. I thought that was kinda how I was going to process it. And so I would see people perk up or what they would type, or listen when they would shout a question to someone. I could tell it was going well. You just got the feeling in that huge filing center. You just felt comfortable and confident as it was going on, because the senator felt confident. You could just see it in his demeanor.

JENNIFER GRANHOLM

On September 28, Barack, Michelle, and Joe and Jill Biden came to downtown Detroit. This was right in the middle of the crash, and the auto industry was about to go under. All of this was happening at once, and when they visited, there were tens of thousands of scared and angry people. Obama was speaking in these rolled-up shirtsleeves. He targeted his speech to the people who had been laid off—people who really needed to believe that a new administration could actually give them hope, because we were just in the middle of this vortex. And, you know, he said, "We don't just need a plan for bankers and investors. We need a plan for auto workers." The crowd went crazy.

---

9   University of Mississippi, September 26, 2008.

JOEL BENENSON

I remember in prep sessions Jennifer Granholm was playing Sarah Palin for the debate against Biden, and she was just magnificent, and I think [Biden] was ready for what she threw at him.

JENNIFER GRANHOLM

We wanted to make sure that he did this right, and Ron Klain, who was the key preparer of this debate, said to me that if Joe makes mistakes or gaffes, we lose, because . . . Joe's a seasoned guy and she's an outsider. So he couldn't goof this. If he's seen as condescending to a woman, we lost. If he took the bait if she tried to go to him, we lost. We thought the best scenario would have been a draw. If it were a draw, we figured we'd win. So our goal was to throw everything at Joe and make sure he could stay on an even keel no matter what would happen.

JOSH LIPSKY

The third debate in Long Island . . . was more intense.[10] There was an argument with the McCain staff. It's fuzzy to me. I needed something from their press advance team—something about a kind of logistical arrangement—and I went over to their room and knocked on the door. I think it was Nicolle Wallace, or one of them, like "What are *you* doing here?" I said, "Oh I need to talk to the advance staff," and they kind of shut me out.

ADAM HITCHCOCK

People on the campaign were cautiously optimistic going into the end. We felt like everything had come together, and that was a testament to all the things we'd been doing since early 2007 and that we believed in this strategy. All that work and preparation we had put in place on the ground, at that point it was just executing on what we knew would work.

---

10 Hofstra University, October 15, 2008.

JOSH LIPSKY

It was just a feeling of *As soon as the end of this debate happens at ten thirty, it is go time. It is an all-out sprint.* That night we all got on planes all over the country. I remember people saying to each other, "I'll see you in Chicago." And it was just that moment: *Whatever happens tonight happens, and we'll see you when we see you, and it'll be election night and don't plan on sleeping till then.*

BRANDON HURLBUT

We felt we built the greatest grassroots operation ever. We felt that people were inspired by this guy in a way they'd never been inspired since maybe Jack Kennedy—but there was the uncertainty of *Are people really going to make this leap?*

2008–2009

It was ten p.m. Chicago time when the network feeds cut to Grant Park. The Chicago Transit Authority had upped the usual number of trains and buses to usher some 240,000 people eager to witness the acceptance speech of the first African American elected president of the United States. Jesse Jackson Sr., among several others, had broken into tears. At campaign headquarters, staffer Brandon Hurlbut "collapsed on the ground" in relief. Even McCain surrogate Joe Lieberman, who was in Arizona with the Republican nominee, admitted to "a kind of excitement in me that this had happened."

November 4 was a night the world had long awaited, to witness the US break a racial barrier and rid itself of the stench from the Bush era. New Delhi's TV channels broadcast wall-to-wall coverage of American news. Citizens in a war-torn eastern Congo cheered in the streets. In Berlin, a twenty-nine-year-old architect had rushed to her radio in anticipation that the election would "give America a new face." The president-elect's victory speech echoed the sentiments that democracy had demonstrated that evening, with returns putting him at 365 electoral-college votes over McCain's 173. Approximately 130 million Americans showed up to the polls—more than in any other presidential election in the nation's history.

> If there is anyone out there who still doubts that America is a place where all things are possible, who still wonders if the dream of our founders is alive in our time, who still questions the power of our democracy, tonight is your answer. It's the answer told by lines that stretched around schools and churches in numbers this nation has never seen; by people who waited three hours and four

hours—many for the first time in their lives—because they believed that this time must be different. That their voices could be that difference. It's the answer spoken by young and old, rich and poor, Democrat and Republican, black, white, Hispanic, Asian, Native American, gay, straight, disabled and not disabled. Americans who sent a message to the world that we have never been just a collection of individuals or a collection of red states and blue states; we are, and always will be, the United States of America.

President-Elect Obama's remarks continued with several shout-outs, among them to his wife, Michelle ("the love of my life, the nation's next First Lady"); daughters Sasha, age seven, and Malia, age ten ("you have earned the new puppy that's coming with us to the White House"); his sisters, Maya and Auma; and his eighty-six-year-old grandmother, who, in a cruel twist of fate, had died twenty-four hours prior ("I know my grandmother's watching, along with the family that made me who I am"). He also acknowledged campaign brain trusts Davids Plouffe and Axelrod, once colleagues at a Chicago political-media firm who would, for a while at least, go separate ways. "Right after the election," Plouffe said, "my arrangement with the president . . . was I would take two years out and then come back in. That was always the plan." As for Axelrod, he would accompany his star client to the west end of Pennsylvania Avenue. According to campaign staffer Eric Lesser, Axelrod, in his capacity as senior advisor to the president, said he needed "a grunt"; Lesser said he would "be honored" to assume the role.

But getting security badges was more than two months away. The priority was setting up transition headquarters—one inside a nondescript office building in DC, another in Chicago's Kluczynski Federal Building—to build a new government and deal with the multiple financial crises. And, despite the ocean of revelers chanting "Yes we can!" past one a.m. at Grant Park, those issues were still on people's minds. "This is just the beginning," one onlooker told a reporter. "Now comes the hard part."

JOE LIEBERMAN

The day after the election, one of the first calls I got was from [Senate Minority Leader] Mitch McConnell. "I know the Democrats are angry at you, and I just want you to know that we'd love to have you in our caucus. We'll arrange a package for you." I thought it was great. So by the end of the morning, [Senate Majority Leader] Harry Reid called. "Joe, I'm gonna be in my office Thursday. Please come in as early as you can." So I did, and basically Harry told me that people were really upset that I had supported McCain, and that there would be a move in a closed caucus to deny me seniority, which meant that I would lose my chairmanship on the Homeland Security Committee.

BILL DAUSTER
Deputy Staff Director and General Counsel, US Senate Finance Committee (2003–2011)
Deputy Chief of Staff, US Senate Democratic Leader Harry Reid (2011–2017)

We were working hard to try and keep all of our Democrats together, and Senator Lieberman was one of the more difficult ones.

JOE LIEBERMAN

So he said, "I wanted to ask you to avoid that and step down as chairman of Homeland Security. I think I can make you chairman of the Small Business Committee," which was a nothing committee. So I said, "Harry, I've been a good member of the caucus. You've been able to count on me." "Yeah, yeah, yeah." "And McConnell's talked to me." "Well what is *he* going to offer you?" "I don't know, but maybe I'll see." "So you won't step down as chair of Homeland

Security?" I said, "I can't." So Harry, as was his wont, lowered his head. He looked down probably for what was ten seconds, but to me seemed like three minutes. Then he raised his head and said, "All right, let's figure out how we're going to get you the votes to keep your seniority."

HERBIE ZISKEND

The Democrats ensured that Lieberman stayed enough in their camp that he kept his committee assignment in the Senate. That didn't happen accidentally. He's from the critical state of Connecticut, which has Hartford, the insurance capital of the country. People understood how the system worked.

BRIAN DEESE
Special Assistant to the President, National Economic Council, White House (2009–2011)
Deputy Director, National Economic Council, White House (2011–2013)
Deputy Director, Office of Management and Budget, White House (2013–2015)
Senior Advisor to the President, White House (2015–2017)

The morning after the election, both Jason [Furman] and I returned to the office after having been in Grant Park the previous night and thought that we would have a kind of leisurely day.

JASON FURMAN
Deputy Director, National Economic Council, White House (2009–2013)
Chair, Council of Economic Advisers, White House (2013–2017)

We got in late [on Wednesday], and I think there was one other person in the entire headquarters. Up until then, [we] never had fewer than several hundred people there at a time.

BRIAN DEESE

David Axelrod came by our little area. "President-elect's gonna have a press conference on Friday." I remember this was right around ten o'clock. "We need to announce the president-elect's economic recovery council, and we need to have our first meeting with those people." And we said, "We don't have an economic recovery council." And he said, "Exactly, so we need to create one and we need to get them here."

JASON FURMAN

We started working on the president-elect's first meeting with his transition economic team, which happened on the Friday after the election. That was also his first press conference.

BRIAN DEESE

That kicked off a flurry of activity in the subsequent forty-eight hours. Before the press conference at a hotel down the road in Chicago, [we held] a meeting with a group [that] included Governor Granholm and a long list of eminent economic thinkers. That was largely a kind of broad-strokes *Where are we and what are we going to need to get done?* conversation.

JIM MESSINA

You've heard this famous thing where Obama heard the news about how bad the economy was, and looked at Axelrod and me and asked, "Is it too late to ask for a recount?"

JAMES KVAAL
Special Assistant to the President for Economic Policy, White House (2009–2010)
Policy Director, Obama for America (2011–2012)
Deputy Director of Domestic Policy, Domestic Policy Council, White House (2013–2016)

People joked among themselves about the bad timing for this administration. It was true that the president ran for office with a long list of things that he wanted to do, [but] was handed a to-do list which included this great economic crisis, restarting the financial markets, digging out the housing markets, creating jobs—plus ending two wars overseas—and that all needed to happen before he could get to the things he always wanted to do. On the other hand, I think folks go into public service because they're eager to make a difference, they're eager for a challenge, and a situation like that, where it really felt like every hour of every day was critical in terms of the impact you were having, could be rewarding.

CHRIS VAN HOLLEN

D-Maryland, Eighth District, US House of Representatives (2003–2017)
D-Maryland, US Senate (2017–)

I had worked with Rahm at the [Democratic Congressional Campaign Committee]. When he was chair, I was the candidate-recruitment chair. I don't have any stories beyond what you already know—every other word is a four-letter word, and he's an intense, hard-driving guy. And when he took the job as chief of staff, they were determined to get as much stuff done as possible. You remember his quote, "A crisis is a terrible thing to waste."

RAHM EMANUEL

Senior Advisor to the President, White House (1993–1998)
D-Illinois, Fifth District, US House of Representatives (2003–2009)
White House Chief of Staff (2009–2010)
Mayor of Chicago (2011–)

How I was approached? I didn't really have much of a choice.

JIM MESSINA

After Rahm had been selected, I remember being sent to the Senate, where I had worked for thirteen years for the most powerful Democrat, to talk about the stimulus bill. And the stimulus bill was supported by the Bush administration. They helped draft it . . . and I was having a discussion with one of the key Republican staffers who I had dated from time to time. I remember her saying, "Jim, we're not going to compromise with you on anything. We're going to fight Obama on everything." And I said to her, "That's not what we did for Bush." And she said, "We don't care. We're just going to fight."

BARNEY FRANK

D-Massachusetts, Fourth District, US House of Representatives (1981–2013)
Chair, House Financial Services Committee (2007–2011)

Obama was unprepared for it. It took him a while to realize the nature of his enemy. He did have that comment which made me crazy, that he was going to be "postpartisan." At the time when he said that he gave me postpartisan depression.

RAHM EMANUEL

The president asked me to be the chief of staff based on three, I suppose, core qualities that he wanted. One, he said, was our personal relationship that went beyond professional. Second, my entire White House experience at a senior level, so I knew the way the building operated. Then third, my legislative background from the Hill. I would say, on the latter part, I brought, obviously, not just [having been] a member of Congress, but [also] a member of leadership who had something to do with both taking back the House [in '06] and building on that majority [in '08]. But I purposefully went out to build a White House team that had a deep legislative bench.

JIM MESSINA

I was very worried about the relationship at the very beginning, because Obama hired me to be the deputy chief of staff before Rahm had agreed to be the chief of staff. And I remember Rahm had said to him, "I'll take it, but I want to appoint my deputies." And Obama said, "Well, that's fine, but I already picked one of them." I'd met Rahm, but I had no relationship with him. It was fair to say he was not happy to be handed a deputy.

JENNIFER GRANHOLM

The president [-elect]'s meeting in Chicago was the first meeting of economic advisors. There were all these notable individuals around the table, and obviously some of this was staged for the media to show he was on it, but you know, Larry

Summers and Paul Volcker—all of these economists—were present, and I was the only governor. He asked me to say a few words about what was happening in Michigan to set the stage, and the quarterly earnings of the automakers had come out that very day. They were through the floor.

AUSTAN GOOLSBEE

Both Chrysler and GM were in big trouble. Ford had gotten some cash right before the financial crisis and decided they were not going to ask for rescue money. And presumably, by showing they were stronger, I think they were thinking they would get more demand. So you had GM and Chrysler, and the real question, from the beginning, was twofold: One, could the economy handle a shutdown of these massive manufacturing enterprises, and the second part was, If you wanted to save them, was it feasible?

BRIAN DEESE

There was a meeting about two weeks later in Chicago, and this was before any of the president's economic team members had been named. It was a meeting of advisors, including folks who had been working on transition economic policies, a sort of initial *Where are we?* with respect to the handful of core challenges we faced.

JASON FURMAN

We went over a provisional stimulus plan with the president-elect that was about $300 billion. As soon as Larry [Summers] and Christy [Romer] came on the team in late November, they both started pushing for a much larger number than that.

BRIAN DEESE

That meeting was not decisional in any way. It was more just an update for him. Jack Lew was there. Jason and I were there. Austan Goolsbee. It was a combination of the campaign economic team—Jason, Austan, and me—and then some advisors. That meeting was sort of like, *Here're where things stand. Here're the big challenges we're sorting through, and we'll come back to you in roughly a month, once you have your economic team in place, and give you a serious rundown with recommendations.* Between then and Thanksgiving the president [-elect] would nominate the four members of the economic team.[11]

TED KAUFMAN
D-Delaware, US Senate (2009–2010)

They had charts up on the wall. I went with the vice president [-elect to the Chicago meeting]. I was the cochair of his transition, and it was a small group. Valerie Jarrett and Mark Gitenstein, and I think Rahm was there and Axe, and some really top-flight economists. We sat and went through the charts, and it was like, *Ohhhhh my God.*

DAVID AXELROD

There were overlapping economic crises. One was a slow-rolling crisis that had been unfurling for decades, and these were the changes in our economy that marginalized a lot of middle-class jobs that didn't require high levels of education. There had been a flattening of wages for some time, and you had a lot of people who were working but working for far less. And so there had been this restiveness. It obviously crested in 2016, but there had been this restiveness for decades that was exacerbated by the crisis.

BRIAN DEESE

I was working on the auto stuff in particular, and so we presented a broad sense of *Where are the companies? What are they asking for? What's likely to happen to them and what are the choices they're going to have to face?* [Obama] took it all in, and the only question he had was along the lines of "Why can't the American car

---

11   Timothy Geithner, US Secretary of the Treasury; Larry Summers, Director, National Economic Council; Christina Romer, Chair, White House Council of Economic Advisers; and Peter Orszag, Director, White House Office of Management and Budget.

company make a Corolla?" His point being, Why is it that American companies can't figure out how to produce a car that has safety and reliability and that people want to buy? It's a good example of him getting right to the core of the issue. We were talking about how much cash GM had left, what they were asking Congress to do, and what might happen in the next couple months.

AUSTAN GOOLSBEE

Chrysler and GM were not going to be able to make their payments, and the Bush administration ended up giving them [$17 billion] just to burn to keep themselves warm before the Obama administration came in.

ARUN CHAUDHARY

The transition in Chicago was a very small group, the president-elect and the immediate people around him who needed to help him function. In general the team was already in Washington working on policy, so the fewer people who were around you—the "you" being President-Elect Obama—the less you're going to feel that panic. When you were around him—and in Chicago you just were, because there were so few of us around—you felt absolutely calm. He was going through the things he needed to do methodically and surely. You're rolling people out. It's still the land of potential. You're still talking about what can potentially be done with all of these players you're putting in place.

JIM MESSINA

The picks we made, it's important to think about that time, because we were watching the economy fall off the end of the table, and you had this president-elect who was brought in to change Washington. He really viewed the cabinet selections as his first chance to do that. And so he wanted, from the very early conversations in the transition, to do two things: hire the best-qualified people, no matter their politics, and send a message of unity, because the country was freaking out about the economy. And so that's why he made a couple early Republican picks in Gates and LaHood.[12]

JOSH LIPSKY

The way [Senator] Clinton took the job at the State Department was just amazingly healing in terms of the Obama and Clinton worlds. It didn't happen overnight. In the beginning, there was always this *Oh, is that a Clinton person? Is that an Obama person?* That faded over time, but everyone's experience was different. I mean, fifteen Obama people would tell you fifteen different things.

GENE SPERLING
Director, National Economic Council, White House (1996–2001)
Counselor to the US Secretary of the Treasury (2009–2010)
Director, National Economic Council, White House (2011–2014)

There's no question there were some hard feelings right after the election, right after Obama defeated her in 2008, but everyone put on their big-boy and big-girl pants and worked together for the greater good, even if not all of the hard feelings had gone away . . . In the first couple of years, I felt that there were more occasional misunderstandings among the staffers who looked out for them and were protective than there were between the principals themselves.

TOM VILSACK

It certainly made sense for the president-elect to look for an opportunity to use Hillary Clinton's abilities in his cabinet. That would have been sufficient, I think, to send a clear message to folks who had been loyal to Clinton that this was a president who embraced former opponents. But he went far beyond that. You would think that, traditionally, the Department of Agriculture would be

---

12 President-Elect Obama retained US Defense Secretary Robert Gates, a holdover from the previous administration who had been nominated by President Bush in 2006. Gates served in Obama's cabinet through 2011; Ray LaHood served the Eighteenth District of Illinois for fourteen years before the Republican moderate became Obama's US Secretary of Transportation from 2009 to 2013.

run by someone who had deeper roots in farming than I had had. Obviously I was governor of a state that was predominantly agriculture based, but that, in and of itself, may not have been enough to get you nominated to that cabinet position. So I was surprised on that score.

MELODY BARNES

The president-elect was looking for individuals who had both the intellect for the job ahead but also a passion for these issues—real-life experience related to the issues in the position that they would hold. Arne [Duncan] was a perfect reflection of that. He's someone unconventional in the sense that he wasn't a national political figure but someone who understood, because of hands-on experience, what it meant to work in an education system.

ARNE DUNCAN
Chief Executive Officer, Chicago Public Schools (2001–2008)
US Secretary of Education (2009–2015)

He and I talked much earlier. Some communication, more socially in the interim, but it wasn't like the offer was there. You just didn't know, and I really did not want to go to DC. To become education secretary was not my life's ambition, but it was really a chance to be part of his team, and to help someone to whom I was a friend, that I just believed in. If he said, "Come to the White House and take out the garbage for me," I would have said yes. Frankly, had anyone else asked, I would have said no. But for him it was a no-brainer.

DR. STEVEN CHU
US Secretary of Energy (2009–2013)

I didn't think many people appreciated how he made his cabinet-held appointments. He picked a lot of people not as kickback favors—he picked people he thought would be good at the job. He wanted me to make decisions based on knowledge, science, and all the other things that seemed a little bit more removed . . . unless you called acknowledging that the climate was changing and we should do something about it "political," but I didn't regard that as "political."

JIM MESSINA

You had a couple picks blow up in the process. We had two commerce secretaries we had decided to pick but in the end couldn't, because of vetting issues. Tom Daschle's [Health and Human Services nomination] blew up during confirmation. Tim Geithner's [Treasury Secretary] confirmation hit a snag in committee. All these things were swirling around at the same time when we were trying to deal with the economy. [It] was just unbridled exhaustion in attempting to grasp the changing situations in a nanosecond. I kept saying to John Podesta, the chair of the transition, "Where the fuck is our honeymoon?"

ARNE DUNCAN

Podesta was involved. Axe was involved. I think [Obama] felt it was important that he had a cabinet that reflected the country. When you look at Secretary Clinton, Bob Gates, and others, these were the best people not just in the United States, but arguably in the world. There were early cabinet meetings where I used to pinch myself. *What's a kid from the South Side of Chicago doing here?* There was definitely a piece of it that was exhilarating but also surreal.

LUIS GUTIÉRREZ

I still had his personal phone number, and I called him up. "Look, we should talk." I met with him over in the [Kluczynski] Federal Building in Chicago— and it's days after Blagojevich was arrested—and he basically told me that we're hemorrhaging jobs and couldn't do immigration reform. I kinda said, "I thought I was important." He said, "You *are* important. That's why you're here." In retrospect, I guess you are pretty important if you get to see the president all by yourself in his transition-team office one evening and you get to chat.

ARUN CHAUDHARY

Governor Blagojevich had done some crazy stuff with Barack Obama's Senate seat. People were going to be subpoenaed, including Valerie Jarrett and possibly the president-elect, and it seemed like not a great situation. And I remember we were all huddled around those TVs and Obama came out of his office. He surveyed the screen and was like, "Huh. That doesn't seem like it's any good. We're gonna figure that out," and walked back into his office. To make a phone call and figure it out, you know, not to start yelling, "What's the hell's that guy doing?" or "Rahm needs to fix this!" or whatever. He didn't feel the need to start a tweet storm.

BRIAN DEESE

We were thinking as hard as we could and trying to be as docile as we could, but it was a harrowing time. It's actually hard to take yourself back, because, present circumstances aside, there was just such existential uncertainty across the board . . . We all took our places in the transition office in Washington, and then got down to the business of preparing for that December 16 meeting.

JARED BERNSTEIN
Chief Economist and Economic Policy Advisor, Office of the Vice President (2009–2011)

That meeting was largely about the recession and how deep we thought it was; basically that meeting was diagnosis and prescription vis-à-vis the recession . . . That's when [Council of Economic Advisers chair Christina Romer and I] started working on that paper. That was published before the president took office.

BRIAN DEESE

That's the meeting where we wrote that fifty-some-odd-page report which leaked,[13] and then that was the meeting where, respectively, Tim [Geithner],

---

13   The fifty-seven-page internal memo that Larry Summers submitted to the president-elect proposed a stimulus ranging from $550 to $890 billion in spending and tax cuts; earlier drafts recommended figures as high as $1.7 and $1.8 trillion, which Summers deemed "nonplanetary." (The memo was eventually leaked to the press and published in 2012.) The Bernstein-Romer paper, intentionally distributed to media in January 2009, proposed a "package just slightly over the $775 billion" mark.

Larry [Summers], Peter [Orszag], and Christy [Romer] walked through different aspects of the crisis and where Christy said, "This is your *holy shit* moment."

ERIC LESSER

They basically gave a run-through of how serious the economic crisis was and what would happen if the measures that needed to be taken weren't taken. You would have seen Depression-era unemployment figures in certain parts of the country. There would have been a continuing bleeding of credit. The deficit would have exploded. It was very dour.

DAVID AXELROD

We needed to fill the huge hole that the economic collapse had created in the output of the economy, and so the Recovery Act would be a large and expensive program by design, as big as we could get it.

ERIC LESSER

I was one of the junior people making photocopies for it, and I remember seeing everyone walking out, just the seriousness and the pressure.

RAHM EMANUEL

I mean you were literally shedding hundreds of thousands of jobs a month. You didn't have to artificially create a crisis or sense of urgency off that crisis. It was there. The harder challenge was getting the policy people and the political people [on the same page], and this was what happened with any big policy. What could the political system absorb?

JARED BERNSTEIN

Even at the time I probably would have had a hard time telling you what was going on. The economics team—at least those of us who recognized this as very much a Keynesian moment—believed that we needed as large a stimulus as the system could bear, politically, and absorb without wasting money.

JASON FURMAN

It was $300 billion before [the economic team] got there. They pushed for a larger number, and the number got larger over the course of December, and almost everyone agreed that the largest number we could get through Congress was what we wanted. And the political people thought—and I think [their] judgment was reasonable—that we couldn't get anything above $1 trillion through Congress.

BRIAN DEESE

The president [-elect] had a mantra early on that he started in both of those early meetings with his economic team and then continued it in the White House. *I want to focus on the policy first. I want to understand the issue, and then we'll get to the politics.* He wanted the team's best analysis and assessment, and he didn't want them to put politics on the front of it.

JASON FURMAN

If you remember the context at the time, Congress was talking about numbers like $200 billion. There were a lot of lefty progressives who were pushing for numbers more like $300 billion, $400 billion, $500 billion. So going for $800 billion or $1 trillion was way outside the bounds of what anyone else was talking about.

BRIAN DEESE

It was hard to find windows of time to sit back, reflect, and really freak yourself out. From that minute we got in at ten o'clock after election night, we were sprinting for what turned out to be months. So you were up really early in the morning. Then you were just sprinting all day, then going to bed very late at night, and then doing it over again. The rhythm of the crisis didn't allow for a lot of time to just freak out. But we were full of extraordinary levels of anxiety, in large part because on all of those fronts—on the financial crisis, and the crisis response on the stimulus, and the fiscal response on the autos—we didn't know whether either the politics or the policy were going to work.

JON CARSON

So there was that side of it, and then there was the interaction with the outgoing George W. Bush [administration]. I was going in as the chief of staff of the Council on Environmental Quality, and Marty Hall was the outgoing Bush staffer. He walked me through everything. He walked me through the budget. He literally walked me through the West Wing while the White House Christmas party was going on.

HERBIE ZISKEND

The last time the parties had swapped was eight years ago, so if you're in your twenties, you didn't really know anyone who could walk you through a transition. And a couple of weeks before [Inauguration Day], a young staff assistant had taken us around the White House—introduced us to the Secret Service agents. She brought me into Vice President Cheney's office and showed me where things were. I didn't see Cheney or Bush. This was late at night, but everyone [was] working really hard because they [were] dealing with a lot of issues, and Keith Hennessey, the advisor who was overseeing the economic operation for Bush, said, "Welcome" and "It's going to be an amazing experience." He put his arm around me. "Go to the White House mess on Thursdays. It's the best food that day."

ERIC LESSER

I obviously did not agree with their decisions, but the Bush people were very polite to us in the transition process. I had a friend, Elise Stefanik, who became the youngest female Republican ever elected to Congress. She had a job similar to me for Josh Bolten, who was Bush's chief of staff, and she had invited me to the White House. She introduced me to some of the civil servants and the professional staff, and that was happening at every level. So Axelrod, I knew he met with his counterpart, and obviously Bush and Obama were speaking. I really do have to give them credit, that they were very professional about it.

DAN SHAPIRO

So all through the transition we were watching this very bloody conflict unfold in Gaza, the Cast Lead, and the president-elect was determined on that issue and others . . . to not get involved in diplomacy other than to say he wasn't president at the time. So we knew we were going to have to deal with this . . . By Inauguration Day, the guns were quiet. There was a cease-fire in place that was shaky, and so we knew that one of his first things that he should be engaged in was to do what he could to stabilize the cease-fire. So it was decided that he would call those four [Middle East] leaders.[14]

DAVID CUSACK

Director of Advance, White House (2009–2011)
Executive Director, Presidential Inaugural Committee (2012–2014)
Director of Operations, White House (2015–2017)

The morning started off across the street at the church. I was the director of events and ceremonies for the [Presidential Inaugural Committee], and . . . ended up doing the tea that morning. It's a traditional tea at like nine thirty in the morning in the Blue Room. So both the president-elect and the president would go to church, and they'd come back across the street and do the welcoming tea between the two families. So I was responsible for that, and so my day started at like four thirty in the morning at Secret Service headquarters, because we were preparing the Mall for all the people who were gonna come.

---

14 President Mahmoud Abbas of Palestine; King Abdullah II bin Al-Hussein of Jordan; President Hosni Mubarak of Egypt; and Prime Minister Ehud Olmert of Israel.

TED CHIODO

Deputy White House Staff Secretary (2009–2014)

On the first day, January 20, 2009, I couldn't go in until noon, so I watched the inauguration from the downstairs bar at the Hay-Adams across the street. I just had a cheeseburger. This was after working pretty extensively on the campaign. I don't think I had a day off since, I don't know, February or March of 2007?

DAVID CUSACK

I got to the White House around probably eight or eight thirty, and they had me sit in the West Wing lobby for like an hour. So I literally sat by myself, and it was weird because the two doors that were usually opened were both closed, and I sat on the north wall looking at the huge bookcase from the late 1700s. There was no ROTUS.[15] There was one UD officer.[16] There were no photos up. There was nothing, and I sat there quietly by myself for about forty-five minutes, and all of a sudden the door to my right opened up and in came Vice President Cheney in his wheelchair. He had hurt his back a day or two before. I know it's bad, but he totally reminded me of Mr. Potter from *It's a Wonderful Life*. I stood up. "Good morning, Mr. Vice President," and he just went, *"Urff."* Like, he just grunted, and he kept on being rolled through the West Wing lobby. And I sat back down.

DAN SHAPIRO

I went down to the Mall to hear the president take the oath of office, and about one hour after he did, I walked a few blocks north and went through a checkpoint. My name was on the list, and I was one of the very first Obama staffers admitted into the White House.

---

15   Receptionist of the United States.
16   Uniformed Division of the Secret Service.

TED CHIODO

You go in, do the security check, and take a little mini oath of office. They swear you in as a government employee. They're like, "Are any of you guys working on security stuff?" I raised my hand. "I do the president's briefing book now." And the security officer, who was a nice woman, was like, "Okay, let me give you the briefing." She literally pulled out this old monitor, and it squeaked as she pulled it over. It had, like, bungee cords holding it down. She put in this VHS tape. "Welcome to the government!" It's ridiculous. She was like, "Watch this tape and retain everything you hear. The penalties for misusing the type of classified documents that you'll be handling can be up to life in imprisonment, or, in time of war, death. Just so you know, we're considered at war right now." I was like, "Thanks, Jan!"

ERIC LESSER

We were all ushered onto a bus and driven down Pennsylvania Avenue with a police escort, and we walked into the White House and they handed me a BlackBerry and a badge, and I walked into my little cubby where my desk was going to be. Everything was empty. The computer was there, and the phone was ringing. I was like, *All right, I guess I gotta get started.*

BRANDON HURLBUT

There's no orientation manual. On day one we had a swearing-in ceremony for seven cabinet members that were confirmed during the transition. We didn't even know where the bathrooms were. We didn't even have computers set up. We were just making this up as we went along.

DAN SHAPIRO

I went straight to work in the West Wing. I had to borrow somebody's computer to write the briefing memos and call sheets for those four calls. So I did that throughout the day. Obviously, at night were the inaugural balls, and we were told to be at the Oval Office at eight thirty the next morning for these calls.

HERBIE ZISKEND

The vice president and the president had what's called military aide-de-camps, a different person from every branch of the military, and those were the people who carried the nuclear football. You always saw the president near a military person who's carrying a briefcase. So I was connected with the people who were Cheney's military aide-de-camps. They're not political appointments. They serve specific terms, and so all the people who were Cheney's aide-de-camps became Biden's aide-de-camps as soon as Obama took office. And I was communicating with them before he took office earlier in the day. Think about it from their perspectives: they went to the Mall with Cheney, Obama took the oath, and then they left with Biden . . . We were at the inaugural balls that night.

ALLYSON SCHWARTZ

I went to one of the inaugural balls. Inaugural balls were what they were. That was not extraordinary. What had been extraordinary [were] the moment and the feeling.

CHRIS VAN HOLLEN

That night I celebrated at a Maryland party. It was obviously a moment of high spirits, and I don't mean alcohol only. It was only later, of course, that we read that, while we were celebrating this great victory, Republicans were plotting to bring down our next president.

TED KAUFMAN

The evening of January 20, 2009, at the Caucus Room—the restaurant in Washington—they all got together: Eric Cantor, Kevin McCarthy, Paul Ryan, Pete Sessions, Jeb Hensarling, Pete Hoekstra, Dan Lungren, Jim DeMint, Jon Kyl, Tom Coburn. And they're having dinner together, okay? They basically decided, led by Gingrich, who kind of did this in 1995, that the only option they had—opposite extinction with the Democrats having the presidency, a majority in the Senate, and a majority in the House—was to agree, as a group, not to do anything. Anything Obama came up with, they were gonna say no to it.

PETE HOEKSTRA

R-Michigan, Second District, US House of Representatives (1993–2011)

I think people have blown this meeting into more than it was, talking about how we were going to obstruct Obama.[17] At least the parts of the dinner that I was at, that's not how I left that meeting. It was kind of like, *Hey, this is a brainstorming meeting where we're talking about, now that we've got a new president, what do we need to do? How do we move forward?*

MARY BONO

R-California, Forty-Fourth District, US House of Representatives (1997–2003)
R-California, Forty-Fifth District, US House of Representatives (2003–2013)

Both parties are the Party of No against whoever's in power. So, long ago, far, far away, when control of the House was so lopsided because the Democrats had such high numbers of seats, Tip O'Neill, the legend went on, decided both parties should work together because there really was no direct political threat. There used to be an unwritten rule that you would not campaign against anybody in your own state—you needed to work together on behalf of your constituents. After a certain point, maybe 104th Congress, everything was a battle.[18] There was no gentleman's agreement that you didn't campaign against your neighbor. You actually expected to. I mean, it was a real battle.

TED KAUFMAN

In 1995, Gingrich came up with this idea of blaming everything on the Democrats. At the same time, he was throwing sand in the gears to keep everything from working. Well, nobody's going to blame Gingrich and the Republicans when the

---

17 Also in attendance at the dinner: John Ensign, senator from Nevada; Bob Corker, senator from Tennessee; Fred Barnes, editor of the *Weekly Standard*; and pollster Frank Luntz.

18 1995 to 1997, led by Speaker of the House Newt Gingrich.

Democrats controlled the House, the Senate, and the presidency. So he pitched the same thing to the [Republican] congressional leaders in 2009, and essentially said, *Look, if we do this, we'll win the House, we'll win the Senate, and then in 2012 we'll win the presidency.*

CHRIS VAN HOLLEN

Right off the bat, you had incredible resistance from Republicans, even on something like the recovery bill.

BARNEY FRANK

I was always for the stimulus. In fact, I continued to call it "stimulus." As you know, they convened my least favorite group, these focus groups, and to be in a focus group you have to be an airhead by definition. You can't be in a focus group if you know anything or have any opinions. So, as a result of the focus groups, they decided they couldn't call it "stimulus." They had to call it "recovery." I've since said that I was puzzled by that, because most of the people I know would rather be stimulated than recovered.

DAN SHAPIRO

I got [to the White House] at 8:20 [a.m.] and walked right in. The president was there—he was businesslike. Rahm Emanuel walked out, having briefed him on the schedule of his day. He looked like he was completely at home, completely just where he had always been sitting and doing his business. We went through the calls. The first was to President Mubarak, thanking him for Egypt's role in arranging the cease-fire. Second call to Prime Minister Olmert, expressing our support for Israel's right to self-defense and concern for its losses in the conflict. Third, the call to President Abbas, thanking him for the Palestinian security forces helping keep the West Bank quiet during the conflict, and then the president had to leave. On the way to the National Cathedral for prayer service for his first full day, he made his call to King Abdullah [II] of Jordan— just to check in and express support. Later in the day, Robert Gibbs put out a summary of the four calls. It did not specify the order.

NICK SHAPIRO

Assistant Press Secretary, White House (2009–2011)
Senior Advisor to the Assistant to the President for Homeland
Security and Counterterrorism, White House (2011–2013)
Deputy Chief of Staff, Central Intelligence Agency (2013–2015)

So Gibbs was the press secretary. Bill Burton and Josh Earnest were the two deputies. Jen Psaki was a deputy as well.

DAN SHAPIRO

[The call summary] listed them in alphabetical order by country. So Egypt, Israel, Jordan, Palestinian Authority—the last two were reversed from the actual sequence—and at some point later in that day the Palestinian Authority spokesman, Nabil Abu Rudeina, said the president told Abbas that this was his very first phone call on his very first day. He sort of put that out to the world's media, which seemed to be a play for relevance . . . I don't know if they actually thought that was true [or] if they were spinning something they knew was not true, but it got picked up by people all too ready to argue that Obama was trying to show distance from Israel.

JACKIE NORRIS

Going into the White House might have been different for me because I had worked in a White House before, when I worked for Al Gore. Also, I was on the First Lady's side, on the East Wing side. The stakes were a little lower than, you know, war.

DAN SHAPIRO

At some point I asked my colleagues, "News people are incorrectly describing the call. Should we correct it?" And, you know, nobody ever made a hard decision, "No," for any specific strong reason—"We need to not correct it." Rather, it seemed kind of petty. Everybody in those early days was focused on much more important things.

BRANDON HURLBUT

I remember Rod O'Connor, who was the chief of staff at [the Department of Energy], called me and said, "Hey, we had some beryllium leak at one of our labs. Who needs to know? What's the process here?" And I remember being like, "What's beryllium?" He's like, "I don't know!" We're, like, Googling *beryllium*. Those were the kinds of questions you would get.

MARGARET RICHARDSON
Counselor to the Attorney General, US Department of Justice (2009–2011)
Deputy Chief of Staff to the Attorney General, US Department of Justice (2011–2012)
Chief of Staff to the Attorney General, US Department of Justice (2012–2015)

This was true at the beginning of every administration. There're like thirteen or so political appointees who start, and then there are people at the White House who are trying to figure out who you call and when you call and who clears things. I had a friend at the Treasury Department who forwarded me an email two or three days in that said, like, *Oh, let's reach out to Margaret Richardson to clear this regulation through the Justice Department.* I was like, "I don't know what this is, but I am not the right person to clear it." Those kinds of things, that's just getting your sea legs in government.

MATTHEW MILLER
Director, Office of Public Affairs, US Department of Justice (2009–2011)

A lot of the things we thought on January 20 just turned out to not be totally true. What we didn't understand was that the Republican Party had bet the entire previous presidency on their handling of national-security issues. After 9/11 they had reoriented the party around, more than anything else, fighting terrorism. Flowing from that was Gitmo, was torture, more renditions—all sorts of issues, each [of] which had fifty tails to it. So if you had renditions, then you also had civil litigation over it. You had to use the state-secrets privilege to block some of that, which has its own thorny history.[19] Same with Gitmo—you had all these habeas cases where people went before courts. You had to decide, if you had someone who you thought was dangerous and couldn't let go, were you going to rely on evidence that might have been obtained through torture to keep them locked up? There were all these thorny questions.

DAVID OGDEN

Deputy Attorney General, US Department of Justice (2009–2010)

One piece of closing Gitmo was [figuring out] what you would replace it with. There was massive resistance to the idea of doing real trials for these folks, and there was the whole controversy over whether there would be military tribunals, which ones would we try [at Gitmo] and which ones would we try in federal court. There was a whole interagency process set up under the attorney general's supervision to figure that out.[20]

SHOMIK DUTTA

Gitmo was such an enormously complicated political decision. There was a class of prisoners you could definitely release and just watch. There was a class of prisoners that you could bring to the US, and there was a class of prisoners who were too dangerous to be [brought] to the US.

---

19   In 2009, the Obama Justice Department argued state-secrets privilege to bat away civil lawsuits, backed by the ACLU, related to the CIA's "extraordinary rendition" program, i.e., the alleged transferring of prisoners to overseas detention centers, where they were tortured. The state-secrets-privilege argument was used by the Bush administration, which candidate Obama criticized during his campaign. "It is vital that we protect information," Miller wrote in 2009, "that, if released, could jeopardize national security."

20   Executive Order 13493, signed by President Obama on January 22, 2009, called for "a comprehensive review of the lawful options available to the Federal Government with respect to the apprehension, detention, trial, transfer, release, or other disposition of individuals captured or apprehended in connection with armed conflicts and counterterrorism operations, and to identify such options as are consistent with the national security and foreign policy interests of the United States and the interests of justice."

MATTHEW MILLER

People didn't know, at the gut level, that the Republican Party would go to war over every inch that we would move on those issues.

DAVID OGDEN

It was strange, of course, because McCain had supported closing Gitmo.[21] There was a consensus that Gitmo was a terrible black eye for the United States. Whatever the realities on the ground were, the perception of Gitmo was [that it was] a bad thing, but it immediately changed overnight and became a point of enormous contention. The idea of moving the real bad guys to high-security federal prisons in the United States, there was panic on Capitol Hill about that.

BEN LABOLT

The president wanted to shut it down. John McCain wanted to shut it down. Bush said, toward the end of his presidency, that he wanted to shut it down. The intelligence community had heard a kind of chatter out there about Gitmo— [al-Qaeda] using it as a propaganda tool against the United States.

DR. HAROLD KOH
Legal Advisor, US Department of State (2009–2013)

Every other established democracy, when they suffered an attack, they tried them in the very place that the attack occurred. The point to be made was that, you know, *You haven't hurt us.* The French, when they had an attack in Paris, they tried the terrorists in Paris. We were doing the opposite. We were effectively

---

21 "Yes, I would close Guantanamo Bay, and I would move those prisoners to Fort Leavenworth. And I would proceed with the tribunals . . . Whether we deserve it or not, the reality is Guantanamo Bay and Abu Ghraib have harmed our reputation in the world, thereby harming our ability to win the psychological part of the war against radical Islamic extremism." —John McCain to *60 Minutes'* Scott Pelley, April 6, 2007.

saying they're so powerful and frightening, we had to keep them locked away somewhere. And that's just playing to this paranoia.

MICHAEL FROMAN
Deputy National Security Advisor for International Economic Affairs, National Security Council and National Economic Council, White House (2009–2013)
US Trade Representative, White House (2013–2017)

The Bush administration had gotten so bogged down in Afghanistan and Iraq and had been so focused on those countries that [it] had ignored important developments elsewhere in the world. Early in the [Obama] administration, the president was focused on the importance of rebalancing [the focus] towards Asia. It was to have multiple dimensions, certainly a security dimension. There're some important treaty allies—Japan, Korea, New Zealand, Thailand, Philippines— and it had a political dimension with the president, for example, being the first US leader to engage with the ten ASEAN countries as a unit.[22]

JEFFREY BLEICH
Special Counsel to the President, White House (2009)
Ambassador to Australia, US Department of State (2009–2013)

The rebalance to Asia was an obvious need, and was part of the discussion in the White House and in the State Department from the beginning. The State Department favored the term "pivot" and the White House favored the term "rebalance," but in both cases, the concept was to focus assets in the Indo-Pacific, where we were facing strategic competition and where our future economic growth would be centered.

MARK LIPPERT

This was something that Obama walked in with in his head, on day one. There's a lot of credit to be spread around here, but I really did feel that this was the

---

22   The Association of Southeast Asian Nations was formed in 1967 by founding members Indonesia, Malaysia, the Philippines, Singapore, and Thailand, and had since expanded to include Brunei, Cambodia, Laos, Myanmar, and Vietnam.

president himself, with his Asia background, realizing what the basic strategic play was. As important as the Middle East was, Asia was far more important in terms of economic viability and its impact on the next century. It's hard to measure things like that, but look at the first couple of months in the Oval Office. The prime minister of Japan was the first head of state of a government to visit.[23] He had the prime minister of Australia in the first six months.[24] Then couple that with the first state dinner with the prime minister of India.[25] You could quickly see, just in schedule alone, how much emphasis there was on this, even from the earliest times.

JEFFREY BLEICH

The rebalance to Asia was crucial, and we recognized early that Australia would be critical to that for a variety of reasons—its location, its positive relations across a number of nations, its weight in Southeast Asia, and various other factors. So Australia was going to be a very important country for us. It was one that I knew well, and where I expected the ambassador role would matter.

MARK LIPPERT

There was talk that the US and China should just get together, form a G2 and divide up how which countries' core interests would be respected in which parts of the world.[26] The president rejected that approach and ultimately went with an "alliance first" strategy. Remember, too, decisions on Asia confronted him in the midst of the financial crisis.

---

23 February 24, 2009.

24 March 25, 2009.

25 November 24, 2009.

26 The Group of Two (G2) proposal gained traction among Washington think tanks during the Bush years. Its broad concept—to forge an unofficial partnership between the United States and China—would use a trade agreement as the pretext to prompt the world's two largest economies in solving issues related to financial crises, climate change, and global security, among others. A G3, also discussed, would have included the European Union.

ADAM HITCHCOCK

At that point, even if you weren't working in [the Office of] Legislative Affairs, you found a lot of your time was spent supporting efforts focused on Capitol Hill.

JIM DOUGLAS

Governor of Vermont (R) (2003–2011)
Chair, National Governors Association (2009–2010)

I was headed to DC to speak at a health-care policy conference, and we didn't have a lot of flights from Burlington to DC. So I said to my team, "Make a day of it. Why don't we see if we can set up a meeting with the new Intergovernmental Affairs folks in the White House to get acquainted?" Well, the Sunday night before we were going, my assistant got a call. "Our meeting tomorrow has been upgraded. You're meeting with the president!" I said, "Oh, okay. I hope our flight's on time."

TED CHIODO

The actual physical shell of the place—outside of the Oval Office, the Cabinet Room, the Roosevelt Room—was sort of just like a beige old government building, but the Oval Office was different. That's the one place that was like, *Oh, it's bigger than it is on TV.*

JIM DOUGLAS

We chatted about his new digs and stuff, and then we got ready for a brief press spray, as they called it, and we sat there, all the press came in, did their thing, and then cleared out. Well, I hadn't noticed that the two couches had been moved back to accommodate the media. So after they left, the president went over to one end of one of the couches, and I instinctively went to the other end to help him move it back into place.

President Obama and Governor Jim Douglas in the Oval Office, February 2, 2009. Pete Souza, White House

PETE SOUZA

Chief Official White House Photographer (2009–2017)

His hands were actually not touching the couch. The president was actually moving it himself.

JIM DOUGLAS

He hadn't been there long, twelve days or so, but the context was the Recovery Act. There was a lot of Republican pushback that this was too big. It was wasteful spending. It was more debt, but among the governors, frankly, there was a lot more bipartisan support. We're the ones who're facing drastic shortfalls in our state budgets and trying to figure out how to dig ourselves out of a hole, fiscally.

JASON FURMAN

The pressure we were getting from the president was to do something bold for the economy, but also something visionary and transformative that would last. If we had a problem, it's almost as if we did too much. It was like twenty different things, any one of which would have been decided a big deal, but they all happened at the same time, and as a result, I think it became harder [for the public] to understand any of them. But the goal wasn't to have people understand. The goal was to have it actually happen.

CAROL BROWNER

Administrator, Environmental Protection Agency (1993–2001)
Director, Office of Energy and Climate Change Policy, White House (2009–2011)

It became clear that one of the important things to do in the Recovery Act was invest in clean energy. This was a nascent industry in many instances. It was struggling. It couldn't go to Wall Street and get the kind of investment resources that more established sectors could get. So we started to build out the program with people in the industry—the environmental community, the academic community, the scientific community, and then ultimately Congress.

JAMES KVAAL

The stimulus included a big increase in Pell grants, college scholarships for low-income students, and we also worked to try and encourage colleges and universities to recognize students who might not otherwise have been eligible for a Pell but had recently lost a job, or one of their parents had recently lost a job. We wanted to make sure that colleges would consider economic circumstances when they were putting together financial-aid packages.

CHRIS VAN HOLLEN

In the House, our members were interested in investing in areas that they thought would be important for the economy but also long-term economic growth. There was a major investment in clean energy. I do recall there being a major effort for an electronic-health-records investment. Now, the one area where there was disagreement was in modernizing our infrastructure—more money into the roads, bridges, light rails, transit, broadband—and it was the view of some folks in the administration, especially [National Economic Council

Director] Larry Summers, that because the spend-out was not so fast, that we shouldn't put as many resources into that.

GLENN NYE
D-Virginia, Second District, US House of Representatives (2009–2011)

It's fair to note that a huge portion of the Recovery Act was tax cuts. So one of the reasons why it was slow to take effect was that it wasn't all infrastructure spending and money flowing directly into the economy.

CAROLYN MALONEY
D-New York, Fourteenth District, US House of Representatives (1993–2013)
D-New York, Twelfth District, US House of Representatives (2013–)

We started a whole series of tax credits and considerations on wind, solar, electric cars—you name it—incentives to help that industry. And it just bounded forward. It's something you didn't read about and you didn't see, but that was a phenomenal move toward renewable energy.

CAROL BROWNER

Well, that whole market of selling tax credits had disappeared. Clean-energy companies were taking advantage of an existing credit that made the energy they produced cost-competitive to older forms of energy production. It had a monetary value in the public markets, but the public markets had dried up. So we figured that out by allowing them to monetize it by taking that credit and letting them basically go to the Treasury Department and get a check for the value of it. That allowed them to keep a footing through those dark times, and, as other things unfolded, to actually grow. It was a hugely important part in how we produce clean energy in this country.

JAMES KVAAL

There was a strong sense from the president down that we wanted to handle this aggressively, that it was a situation where you're losing eight hundred thousand jobs a month and it's hard to know where the bottom was. Now, in large part, the issues were, what kind of plan you could get through Congress, and what were the moderates, particularly in the Senate, willing to accept in terms of the size of the package. That was probably the biggest single constraint.

TED KAUFMAN

We had fifty-eight [Democratic-controlled] Senate seats then, and we needed two votes for the stimulus.

HERBIE ZISKEND

Al Franken didn't take office for a number of months because there was a recount in Minnesota.

TED KAUFMAN

My chief of staff suggested I join this bipartisan caucus group since I was going to be there for two years. "The people in the middle are going to have a lot to say about what goes on." He was right. So I went to my first meeting. I listened for a while, and I think it was [Maine Senator] Olympia Snowe [who] got up and said, "Well, you know, $250 billion is max." I thought to myself how absolutely ridiculous that was, and so I walked out the door. That was the end of the bipartisan caucus for me, but we needed to get those two Republican votes.

JOE LIEBERMAN

Ideologically, I was very much in favor of the stimulus act. The economy needed it, so I was never a problem on that one. Harry [Reid] and the White House, particularly Rahm, engaged me and used me pretty well. [Maine Senator Susan] Collins really was the key. She was asked to go see Harry, and Harry asked [me] to come with her. So we walked in the door of Harry's office. Harry was there. Probably [Illinois Senator Richard] Durbin was there, but Rahm was there, and Rahm said hello to Susan, might have given her a kiss, and then looked to me. "Oh, you wouldn't meet us without your Jewish lawyer." That's Rahm.

MONA SUTPHEN
Member, National Security Council, White House (1991–2000)
Deputy Chief of Staff for Policy, White House (2009–2011)

The Party of No was under way. The fact that we barely got any Republicans on the Recovery Act was kind of the warning shot.

JARED BERNSTEIN

I had been to that kind of rodeo before, but when the economy was contracting at a rate of 8 percent, I was surprised that they lacked a sense of urgency. But I think where I probably wasn't surprised was the ways in which the legislators tried to muscle us. A lot of Republicans went, *Aha, this is an opportunity to cut some taxes*, and so they pushed very hard on that. Grants to businesses and things like that, whereas some of the folks on the left were pushing more for a safety net—employment insurance, food stamps—measures like that.

RAHM EMANUEL

It was hard because nobody had ever spent that type of money, a quote-unquote stimulus. We had just come off a quote-unquote bailout of the banks, and it *was* a bailout. And people were exhausted by the size of the number. And so all of a sudden the pushback came: *That's not what you need—a tax cut is what we need.* So there were all those complications, and then you had to assemble what people wanted: tax cuts, government spending, and investments—which made it, from a messaging standpoint, a difficult thing to sell.

JOE LIEBERMAN

It got down to some real classic horse-trading. Originally, the gross number was up to a trillion dollars—but Susan [Collins], Olympia [Snowe], and Arlen [Specter] wanted it under $800 billion, maybe under $900 billion, I forget which. It's only $100 billion here or there. Susan was bothered by a particular $1 billion for something. It might have been health-care grants of some kind that she thought were wasteful. Anyway I remember suggesting to Rahm, because

I knew [what] she liked, and I was with her and Rahm in the anteroom off of Harry's office. "What if we take that billion out and we give it to the community health centers?" She said, "Oh that's a good idea," and then we went to Rahm, and he said, "Great."

RAHM EMANUEL

That number kept growing until eventually it got to around, I think, just shy of $800 [billion], because I think at that point there was the political argument [that] you couldn't go north of $800 [billion], even though the policy people would have liked to have seen overwhelming force at all levels.

JOE LIEBERMAN

The most noble political quid-pro-quo negotiating session I had ever seen: When [Pennsylvania Senator] Arlen Specter said that he would not support the bill unless an adequate amount of money for cancer research was given to the National Cancer Institute at NIH.[27] Of course, Arlen was a cancer survivor, and Harry or Rahm asked, "How much do you want?" "Ten billion." "Ten billion—are you kidding? I mean, obviously, we want to help cure cancer, but how do we come up with ten billion? Besides, your people are screaming the total is too high." And he held his ground. It was fascinating . . . That was a big boost to research on cancer.

HERBIE ZISKEND

Three Republicans ended up voting for the stimulus—Snowe and Collins from Maine, and Specter from Pennsylvania.

TED KAUFMAN

The idea that we could have gotten more than what we got is ludicrous. It took everything we had to get to [$787] billion. I listened to Republicans come to

---

27   National Institutes of Health.

the Senate floor and say, "We shouldn't do the stimulus. It's waste." But . . . how would the economy get running again? I mean, two or three years after the stimulus was passed, the banks still were not lending and the corporations were not investing. How would we ever get going if we hadn't put the money in?

GENE SPERLING

The Recovery Act was passed on February 17, major decisions on the stress test[28] and the auto rescue were made within the first two months, and the reality that the United States was moving with unprecedented speed to prevent a global slide into depression was so consequential.

BARNEY FRANK

I was strongly supportive of a large stimulus package and critical of the people unfair to [Obama] that it was too small. Yeah, it was too small. It was $80 billion smaller than it would have been if the three Republicans whose votes were needed—Specter, Collins, and Snowe—hadn't insisted on shaving the $80 billion. So it's ridiculous to blame Obama for that. He wanted it to be bigger. What we got was the maximum you could get and have sixty votes. You only needed [two Republican votes], but the three Republican moderates basically agreed that they'd go all or nothing. So he either got zero of them or three of them.

---

28   In February 2009, Secretary Geithner announced a plan purported to instill
     confidence in the nation's largest banking firms: Regulators from the Federal
     Reserve and Treasury would review the assets of nineteen financial institutions
     and determine if they could potentially withstand the recession. If, during the
     process, regulators discovered assets deemed too risky, organizations would then
     be required to raise capital to back them—either by selling shares to private
     investors or, if unable to do so, borrowing from the US government. (Congress
     approved Obama's ability to use the second tranche of TARP funds days before his
     inauguration.)

GLENN NYE

As a Blue Dog,[29] I had some difficulty supporting the Recovery Act. We didn't have a plan attached to it to pay back the money. That should have been something we included. That might have helped the American people understand, number one, that we understood spending a lot of money to try to invigorate the economy was both important and expensive, and that we would make the difficult decisions up front, to decide how we were going to pay for that in the future.

DAVID AXELROD

That came at a time when we already had a trillion-dollar deficit, which was what the Bush administration left us. And so the country was very sensitized to spending, skeptical about whether government spending—or, at least, large parts of it—could be constructive, or whether it would be just wasted money. So that was a barrier toward selling the program, and there's no doubt that the Recovery Act did enormous good. I mean, oftentimes, as our economic advisors told us in that room in Chicago on December 16, 2008, crises that are caused by financial meltdowns tend to produce slow recoveries, and U-shaped recoveries rather than V-shaped recoveries.

BRANDON HURLBUT

So the president put Vice President Biden—the sheriff—in charge of helping administer the Recovery Act, making sure that money was going out the door. We needed to do it quick. We knew the Republican opposition was waiting for the story of how that money got into the wrong hands and ripped off the taxpayers, right? And so the vice president held these weekly meetings. How

---

29   The Blue Dog Coalition was formed in the House of Representatives in 1994 and made up of fiscally conservative Democrats, largely hailing from Southern districts. The caucus had been named after founding member Congressman John Tanner of Tennessee said he was "choked blue" from his liberal colleagues' desire for more government spending.

fast was this money going out? Where was it going? Did we have the safeguards in place?

SETH HARRIS

One of the best things that Barack Obama did in his presidency was pick Joe Biden to lead the implementation of the Recovery Act. It was an under-written story of the Obama presidency, what a fantastic job the vice president did on implementation with the full authority of the president. We were carefully monitored. We were forced to work together.

VAN JONES

Special Advisor, Council on Environmental Quality, White House (2009)

There were more than ten agencies that I was helping coordinate $80 billion out the door, and I was able to use my community-organizing skills inside the federal family—identifying allies in the Department of Energy, at HUD, creating these memoranda of understanding between different departments so that things could work better with this kind of one-time windfall of dollars that needed to get out fast.

BRANDON HURLBUT

The Department of Energy got a ton of stimulus money, something like $30 billion. The annual budget was $29 billion, so you're essentially doubling their budget right away. That's a lot for an agency to handle, especially because most of the budget went to nuclear-weapons management. Making sure nukes didn't get in the hands of the bad guys, and also in the nuclear-waste cleanup—all these weapons in the Cold War, there was some nasty stuff that happened. We're still cleaning up these giant toxic sites, like Hanford in Washington State. So to put $30 billion into real, clean energy, that was a lot. A good example was [how] the Office of Weatherization went into low-income homes and retrofitted them [for] the cold winter. Because these low-income folks were paying high electricity bills, and they're the ones who could least afford that, so some government help could reduce their utilities and keep 'em warm during the winter. Who's against reducing people's bills? This was simple stuff. Caulking windows, putting in some insulation—this was like an $8 billion program, a lot to drop on this tiny office in the DOE.

TOM VILSACK

What I was hoping to do with our [Department of Agriculture] was to make the case that government did, in fact, work. That there were many decisions a government made every single day that were helpful to people, not harmful. That money was not being wasted, that it was actually going into improving people's lives, and into the quality of life of their communities . . . We had our team in each state look at shovel-ready projects to jump start, whether it was a water project, or an extension of a utility line, or opportunity to expand broadband, or a business development.

BRANDON HURLBUT

Of that $30 billion that went out of the DOE, I think to like seventy-five companies, the amount of failures, you could name them. A123 batteries. Solyndra. The amounts of money that went out to successful companies or helped companies succeed had catalyzed the entire clean-energy industry. There was no utility-scale solar farm before the Recovery Act. The banks wouldn't lend to them. *This looks risky. We don't understand solar.* The banks didn't want to go first. So the DOE did the first six! Lent that money, showed how it could be done. Those loans were repaid, and those projects were hugely successful. They created jobs, cleaned up the air, and demonstrated how to finance a big solar farm. The banks did the next twenty solar farms in the country after that. That was an amazing use of money.

DR. STEVEN CHU

If you tally all the losses, like Solyndra, where there were no politics involved, and all the loans that we knew would be paid back and you took all the losses and all the gains, there was a net gain . . . The hullabaloo about one or two failed loans was very sad. It was political posturing. It served the country very well. It not only created jobs but a bankable industry, and it drove the prices down.

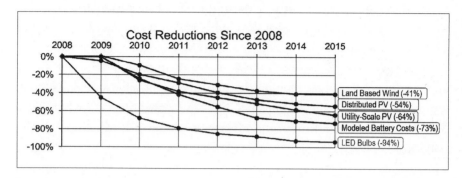

From 2008 to 2015, the cost for clean technologies, ranging from solar- and wind-based energies to batteries and LED lights, dropped between 41 percent and 94 percent. US Office of Energy Efficiency & Renewable Energy

BRANDON HURLBUT

We were so far behind on clean energy when the president took office . . . We got back in that game and made progress at a rate faster than anybody could have imagined. People expected results right away, but in reality, the president was making a long-term bet. It took them time to perfect their technologies, to grow the companies, to scale up and commercialize it.

ARNE DUNCAN

The fact that, out of the stimulus, there was about $800 billion and that we got $100 billion for education? That was amazing. I had these literal nightmares, images of hundreds of thousands of teachers in an unemployment line, and not just not teaching in the classrooms, but not able to pay their bills or make their house payments or car payments. I worried about all the ripple effects in the already-hard times of having teachers unable to meet their obligations. We were able to save a couple hundred thousand teachers' jobs. We didn't save all the jobs we could have saved. Many teachers still got laid off in that time.

BRIAN DEESE

Living through that period, it was low in the sense that it was harrowing, but we had a mandate to try to solve these problems, as painful as they were, and all of the solutions were so terrible that there was a certain freeing sense: *Let's just figure out what's the right thing to do and do it.* In January-February-March of 2009, any potential decision on the autos was, politically, terrible. Nobody wanted us to bail out these companies. Nobody wanted them to go bankrupt. They had different constituencies across the government. It was just all deeply politically unpopular.

AUSTAN GOOLSBEE

They were running out of their $17 billion. They hadn't made really significant efforts at restructuring or even identifying how much the restructuring was going to need to be, and so we were jammed again.

GENE SPERLING

When we were early in the auto bailout, we were about to make calls to several leading politicians in Michigan and Ohio to go through some of the tough things we were going to deal with. Somehow, I was the first person to arrive in the Oval and the president said to me, "Geez, you've been in the White House for eight years. Is it always like this?" And I said, "Mr. President, when I used to consult on *The West Wing*, people would ask me, 'Is it realistic?' And I'd say, 'It's pretty realistic, except that you have to condense what normally happens in a year and a half to sixty minutes.' That's kind of what the beginning of your presidency feels like."

JOHN DINGELL

D-Michigan, Sixteenth District, US House of Representatives (1965–2003)
D-Michigan, Fifteenth District, US House of Representatives (2003–2013)
D-Michigan, Twelfth District, US House of Representatives (2013–2015)
Dean, US House of Representatives (1995–2015)

He had to save it. If the auto industry collapsed—and it would have collapsed all three of the major US companies—[so would] the manufacturers and suppliers. The wheel makers, the seat makers, the glass makers, the steel manufacturers, and the rubber-tire makers. There's only one state that didn't make parts for automobiles. That's how bad it was. They had to do it.

BRIAN DEESE

It took [GM] a while to fully absorb the magnitude of the dire financial straits that the company was in, and, then, the degree of reform and restructure that was going to be necessary. So, in that November–December 2008 period, there was a certain amount of denial and unwillingness to accept certain hard realities, and, you know, it evolved over time. By February, when the management team submitted their first version of their viability plan, they'd progressed to the idea of *Okay, we're going to have to restructure. It might well require using the bankruptcy code*, but [had] not accepted the degree of the fundamental reform that needed to happen.

JENNIFER GRANHOLM

All of the factories were shutting down before the president took office. The suppliers were not getting orders. Nobody was loaning to the suppliers . . . Our [state's] unemployment rate was [10.1 to 12.2] percent. This was December-January-February that we were just in the middle of this unbelievable vortex.

JOHN DINGELL

The one company they couldn't make walk and do well was Chrysler. Chrysler first fell in the hands of the German company,[30] and that German company sucked 'em dry with their large technology and then said, *You're on your own.*

BRIAN DEESE

With respect to Chrysler, there was more acceptance of the reality of their dire circumstances, in part because Chrysler had been in a much more precarious operating state for a longer period of time. They recognized that they were in a really tough bind. They needed a partner, and they were struggling to find one. And so, with Chrysler, it was more an acknowledgment of the straits but not having many cards on the table in terms of alternative plans that might work.

GENE SPERLING

I didn't live the auto rescue every moment of the day like Brian did, but we would consult almost every day. He said that there was no way there would be a Big Three—that it's not going to happen—then he said, "There's just one slim possibility that somehow, in the next couple of months, there would be a potential merger partner with Chrysler." So, you were having somebody tell you something deeply scary and then telling you that there was one potential way out. That one potential way out started to emerge with Fiat.

---

30 In 1998, Daimler-Benz AG purchased the majority stake of a profitable Chrysler Corporation for $36 billion. The acquisition was framed as a "merger of equals," but several factors had proven otherwise, from a deterioration of manufacturing quality control to forcing out American executives. The automaker posted billions of dollars in losses in the coming years, and in 2007, Cerberus Capital Management took the American property off Daimler's hands for $7.4 billion.

STEVEN RATTNER
Lead Advisor, Presidential Task Force on the Auto Industry (2009)

We were simultaneously fielding inquiries from people who wanted to partner with Chrysler or, for that matter, GM, as well as deciding what to do about them. Chrysler was a marginal case, and there was a very spirited discussion about whether a number-three competitor that was in a weakened stage should be saved or not. But at the same time, we were in parallel talks with Sergio Marchionne [of Fiat] about his ideas for an alliance or an affiliation or whatever you wanna call it.

AUSTAN GOOLSBEE

The whole industry was about the SAAR, and that's basically just, "What's the total sales of cars in the nation, in the aggregate?" The SAAR was averaging about sixteen million a year through the 2000s and then, in the recession, it went down to the lowest in decades.[31] So then the question was, What is the national sales of cars going to go back to? If it's going to go back to sixteen million a year, then it's conceivable to have all three of those companies, if they could get their costs down enough and be viable. But if you thought it would come back to, let's say, twelve million, then it's not at all clear that there's enough space to preserve three companies. If you insisted on keeping Chrysler alive, you might actually endanger Ford and GM.

BARNEY FRANK

I was supportive of using the TARP money for the auto bailout.

---

31   In February of 2009, the Seasonally Adjusted Annual Rate dipped to 9.6 million, a sharp decline from 15.4 million in 2008. This was the first time in more than twenty-six years that the SAAR hit below the ten-million mark.

JARED BERNSTEIN

It was pretty clear that the public didn't always distinguish between the Recovery Act and TARP, and TARP was pretty unpopular. So there was some nervousness there. Some real dissension built up after that.

BARNEY FRANK

There was increasing resentment, and that was the problem of the [home] foreclosures . . . When you had Santelli go on television . . . what you had was this anger because, even with foreclosures, most of those people were paying off their mortgages.[32] And it was also true that some of the people facing foreclosures had been irresponsible. People took out home-equity loans to buy boats because the value of their houses went up, so it became politically impossible to use any public funds to alleviate foreclosures, and I saw great resentment, misunderstanding about what we were doing with the banks with TARP . . . The critical point came when AIG announced that it was giving bonuses to the very people who had incurred the huge losses. I had never seen such anger on the part of the public. They were out there with their knives and pitchforks and torches. I understood. It was March of '09 when I realized we were getting the blame for all of this.

---

32 "The government is promoting bad behavior, because we certainly don't want to put stimulus forth and give people a whopping eight or ten dollars in their check and think that they ought to save it. And in terms of modifications, I'll tell you what: I have an idea. You know, the new administration's big on computers and technology? How about this, President and new administration? Why don't you put up a website to have people vote on the internet, as a referendum to see if we really want to subsidize the losers' mortgages? Or would we like to at least buy cars and buy houses in foreclosure and give them to people that might have a chance to actually prosper, down the road, and reward people that could carry the water, instead of drink the water? . . . How many of you people want to pay for your neighbor's mortgage that has an extra bathroom and can't pay their bills? Raise their hand. President Obama, are you listening?" —CNBC's Rick Santelli, broadcasting from the Chicago Mercantile Exchange floor, February 19, 2009.

GLENN NYE

Because of the Great Recession, because of the rawness that was created among the American people, their worries about their jobs, whether they were going to be able to pay their mortgages tomorrow, it was a very difficult time . . . I think, sadly, Republicans capitalized on that worry and turned it into cynicism. They created a really difficult political well for Democrats to climb out of.

BARNEY FRANK

That, I thought, was the turning point. All of us were in a panic trying to alleviate the anger at government. We were in power when [the bailouts] happened, even though the decisions were made in the Bush administration. Today, if you ask people who's responsible for bailouts, "It's the Democrats!" All five bailouts were started by Bush,[33] but the anger over that, and particularly the AIG bonuses, just sunk us. That's a major reason why Chris Dodd couldn't run again. He was unfairly blamed for that.

CHRIS DODD

I was hardly the guy who's going to argue with the administration about what they wanted to do. The point is, these things happen. It's not unique. I realize they had a point of view that they were trying to get the things done, and I paid the price for it.

BARNEY FRANK

[The media] got it backwards. Chris originally founded the [Recovery Act] amendment to ban the bonuses retroactively, and Treasury said to him that you couldn't do that constitutionally. Unfortunately, they were right. So Chris said, *All right, I'll do the best I can. Let's ban any more being included,* and then

---

33   In 2008: investment bank Bear Stearns (March), mortgage lenders Fannie Mae and Freddie Mac (September), insurance conglomerate American International Group (AIG) (September), preferred stock from eight commercial banks (October), and the auto industry (December).

he was totally unfairly accused of having legitimized the retroactive ones which he *wanted* to get rid of but couldn't constitutionally. It was a totally unfair accusation against him—absolutely ass-backwards.

CHRIS DODD

It's not complicated. Tim Geithner felt that there were constitutional issues on a clawback. We disagreed. And I recall very vividly going to some meeting in the basement of the Dirksen garage, and my old friend Rahm Emanuel called—he spent fifteen minutes working for me back in 1992—and we had a shouting match. Rahm was arguing very strenuously that he wanted that whole [retroactive] provision out, and I vehemently disagreed. Anyway, the administration didn't give up and, unbeknown to me entirely, they convinced a person on the [Senate Banking Committee] staff to delete a section of that sentence of the amendment. I never knew about it.

ED SILVERMAN
Staff Director, US Senate Committee on Banking,
Housing, and Urban Affairs (2009–2011)

I wasn't there during the AIG thing. I had been Chris's chief of staff back in the '80s and had gone off to the private sector. I didn't come back to the committee until April of 2009, although once I got back, I did try and piece it together. It was a staff guy, who will remain nameless, who basically acquiesced to the Treasury. We were, quite frankly, in between staff directors. So the committee was not functioning well, and certainly not with anybody in charge who was aligned with Senator Dodd.

NICK SHAPIRO

The tone was really set by Rahm. He was the chief of staff on day one. Most of us hadn't worked in the White House before.

JOE LIEBERMAN

Rahm knew Congress. He knew how to cajole and coerce and swear at you, laugh with you, whatever, and he made a big difference.

JEN PSAKI
Deputy Communications Director, White House (2009–2011)
Traveling Press Secretary and Senior Advisor, Obama for America (2012)
Spokesperson, US Department of State (2013–2015)
Communications Director, White House (2015–2017)

You know, I loved working for Rahm. That wasn't the case for everybody, but he was completely straightforward and a straight shooter. He would come to you—this was so abnormal for a chief of staff—come into [your] office and say, "What the F is happening with" whatever it was, and he'd do that to people around the building. He would go directly to the person who he thought knew the most about whatever it was. Now, that wasn't always the most senior person in every department, which ruffled some feathers, but that was his style. And, you know, there were always reports about how he offended people. He never offended me.

DANIELLE CRUTCHFIELD
Director of Scheduling, White House (2009–2014)

If you ask any White House staffer, their jargon's pretty similar.

JIM MESSINA

Very early on, we both found respect for each other. I'd heard of the great Rahm Emanuel, but I didn't realize how deep he was on the issues. I remember one of the first [Office of Health Reform Director] Nancy-Ann DeParle health-care briefings, Rahm got way into the weeds. The very first weekend of the administration, I read his book and was like, *Holy shit, he really knows this stuff.* And he could see how well I knew those guys [in the Senate] and how close I was to them. He could also tell that I was on Obama's side. I just wasn't going to be a whore for the Senate Dems.

TOM DASCHLE

The president was accused of being somewhat naive, but I really felt he could break the mold and, by his own deportment, set an example that would ultimately catch on and help create a new climate. After he got elected, we were in the room with him on many occasions when deciding how to position his administration on health care. He got a lot of advice to start on the left and recognized that, as time went on, he would have to compromise and move to the middle. I remember how determined he was to demonstrate his good faith by actually doing something incredibly counterintuitive, to take the 1993 Heritage Foundation draft and use that as his opening bid for health reform.[34] He thought it would make a statement with an exclamation point about his desire for bipartisanship.

VALERIE JARRETT

What President Obama set out to do was what seven presidents before him had been incapable of doing. Many were concerned about the political risk of doing something like that, particularly when we were faced with a challenging economy. There were folks who thought, when it was hard, that perhaps we should compromise, and many thought we would never get bipartisan support, so why bother?

CHRIS DODD

Rahm Emanuel, again, was rather outspoken. He thought it was a mistake to take on health care—in light of all the other issues, dealing with the collapsing economy, that we took on too much. So there was an internal debate in the White House about whether or not it should be a slimmed-down bill or a larger bill. Teddy [Kennedy] was really in many ways the spiritual leader.

---

34 In November of 1993, Republican John Chafee of Rhode Island introduced the Health Equity and Access Reform Today Act (S. 1770, a.k.a. HEART) on the Senate floor. The Republican majority did not take up the bill for a vote, despite having twenty GOP sponsors. Many provisions in the bill were based on economist Stuart Butler's work at the Heritage Foundation, a conservative think tank.

RAHM EMANUEL

This will be the thirtieth time I'm going to correct the record, even though it was written contemporaneously at the time. I said to the president, which was what he asked for, "Look, this has been tried for a hundred years. It's going to be a lot of politics—political capital that you won't get back—and there will be a lot of time, given the robustness of the agenda. Time is the most valuable asset you have, because of your political standing."

DAVID AXELROD

I was conflicted, because I have a child with a chronic illness. I almost went bankrupt because of flaws in our insurance system, and yet, as his political advisor, I was frightened about taking it on, particularly in the midst of everything else. But when we had this discussion, he said, "If we don't do this in the first two years, it probably won't get done. If it doesn't get done, we're going to continue to have this runaway health-care inflation. We're going to have tens of millions more without coverage, and the whole thing will implode." And he looked at me and said, "What are we here for? Are we here to put our approval rating on the shelf for eight years and admire it, or are we here to draw down on that capital and do things that are important for the long term?"

RAHM EMANUEL

I said early on, "If we're going to go all in, go in with a big universal. But, given the complexities, you should have [another plan] in the drawer." This had come from my Clinton days. If you look at history, the successful plans were the ones that universalized populations: Medicare for seniors, Medicaid for poor, veterans, children's health care. And I said, "My recommendation is, there may be a point in time we're going to want to do back-offs." I said, "I would universalize small business and family. [It's] smaller, cheaper, more affordable, and you'll get in and out of it, and you'll have the political capital to do other things." It was not like "Don't do health care."

ROB ANDREWS

D-New Jersey, First District, US House of Representatives (1990–2014)

The public side of it would have been when the president held a White House summit, and Senator Kennedy made a dramatic appearance at that.[35] He was ill at the time but wanted to indicate his support. But the private work really started in the House where Speaker Pelosi decided to convene three committees to meet on essentially a weekly basis, and the staff would work around the clock. And that, of course, was the Ways and Means Committee, at the time chaired by Charlie Rangel; it was Energy and Commerce, chaired by Henry Waxman; and Education and Labor, chaired by George Miller. I was the subcommittee chairman under George Miller that had the health jurisdiction for Education and Labor.

DAVID BOWEN

In the spring of 2009, I distinctly remember sitting at a table by a window in our then temporary offices in a Russell courtyard and having this moment of realization of what a privilege it was to take a blank sheet of paper and start the process—obviously, there were many others involved—but to start the process of what became the Affordable Care Act.

ROB ANDREWS

We would meet at least once a week—the three committees—usually in a room off of the House floor. The staff would talk about the policy choices that were incumbent in making that decision. That was a process that began in March of '09 and came to ultimate fruition in either late June or early July of '09. Where that group, the so-called Tri-Committee Group, decided it would sign off on a draft.

---

35   March 5, 2009.

DAVID BOWEN

We had talked to a lot of people. We had done a lot of thinking. One of the [realizations] we made vis-à-vis the Clinton effort in '93 was that their effort was viewed, perhaps mischaracterized, as kind of sweeping away the former structure of health care and replacing it with something new. We consciously decided to build on the existing structure, because one of the things that sank the Clinton effort in '93 was this organized attack [claiming] that it would take away what you had. There's this funny duality in people's minds, like they hate Congress but they're a member of Congress—they sort of hate the health system, but most, especially those with employer-based health care, are generally satisfied with the coverage they have and are loath to change it.

BARBARA LEE

D-California, Ninth District, US House of Representatives (1998–2013)
D-California, Thirteenth District, US House of Representatives (2013–)

I was chair of the Congressional Black Caucus, and we put together what we called the "Quad Caucus." It was the Black Caucus, the Hispanic Caucus, the Asian Pacific American Caucus, and the Progressive Caucus. And we wrote to the president and Speaker Pelosi and laid out our principles, what we wanted to see in the bill. I led the effort in the negotiations to get our health disparities based on race and ethnicity [addressed] as part of the Affordable Care Act and expanded the Office of Minority Health.

DAVID BOWEN

So what we did to build on this structure of the current system was the Medicaid expansion—to expand Medicaid as the floor, and build from that with existing employer-based coverage. Plus the ACA exchanges would act as regulated marketplaces along the lines of—ironically, in retrospect—the Mitt Romney bipartisan bill only in Massachusetts.³⁶ So, coming back to that moment where I was sitting with a cappuccino and a blank piece of paper, I wasn't making things up from a blank slate. I had a sense of what we wanted to do, and literally the first thing I wrote was a table of contents. That was the framework.

CECILIA MUÑOZ

Director of Intergovernmental Affairs, White House (2009–2012)
Director, Domestic Policy Council, White House (2012–2017)

One of the reasons, ultimately, that health-care [legislation] moved in the way that it did was because of our deep understanding that health care was essential to fixing the economy—that the cost of health care, both to the government and the people, was unsustainable and was a huge drag on the economy . . . It was not a given that immigration reform was low on the list. In fact, it was high on the president's list.

President Obama meets with the Congressional Hispanic Caucus in the State Dining Room, March 18, 2009.
Pete Souza, White House

---

36   In 2006, Governor Mitt Romney signed healthcare reform legislation crafted by a Democratic-majority state legislature, which aimed to provide coverage to nearly all of Massachusetts's residents without the use of a public option, and later became colloquially known as "Romneycare." Senator Edward Kennedy worked closely with Romney on the effort, and was present when the Republican governor signed the bill into law. The legislation would inspire several provisions of what would become the Affordable Care Act, including essential health benefits, coverage for preexisting conditions, and out-of-pocket limits.

LUIS GUTIÉRREZ

He wasn't thinking about immigration. The Congressional Hispanic Caucus's first meeting with Obama at the White House, I brought about three of those banker boxes, because I'd gone and collected petitions in Providence, Boston, Atlanta, Chicago. *Obama. Keep your promise. Immigration reform. Keep the families together.* He's not too happy. Here's exactly what he said to me: "Luis, I'm gonna assign that to Rahm Emanuel," which basically meant, "This is bullshit to me," and on that day, he called me to the side. He said, "You're from Chicago. I'm from Chicago. We should be working together. You shouldn't be getting on my ass all of the time."

JARED BERNSTEIN

There was no space between Obama and myself on issues around the Recovery Act or the need for Keynesian stimulus. Most notably where I saw this was around the auto sector. There were a lot of people, even on the economic team, who were pushing him not to bail out the auto sector. They just felt that was an economic mistake. A number of us pushed in the other direction.

AUSTAN GOOLSBEE

So the vote that took place at the [National Economic Council] meeting in Larry's office was about the narrow question of *Two years from now, if we do this, where will Chrysler be, alive or dead?* And it's fifty-fifty whether Chrysler could survive or not if they got the money. That became the question: *Do you think we should do this?* We went back and forth.

STEVEN RATTNER

We held a whole series of meetings, and then there was the one in the Oval Office.[37] We started to have this discussion with the president, and the president

---

37   March 26, 2009.

first said, "Well, somebody doesn't want to do this. Where's Austan?" And somebody went and got Austan.

AUSTAN GOOLSBEE

We're trying to answer the questions. *If Chrysler did not exist, would the people who buy Chrysler cars not buy a car? Would they be likely to buy a Ford or a GM car?* In which case, the job-loss impact of just Chrysler going under would be far smaller on the nation than it would at first seem.

STEVEN RATTNER

Then the president ran out of time and said, "Let's get together again at the end of the day and figure it out."

GENE SPERLING

When we had the big meeting with the president in the Roosevelt Room that afternoon, the economic team was evenly split. Three or four people spoke on behalf of letting Chrysler go under. Brian Deese, Ron Bloom, and I—the three of us—each separately made the case for why we would go forward. Some people might have thought, perhaps, I had too much emotion in it because of where I was from, but I would have felt the same way if I'd grown up in Wyoming instead of Ann Arbor.

STEVEN RATTNER

Deese, Ron Bloom, and Sperling were probably the most passionate on the side of saving Chrysler.

GENE SPERLING

So when someone said, "Well, if Chrysler goes under, the other two will pick up the demand," that, to me, was very static. You're dealing in a world, at that time, of enormous economic fear, of unknown negative cycles that could happen, and so that was a moment where the president had a split team. He heard from everyone. He heard from his political advisors. I think David Axelrod's heart was completely with saving Chrysler and [he] was hoping that side [would win], and yet had to tell the president that the polling was totally against it. That was his job. He had to tell the president that this was going to be a time that he should do the right thing, but it was going to be, in the short term, an unpopular thing.

STEVEN RATTNER

I didn't think the public was *that* emotional about the auto rescue. I think, on balance, they were negative about it. At the time, polls showed people *would* be negative about it, but people were not marching in the streets saying, "How dare you bail out the auto industry?!" In general, people kind of thought to themselves, *I wish we weren't doing this, but this is not the end of the world.*

AUSTAN GOOLSBEE

The president heard all sides. He said, "I hear ya. I know it's risky, but I don't think we can afford not to do this." So they extended the loans to Chrysler.[38] The president decided that we had to try.

JENNIFER GRANHOLM

March 29, [President Obama] said the plans that he had received from Chrysler and GM, which they had been required to put forth, were "unacceptable" and that he was going to announce that he was giving Chrysler thirty days and GM sixty days to revise them. Otherwise, he would put them into bankruptcy. And

---

38   After the government approved $17.4 billion in loans to Chrysler and General Motors in 2008, the Obama administration demanded that, in order to continue receiving federal aid, the manufacturers submit rigorous viability plans to his auto task force. In addition, President Obama pressured General Motors' CEO Rick Wagoner to resign and insisted that Chrysler agree to a deal in thirty days wherein Fiat would own no more than 50 percent stake of the company. (Fiat could purchase more of Chrysler once Chrysler's loans were repaid to the government.) The administration would provide operating funds for Chrysler as they ironed out the details of the partnership.

he told me that Rick Wagoner, GM's CEO, was stepping down. I went into my *Please don't put them into bankruptcy, they won't buy cars from a bankrupt company* pitch, and he was totally compassionate . . . "I get it. I really understand. This is really difficult."

GENE SPERLING

We were on the phone with some of the congressional delegation from auto communities,[39] and one of them said, "Whatever you do, sir, don't use the word *bankruptcy.*" And President Obama said, "You know I can't do that. I'm going on TV,[40] and I'm going to be clear that there are bankruptcies that lead to resolution and there are those that lead to restructuring in a stronger economy. We're going to be the latter. I can't get into the game where I'm afraid to use words or look like I'm not being straight."

JENNIFER GRANHOLM

And so they had thirty and sixty days, and so he called me again to say that he was putting Chrysler into bankruptcy. This was on April 30.

GENE SPERLING

The auto rescue was really the president at his best, in terms of allowing a robust discussion, and I thought Larry Summers did a good job. At the end of the day, Larry sided with the "save Chrysler" side, but the president saw that there was an evenly divided economic team, made sure he had the sharpest presentation;

---

39 March 29, 2009.

40 "My Auto Task Force has been reviewing requests by General Motors and Chrysler for additional government assistance, as well as plans developed by each of these companies to restructure, to modernize, and to make themselves more competitive. Our evaluation is now complete . . . My administration will offer GM and Chrysler a limited additional period of time to work with creditors, unions, and other stakeholders to fundamentally restructure in a way that would justify an investment of additional taxpayer dollars . . . That may mean using our bankruptcy code as a mechanism to help them restructure quickly and emerge stronger." — President Obama, in the White House Grand Foyer, March 30, 2009.

he made the decision fully informed of the upside and downside risks, and I thought he communicated in a way that showed somebody talking straight.

AUSTAN GOOLSBEE

A couple of things on the economic side proved somewhat decisive. One was, Ford's a direct competitor to Chrysler and GM. So, the normal economist model of an industry would say, "The last thing Ford would want to do would be to keep its competitors alive"—that, if anything, they should be trying to *prevent* the rescue of their competitors. But Ford thought GM and Chrysler should be rescued. All three of the big automakers shared tons of suppliers. So they said, "If Chrysler fails, and if that leads to the brake manufacturers going under, then we're doomed, because we're not going to be able to get brakes for our cars."

STEVEN RATTNER

Probably a defining moment, although there were several, was getting Chrysler out of bankruptcy on June 9, because that did go to the Supreme Court. But besides that, we were using a bankruptcy process that had never really been used on something of this scale or on this kind of a timetable, and we weren't sure it would work. It would have been like putting an airplane together in your driveway and then wondering if it was going to fly. So when the Supreme Court refused to deal with it and we got [Chrysler] out of bankruptcy,[41] [when]

---

41   With Chrysler LLC facing bankruptcy, the Treasury arranged for an asset sale that would allow the auto company to emerge as a new Chrysler Group LLC, jointly owned by the United Auto Workers union, Fiat, and the US and Canadian governments. The Indiana State Police Pension Trust—a group of some 100,000 retired police officers and teachers that had obtained Chrysler bonds in July 2008 at forty-three cents per dollar—filed a lawsuit to block said sale. The lawsuit argued that the sale redistributed value to unsecured creditors (the UAW) in a manner contrary to US bankruptcy law. (The US Treasury set the debt-exchange offer to twenty-nine cents on the dollar.) The plaintiffs appealed a Second Circuit ruling that had approved the sale, but on June 9 the Supreme Court declined to hear the case, stating that the trust had "not carried the burden" of proving that the court needed to intervene, while clarifying they were not ruling on the merits of the pensioners' challenge. The decision pulled Chrysler out of bankruptcy and allowed the sale to go through.

GM went into bankruptcy on June 1, at that point we assumed that if Chrysler had worked, then GM would work. And so that was probably the most exciting moment of the whole thing. If you will, the most monumental point.

ERIC LESSER

For the most part, everyone at the White House had clearly delineated lines of authority. The economic advisor handled banking regulations and financial issues. The press secretary answered questions from the press. The domestic policy advisor managed the domestic-policy portfolio. The energy advisor did climate change, and on and on and on. David [Axelrod]'s role was unique. He kind of floated at thirty thousand feet and took into consideration the whole picture of policy and political implications, the public-affairs and press considerations, of every single issue at every dimension, and synthesized all of that into coherent broad advice. As a result, he really was kind of involved in everything.

DAVID AXELROD

It was like being in a submarine, in that, when you worked there, you rarely left. You went in at dawn and had breakfast, lunch, and often dinner there. You'd just go serially from one consequential meeting to another, and you'd see many of the same people throughout the day, and . . . you do feel sort of insulated there. The other reason the submarine analogy appeals to me was that you also looked at the world through a periscope.

MELODY BARNES

You're the consummate insider because it's the White House, the center of power in a city very much focused on power. There's an interesting tension with that. For those of us who did the work day-to-day, you were so immersed in that, for better or for worse, and in what people would call "the bubble." My husband would say, "It's not a bubble. It's a cave." A bubble is transparent. You can see out. A cave is not. And you went in that building and felt all of the pressure, whether it's the news being spun about you, or the very real and challenging problems that were coming to you every day.

DAVID AXELROD

You're never sitting there making paper dolls or looking at the clock and waiting for it to hit five. Whenever I looked at the clock my question would be, "Where did all the time go?" But the downside of it was, it was very insular.

MELODY BARNES

One of the challenges was to stay attuned to what's happening outside the White House.

TED KAUFMAN

I was only going to be [in the Senate] for two years. I had gone to Wharton School. Finance was natural for me, and, even though I was not in the finance committee areas, I was concerned about the crisis. There had to be a way to send a message. So I found out on the Judiciary Committee, the chair, [Patrick] Leahy, and [Republican member] Senator Grassley had this bill, the Fraud Enforcement and Recovery Act. So I got involved to do the kind of legwork, to write op-eds and go on TV shows, stuff like that. Then after the bill passed, Leahy let me chair two oversight hearings on how it was being implemented.[42]

DAVID OGDEN

There were all the various initiatives with the economy. The Chrysler and GM situations were very complicated legally, and then you had the ongoing investigations, which were getting under way, of the various institutions that had been at the heart of the crisis. They were run by the career prosecutors who were experts at financial crime . . . There was, in general, an appetite, I would say, for bringing those cases if they could be made.

---

42   May 20, 2009.

TED KAUFMAN

Lanny Breuer[43] and Robert Khuzami and the number-two guy in fraud enforcement in the FBI, testified. I met with them before the hearing, and they said, "Look, you know, we're really into this stuff." And by the way, the one thing you couldn't do was ask them about specific prosecutions. It's just not right for Congress to talk to prosecutors about whether they're going to prosecute a case or not . . . They hadn't done anything yet, which was okay at the time. It was brand new.

CAROLYN MALONEY

Anytime you take on the banks, it's difficult. I started working on the Credit Cardholders' Bill of Rights in 2007, and I could not even walk down the street or even to the floor of Congress without people coming up to me about how unfairly they were treated by credit-card companies. Everybody had a story, and when members of Congress started telling you about *their* credit-card stories you knew it's just a horrible thing. So I put together the consumer groups with the banks to come up with a list of goals that we wanted to put in the bill. We came up with the list, and, little did I know, the banks would fight it tooth and nail.

CHRIS DODD

Of course, the credit-card companies didn't help themselves—the *Frontline* stories about the abuses, and all of these various provisions that were six different ways to take consumers to the cleaners. You know, they used to call those who paid their monthly bills on time "deadbeats." There was no financial value in having you as a card-carrying member. They loved the people who would make the minimum monthly payments. Those were the ideal customers, in a sense. And so they were a major asset in getting the legislation passed, and, obviously, having the president and the administration on your side didn't hurt either.

---

43   US Assistant Attorney General, Criminal Division, US Department of Justice
     (2009–2013).

CAROLYN MALONEY

They had all kinds of ways to trap people into huge amounts of debt. The CARD[44] Act would effectively eliminate [hidden and excessive] fees by requiring them to get an affirmative opt-in from consumers, and when President Obama adopted it and it became an issue that he ran on, that started a whole new momentum.

CHRIS DODD

The credit-card legislation went flying through.

CAROLYN MALONEY

I was the only woman at the bill signing,[45] and all these male senators started standing in front of me. I literally wrote this bill and worked on it nonstop for a long time, and they started pushing me out of the way. And President Obama came over, grabbed my hand, pulled me up and said, "No, it's her bill." He had me stand right behind him.

DANIELLE CRUTCHFIELD

President Obama was, for the most part, very punctual. As a scheduler it's the best thing ever. You could make a schedule, and of course things always came up that you had to change, but President Obama was always conscious of the fact that he needed to get to the next thing, which was one of the things that separated him and made him very different. President Clinton would linger out on that tarmac forever.

---

44   Credit Card Accountability Responsibility and Disclosure.
45   May 22, 2009.

MARK LIPPERT

We went to Saudi and then to Egypt. I think the thinking was to go to the Saudis, meet with the king, get that bilateral relationship—as sticky as it can be—in good order, then the Egyptians were next. So the Saudis got the order number one in terms of the stops, and the Egyptians got a significant speech.

DAN SHAPIRO

There was a question of where he would [give the speech]. People advocated a Muslim capital that might be less fraught. Some thought Indonesia, because he had his own early-years experience there, and it's a way of taking less risk to go to a country that's not quite at the center of the issues around terrorism. Others thought he'd split the difference and go somewhere like Morocco. He argued that if you were going to do this, you'd have to go where the problem [was]. You had to go right to the heart of it, Cairo being the heart of the Arab world and where Islamic extremism had been playing itself out.

MARK LIPPERT

[Speechwriter] Ben [Rhodes] was the driving force on that one. He did a lot, as I recall, working with Dan and a few others. I think John Brennan also, because John was the counterterrorism advisor but also had a lot of experience in the Arab world. He had been the [CIA] chief of station in Saudi Arabia. I was more of the logistics guy, so [I took care of] the planning and travel associated with it.

DAN SHAPIRO

He wanted to say to an Arab audience in an Arab capital, *You need to put aside your dreams of Israel's disappearance or of somehow convincing the United States to separate itself and weaken our commitment to Israel. That's not going to happen.* And, at the same time, he demonstrated his understanding of Palestinian aspirations—that that was also a commitment that we could maintain, that those could reside together. That meant, among other things, we were going to advocate ending [Israel] settlement expansion as one of the things that contributed to the stalemate that we inherited.

DAVID AXELROD

I was there. It was an extraordinary moment. Of course, it was tricky because he was doing something that hadn't been done before. Obviously there were some domestic political issues surrounding that, and unhappiness in Israel and some of the American-Jewish community about it.

DAN SHAPIRO

The idea was to do some truth telling to all sides. That was very much Obama's kind of concept. *Let's stop dancing around certain taboos and talk hard truths and get on with some improved relationships and hopefully some improved prospects.*

DAVID AXELROD

He felt strongly that we needed to make the Muslim world allies in this fight against extremism. He wanted to signify an open hand to those who wanted to work with us. And the speech was challenging in places, challenging to Israel about the settlements [and] challenging to the government of Egypt over corruption and the treatment of women.

DAN SHAPIRO

This obviously didn't just pop up as a momentary afterthought of a policy. This was a very well-thought-through decision that he, having observed the difficulties we were having in relationships with many Muslim societies and many Arab Muslim countries—in large part because of what had gone on during the Iraq War—that there was an opportunity and need to begin a different kind of conversation.

ERIC LESSER

Obama is very deliberative. He's open minded. He liked to seek out alternative viewpoints. He thought about things on very granular levels but also intellectual levels, and that style suffused the team. Even the very junior people like me, you couldn't help but absorb that.

JACKIE NORRIS

I was lucky to have had a seat at the table during the most historic, in my lifetime, moment in time.

TED CHIODO

The first two years were hot and heavy with everything. You had staffing of the government. We were trying to implement our policy. The Recovery Act was going on. You had the health-care bill. Everything was taking off at the same time.

ROB ANDREWS

I read a draft [of the health-care bill] on a trip to Las Vegas. It was enormous. I carried it onto the plane, and I couldn't throw out the pages because they were sensitive and private. I had to carry them in a bag until I could find a shredder, but [around] then the committees in the House proceeded to mark up the bill.

CHRIS DODD

We went through the longest markup [in the Senate Health Committee]. It began in June of '09 and we finished on July 15 of '09. The big debate items were more in the Finance Committee.

DAVID BOWEN

There were two committees in the Senate and three committees in the House that had significant jurisdiction over the ACA. Someone had to go first, and we went first. That was very much a product of Senator Kennedy's desire to move things forward quickly. As you know, he was quite sick and wasn't able to come back to Washington that often. And when he came back in May, he met the whole staff. For everyone else, he'd say, "Oh, Jeff, hi. How are you doing?" and "Oh, hey, Melanie. How are you doing?" He came to me and just said, "Where's my bill?"

CHRIS VAN HOLLEN

A priority of House Democrats was [also] doing something on the clean-energy front. So there were timing issues about whether we should take up the Affordable Care Act or the clean-energy legislation first, because Nancy Pelosi was interested in moving the Waxman-Markey bill.[46] Rahm and I were on the same page and urging that we take the Affordable Care Act first because we recognized the Senate did not have the bandwidth for both.

JOHN TANNER
D-Tennessee, Eighth District, US House of Representatives (1989–2011)

[The Waxman-Markey bill] wasn't going anywhere in the Senate, and although it's an important issue, it was not the issue du jour. When Obama got elected in '08, we were in the midst of a horrible recession. The life of the planet was secondary to the economic life of the United States. And cap-and-trade [legislation] had more to do with the economic life of the planet than it did

---

46 In May of 2009, Representatives Ed Markey (D-Massachusetts) and Henry Waxman (D-California) introduced the American Clean Energy and Security Act (H.R. 2454). The "transformational legislation which takes us into the future," as Speaker Pelosi asserted in 2009, would set higher standards for emission-reduction targets by enacting a national cap-and-trade program. The system would incentivize private companies to reduce pollutants with the purchasing and trading of permits that regulate quotas (caps) on carbon and greenhouse-gas emissions.

the economic life of the United States. I think that the [House] leadership and the White House lost the connection with the people that led to the election of Obama. They said, *Wait a minute. What are y'all doing? We want to get out of this recession, then we'll worry about this.* So it was an important issue, but it was the wrong issue at the wrong time. That poisoned that Congress.

JON CARSON

Waxman-Markey passed through the House before health care.[47] That was a transformational bill, and then it got stalled in the Senate . . . There just wasn't the political infrastructure across the country to get it across the finish line through the Senate like we saw on health care. I think health-care advocates had done a better job over the years of building an on-the-ground infrastructure, so that when it was nearing the finish line, they got it across. That wasn't there for Waxman-Markey—particularly when you were talking about needing sixty votes.

ROB ANDREWS

The Senate never voted on cap-and-trade, or at least it never passed the filibuster.[48] It was important to House leadership and the president, and so we got it through the House. A lot of members suffered because of that. There's no question about it.

MARY BONO

President Obama had worked really hard to court Republicans, and certainly centrist Republicans, to find—I don't know if I should say "common ground"— but persuade them to support his agenda. So after cap-and-trade, which, I was

---

47 The American Clean Energy and Security Act passed on a 219–212 vote June 26, 2009. Forty-four House Democrats voted nay.

48 A maneuver that empowers the Senate minority, or individual senators, to prevent a motion to vote on a bill by giving floor speeches for an indefinite period of time. To end a filibuster, the legislative body must invoke *cloture*, a procedure that requires a three-fifths majority (sixty votes).

one of six Republicans to vote for the climate-change legislation, he had a definite change of heart and approached the Congress differently, beginning with Obamacare.

MICHAEL STEEL

Press Secretary, House Republican Leader John Boehner (2008–2009)
Press Secretary, Speaker of the House John Boehner (2011–2015)
Press Secretary, Vice-Presidential Candidate Paul Ryan (2012)

The president's promise of bipartisanship really fell apart within weeks of him taking office. The sort of original sin of the administration was their handling of the stimulus. They blocked Republicans out of consideration on the policy of the stimulus bill, which resulted in House Republicans unanimously voting against it, and they basically didn't bother talking to us seriously again until we won the majority.

MARY BONO

It's not unique to them. If you look back to when Newt Gingrich was Speaker of the House in '95, the class that Sonny [Bono] was elected in, he, too, did not believe he needed the other side. It's really typical of a new party in power to overplay their hand, but there was a certain hubris, and one thing that I was really frustrated with [was that,] as I was invited to the White House for a meeting, [there were] about ten or twelve of us, I hand delivered to Rahm and the president—but Rahm took it—a packet about the opioid epidemic. It was gonna hit us smack dab in the face in the worst possible way.

LUIS GUTIÉRREZ

Giving it to Rahm was basically like saying it's going into a black hole.

MARY BONO

It was occurring in Southern California. It was occurring in Appalachia. I couldn't convince anybody at that time, even in my party. Again, there are lots of different reasons people do what they do. Calculus everywhere. It's just frustrating because, had we jumped on it then, we probably would have been a lot better off.

DR. HAROLD KOH

Also, and very important, by July of '09 the president had said dozens of times he wanted to close Guantanamo. It was either going to happen early or it was going to bleed out and happen in a slow, painful process. In July 2009, I thought there was no chance it wouldn't happen before eight years were up, but [after] our eight years [in office] were up, and we still had forty-five people in Guantanamo, it's a very sad situation.

DAVID OGDEN

There was a process to figure out where the new facility would be and the whole issue of relocating people, either to the United States or to other countries. The administration was working hard to convince other countries to take some of these prisoners, the ones where the cases against them were weak or nonexistent. But we felt we needed to show that we would take some too. The Uyghurs were the plan for that, but that fell apart politically.

BEN LABOLT

There was the plan to bring the Uyghurs, one of the groups of detainees reviewed as nonthreatening, to Virginia. They're from the western part of China, and, basically, they had an issue with the Chinese government, not with the American government. Frank Wolf had been viewed as an ally on the issue, but when he was notified of the plan, he went public and came out against it.

FRANK WOLF
R-Virginia, Tenth District, US House of Representatives (1981–2015)

They were going to move them to northern Virginia. They were going to be in the Seven Corners area. They were going to live close to the mosque that Anwar al-Awlaki went to,[49] and Anwar al-Awlaki was the one who was radicalized. Major [Nidal] Hasan, who was involved in the shooting down in Fort Hood, had gone to that mosque. That mosque had been known for radicalization. So, to take people who had been arrested in Tora Bora, a training camp run by Osama bin Laden, then put them there in Guantanamo, where they were mixing with Khalid Sheikh Mohammed and all the other guys, and then bring them here to the United States? They were going to release them. They were not moving them to a supermax.

BEN LABOLT

Some of the plans [included] bringing some detainees into a facility in the United States that resembled ADX Florence, where you never had somebody escape. Some states wanted to open a facility like that, like in Michigan and Illinois. It's just the political climate changed after that moment with Wolf, and it became very difficult to get done.

FRANK WOLF

So you had an issue of closing Guantanamo, but you had an issue of *Where do you bring them?* They were released, and a number of very dangerous guys were sent back to Yemen, sent back to Saudi Arabia and some other places. You wouldn't want to risk the opportunity of bringing a guy here within seven miles of the Pentagon and nine miles of the Capitol and nine miles of the White House and seven miles of the Chinese embassy. Particularly since we've had radicalization of people who were born and raised here in the United States.

---

49   The Dar al-Hijrah Islamic Center, located in Falls Church, Virginia, was founded in 1983 and affiliated with the North American Islamic Trust, a foundation that provided places of worship for Muslim American students. Anwar al-Awlaki, a US citizen whom the US government alleged was a recruiter for al-Qaeda and helped plan or inspire a number of terrorist attacks, including the 9/11 plane hijackings, served as imam at the center prior to April 2002. Two of the 9/11 hijackers, Nawaf al-Hazmi and Hani Hanjour, attended services at the mosque during this period. Fort Hood shooter Nidal Malik Hasan also was present at the mosque for his mother's funeral in May of 2001.

BARBARA LEE

What members of Congress could not come to grips with was that we're in more danger by allowing these types of prisons to continue. Not closing Gitmo gave rise to more anger and made our national security *more* at risk, not less. It was Democrats and Republicans.

DAVID OGDEN

From both sides of the aisle, yeah, [and] you had high-security prisons that would handle the worst of the worst forever and we never had an issue with it, including very serious terrorists who were held in the highest-security federal prisons. It was never an issue of any kind and never would be.

DR. HAROLD KOH

Supermax prisons cost $80,000 a person and nobody ever escaped them. So, even if you were positing that they're equally dangerous as supermax inmates, there's a place to hold these people onshore. Why invest in detention offshore at $1 million per person? I think the original reason for the Bush people to hold them offshore at Guantanamo was the thought that they couldn't have any rights to assert, but then the Supreme Court held that they did.[50] Whatever value there was in having an offshore prison camp was negated. You had might as well bring them onshore and let them contest their detention.

---

50   In 2004, the Supreme Court voted 6–3 in *Rasul v. Bush* that detainees in Guantanamo had a right to petition the American judiciary for legal review. The plaintiff, Shafiq Rasul, spent two years in the Cuba detention camp after being captured during the US invasion of Afghanistan. He denied any allegiance to terrorist organizations but did not deny fighting with the Taliban. "They are not nationals of countries at war with the United States," read the SCOTUS decision, "and they deny that they have engaged in or plotted acts of aggression against this country; they have never been afforded access to any tribunal, much less charged with and convicted of wrongdoing; and for more than two years they have been imprisoned in territory over which the United States exercises exclusive jurisdiction and control."

BEN LABOLT

My understanding was that one of the things that delayed [closing Gitmo] was that the administration expected that the detainee files left over from the Bush administration would be in better shape to bring to court, and bring swift justice in the process. They needed to spend time getting the detention cases up to date, and also making sure we had a military-tribunal process that passed constitutional muster.

MATTHEW MILLER

Bush let more people out of Gitmo than Obama ever did.[51] But every time we did it, the Republican Party decided they would win politics going forward by never letting us be equal to them on terrorism. So if we would move their direction, they would keep going to the right.

MARY BONO

It seemed that [the Obama administration] really felt that they were just riding on a wave of popularity, and that they did not need us. I clearly remember sitting on the floor of the House on the Democrats' side to try to talk to the Blue Dogs about finding common ground on health-care reform. And one of the Blue Dogs' exact answers to me was "Are you kidding? If Nancy Pelosi knew we were talking to Republicans, she would shoot us." They had been given a mandate that, with the president in the White House and Speaker Pelosi, it was going to be their way and their way only.

---

51   Number of detainees from 2001 to 2009 released or transferred under Bush: 500.
     Number of detainees from 2009 to 2017 released or transferred under Obama: 197.

BEN NELSON

Governor of Nebraska (D) (1991–1999)
D-Nebraska, US Senate (2001–2013)

I'm not taking sides in saying the Democrats continued to try to reach out. I think they gave up. Just before the August break, both sides were legislating in the [Senate] Finance Committee. Olympia Snowe had a number of amendments that were accepted. Others had amendments accepted.

DAVID BOWEN

There was a long process during which Senator Baucus, the chair of the Finance Committee, was trying to find bipartisan compromise to allow a bipartisan markup in the Finance Committee. And so that dragged on through the summer.

CHRIS DODD

Max Baucus's dog bit Orrin Hatch's leg. Orrin Hatch didn't think it was terribly amusing, but everyone else thought it was rather funny that the chairman of the Senate Finance Committee's dog went after the ranking Republican's leg in the process.

BILL DAUSTER

Senator Baucus's dog bit a number of people . . . Throughout most of those sixty hours of meetings on multiple days over the summer, everybody worked together, and the difficulty came at the end of the summer when we tried to bring it to a conclusion. It became evident that Senator McConnell and [Republican whip] Senator Kyl were working hard to prevent any of the Republicans in the group from agreeing to anything. [Republican Senator Mike] Enzi begged off and then Grassley said, "Well I can't be just the only one. I need cover," and Snowe's being there was not enough, because she was too moderate.

CHRIS DODD

Max, I think, was so determined to get Olympia Snowe or Chuck Grassley on the bill, that I felt we made a mistake. We should have just finished and marked up the Finance Committee bill in July and then used August to start melding the two [Senate] bills, which we ended up doing in the fall. By the time we came back after the August break, the damage had been done.

BEN NELSON

When we went home for the recess, they encountered the Tea Party. Republicans were being skewered by anxiety-ridden conservatives about what was going on in Washington. Basically, when they came back, it became a one-party process. All cooperation across the aisle just stopped.

CHRIS DODD

"Death panels" and all those other silly words were being bandied about as part of the lexicon in describing the bill, and we never really regained our footing.

BARNEY FRANK

They waited too long and played with Grassley and Olympia Snowe, and, in the end, got nothing for it.

VALERIE JARRETT

We were trying very hard to get the Affordable Care Act passed, and . . . one offhanded comment was hijacking headlines every day.

ROY AUSTIN JR.

Deputy Assistant Attorney General, Civil Rights Division,
US Department of Justice (2010–2014)
Deputy Assistant to the President for the Office of Urban Affairs, Justice,
and Opportunity, Domestic Policy Counsel, White House (2014–2017)

The president's comments with respect to Henry Louis Gates created this false narrative that the administration was anti-police.

VAN JONES

When Obama said that the police officer had behaved "stupidly," my heart stopped for a second. I was so proud. I was shocked to hear a president of the United States say something that forthright and commonsensical. Don't forget, at that point, Skip Gates was by far the most famous professor at Harvard, and he was arrested in his home for being in his home.[52] He wasn't brandishing a knife. He wasn't carrying an AK-47. He didn't have a hostage. But there's this unspoken rule about any kind of abuse against black people. Black people can't say anything about it or we're somehow the problem. And for the president to break, that was great. Then, a week later, he had to sit down with an arguably racist white beat cop, chaperoned by Joe Biden. I thought it was the low point in his presidency.

---

52   July 16, 2009.

LUIS GUTIÉRREZ

Obama had to invite the white guy to have a beer and everything. What was he apologizing for? Because he said the cop shouldn't have been targeting that black professor?[53] I mean, come on.

VAN JONES

It just sent the signal. Even if you're the president of the United States, you couldn't tell the truth about transparently obvious acts of at least racial foolishness, if not antagonism. I thought it opened the door for a whole bunch of other problems.

VALERIE JARRETT

My lesson there was not what Van concluded at all. The voice of the president of the United States carries a weight, and on issues where there is history of sensitivity, people are hypersensitive. That's just human nature, and it took a while for me to appreciate how people hung on his every word and blew things way out of proportion from his intent. That comment was at the end of a very long press conference about the Affordable Care Act, and it was the last question

---

53   "The guy forgot his keys, jimmied his way to get into the house, there was a report called into the police station that there might be a burglary taking place . . . But so far, so good. They're reporting. The police are doing what they should. There's a call, they go investigate what happens. My understanding is at that point Professor Gates is already in his house. The police officer comes in. I'm sure there's some exchange of words, but my understanding is, is that Professor Gates then shows his ID to show that this is his house, and at that point he gets arrested for disorderly conduct—charges which are later dropped.

"Now, I don't know, not having been there and not seeing all the facts, what role race played in that, but I think it's fair to say, number one, any of us would be pretty angry; number two, that the Cambridge Police acted stupidly in arresting somebody when there was already proof that they were in their own home; and number three, what I think we know separate and apart from this incident is that there is a long history in this country of African Americans and Latinos being stopped by law enforcement disproportionately. That's just a fact." —President Obama, news conference in the East Room, July 22, 2009.

from [*Chicago Sun-Times* columnist] Lynn Sweet . . . From the perspective of members of law enforcement, they thought that he was not being supportive of them, and I think what he was wise to recognize was that, as president, you couldn't afford to alienate our nation's men and women in blue who were putting their lives at stake each and every day for our country.

ROY AUSTIN JR.

The police unions, in particular, kept driving at how the president commented on that matter—despite the fact that [over the years] we gave more money to law enforcement through the COPS program, through the Office of Justice programs, despite the fact I couldn't even tell you how many meetings I had in the White House with the law-enforcement organizations.

VALERIE JARRETT

There were people who thought somehow he was retreating by inviting the officer and Skip Gates [to the White House]—he wasn't doing that. He was saying that, when these things happen, the best thing to do is bring people together. And he had said since, "I have to watch my words, because I'm the president of the United States." But he could have easily said that if it had been in a totally different context, which was why I think Van read too much into it.

ROY AUSTIN JR.

But that one incident where the president spoke his mind on what had happened colored our relationship with law enforcement, sadly, in a way that we were never able to fully get out from under.

2009

The Senate debate on health-care reform remained in committee, but during the summer recess, the lower house's latest iteration of the bill, H.R. 3200 (a.k.a. America's Affordable Health Choices Act), had been disseminated among an anxious electorate. The biggest takeaway? Misinformed hearsay on supposed "death panels."

Viral email chains cautioned of a Democratic Party that would "require EVERYONE who is on Social Security to undergo a counseling session every 5 years" and "push SUICIDE" on senior citizens to offset the costs of Congress's Medicaid expansion. Republicans such as Chuck Grassley fanned the flames. "I don't have any problem with things like living wills, but they ought to be done within the family," the senator told a morning crowd in an Iowa town. "We should not have a government program that determines you're going to pull the plug on Grandma." Grassley failed to mention how the bill's language had been twisted—that "advance-care planning" was designed to assist families with legal consultations for drafting wills and powers of attorney, not with killing loved ones.

Overrun by panicked constituencies, Democrats lost their grasp on the narrative. "I was at a town hall in a very safe part of my district with mostly seniors," recalled Allyson Schwartz of Pennsylvania's Thirteenth Congressional District. "They were holding up pieces of paper and saying, 'I read that you're going to take away my Medicare.' It was really hard to address all of these things that were not true, and the scare tactics that people were misled on." Voters trailed Congressman Lloyd Doggett out of a scheduled event at an Austin grocery store while chanting, "Just say no!" After a forum in Long Island, police escorted Congressman Tim Bishop to his car. David Bowen, staff director for the

Senate's health committee, attended one of Senator Bob Casey's get-togethers in Pennsylvania. "My view was that the opposition was to the president himself," Bowen said. "I think it would have manifested had it been climate change or anything else."

As for the commander in chief, he headed out west to combat the euthanasia fear—and to address the less conspiracy-theory-based concerns. At a town hall in Grand Junction, Colorado, attendees asked about the bill's public option, which would provide affordable, government-backed health care to individuals who couldn't access a private insurer's plan. The program would "keep the insurance companies honest," the president explained to an industry veteran who worried about diluting competition. Other critiques circled around individual mandates, the cost of premiums, and whether the scale of this legislative undertaking was too much—or not enough. One wondered if all these questions had only magnified the anxieties that continued to linger from the last year. After witnessing the United States Treasury bail out the banking and auto industries, and Congress approve $787 billion to nurse an economy back to life, America's heartland had difficulty stomaching another major reform. It seemed like too much, too fast— if not immediately to voters, then to their Republican representatives, because the GOP never lost sight of the fact that Obama could use the Democratic majorities and pass the bill through both houses without them.

"The Republicans were worried that the president would use the [Senate] reconciliation procedure and move ahead with only Democrats," said James Kvaal. "His preference was to try and do something that would include the Republicans."

HERBIE ZISKEND

Obama and, really, Biden got Arlen Specter, Republican stalwart senator from Pennsylvania, to flip and become a Democrat—and not just a Democrat but a strong proponent of health-care reform. I remember, early on, Biden met with Specter and lobbied him to flip parties, and that was no easy thing to do. That was savvy. It doesn't necessarily fit into the narrative, that those guys did backroom deals the way Lyndon Johnson did, but they successfully had been able to flip a Republican and could ensure that the bill got passed after Senator Kennedy died.

DAVID BOWEN

He died after his committee had voted, but I essentially did my same job. I stayed on through the whole process. And during that time, you know, I was sort of working for the memory of Senator Kennedy. Then Senator Dodd took over [the Health Committee] in a kind of shepherding role. Then [Iowa] Senator Harkin took over as chair. Really, I was just kind of working for the bill.

MARTHA COAKLEY
Attorney General of Massachusetts (D) (2007–2015)

Certainly everybody dreaded his death. Ted Kennedy was synonymous in many ways with the Democratic Party in Massachusetts. His death was a shock. It was also an open Senate seat that people realized needed filled, and I made a decision with some close advisors to run for the office.[54]

JON FAVREAU

I was sitting in Axelrod's office . . . They decided they wanted to give that [joint session of Congress] health-care speech in less than a week. It was a very last-minute decision to do a speech like that. I think they told me that Tuesday or Wednesday, and as we're sitting there trying to figure out this speech, Axelrod's assistant came in. "Vicki Kennedy called. She has something she needs to send over." It's a letter Kennedy wrote before he died that he asked to be delivered to Obama, and it's all about health care. And Axelrod said, "Well, she's going to mail it, because she wants to give him the original," and I was like, "Could we get her to fax it over or something? We've got this big speech."

ERIC LESSER

David's office was adjacent to the Oval Office . . . and the president's a pretty scrupulous writer. So we knew if a written product was going to be put in front of him, it had to be good.

JON FAVREAU

Vicki faxed the letter over, and Axe and I sat there reading it in his office. We're both tearing up. At the end, Kennedy talked about [how] this was more than about health care—this was about "the character of our country."[55] I sort of seized on that phrase.

---

54   Coakley announced her run for the Senate special election on Tuesday, September 1, 2009.
55   "What we face is above all a moral issue; that at stake are not just the details of policy, but fundamental principles of social justice and the character of our country." —Letter from Senator Edward Kennedy to President Obama, May 12, 2009.

CODY KEENAN

We were all at Ben Rhodes's wedding the weekend right before the speech. It was Labor Day weekend '09, and I had been working on Walter Cronkite's eulogy. Both speeches were on September 9.

JON FAVREAU

I finished a draft, went to Rhodes's wedding, woke up on Monday in Los Angeles. At six a.m. I got a call from Reggie Love, and he's back in DC. "Hey, Boss wants to see you about the speech. Can you come upstairs?" I was like, "Reggie, I'm in Los Angeles." He's like, "Oh, he's got a bunch of edits. Can you get here soon?" And I was like, "I don't know. How fast can a plane go from Los Angeles to DC?"

REGGIE LOVE

I was calling people all the time. It never really occurred to me that they wouldn't be available.

JON FAVREAU

I immediately got on a plane—[was] running through Reagan Airport sweating in ripped jeans and a T-shirt. I looked like a mess. I got to the West Wing of the White House and didn't have my badge. "I got an appointment." [Security] was like, "With who?" I was like, "With the president." They looked at me like I was fucking nuts. And so I finally got in to see the president, and he looked at me and was like, "Well, you look well. Have you showered today?"

Obama and Favreau (left), reviewing the final page of a speech draft on health care days before the September 9, 2009, address to Congress. Pete Souza, White House

PETE SOUZA

I made that picture. It's interesting because, even though you don't see the president, and you don't see Jon Favreau, it tells you about not just how he edits but how he thinks. It also tells you about his relationship with his then chief speechwriter, in that he could easily have done his edits, made notations, and then just handed it to Jon Favreau: "Here are my changes." Instead, he called Jon into the office—nobody calls him "Jon," everybody calls him "Favs"—and he called Favs into the office and sat down with him for like an hour.

JON FAVREAU

He sat down with me and did two major things to the speech. Number one was, he was like, "Look. There're all these crazy arguments out there about health care: death panels, free health care for illegal immigrants"—a couple other things—"and I know you're not supposed to talk about the arguments that your opponents have against you and repeat them, that's not a good communications practice. But if we don't knock down every single one of their arguments and their myths about this bill, then we're never going to pass it."

PETE SOUZA

He went over his thinking and reasoning for why he's using this clause instead of that clause. I thought it was bold of the White House to allow me to release this photo not much later. Here, you got a chance to see what the president of the United States crossed out and what he put in its place. You could easily have seen people really nervous about releasing a photograph like this to the public.

CODY KEENAN

I traveled with the president that day up to New York for the Cronkite eulogy and remember flying back with him on Marine One while he was making edits to the joint-session [speech] for that night.

JON FAVREAU

The other thing was, he had also seized on that phrase "the character of our country," but he basically wrote almost an entire new ending around that. That was one of my favorite endings of any speech. It's an ending about the role of government in our lives and how certain things shouldn't be Democratic or Republican or liberal or conservative.[56] Ted Kennedy realized that, and Ted Kennedy's passion wasn't just a passion for big government. It was a passion for the idea that there are some things that we cannot do on our own.

MELODY BARNES

It's a combination of the personal as well as the pragmatic. Given all the things that we knew—GDP just being gobbled up by the cost of health care—and the fact that in our country, we're not providing to the number of people that needed it, Senator Kennedy and President Obama understood the very real effects of that, not only on our economy but on individuals and families. It's a mixture of those things, the individual as a policy maker—someone who understood more broadly the effect on our economy, but also an individual who, with his family, had seen how our health-care system worked and didn't work.

---

56 "Ted Kennedy's passion was born not of some rigid ideology, but of his own experience. It was the experience of having two children stricken with cancer. He never forgot the sheer terror and helplessness that any parent feels when a child is badly sick; and he was able to imagine what it must be like for those without insurance; what it would be like to have to say to a wife or a child or an aging parent, 'There is something that could make you better, but I just can't afford it.'

"That large-heartedness, that concern and regard for the plight of others, is not a partisan feeling. It is not a Republican or a Democratic feeling. It, too, is part of the American character. Our ability to stand in other people's shoes. A recognition that we are all in this together . . . A belief that in this country, hard work and responsibility should be rewarded by some measure of security and fair play; and an acknowledgment that sometimes government has to step in to help deliver on that promise . . .

"Our predecessors understood that government could not, and should not, solve every problem . . . But they also understood that the danger of too much government is matched by the perils of too little; that without the leavening hand of wise policy, markets can crash, monopolies can stifle competition, the vulnerable can be exploited. And they knew that when any government measure, no matter how carefully crafted or beneficial, is subject to scorn; when any efforts to help people in need are attacked as un-American; when facts and reason are thrown overboard and only timidity passes for wisdom, and we can no longer even engage in a civil conversation with each other over the things that truly matter, that at that point we don't merely lose our capacity to solve big challenges. We lose something essential about ourselves." —Obama to the 111th Congress, September 9, 2009.

SCOTT BROWN

R-Massachusetts, US Senate (2010–2013)

They were taking everybody for granted. I'm not trying to have bravado, but I could feel it. The people were really pissed off at this whole *It's the Kennedys' seat. It's the Democrats' seat, and Martha's going to be the next one*, and really wanted to send a message. So, yeah, I was eating a bowl of Rice Chex and reading the paper, and I said, "You know, honey, I think I'm going to run." She said, "Heh. That's the Democrats' seat." I said, "No, it's the frickin' people's seat." And she said, "You know what? You're right." That's how it started.

MARTHA COAKLEY

It's not the Kennedy seat. It's the people's seat. That became a mantra, and he was able to wage a good campaign, particularly around health care and fighting these Democrats . . . That was increasingly becoming a national focus, and I took a strong position that we should have a public option. And we saw increasing outside money coming in to support Scott Brown and that maybe—maybe even in Massachusetts—this could be a place where Republicans could put a halt to that in ways that people hadn't anticipated.

ROB ANDREWS

The decision was made to go full speed ahead when the House came back in September. [Speaker] Pelosi really took over the process, wanted to have a meeting with the [Tri-Committee] Group once a week but also with the freshman and sophomore members who would be critical to getting health care passed. I sat in on those meetings.

ALLYSON SCHWARTZ

The Progressive Caucus was pushing the public option. Most Americans had coverage through their employers. That was going to be maintained. That, the president was clear about. And whether there would be a public option or not, he was more mixed about . . . I became a supporter, but I was not one of the people who initially fought to make sure that that was included.

BARBARA LEE

We were pushing for a public option, and we *did* get it into the [House] bill that states had the option if they wanted to do it, but there were many provisions we pushed for that we didn't get. But I'll tell you one thing: Medicaid was expanded, we expanded community clinics, and I really believed that this would be the reason for the decline in the uninsured rates.

ALLYSON SCHWARTZ

Not everybody's in the same place as Democrats, and health care's done a lot of different ways across the country. How's it going to affect a district? How do we have choices for Americans? There's no single model. We were really building on a system of American health care. We were going to build in accountability for the private sector but were going to offer options. That was actually exciting to me.

ROB ANDREWS

We reached a point in late October, after a lot of input from people, where Pelosi closed the bill, meaning this was it—this was what we're going to put up for a vote. We voted November 7 to pass the House version of the bill.

VALERIE JARRETT

In the nature of any White House, the stakes are high. The opportunities and the risks are plenty, and you need a leader with an even temperament and a clear vision of what true north is to steer the ship. Through all of that, it's inevitably going to be choppy.

PETE SOUZA

Usually in the Residence, I wouldn't ever bother him. That was kind of his private time. There were few occasions where, if John Brennan or Tom Donilon[57] would need to go upstairs and brief him on something late at night, I would go up with them. I had one or two [photos] close to midnight if he was going to make calls to the Japanese prime minister or a couple other people. I would just work it out with him that I would come upstairs when he would be doing those calls, but for the most part, I figured my day started when he left the Residence and [ended] when he went upstairs to the Residence.

TED CHIODO

I was always around at odd times. He needed to make a congratulatory call to a Greek prime minister who had just won an election.[58] It was a Sunday. No one else was there, and I was like, *Has anyone delivered him his call sheet?* It was hot out. I was wearing ridiculous flip-flops and shorts, and I didn't think I actually had to see the president. I was just going to deliver stuff to the Residence and go on my way. So you go up. Package it all secured in a sealed envelope. If he was around, you'd give it to him, but if he wasn't, you'd either place it upstairs on the table or you'd give it to an usher walking around on duty: "Hey, we can't leave this on the table. You have to hold this until he comes back." Some stuff you couldn't even give to the usher. You'd have to chase the president down.

REGGIE LOVE

You carry around whatever he needs.

---

57 Deputy National Security Advisor and National Security Advisor, White House (2009–2013).
58 October 4, 2009: George Papandreou and his social-democratic PASOK party won by nearly ten points in the Greek snap election against the conservative New Democracy party.

TED CHIODO

Plenty of times you'd have to wake up the president, or make sure he didn't go to bed at a certain time, to sign something. He'd have to sign a foreign-surveillance act. There were plenty of examples where he had to do that, but that's the exception, not the rule. We'd plan this out so we didn't inconvenience him, but sometimes world events happened and you gotta get call sheets up. Whenever you're on call, something like that could happen.

REGGIE LOVE

The job was very much a consistent job. Not like a rocket scientist, right? Not like having to solve the most complex problems, but you're often trying to deal with problems around logistics, or food, or staffing, or setup or lighting. Very human-type challenges, but it's all day.

TED CHIODO

So that day I couldn't find him at the Residence, so I went back downstairs. He and the First Lady were playing tennis down on the tennis court / basketball court on the South Lawn. They saw me. "Chiodo, what are you doing?" So that's great. It went from *I have to bother the president on the weekend* to *Now I'm breaking up family time*. I was just, "Oh, sir, you have to make this congratulatory call." I was always the person bringing homework, and he was like, "Oh, they scheduled it so fast. We got a phone down here?" You'd have to think about all those logistics. "Yes, sir, we have a secure line right here. The Sit Room will transfer you through."

MONA SUTPHEN

He's always that Rorschach-test kind of guy, and I remember that during the campaign. I had friends that were die-hard Obama fans who essentially would not even sit in a room together . . . I mean, politicians always disappoint on some level. You can't help it. Because you are a vessel for people's aspirations, but half the time they're not even articulated. The Nobel thing just added to it. Somehow the whole world's giving you this prize and you're like, *Great.*

JON FAVREAU

There was a big gap, obviously, between the day we found out[59] and the day we went to Oslo—a couple months. But right around the time it'd been announced, the president wanted Axe, Ben [Rhodes], and me to come see him. He directed the research for that speech in a way that he hadn't for any other speech. "I want you to look at Gandhi and King and Eisenhower and just-war theory." He had all the different theories of war and peace and readings that he wanted us to look up, and so we put this big binder together. We researched. We'd done all this kind of stuff, and then he had all these other crises intervene.

MONA SUTPHEN

Yes, being in two wars, and also the sense of *We just got into office.*

DAVID BOWEN

Then the Finance Committee marked up [health-care legislation].[60] So there were two Senate bills. We merged the two, and of course we needed sixty votes, and there were sixty Democrats plus independents. So we needed to make sure that every single one of them would be okay with it, or find a Republican who would provide one vote if we lost one of the Democrats.

JOE LIEBERMAN

I was on a Sunday-morning TV show.[61] I remember it was *Face the Nation* with Bob Schieffer, and at one point he asked me about the public option. I told him I was opposed to it, and he asked if I was opposed to it enough to vote against cloture on the bill, and I said I was, and the show was over. I walked

---

59   October 9, 2009.
60   October 13, 2009.
61   November 1, 2009.

out, got in the car, and my cell phone rang. It was Harry. He said, "Did you just say on *Face the Nation* that if the public option is in there, that you're not going to vote for cloture?" I said, "That's what I've been telling you and [New York Senator Chuck] Schumer for the last two weeks." So he said, "Come into my office at two."

JON FAVREAU

We didn't get a public option because of fucking Joe Lieberman.

CHRIS DODD

I thought the public option should have been part of the bill, but when Joe made that decision, I heard him say it [when I was] at home, and before the show was over, Harry Reid was on the phone to me. I was in his office maybe a half hour or an hour later.

JOE LIEBERMAN

I came in and there was the normal cast of characters: Harry, Schumer, Durbin, and some staff. Rahm was there. We went back and forth on it, and Rahm said, "So are you telling me that if we promise you the public option is out, you're going to commit to us to vote for the bill?" I said, "Well, look, I gotta read it, but from everything I know, from everything else that's in the bill—a lot of which is controversial—if you take this thing out, you got my word. I'll vote for the bill." And he said, "Okay."

CHRIS DODD

Literally that was the vote that broke the back. We were working on margins, getting this bill done, and decided that [we wouldn't] give up on the bill, although, going forward, we blew off a major provision. It was a loss.

JOE LIEBERMAN

The public option was clearly an attempt by the leadership to pacify the people who really wanted government health insurance for everybody as kind of a door opener . . . There's no question that Ben Nelson felt as strongly as I did about it.

BEN NELSON

There was never a deal-making process. I told them what I was interested in, and that I would continue to work with them if we could get the public option out, get the medical loss ratio in,[62] and get in appropriate language regarding abortion consistent with the Hyde Amendment.[63] Because there was nothing in there until I worked with Senator Boxer and her staff to try and come up with appropriate language so you didn't have government money funding abortion by subsidy under the act.

JIM MESSINA

At one point we were talking about the health-care bill with the president and I blew up and started screaming about some senator, and Obama said, "Hey. Stop. Rahm's supposed to be the screamer. You're supposed to be the calm one. Don't switch roles."

---

62 A medical loss ratio (MLR) determines the percentage of premium dollars that health providers would put toward medical claims, with the remaining revenue applied toward operation costs. A medical loss ratio of 90 percent, for example, would mean the provider appropriates 90 cents on the dollar toward customer costs, as opposed to payroll or advertising. The provision was included as an attempt to sort of Band-Aid progressive lawmakers who were aching over the removal of the public option.

63 In September of 1976, Republican Congressman Henry Hyde of Illinois introduced legislation that banned the use of federal funds for abortion services to Medicaid recipients. The amendment passed on a 207–167 House vote.

VALERIE JARRETT

The president just was determined to push, and there were times when his senior team was pretty beat up and bedraggled. He picked us up and said, *Get back to it.*

JIM MESSINA

Rahm and I both, very early, became frustrated with long decision-making processes. I think we bonded over that.

JOE LIEBERMAN

Toward the end, they brought the closer, William J. Clinton, into the Senate Democratic caucus.[64] Basically his argument was, "You all understand how much our system needs reform, how many people are uninsured. It's outrageous, and I believe you want something different from the status quo, right?" And everybody said, "Yes, Mr. President." He said, "It's too complicated to get it right on the first shot, but if you can get it to a point where you're absolutely convinced that it will improve the status quo and cover a significant number of people who don't have insurance, then vote for it. But know that you will have to come back, or Congress will have to come back, to every session probably for the next twenty years, to fix something that experience will show you wasn't quite working as you thought."

TED CHIODO

Within the White House there were disagreements all the time, but that was good. That meant a rigorous process was happening. If everybody agreed, then they're not really serving the president. People had points of view. Sometimes the debates were hearty. That's why the president wanted them in the first place.

---

64   November 10, 2009.

JON FAVREAU

Even the week before we went to Norway [to accept the Nobel], he had to give this West Point speech on Afghanistan. So he and Ben were working on that, and I was working on the Nobel speech.

TERRY SZUPLAT
Presidential Speechwriter, White House (2009–2017)

West Point was the speech where they rolled out the Afghan surge and timetable. Ben was very much the lead on that one. That was the moment where he stood up in front of the country and in front of the military and made the single-largest commitment of troops of his presidency. That's what helped shape the Oslo speech. Here he was getting the Nobel Peace Prize while at the same time leading a nation at war, and he'd just made the decision to commit more troops to a fight. So he was very much aware of the apparent contradiction in that.

MONA SUTPHEN

I do remember him being quite thoughtful about this challenge. It just added to the expectation burden that we all felt already for the economy, for two wars, for the world, for restoring popularity and credibility of the US government.

JON FAVREAU

We got him a draft. He didn't start working on that speech until the night we left for Oslo. So the day that we were leaving, Obama came down from the Oval and had like thirty handwritten pages of a speech plus our draft. "I'm not finished at all, and what I wrote is way too long, and I also like a lot of parts in the draft you guys sent me. So now we need to combine them all together in a speech by the time we leave tonight."

MONA SUTPHEN

Favs will tell you the president had a very strong view of what it was he wanted to say, and he spent a lot of time, back and forth, editing multiple versions.

JON FAVREAU

Ben and I panicked. We spent all day trying to put this thing together. Sam Power was helping us, too,[65] and then we all got on the plane. We didn't have a speech finished, and the whole flight Rahm, Axe, and everyone else passed out. The only people up were Obama, Rhodes, Sam Power, and me. Ben and Obama worked on the policy, I was off in the corner trying to write the ending, and it's the worst turbulence ever. And I'm a bad flyer and I was just sweating and trying to finish this thing. Sam's trying her best to help me. It was the closest we ever came to not finishing a speech. And Obama handed me his last page of edits while he was in the elevator on the way to the venue, and so we were directly typing in the last page of edits in the prompter as he was walking up to the stage. It was crazy.

MONA SUTPHEN

It's one of his better speeches, by the way, and got no coverage. He wrote a fair amount of it.

JON FAVREAU

I totally agree with Mona. It's one of my favorite speeches of his whole presidency.

---

65 Samantha Power was on the National Security Council from 2009 to 2013 as a senior director for multilateral affairs with a focus on human rights. In 2013, President Obama nominated her for UN Ambassador, a role she served through 2017.

JEFFREY BLEICH

If you reread the speech you'll find real consistency in what he said he would do, and the policies that he pursued throughout his presidency.[66]

JON FAVREAU

Whether they were foreign-policy successes or failures, he sort of saw all the limits of American power, of what we could do to stop war, what we could do to achieve peace and the possibilities as well. It was also a speech about human nature at its core, and what it is to live in peace with each other, and what it is to live in a world that will never be perfect but that we have to constantly strive to perfect.

TERRY SZUPLAT

If you made a list of his ten most important speeches of his presidency, that would certainly be one of them. I've never really thought about whether it got the coverage or attention it deserved. Within national-security and foreign-policy

---

66 "We must begin by acknowledging a hard truth. We will not eradicate violent conflict in our lifetimes. There will be times when nations, acting individually or in concert, will find the use of force not only necessary but morally justified.

"I make this statement mindful of what Martin Luther King Jr. said in this same ceremony years ago: 'Violence never brings permanent peace. It solves no social problem. It merely creates new and more complicated ones.' As someone who stands here as a direct consequence of Dr. King's life work, I am living testimony to the moral force of nonviolence. I know there's nothing weak—nothing passive, nothing naive—in the creed and lives of Gandhi and King.

"But as a head of state sworn to protect and defend my nation, I cannot be guided by their examples alone. I face the world as it is, and cannot stand idle in the face of threats to the American people. For make no mistake: evil does exist in the world. A nonviolent movement could not have halted Hitler's armies. Negotiations cannot convince al-Qaeda's leaders to lay down their arms. To say that force may sometimes be necessary is not a call to cynicism—it is a recognition of history, the imperfections of man and the limits of reason." —President Obama, inside Oslo City Hall, Oslo, Norway, December 10, 2009.

circles, there's a widespread recognition that that was a defining moment and laid out some of the core themes of his presidency.

CAROL BROWNER

One of the [themes] the president had run on was a commitment to building a clean-energy future.

BEN LABOLT

The Copenhagen Climate Agreement started the process that allowed the Paris accord to happen.

JAKE LEVINE

There was a lot of prep. You had to remember that the Conference of the Parties happened every year, and Copenhagen was COP 15. So the one before it and the one after it were not that remarkable. Of course, Paris would be remarkable. That was COP 21, six years later. COP 15 had a lot of hype and anticipation because we had Obama, this new president, a Democrat who campaigned on climate. This was his first major foreign-policy venue for which climate was the focus.

JONATHAN PERSHING
Deputy Special Envoy for Climate Change, US Department of State (2009–2012)
Senior Climate Advisor and Principal Deputy Director of the Office of Energy
Policy and Systems Analysis, US Department of Energy (2013–2016)
Special Envoy for Climate Change, US Department of State (2016–2017)

We had gone into that [conference] where developing countries were insisting on separate levels of treatment, that they should do less because they were developing.

MICHAEL FROMAN

In my view, it really was the critical moment of breaking down this artificial barrier between developed countries and [developing countries] to establish that all countries would have to contribute to solving the climate-change problem. It would take several years and subsequent conferences in Durban, Cancún, and ultimately in Paris for that to be refined in what became the Paris accord. But the Paris accord wouldn't have been possible if it hadn't been for that breakthrough.

BRIAN DEESE

It was a total disaster as a conference, but . . . Copenhagen was the beginning of Paris. That gave a clear sense of what was going to be necessary in terms of changing the diplomatic tectonic plates.

MICHAEL FROMAN

I didn't think of it as a disaster. It was highly chaotic, but we got an important outcome that laid the groundwork for Paris several years later. When people arrived in Copenhagen . . . It was unclear what the respective roles of the Danes, the UN Secretary General, [or] Yvo de Boer were.[67] Who was running the show? Who had responsibility to forge an agreement? . . . By the time Secretary Clinton arrived,[68] the question was, what could she do to change the dynamic and increase the focus?

JONATHAN PERSHING

Clinton's role, she came as the bearer of money . . . I don't mean to make it in crass form, but people were worried about what the costs were gonna be . . . Put this in the context of the entire global development budget—all of the AIDs of the world.[69] Ours, Germany's, the Brits, Japan—everybody's combined was about $130 billion. She came with a commitment for another $100 billion [in

---

67 Chairman of the United Nations panel on climate change.
68 December 17, 2009.
69 Agencies for international development.

financial aid] that we were gonna try and mobilize, and that was insufficient. It gave you some sense about the worries that people had then, about how hard this was gonna be to do, and the lack of real political commitment.

MICHAEL FROMAN

We were still far from any agreement.

JONATHAN PERSHING

The White House got into this internal debate where we on the ground were saying, "We think we could perhaps unlock it if Obama comes [to COP 15]. If he doesn't come, we know that it fails," and all the people back at home were saying if it failed, it [would be] a disaster for a new presidency. "He's committed himself to working on health care. This is not gonna go anywhere. We don't want him to go." That was a really interesting debate, and, from what I had heard, he decided he was gonna come anyway, even though there wasn't a deal.

TODD STERN
Special Envoy for Climate Change, US Department of State (2009–2016)

Obama arrived on Friday morning, the eighteenth, and went into the Arne Jacobsen room, where the group of [twenty-eight parties] had been meeting and had first convened around eleven on Thursday night[70] . . . The Chinese were not represented at the top level. They had a bureaucrat there, and he at least once said that he had to leave the room to consult with his superiors, which was thoroughly annoying to most every other country because the other countries had their leaders there. President Hu was not in Copenhagen. Wen Jiabao, the

---

70   Danish Prime Minister and COP 15 chair Lars Løkke Rasmussen hosted a "Friends of the Chair" group to preside over a number of issues. Joining UN Secretary General Ban Ki-moon and Rasmussen were representatives from Ethiopia, US, UK, Sudan, Saudi Arabia, South Africa, Russia, Mexico, Lesotho, Korea, Japan, Indonesia, India, Maldives, Grenada, Colombia, Germany, France, China, EU, Brazil, Bangladesh, Australia, Algeria, Norway, and Spain.

Chinese premier, *was* in Copenhagen but still didn't attend that meeting of leaders. The Indian prime minister, Singh, did not attend either.

JONATHAN PERSHING

[German chancellor Angela] Merkel was more or less throwing up her hands and saying, "If you can go in and get the BASIC countries to buy in, good.[71] But we've given up."

TODD STERN

The biggest issue that was open at that point was the issue of transparency, the language on that issue. And Obama wanted to talk to the Chinese again, and we weren't able to locate them for a considerable period of time.

BRIAN DEESE

That summit's become a little famous because Obama and Clinton ended up literally chasing the heads of states around the conference center.

JAKE LEVINE

We had learned that the Chinese were leaving the conference and that they were on their way to the airport, and then, of course, we stumbled onto a room full of Chinese negotiators.

MICHAEL FROMAN

Ultimately we found the room where we thought Premier Wen of China was. We spotted the Chinese bodyguards outside, and the president said, "Well, let's just go there." He, Secretary Clinton, and a group of us presented ourselves at

---

71 The four large newly industrialized countries (NICs) Brazil, South Africa, India, and China made a pact one month prior to the conference with the intent to collectively negotiate their responsibility for climate change.

the door, pushed our way in, and found not just Wen but all of the leaders we had been looking for.

TODD STERN

We get to the room and there were like a zillion reporters and news-camera guys. I don't know if they had been there before or they had just started to collect when they had seen Obama—probably some combination of the two.

JAKE LEVINE

[Press secretary Robert] Gibbs ended up getting pushed around by some of the Chinese. Either they were security guards or maybe [part of the] negotiating team, but they were clearly not welcoming others into the room. Meanwhile, there was the impression that they had purposefully misled our team as to their whereabouts.

TODD STERN

Everybody had to kind of muscle their way into the room and, you know, Obama just asked if they were ready to see him or if they wanted to wait.[72] And everybody all started scrambling around to make room for Obama and Hillary Clinton at the table.

MICHAEL FROMAN

Sort of hidden away in this room, you had President Zuma of South Africa, President Lula of Brazil, and Prime Minister Singh of India. The president and Secretary Clinton pulled up chairs at the table and the rest of us hovered around them. And over the course of the next hour or so they worked out the final agreement, including the fact that those countries—particularly China—would

---

72 "Are you ready for me or do you guys need to talk some more? . . . It's up to you . . . Come on, what do you think? . . . Premier, are you ready for me or do you want to wait?" —President Obama to Premier Wen inside the Bella Center, Copenhagen, Denmark, December 18, 2009.

have to indicate how they specifically would address climate change just like the developed countries. That was a key breakthrough.

BEN LABOLT

The president played a big role in making sure that China, South Africa, India, and Brazil didn't crush the deal and go off to do their own thing. That was kind of the first time where he really brought China into the process of acknowledging that they had to reduce their emissions. They were the world's largest polluter and had an obligation as well.

TODD STERN

That famous meeting was mostly focused on getting language on the transparency point . . . that they would be subject to international consultation and analysis. There was lots of back-and-forthing before those words got landed on, because the Chinese were seeking language that kind of avoided that in various ways. We were pushing for language that was strong enough.

JONATHAN PERSHING

I have a sense that it was a very personal appeal. It's funny that the analogy that's often brought up was that he treated [the meeting] like a community-organizing structure. You went in and you talked to people, and you engaged them. And he was incredibly effective, because when he went in there was no outcome, and when he came out, there was a deal . . . The structure was essentially that all countries would individually have to take an action. It would be self-determined, but it would have to be an action.

TODD STERN

The meeting went on for about an hour or so. The main part of that discussion was what everybody was going to put forward in terms of what amounted to a target . . . That might not sound like a big deal. That was a *really* big deal for China.

JAKE LEVINE

I think the fact that the president decided to come was what, in turn, got all the other heads of state to sit down at a table, even though it was a table that was literally hard to find.

TODD STERN

When that meeting's over, Obama went back and sat with developed-country leaders and walked them through what happened in the meeting with China, India, Brazil, and South African leaders. That was probably in the range of sixish, six thirty [p.m.].

JONATHAN PERSHING

They're in a room that's about thirty feet long, around an open rectangular table. The place was hot and sweaty. There's no airflow, and there's a space for the senior person from each country at the table, either the head of state, sometimes it's the secretary of state or foreign minister. You had like [twenty-eight] countries around this table arguing for *hours* over the nuance of the deal, which at this point was only a couple of pages. And Obama's doing this himself. He's sitting at the table, and Todd's advising him. Mike Froman's advising him. Clinton's sitting next to him advising him, and there's this team of people coming in and out, the US delegation providing input to this small room upstairs.

TODD STERN

When Obama left, he left Copenhagen altogether, because there was this gimungo snowstorm which was predicted to come to Washington, and they were keen to get the president out of there.

JAKE LEVINE

A snowmageddon was coming to DC and we had to depart, and the negotiations were still ongoing at that point. We had announced the accord and felt really good about that, actually, but there was still a huge amount of work in order to get the emissions-productions commitments from each individual country.

TODD STERN

The leaders around that table at that point had agreed on all the elements of this two-and-a-half-page Copenhagen Accord, [but] that's just done among a group of [twenty-eight] countries. It still had to go to the plenary meeting of everybody—all 190-plus countries—and so at some point, not immediately thereafter, the plenary reconvened. There was a period of time when those of us who were still there knew that there was a very live issue . . . In theory, any one country could break consensus.

JONATHAN PERSHING

The Danes were having this enormous problem making things work. The world was focused with its attention on this as it's never focused before on any international environmental agenda. A stunning level of global attention, and it's not going very well. What partly seemed to have happened was that all the heads of state that Obama met with in that small room, they went back to the delegations: *Here's the deal we want.* Even though you had the deal with China, the Chinese in particular felt that it was not good enough. Their technical guys were not happy with Wen's commitment.

TODD STERN

There were all sorts of objections, and you could hear from the applause there were more countries semipassively supporting the objectors. It seemed there was potential for the entire Copenhagen Accord to be rejected outright . . . I was sitting with the UK and proposed that we needed to seek a pause, just a timeout from the proceedings to avoid Prime Minister Rasmussen literally slamming down the gavel and declaring the meeting over. So the pause happened, and there was a lot of consulting and agitating in the corridors of the plenary room to try and produce a result, and the proposal was that the accord not be adopted, but taken note of. There are all sorts of UN-ese, several different buzzwords that get used. "Taken note of" was one of those,[73] and Rasmussen had to go somewhere for a short period. So in his absence, a lead negotiator from the Bahamas acted as the de facto president and slammed the gavel down fast on that proposition. There was some discussion, but he moved pretty quickly, so there wasn't time to start rebelling. That's how the Copenhagen Accord had been kept alive.

JAKE LEVINE

That's ultimately what would lead to this novel approach of seeking the individually determined national contributions . . . To the extent that health care dominated the agenda, it was more a sense that it had dominated the domestic-policy agenda rather than the international stuff.

BARNEY FRANK

One frustration people forget: We were close to getting the votes to extend Medicare down to [age] fifty-five, which would have been a great thing and made it much more popular. Joe Lieberman, who'd been for it, for some reason backed away from it.

CHRIS DODD

There were other issues. A great job that Barbara Boxer did [dealing with] Ben Nelson on the abortion issues.

---

73   "Normally, the COP would adopt something by consensus," explained State Department lawyer Susan Biniaz, who attended COP 15. "Consensus requires the absence of a formal objection. After the Copenhagen Accord was drawn up by a subset of parties, a handful of parties (including, e.g., Venezuela) formally objected to its adoption. So it wasn't possible to adopt the accord by consensus. But the proponents of the accord (most parties) didn't want it to have zero recognition at the conference. So the compromise was to have the COP 'take note' of it, i.e., recognize its existence while not actually endorsing it."

BARBARA BOXER

D-California, US Senate (1993–2017)

I played a big role at the end. Harry [Reid], Chuck [Schumer], and Dick [Durbin] were stuck on the abortion provision in the Senate version of the bill. We couldn't get our sixty votes unless I was able, as it turned out—because this was the role Harry gave me—to ensure that federal funds would never be used for abortion. So we had to figure out a way for people to be billed separately for their abortion coverage, but we really came close to losing the Affordable Care Act over this, because Ben Nelson was pro-life . . . So I came up with a way to fix it at midnight. It was a snow night, and I remember driving to Harry's office. Chuck was the go-between, and we resolved it.

BEN NELSON

I decided to be the sixtieth vote for cloture,[74] to continue to move the bill forward so that the Senate could legislate. They could have stopped at any time and used the reconciliation process, but I didn't want the process to stop too early because, among other things, I wanted to get a medical loss ratio in—80 to 85 percent—to deal with the question of whether or not the rates would be adequate or excessive. Consequently, that's why I continued to push forward and legislate in addition to getting the public option out. These things all progressed along the way as long as they had cloture to continue to deal with it.

DAVID BOWEN

The Senate bill passed with no Republicans on Christmas Eve. If Hollywood wrote the script, you wouldn't believe it, with members getting snowed in and having to be dug out so they could make the vote. It was completely *Mr. Smith Goes to Washington*. And then there was a process. We had a Senate bill and a House bill, and the sort of Civics 101 plan would be that the House and Senate would get together and enact a compromise bill.

---

74 December 19, 2009.

ROB ANDREWS

The plan was to go conference, and, you know, everyone would admit that there were imperfections in the Senate bill that were meant to be corrected.

JOE LIEBERMAN

I thought Rahm was pretty happy. We didn't exchange high-fives or anything after I committed to him, but, of course, that's the way it went.

CHRIS DODD

After we did the health-care bill at seven o'clock in the morning on the floor of the Senate, I had gone up to Connecticut, and I stopped on the way to see Teddy Kennedy's grave at Arlington Cemetery. An incredibly beautiful, crystal-clear morning, December 24, 2009, and this was eight o'clock. And looking out over the city with the sun coming up, and I just, I didn't know why at that particular moment, I said, *Do you want to do this again for six or seven years?* And the answer was quicker than the question was. I said, *I've had enough.*

2010

Khalid Sheikh Mohammed, the mastermind of the attacks on September 11, was still awaiting his day in court. He had been in US custody for almost seven years, ever since the CIA picked up the al-Qaeda operative in Pakistan and applied "enhanced interrogation techniques" at multiple black sites on foreign soil. (Said techniques, ranging from "stress positions" to waterboarding to a medical procedure known as "rectal rehydration," had yielded no valuable information from the subject, per intelligence reports.) Mohammed had been moved to the Guantanamo Bay detention camp in Cuba; five years had passed between the time of his capture and the Bush administration's charging him with war crimes. Evidence of any concerted efforts to successfully try him in a military tribunal was slim.

Attorney General Eric Holder, on the other hand, made prosecuting the Gitmo detainee part of his agenda. Over the administration's first year, Obama's top cop had recruited several lawyers in preparation for trying Mohammed, and four of his accomplices, in a civilian court. It was during the National Mall's Fourth of July celebration when Holder told the president his intention to try the group in New York for the murders of 2,976 people. "It's your call," an expressionless Obama responded, as the two watched the fireworks from the White House terrace.

"Just because Holder was close to the president personally, it didn't mean that the president would decide every decision Holder's way on a policy matter," the Justice Department's Matthew Miller explained. "He would often side against him if he felt it was right, and by the same token, Holder was always cognizant that, even though they were friends, he had an obligation on some things—investigative matters, certain legal calls—to make decisions independent of the White House."

It certainly felt as if Holder would go this one alone. Members of the White House Counsel's office valued the AG's initiative, but "didn't have the line of sight into where [the Office of] Legislative Affairs and guys like Rahm were making other decisions," one West Wing aide remarked. Conservative political-advocacy groups launched demonstrations. One New York City protest, held downtown in December, included personal attacks on the attorney general, claiming that he was a "traitor" who "wants to help the terrorists." Then, Michael Bloomberg's comments piled on.

The NYC mayor previously believed it was "fitting that 9/11 suspects face justice near the World Trade Center," but come January of 2010, Bloomberg reversed his support on holding the trials locally. Rather, he endorsed "a military base" as a more proper venue to guarantee security and avoid disrupting civilians. Though the federal government had already committed to covering the trial's expense, Bloomberg also cited the exorbitant costs of such a prospect, claiming the legal proceeding could run up a city's tab north of $1 billion.

Bloomberg's shift opened the door for others to suggest that the state of New York, let alone anywhere within the five boroughs, was an inappropriate location to try the five men. "Chuck Schumer and everybody else came out against it," Congressman Frank Wolf recalled. "They certainly didn't want any trial in New York, because they felt that would tie up New York with threats. Many, on both sides, thought it was a danger, and I think they were right. Because after what New York went through? It was pretty difficult. Have you toured the 9/11 Memorial?"

MATTHEW MILLER

Khalid Sheikh Mohammed was such an episode on its own. That was a case that history will absolutely judge Eric Holder to have been right about. I didn't think, back then, many people thought he was wrong on the substance of it. If that case had gone forward in federal court, KSM would have been on death row. There's just no doubt about it, versus what happened in Guantanamo, where [the military commission] couldn't even get the case to trial.

DR. HAROLD KOH

What we're looking for here was credible justice. You could have a perfectly tried case in a military commission against KSM and nobody in the Middle East would think it was fair, right? So what's the point of doing it? The test of whether it's a reasonable and legitimate, credible system was whether it stood the test of time. And the United States ought to have confidence in its own justice system to do the right thing in a case that had been made complicated because of the mistreatment of the defendant.

MARGARET RICHARDSON

He continued sitting in Guantanamo, and untried for a crime that was an open wound for families and for our country. Attorney General Holder said, if he had been able to have him prosecuted in an Article III [federal] court, this would have been resolved within that year.

DR. HAROLD KOH

Just take a look at the Boston Marathon bomber, Dzhokhar Tsarnaev. He was captured, represented, tried, convicted, and sentenced. You know, it's insane to think that a better way to do it was to do it in a military commission. The problem was KSM was tortured, and nevertheless, even if you excluded all that evidence, a lot of objective evidence connected him to 9/11. Would people seriously contend that the Southern District of New York's US Attorney's Office couldn't get a conviction from a New York jury in a case like that? Even if they admitted error on all of the mistreatment, which they should? So the decision to try him in an Article III court in New York, where many others had been successfully prosecuted and convicted, was correct. And the huge error was to back off of that because of political pressure.

MATTHEW MILLER

The administration wasn't willing to spend all the political capital it needed to on that, because they were in the middle of a health-care fight. I didn't blame them for that. *Trying to get health care? Let's not spend all our capital on KSM right now.* In the meantime, you had the Umar Farouk Abdulmutallab case, Christmas day of 2009, when he tried to blow up a bomb on a plane descending to land in Detroit.[75] That confluence of factors led to the KSM trial being killed, and left him sitting in Gitmo. It's a real travesty. Health care's an important thing, but there's an opportunity cost to that, and it meant KSM was kind of hanging out there. We're nowhere closer to justice for the 9/11 victims than we were at the beginning of the Obama presidency.

---

75   Known as the "Underwear Bomber," Abdulmutallab confessed to attempting to detonate plastic explosives, hidden in his underwear, on Northwest Airlines Flight 253 from the Netherlands to Detroit. (He made it past airport security, but passengers on board the flight were able to subdue him.) The twenty-three-year-old Nigerian was assisted by al-Qaeda in the Arabian Peninsula, which claimed responsibility and stated that the thwarted attack was retaliation for the US's role in a Yemeni military offensive against al-Qaeda. Abdulmutallab was convicted in federal court and was sentenced to four life terms, plus fifty years without parole, at the ADX Florence facility in Fremont County, Colorado.

MARTHA COAKLEY

[Health-care reform] was one issue that people didn't have time to absorb—you're either for it or against it. That was part of what happened in the [special Senate] race. We didn't realize at the time, and I didn't think people in Massachusetts understood the distortion. It wasn't that people were rejecting health care. We didn't have time to frame it properly, and it got miscast by some of the Republican anonymous PACs who came in with the scary music and the awful gray-black pictures. That frightened people.

DAVID BOWEN

I had told one of my colleagues, "I'm getting paranoid that Scott Brown's going to win." And he said, "Oh, no, you are completely crazy. That's not going to happen."

MARTHA COAKLEY

Meanwhile the mantra became that I was "unfriendly." I "wasn't campaigning." One thing that really irritated me was that after the [special-election] primary, somehow I had gone on a weeklong vacation in the Caribbean—absolutely false, never happened, never disputed, and it got traction that I had been taking the race for granted.

JOSH LIPSKY

When the president went to stump for Martha Coakley up in Boston, days before Scott Brown defeated her, I remember vividly just kind of feeling that Brown was gonna win. And we were trying to wrap our heads around the implications of *Wow, this really may not happen. This health-care bill just may not happen.*

MARTHA COAKLEY

We had been outcampaigned and outspent. I thought the Obama White House and many of the staffers, including the president, were terrific. They realized that it might be a tougher race than we thought—that the issue of health care was at stake—and I remember somebody who had been at the senior home had come back to headquarters and said she was really worried because many seniors felt they would lose their benefits. Some of that was due to advertising by outside interests, threatening people that their coverage would be damaged if health care succeeded.

JAMES KVAAL

We were never under the illusion that the Republicans would decide not to filibuster that bill. We sort of always knew that a simple majority in both houses of Congress was not enough to pass that particular piece of legislation, and so we worked very hard to get sixty votes [in the Senate], and there were times that it appeared to be in sight. But with Ted Kennedy's passing and being replaced by Scott Brown, that seemed to move out of reach.

ROB ANDREWS

There was an intense debate at that point about whether to go small, to try and pass a package of insurance reforms, or stick with the bill. And Nancy Pelosi gave her famous press conference about pole-vaulting over the fence.[76] She actually stood in front of the Democratic caucus—this was right after the Scott Brown election—and said, "If the gate's closed, we'll go over the fence. If the fence [is too high], we'll pole-vault in. If [that doesn't work], we'll parachute in, but we're going to get health-care [reform] passed."

DAVID BOWEN

The Senate no longer had sixty votes for the bill, and the only process to pass it was for the House to pass the Senate bill.

---

76   January 28, 2010: Pelosi's weekly address on Capitol Hill.

JAMES KVAAL

The problem was that [the Senate] bill included substantive provisions that the House didn't agree with, and the staff that had drafted it had not thought of it as the final draft that would be enacted. So there was some cleaning up that needed to happen to the language of that bill.

ROB ANDREWS

I dealt with Rahm a lot. Rahm was my friend. When I first ran for Congress, Rahm was the opposition-research director for our campaign. And I will tell you, clearly there were disagreements in the White House, but that's kind of cocktail-party chatter. I mean, any group of smart people would get together and ask, *What are our strategic options and what can we do?* But the consensus, developed with Nancy Pelosi and Harry Reid, was, *Okay, let's go for the end zone.* The first president to try to get a law that would make health care available to all Americans was Theodore Roosevelt. And so it was a hundred years that people had been trying to do this, and there was a sense that this was a window that was going to close and wouldn't reopen again for a long time.

SCOTT BROWN

Harry Reid had a plan in place. They were gonna merge the bills, and they couldn't. So you had two basically screwed-up plans, and they had to pass them through reconciliation—parliamentary maneuvers and the like.

JIM DOUGLAS

[We] had a lot of meetings up there with Speaker Pelosi, who I actually liked better than I was supposed to. She was very accessible and quite engaged, but eventually it just devolved into partisanship. Harry Reid sent the word down that *We're just gonna ram it through*, and that's not the way to do things. That's why half the country didn't like the act.

JAMES KVAAL

There was quite a bit of uncertainty for weeks as the president and Speaker Pelosi and Leader Reid tried to chart a path forward, and ultimately what happened was the House passed that Senate bill. So that became the foundation of health reform, and then the House enacted a second [reconciliation] bill that required only majority support in the Senate. It was a budget bill, and it was filibuster-proof. So they were able to make some amendments, and together those two bills became the Affordable Care Act. I know that's kind of a tricky procedural move.

ROB ANDREWS

In a reconciliation bill, the provisions must principally affect revenue and expenditures, not policy. They had to be primarily budget in nature.[77] So the [House] reconciliation bill that was done had some modifications to the underlying Senate bills. It passed both the House and the Senate, and therefore the package became the law. And that was the bill that was passed in March of 2010.

SCOTT BROWN

Here's what I find ironic. They had two years to do whatever they wanted, and they did hardly anything. They didn't do minimum wage. They didn't do climate change. They didn't do immigration. They didn't do health care. They just assumed that they would always have this supermajority, and when I got there, because I won, they could have fixed up [the health-care bill]—they could have if they wanted to—but we brought up two or three hundred amendments to fix it, and they didn't want to vote on any one of them. As a result, you got a seriously flawed plan, and that's why it failed. I'll take credit for that all day.

---

77 James Kvaal: "Let me try and explain that a different way. Congress had long ago adopted expedited procedures for budget bills, as a way of making it easier to reduce the deficit. It would keep the Senate from filibustering bills that would reduce the deficit, and so those types of bills only need majority support in the Senate. That's how Bush passed his tax cuts, for example. So we were able to get the final touches put on the health-care law without getting that sixtieth vote."

JOHN TANNER

I didn't vote for it for two reasons. It was too much in one bill. I likened it to trying to digest a fifty-ounce steak when really it should be cut up into six-ounce fillets to be digestible by the system. The second thing was, it really didn't save any money until about ten years out, when the majority of the savings, at that time, were predicted. It's been my experience, through the years, that any major legislation—and that certainly qualified as major—had to have some semblance of bipartisanship to be lasting or permanent or accepted by the majority of Americans. And that didn't have any of that.

CHRIS DODD

The last time there was a perfect piece of legislation was the Ten Commandments, and four hundred thousand years later we're still arguing about it. In the summer of '09 in the Health Committee, there were 890 amendments filed. We debated 200 of them, and I accepted 160 Republican amendments. To the point where, one Monday morning, after having worked all weekend, I made the motion that we accept the amendments, and there was a moment of hesitancy about Republicans voting for their own amendments! And they did, but also began to realize, *The guy's taking our amendments, and we're making part of this bill. We're going to have an awful time explaining why we're not for it in the end.*

HERBIE ZISKEND

Zero Republican senators—other than Specter, who became a Democrat—voted for health-care reform.

BEN NELSON

I had voted for cloture to continue to move it, but I didn't vote for it at the end. If you're trying to get provisions put in and put out, you have to continue to legislate . . . You don't take sides in terms of whether you work for the left or the right. You take sides on issues. Let the chips fall where they may.

GENE SPERLING

In many ways it was far easier to talk straight and explain to the American people the pros and cons of the auto industry. Trying to have that level of communication on the degrees of complexity in the financial or health-care systems was never close, even with the brilliance of a communications team that had just won a historic presidency. When people would say, "Oh, you should have just communicated this or that way better," I'd keep thinking of the little plaque the president had on his desk: *Hard things are hard.* I once said, "It's not like Obama, Plouffe, Favreau, and Axelrod went from being geniuses to idiots in two months." Of which Jon Favreau replied to me, "How many months was it, then, before we became idiots?"

Pete Souza: "There were times when he might be having a lunch, and I'd see some scene, still life in the Oval because of the light, so I'd walk in and snap a couple pictures. He didn't have that much stuff on his desk in terms of mementos or anything like that." Peter Souza, White House.

DAVID AXELROD

The God's-honest truth was that plaque was less related to the ACA than it was to Social Security and some entitlement reform, because he was concerned about the actuarial strength of these programs, and I said, "There's a reason they're not fixed and why there's not a winning constituency for it, you know, because hard things are hard to do." That engendered a lot of laughter in the room because it seems like a truism, but the nature of politics is that it's very hard to get hard things done.

JOEL BENENSON

President Obama was aware, all the way through, of the potential political fallout of Obamacare, but he believed strongly that, for the well-being and health of millions of Americans, it was the right thing to do. We had the most developed economy in the world. We could not continue to leave tens of millions of people without health-care coverage every day. He knew that he could pay a political price for it, potentially.

JEREMY BIRD

It's disappointing when people say that he wasn't aggressive enough or that he wasn't progressive enough. To that, I'd like to say, "You look [at] those tens of millions of Americans who now have health insurance and grew up in the trailer park I grew up in, and you tell them it would have been better to be self-righteous and not get that passed by trying to go for something that we weren't going to get."

KAREEM DALE
Associate Director, Office of Public Engagement, White House (2009–2013)

People talk about health care and, if you think about it, it was the left-off arm of the ADA.[78] To get that done was huge for people with disabilities—no preexisting-conditions exclusion, the Medicaid enhancements. Sometimes

---

78   President George H. W. Bush signed the Americans with Disabilities Act into law on July 26, 1990. It was the United States' first comprehensive antidiscrimination labor law for people with disabilities, ranging in civil-rights protections from employment opportunities to public accommodations. The bill's first draft was introduced in Congress in 1989.

people looked at what the administration did for people on disabilities and they just looked at the initiative. But, like so many other things, what the president did in the broader scope benefited people with disabilities. Health care was a huge example of that.

RAHM EMANUEL

[Obama] got it done because of what happened in the '06, the '08 elections that built up big majorities for Democrats. Without the '06 victory or the '08 House victories, a lot of his agenda could not have happened. It was because of the prior elections that he had a majority that could move something like this.

TOM DASCHLE

Both Harry Reid and Nancy Pelosi deserve credit. I didn't think they probably got the attention they deserved. Were it not for the fact that we were the majority and had leaders who really had the capacity to work with the president, we wouldn't have been able to accomplish a lot. Nancy Pelosi, particularly, took an unruly House, a caucus that was not inclined, in some cases, to be that supportive, and found the wherewithal to get it done.

DAVID AXELROD

Politicians shy away from hard things. It jeopardizes their well-being, and it does relate to the Affordable Care Act, because that was a very hard thing to do. A lot of politicians put their careers on the line. Some lost their careers for that.

JOHN TANNER

That was my last year. I didn't seek reelection in 2010, but I remember talking to the Democratic leadership about it. I thought it was not the best way to approach the health-care system. Before so-called Obamacare was passed, the system was in disarray. The burden of the money going out of the tax base was escalating at an unsustainable pace, and so, for all of the problems Obamacare had, it could be fixed. But it had to be fixed by several different bills, not just one . . . I guess their feeling was they had to do it that way and then they'd come back and fine tune it. Anytime you have a two-thousand-page bill, you're going to have some problems.

JIM DOUGLAS

I wouldn't say governors were as united on health care as we were on the Recovery Act. We don't like mandates, as a general principle, and we obviously didn't want something that would put the states in even more fiscal stress. Actually, it was a Democrat, Governor Bredesen of Tennessee, who called the Medicaid expansion "the mother of all unfunded mandates." So, as there was bipartisan support for the Recovery Act, there was bipartisan at least concern about some of the stuff in the ACA.

BEN NELSON

There was the whole question whether you could have state-based regulation, whether you were going to have state exchanges . . . Then that created the whole Burwell case.[79]

JIM DOUGLAS

I thought part of it was the president's patience wore thin on the obstructionism, and so there's blame to go around. The problem, from my standpoint, was that it really divided the governors. All the Democrats who had been saying the right things about states' prerogatives and no mandates all of a sudden fell in line and were loyal to the president. It caused a schism within the ranks of the governors, and that's something that I regret.

---

79 *King v. Burwell* was a 2015 Supreme Court decision that upheld key provisions of the Affordable Care Act to provide premium tax credits to qualifying individuals receiving coverage from both state-run and federally established exchanges. The challengers, led by Virginia limousine driver David King, had sued Secretary of Health and Human Services Sylvia Burwell—arguing that the text describing the calculation of those tax credits referred only to state-run exchanges, and therefore anyone residing in the thirty-seven states that had not set up an exchange was not eligible.

JOHN DINGELL

Look. There's no saint walking the streets—and that includes John Dingell—who could come up with something that's the perfect cure to the problem. But if you look, we had come a long way. Roosevelt intended to do this in 1935. This was a step that had to be taken. It covered millions of Americans who otherwise would not have been covered.

JOE LIEBERMAN

I thought President Obama and Rahm felt, and I agreed with them, that they were to achieve something historic and transformational. Not perfect, by any means, in what they put together, but they wanted to get it done.

ARUN CHAUDHARY

Every meeting someone had with the president was historic. That constantly heightened sense could be exhausting, but what I would find mind blowing were the sort of grounding and interesting meetings that didn't happen every day. [Secretary of Commerce] Gary Locke came into the Oval with the [US] Census, which only got done every ten years. It seemed like another thing he had to sign, but then Gary Locke's like, *You know, there have only been twenty-two of these in the history of our country.* And not just me, but also President Obama kinda looked down and kind of went, *Oh yeah, this is a big deal.*

MONA SUTPHEN

It had been years since Congress had approved a treaty . . . We'd sign treaties all the time, but we didn't necessarily try to ratify them if US law was basically abiding by it already, so we didn't go through Congress. But in the case of New START[80] because you'd be reducing nuclear arsenals, that meant you're taking a step. It needed to be ratified.

---

80   Strategic Arms Reduction Treaty.

ARUN CHAUDHARY

We were in Prague to sign the nuclear treaty,[81] and [Russian President Dmitry] Medvedev's videographer and I asked what the rules were—often in G8s and bilaterals it's very regimented what you can film—and everyone was like, *There hasn't been one of these signed in about twenty years. There really aren't any rules. Just make sure that both of you stick together.* In those moments you get brought out of yourself. Things could seem so routine—the next G20, the next G8, whatever—but then there were these rare important moments. You'd have to be able to differentiate them from the run-of-the-mill historical moments. That's the real problem. Everything was historic. It's just that some of it was extra historic.

MONA SUTPHEN

Everybody knew that Putin was still incredibly powerful. Let's put it this way: Medvedev wasn't going to do something that Putin was strongly against with the United States, but we technically weren't negotiating with him, at least directly. People weren't naive about that.

TERRY SZUPLAT

Medvedev was in the president's position, and Putin was behind the scenes, pulling the strings, so to speak.

MONA SUTPHEN

In terms of warming up the bilateral relationship, even though we disagreed on 1,001 other things, the Russians were interested in doing business with us and us with them. That's kind of where we started things off, and New START was part of that—fewer nukes is a good thing. And obviously, for a bunch of reasons, things went sideways on all of that relatively quickly, unfortunately for everybody. But [we] just thought, *This is important. Let's see how much business we can do with these guys. Hopefully this'll work out and we'll keep the page turned.*

---

81 April 8, 2010.

MICHAEL STRAUTMANIS

The crazy thing about that time was, while we were dealing with the final throes of passing health care, moving through the auto bailout, and probably about four other things, the oil spill was going on.

CAROL BROWNER

We first heard about it on Earth Day. Obama was having all the environmentalists over to the White House, and we were in the Rose Garden. My husband and my husband's eighty-year-old mom were there to meet Obama, and a reporter overheard me. "I have to leave. There's a problem in the Gulf of Mexico. One of the wells has fallen or is on fire. Something has happened."

MONA SUTPHEN

What we just thought of as an explosion we'd have under control relatively quickly turned into what it turned into, which was a major undertaking with all kinds of moves. Early on it was literally, *Okay, what's actually happening? How are we going to come up with a reporting chain that is both timely and relevant?*

JAKE LEVINE

This was an unprecedented disaster. The morning it happened, we really didn't know the scale of the problem. Part of that was we didn't have enough information from BP. This was after seven lives were lost. So you had the feeling of a tragedy. You didn't have the feeling for how large scale of an environmental disaster it was.

CAROL BROWNER

I told my husband that I couldn't go to dinner because I had to meet with the president in the Oval Office, and the Coast Guard was in there. Everyone was there. Half the people were like, *This'll be fine. These things happen.* I just remember saying, "You know what? This is not going to be fine. This is going to be a problem."

DR. STEVEN CHU

After the blowout, they didn't know the state of the valves. All they could see was oil and gas gushing out. They had remotely operated vehicles going down there and trying to figure out what was going on. I had made the suggestion to use gamma rays to try and find out whether the valves were opened or closed, but the BP engineers initially laughed at it. Then they said, "You know, you may be right."

JAKE LEVINE

The president ended up sending Steve Chu down there to sit in the control room with BP and think through solutions. That felt like a real turning point in terms of the kind of information that we were getting. We were able to build trust with BP. He was a constructive partner, arguably critical in helping to design the actual engineering solution to getting this blowout preventer. There was a lot of vocabulary that I've since forgotten.

DR. STEVEN CHU

I wanted a small team of people—maybe four, five, or six—and we'd go down there and roll up our sleeves together. It was not a committee making recommendations.

CAROL BROWNER

The depth at which this was happening was hard to explain. People were like, *Can't you just put divers down there?* and you're like, *People don't actually go down that far.* This was so beyond what anyone had ever focused on. Obviously, when you're working for a president, your first thought was, *Does this become his Exxon Valdez?* We were trying to get the hole closed to get it capped. They're building the technology. There were some dark moments, and Steve Chu might have mentioned where they were actually modeling when the pressure would equalize. At some point enough oil would have spewed out to where it's not going to spew out anymore. And we're sitting there thinking, *Well, this is really frightening.*

DR. STEVEN CHU

It was BP's initial conclusion that the well was damaged and could not be sealed from the top; therefore, you had to wait for a relief well at the bottom two months later. And I said, "No, I think it's equally likely that the well might not be damaged. We don't know from the data." After a day of thinking about that they said, "Yeah, you're right." There were decision points, which always entailed some risk, and so that was actually satisfying because I was there acting in capacity as a scientist with the president's backing.

JAKE LEVINE

There's this hat that was supposed to go on top of the blowout preventer that they weren't able to get back on because of all of the difficult conditions at that depth, and so the oil was just coming out of the bottom of the earth, essentially, and the equipment that was down there to manage and mitigate that needed to be manipulated in a way that Secretary Chu was very instrumental in figuring out.

DR. STEVEN CHU

We had the national weapons labs go through the entire design and make very strong recommendations. You had to right the swivel joint if you put the sealing cap on the way it was tilted. Again, you presented this *This is a concluded analysis from the weapons labs. Here it is.* So the BP engineers again said, "You're right."

MONA SUTPHEN

I was usually just trying to make sure that the president was getting a complete picture, and that the issues on the table were the right ones, that everybody who needed to be involved in something had been involved—side issues that, obviously, Carol and the guys were way too busy to deal with.

DR. STEVEN CHU

In my opinion, we helped them stop the leak in very substantive ways.

CAROL BROWNER

In addition to the environmental concerns, people had rights, under the law passed after Exxon Valdez, to be reimbursed if they weren't able to work. There was a trust fund to pay people like the shrimpers. So I started looking at that and realized only a handful of people worked on the [reimbursement] program. They would be quickly overwhelmed with all the claims, and, secondly, there weren't many resources in the fund. That's when we began negotiations with BP over setting up a fund, which BP, at the end of the day, probably wished they hadn't done.

JAKE LEVINE

You started to see Gulf Coast characters come out of the woodwork and manufacture different narratives that advanced their particular political needs. A lot of that was, frankly, jockeying to get a piece of what would become the settlement. It became known eventually that BP would commit to this gigantic $20 billion settlement, which the president negotiated directly.

MICHAEL STRAUTMANIS

If you think about the Gulf, those were mostly Republicans. So it was a bipartisan effort. We wanted our office to function across party lines, making sure that people on the ground were able to stay connected to their government and the federal government and get things done.

RAHM EMANUEL

The president was [also] implementing the Recovery Act at that point. I, also, was an advocate, after the Recovery Act and after TARP, to tackle financial regulation. Because those two votes were very partisan and on big spending—the Recovery Act and the TARP—financial regulation had no money involved. [It] had regulations the financial industry was gonna fight, and therefore I believed there was some Old Testament justice written into the script.

BARNEY FRANK

I think he wised up by late '09 or early '10, because we had one meeting in the White House[82]—Obama, top staff, Chris Dodd, and myself. There was a point at which Dodd was still hoping, reasonably, to get a bipartisan coalition for the financial-reform bill. [Senator Richard] Shelby sort of switched signals at the end, and the president and I were both worried that, to get Republican support, Chris might water things down.

CHRIS DODD

That was certainly true. I had an awful time. I went down to the fifth member on the Banking Committee to find someone willing to work on drafting a bill. Dick Shelby was a good friend of mine. If he decided to work with us on that bill it would have been a different bill. Not substantially different, but certainly different if I had a partner. [There was] this idea that "You should fight everything" by that time. *Don't give 'em anything. We got a chance to regain control.*

BARNEY FRANK

The president and I both said to Chris, "Hey, let's try to get the votes without them if the cost of getting their votes is too much compromise." Obama joined

---

82   May 21, 2010.

me and said to Chris, "Write them off if that's the way they're going to be, and do our best bill with our own people."

TED KAUFMAN

Shelby, [Senator Bob] Corker, and those guys were saying, "We're going to negotiate." They were never going to negotiate. All they wanted to do was drag this thing for as long as they could. It was the same way with the stimulus.

ED SILVERMAN

It would have been a better bill with eighty votes and Republican help, and, quite frankly, Dodd-Frank[83] had a lot of Republican provisions, which they will disown to this day, but they're there.

SCOTT BROWN

Barney Frank tried to screw me and put stuff in it during the committee wrap-ups. Had it passed in its original form—Harry wanted to do it in a day—it would have included auto dealers, dentists, doctors, and it would affect financial services, which had nothing to do with this. There were really serious flaws, so I told them I wasn't going to [vote for the bill]. So they pulled it back and made the changes.

CHRIS DODD

We did sixty amendments on the floor of the Senate over a period of eight days. Only one of those amendments required a sixty-vote margin. Every other amendment was fifty votes, up or down. But nonetheless, I was determined to prove you could bring a major bill to the floor, conduct it to where people could talk—not endlessly, I didn't shut anybody off—but you could raise your amendments, there could be a full-throated debate, and an up-or-down vote. In fact, Mitch McConnell used to talk about, if you'd bring a bill to the floor,

---

83   Dodd–Frank Wall Street Reform and Consumer Protection Act.

if it could be managed in that way, there would be less obstruction to the consideration of bills. I was a great believer in that.

SCOTT BROWN

I liked the fact that those laws hadn't been updated in half a century, and I was tired of banks acting like casinos. But I never liked that [Dodd-Frank gave] the Consumer Financial Protection Bureau unlimited power with no check and balance, like a runaway freight train, and I didn't like community banks and credit unions being treated like the big Wall Street banks. It would put them out of business. The overregulation's out of control, and the hope was I would get reelected. I hoped to get on the Banking Committee and make it better.

TED KAUFMAN

There're a lot of good things in Dodd-Frank. We got the Volcker amendment,[84] but in terms of the banks, on how to stop "too big to fail," we didn't do anything, as far as I was concerned. Brown-Kaufman didn't pass because the administration came out against it.[85] Again, the administration [had been] so focused on pulling out of [the recession], they didn't want to put more financial burdens on the banks. That's really what it came down to. The Brown-Kaufman amendment would have required the banks to hold more assets and better assets, [a proposal] which had been accused of breaking up the banks and may well have broken up some. They weren't going to pass that.

---

84   The Volcker Rule, named after former US Federal Reserve chair Paul Volcker, was designed to prohibit big banks from "proprietary trading and certain relationships with hedge funds and private equity funds."

85   Democrats Ted Kaufman of Delaware and Sherrod Brown of Ohio proposed Senate Amendment 3733, which would have levied a 10 percent "cap on any bank-holding-company's share of the United States' total insured deposits" and other restrictions that would prohibit "financial institutions from becoming 'too big to fail.'" The Senate voted down the amendment 61–33 on May 6, 2010. Twenty-seven Democrats, plus one independent (Joe Lieberman), voted nay.

AUSTAN GOOLSBEE

The first thing to recognize is, deposits aren't risky. Deposits are the safest things in the system. So capping banks by *You shouldn't be able to take more than* x *amount of deposits* was not really what the origins of the crisis were about; they're about shadow banks, and not real banks, taking a bunch of financing *other* than deposits. Because we have the FDIC, deposits don't tend to cause bank runs anymore. The second thing is, "too big to fail" was a misnomer. It wasn't size that made them dangerous. You could have broken up Bank of America into eight pieces and every one of those eight pieces would be bigger than Bear Stearns was. But Bear Stearns was too connected to fail, because if they failed, they were gonna have this smallpox virus. Patient zero would have spread it to the next one and to the next one, and [the potential for] that domino effect was what made them so dangerous.

TED KAUFMAN

[Not passing Brown-Kaufman] was a conscious decision. So that's the reason why. It wasn't politics or anything else. It was just a difference of opinion about how much the economy could take and how important it was to do something so that this didn't revisit itself at some not-too-distant place—the kind of tough medicine that we needed, based on the fact that we had the most deadly economic turnback since the Great Depression.

PETE HOEKSTRA

A battery plant in Holland, Michigan, got money out of the stimulus bill. We went to the groundbreaking, and the president showed up. It's Ottawa County. It's rock-solid Republican. It's my hometown. My local mayor and folks invited me to come, and so we're sitting in this field on our folding chairs. The president and the mayor were on the stage, and I was the only federally elected official that's there. So I'm sitting front row on the aisle, right in front of the podium. There's maybe 350 people there, and the president went through his nice speech, and about halfway through he made a crack somewhere along the lines of how people who didn't vote for the stimulus bill have no problem showing up for the groundbreaking.[86] I thought about walking out, but you know, it's the president. He's visiting here, and I had 350 pairs of eyes burrowed into the back of my head—people that I knew. They're just wondering what I was going to do, and as soon as the president's done, they all ran up to me. "Hey, the president just took a shot at you!"

SCOTT BROWN

Here's the thing about the president: He blew it in terms of not spending time with any of the Democrats or House members. He just was kind of aloof. He didn't reach out to me. I just took away the supermajority. You would think they'd call me. "Hey, good job. Let's get together and find things." As I told Harry Reid, I'd be the forty-first senator or the sixtieth senator. I didn't have an agenda. I just wanted to pass good stuff.

PETE HOEKSTRA

You know what Bill Clinton would have done? Bill Clinton would have said, "I just want all of you to know how much I appreciate Pete Hoekstra, and when I need some help, I know I can count on Pete Hoekstra." And I would be waving my hand saying, "No, he can't! He can't count on me for anything!" But that's the difference. Bill Clinton would not have taken the opportunity to go into somebody's hometown and use the office of the president to slam the local politician. Bill Clinton would recognize [that] if he was there and being nice to me, he'd have 350 people saying, "Hey, Bill Clinton's an okay guy" . . . That's the story that always captured for me why this president was not successful in getting Congress to work with him.

---

86 "Some folks . . . think that we should return to the policies that helped to lead to this recession. Some of them made the political calculation that it's better to obstruct than to lend a hand. They said no to tax cuts. They said no to small business loans. They said no to clean-energy projects. Now, it doesn't stop them from being at ribbon-cuttings, but that's okay." —President Obama at Compact Power, Inc., July 15, 2010.

BARNEY FRANK

Total and complete bullshit—it would not have made any difference. He was not warm and fuzzy, but so what? I'd never met George Bush or had a conversation with him during the whole time we were doing TARP, and I had worked closely with Hank Paulson. I had worked closely with Ben Bernanke. The only time I had talked to Bush was during that meeting in the White House when he complained to people that I was talking without being called on. It wasn't Obama's style, but you could not have schmoozed your way into any softening their resistance.

ROB ANDREWS

Obama was very friendly, but a more human and reserved person. The challenge of his presidency was to literally rescue the world from potential financial catastrophe, turn the economy from bleeding jobs to growing them, and reduce the deficit. Bill Clinton didn't succeed because he could stay up all night playing cards and learn all about your district. It helped, but if he had done all those things but had a nameless agenda and no sense of where he wanted to take the country, and surrounded himself with incompetents, he would have failed.

BARBARA BOXER

My relationship with the Clintons was different, because my daughter was married to Hillary's brother for seven, eight years. So we had kind of a familial relationship for a while. But I felt very aligned with what [President Clinton] was trying to do on most things. I did not support NAFTA. There were a couple other issues I didn't support, but it was kind of the same thing. I was able to have my knockdown drag-out with the cabinet member. I always had this deep and abiding respect and understanding that the president of the United States literally had the world on his shoulders. So if it didn't rise to the level of life or death, I was usually able to work everything out with the Obama team.

RAHM EMANUEL

The average stay for a chief of staff in modern times was eighteen months. I stayed twenty-one, not counting the transition, and he knew from day one that if the opportunity provided itself for me to run for office again, having given up my own electoral position, I would do that. I wanted to be mayor. He knew it. We talked about it when he asked me to be chief of staff, because he knew that, being in Congress, I was getting off a path from my own career that I wanted. So one day Mayor [Richard M.] Daley announced he wasn't running. We talked about it. There's not a lot of intrigue. I moved back to Chicago on October 3, I think it was.

DAVID AXELROD

I had always lived in Chicago and felt I was a better political strategist because I lived outside of Washington, where the conversation was entirely different. I used to have meetings every week or two with some of the other outside strategists, consultants, and so on who had worked on the campaign, because I felt that I was losing my touch. It's easy to lose your touch, your feel, when you're in that building.

GENE SPERLING

As we went into the fall of 2010, we faced a difficult issue. Even in our own party. I guess you'd call it "fiscal stimulus fatigue." People did not support doing more at that time. And the Republicans were completely opposed to anything, and yet we were still looking at unemployment that was over 9 percent. So at that point we did start asking, instead of what were our ideal policies, what was something that could actually pass to increase demand and help real people in the next year or two?

GLENN NYE

Democrats were stuck choosing between doing things that were pleasing to their base and things that were pleasing to independent voters. And in the political chess game, you don't win by putting yourself in the position of choosing whether to give up your queen or your castle. You win by forcing your opponents to make that tough choice.

GENE SPERLING

We did not consider the payroll-tax cut to be one of our most effective demand policies—we didn't think it was as effective as increasing Medicaid or infrastructure. It *did* feel like it would still be somewhat effective, and if this was something we could pass, shouldn't we focus on getting something done, as opposed to saying, *We're just gonna go forward with ideal message proposals when people are suffering?* That's not being practical or trying to cut deals. That's thinking what you can *actually* do in real life for millions of people.

GLENN NYE

The Republicans observed the worry among the American public, that people were having a hard time digesting a lot of things on the Democratic agenda. They just decided that the best course of action would be to ride the wave of that worry, versus doing things to alleviate the worry. They made it the Democrats' job to explain any policy ideas instead of working to solve major problems in the country. They determined just to play into the cynicism as much as they could, and they were correct in that it really was a successful strategy for them for the 2010 election.

JAMES KVAAL

There used to be a difference between a political season and a legislating season. There was an ethic, even if it was not always carried out in practice, that there was a time to set aside the politics and legislate, and then a time to campaign. It was true that, in our system, ultimately the president was accountable for what happens, and yet he couldn't do it without the cooperation of Congress. So you had an opposition party in Congress that had the incentive to block the president from carrying out his agenda.

JOEL BENENSON

If you went back and looked at President George W. Bush or Bill Clinton, major pieces of legislation passed with Democratic and Republican votes—not always, and not a lot of those from the [opposing] party, but enough, because the majority of the people in Congress supported them. That disappeared under President Obama. It was a new era of obstructionism, and a manipulation of the legislative process on the part of the Republicans, to deny this man normal negotiations and potential for progress that other presidents had always enjoyed across party lines.

JOHN TANNER

Mitch McConnell said his number-one priority in the United States wasn't trying to do something about ending the wars in Iraq or Afghanistan. He said "the single most important thing [we want to achieve]" was to "deny Obama a second term."[87] I'd never seen that.

STUART STEVENS
Chief Strategist, Romney-Ryan 2012

I didn't think that was as historically as unusual as it's made out. I knew [of] McConnell's statement, but pretty much everybody had thought that, whenever the next person got elected. McConnell just said it out loud.

BARBARA BOXER

Mitch McConnell basically said, "My mission is to defeat the president." The only thing I would say, I was able to get a lot done at times, but because it mattered to their states, whether it was a highway bill, a water bill, after-school care—it had nothing to do with the president. It had to do with self-interests and self-preservation.

---

87   Senate Minority Leader McConnell, in an interview with the *National Journal*, October 23, 2010.

BARBARA LEE

I worked with a variety of Republicans. You had to work issue by issue by issue and not let it get personal.

BARBARA BOXER

I did have colleagues to work with on specific issues, but they never disassociated themselves with what Mitch said, which was disappointing.

GLENN NYE

I talked to a number of Republican members in the House who complained [about] Tea Party primary challenges. So when you play with fire sometimes you get burned. I wasn't sure I was sympathetic to their cause at that time.

MARY BONO

It was a movement that didn't have answers. It just had anger. In a tough swing district like mine, I thought they did themselves more harm than good. No Republican was good enough, pure enough, or conservative enough.

ALLYSON SCHWARTZ

I did have a tough reelection. Nobody believed it, but there were so many members of Congress at the time in swing districts leaning Democrat. It was expensive. I won it handily at the end of the day, but I took it seriously. I was glad I did. Many members, whether they voted for the health-care law or didn't, felt the brunt of it.

JOSH LIPSKY

On election night in 2010, I was on advance in South Korea because the president was going there the next week. As we landed we got reports from the embassy about the huge losses, sixty-three [seats] in the House.

RAHM EMANUEL

We had seats in the House level in '06 and '08, cumulatively, that required an extraordinary Democratic year to keep those seats. It was inevitable that you were going to lose some portion. It did not have to be as bad as it was. You could argue there were things that were done that exacerbated what, no matter what, was going to be a challenging year. You could argue there were things you could have done that would have softened it a little, but nobody will ever know.

ERIC LESSER

David [Axelrod] met with members of Congress who had lost, who had taken courageous votes on health care and on the Waxman-Markey cap-and-trade bill. We always talk about beating up on people who don't show political courage, and there's plenty of that, but I remember pretty vividly thinking that a lot of these members stood up and took tough votes in difficult districts, in rural Virginia or in rural Ohio.

GLENN NYE

It's funny to hear the other side of that perspective. I thought the Democratic caucus shrunk because moderates didn't win elections. That process was really accelerated when the House Democratic leadership decided to bring really complicated cap-and-trade legislation in the middle of the Great Recession. That destroyed the political capital that the president and the Democrats had brought in after 2008.

CAROLYN MALONEY

It was horrible to lose the majority. I never would have passed the CARD Act if we did not have a majority in the House and the Senate. We never would have passed TARP without a majority in the House and the Senate. We never would have passed Dodd-Frank reforms. We never would have passed health care. Anytime you bring change, there's always a shift back.

BARBARA LEE

Another part of it was turnout. We didn't invest like we should, and the White House didn't communicate clearly the impacts and achievements that the Affordable Care Act would bring. It was a convergence of a bunch of issues.

GLENN NYE

Health-care reform was much more important to the president than climate-change legislation. Had that been taken up first, things might have turned out a little bit different. A key difference between these two bills, of course, was that cap-and-trade did not have a chance to go through the Senate. Health care did. So voting on cap-and-trade was particularly damaging without the upside of still having a good chance of becoming law.

RAHM EMANUEL

Yeah, I don't know. I mean, look, health care was the main focus. Everybody knew it was the main focus.

ROB ANDREWS

I didn't think it was the health-care bill. I thought it was outrage about the economy being in bad shape. Unemployment started to fall by late in 2010, so when people said he didn't go after the economy first, that's not factually correct. It just didn't work soon enough for the Democratic majorities. The one criticism I would lodge was that they weren't good enough at taking credit for what they did.

DAVID AXELROD

You know, we recovered more rapidly from the biggest crisis since the Great Depression than what was the average for those kinds of crises, and a lot of it had to do with the steps the president took, including the Recovery Act. But all of that was meaningless if you were one of the people who lost their jobs, one of the people whose wages were frozen. So what we learned very quickly was, even when there were signs of progress, if you claimed too much progress, people would recoil from that. They weren't feeling it in their own lives. It was a very tricky path to navigate.

JON FAVREAU

I just don't know that better communication—that telling people *No, no, no, no, you're fine* when they weren't—would have fixed anything.

BARNEY FRANK

Right, I agree. He shouldn't have said how great it was, but to say, *Hey, things are terrible, but we're trying to make them less bad?* I had a slogan I wanted to use in 2010, and one of my friends actually made a bumper sticker for me: *Things would have sucked more without me.* But he should have been blaming [Republicans] more.

VAN JONES

The stupidity of the way that the stimulus package was marketed really hurt us. There was a little emblem next to a bunch of signs all the way across America— a worthless thing. *Paid for by the Recovery Act*, blah blah blah. No American had seen that symbol, before or afterward. Obama's "Hope" campaign symbol could have been put on everything. Or it could have had a picture of Obama. Everybody would have said he was a narcissistic crazy person, but people would have seen that symbol all across the country.

JON FAVREAU

Now, it's interesting to talk about using his picture. The Recovery Act, if we had to do that over again, should have branded that better. Every time there was a new shiny road somewhere, it should have been called "the Obama Road," or I don't know what we could have done. We could have figured out

Payment Receipt

Pikesville Branch (PI)
www.bcpl.info
Thursday, February 07, 2019 10:05:47 AM

65038

Title   : [DELETED] PRAYING BACKWARDS - T
RANSFORM YOUR PRAYER LIFE BY BEGINNING IN JESUS'
  NAME
Item barcode   : 31183189199919
Call number   :
Reason   : Overdue Item
Charge   : $2.00

Total charges : $2.00
Paid   : $1.00

Account balance: $1.75

HOMEWORK HELP
Brainfuse tutoring, Rosetta Stone,
research databases and more
Available at bcpl.info

Shelf Help 410-494-9063   www.bcpl.info

something, but there was a little too much bureaucracy in terms of branding of the Recovery Act.

VAN JONES

It could have been an Uncle Sam. "Brought to you by Uncle Sam." Anything. Instead, in typical blind, deaf, and dumb DC fashion, they invented a completely different symbol that nobody had ever seen before and would never see again.

JON FAVREAU

But you'd be driving around and see, like, a bunch of construction that would stop traffic, and it's like, "Well that's the Recovery Act." Putting Obama's name on that wouldn't have helped. It's a bunch of people stuck in fuckin' traffic. Now, could we have spent every day trying to figure out how we could have come up with a better story? Yeah, maybe. But it always seems to be a communications problem, and communications people don't exist to make problems better. They exist to tell the best-possible story, and the story of the early Obama years was, *We're in the middle of a crisis. We're taking every possible step to fix it that is politically feasible, and yet, even with that, it's going to take a long time to get out of that.*

VAN JONES

The American people are pretty busy. They don't have time to track this stuff. We tend to traffic in symbols, moments, and gestures, and this was Obama's downfall in a lot of ways. That *If you just go in, ignore the politics, and do the hard work, ultimately the country would notice and reward you.* That was where the mythology of the Obama White House translated to "No Drama Obama." In hindsight, it was foolish, but we were that way, and I had a different view the entire time but wasn't in a powerful-enough position for my opinion to matter a lot.

RAHM EMANUEL

I was gone, but it's not like the telephones didn't work. There's one chief of staff at a time, and if the chief of staff wanted your advice for the president, they called you. Not the other way around. I was gone, but obviously after the election I talked to them about what to do, how to structure. There were discussions about his agenda for the 2012 presidential [election] and also in 2010, between the old Congress and the new Congress, what you could get done.

BILL DALEY
US Secretary of Commerce (1997–2000)
White House Chief of Staff (2011–2012)

[Pete Rouse] was going to be temporary, he was only going to be [White House chief of staff] a couple of months . . . You'd just come off a terrible election. There was a sense that things had to be changed. So I think that was part of why they reached out to me and began the discussions in November/December of '10.

MONA SUTPHEN

Before we lost control of the House, we pushed Don't Ask, Don't Tell [repeal], New START, and had immigration on the table. [We thought we could] get two of those three over the finish line. There was a big question of which of those three it would be.

TYLER MORAN

Policy Director, National Immigration Law Center (2001–2012)
Deputy Policy Director, Domestic Policy Council, White House (2012–2014)
Senior Policy Advisor, US Senate Democratic Leader Harry Reid (2014–2017)

Harry Reid was the one who decided to bring the DREAM Act to the [Senate] floor, even though people in the administration were telling him not to do it.[88] Everyone was telling him he was crazy . . . That was after his election, where everyone thought he was a goner, and it was the Latino vote that put him over the edge and he won.

CECILIA MUÑOZ

Senator Reid, who was in a tight reelection race, announcing he was gonna bring the DREAM Act to a vote—that was controversial in the immigration world, because up until then, there had been this sense of *Everybody has to link elbows and go together*. People in the immigration community did not want to break any one piece of the legislation off from any of the others. Every piece of the comprehensive immigration reform is an incentive to move it forward, and if you break off the more popular pieces, the theory went, that might jeopardize the ability to get the whole thing done.

JIM MESSINA

We had lost seats in the House of Representatives. We lost [six] seats in the Senate, and we had to get New START [ratified]. Basically the Senate Republicans and Dems had come together and said they had time to do one issue. And I remember Obama saying, "Uh-uh. We're going to get 'em both."

---

88 The Development, Relief, and Education for Alien Minors (DREAM) Act proposed provisional and eventually permanent residency status for undocumented immigrants who entered the country before their sixteenth birthday and would fulfill a number of other requirements, including either serving two years of military service or attending college.

GENE SPERLING

We also still faced an issue with the economy, which, while technically in recovery, was not in recovery for tens of millions of people. The long-term unemployment rate still reflected the depth of the financial crisis. We knew going into 2010 that Making Work Pay was going to expire.[89] We knew that we had to extend emergency unemployment insurance for millions of families. So the question was, Were you going to do everything you could to help real lives, struggling Americans, or were you just going to stand on principle, even if it meant getting nothing done?

LUIS GUTIÉRREZ

Instead of doing [comprehensive] immigration reform in the lame-duck session of 2010, I led the effort here in the House and we passed the DREAM Act.[90]

CECILIA MUÑOZ

So, Speaker Pelosi passed it through the House. It was the first time the DREAM Act had ever passed the House. [Because Senator Reid was going to introduce the bill] we, and the advocacy world, worked it incredibly hard in the Senate. In fact, in the administration we did so many press calls and conference calls with different members of the cabinet that it became almost a joke in the White House press corps. Like, *Oh, it's Tuesday. Which cabinet member's gonna come out for the DREAM Act today? "We've got an angle for the Secretary of Defense!"*

---

89 The Making Work Pay tax credit was a provision of the American Recovery and Reinvestment Act of 2009, and provided a refundable tax credit of up to $400 for working individuals and up to $800 for married taxpayers filing joint returns. The credit was applied via automatic withholding changes to workers' paychecks, as lawmakers hoped the increase in take-home pay would encourage consumer spending to help stimulate the economy. The credit was not renewed by the House for 2011, and only applied to the 2009 and 2010 tax years.

90 House Democrats passed the DREAM Act by a vote of 216–198 on December 8, 2010. The legislation would fail in the Senate ten days later by a vote of 55–41, falling short of the sixty votes needed to pass.

JAMES KVAAL

Still, at the time there was a lot of concern about the state of the economy. So the president had a clear sense in priorities, and that meant finding legislative common ground with people who didn't always agree with you, and prioritizing that above ideological purity.

GENE SPERLING

Here was the reality: the only way we could get through a House that was going to have John Boehner as its Speaker and Eric Cantor as its majority leader was to allow the top [marginal tax] rate to not kick back up to 39.6 percent. Now, believe me, I was an architect in the Clinton era of taking the top rate to 39.6 percent, but if simply extending [Bush's 35 percent tax rate] for two years was going to allow us to get unemployment insurance, which we had no chance to do without this deal, if it allowed us to extend for two more years the refundable tax credits that could help twenty million low-income families, if it could allow us to do some form of significant middle-class demand policy, like a payroll tax cut, was that trade-off worth it? Our view was that it was.

AUSTAN GOOLSBEE

The Making Work Pay tax credit, which effectively gave you a tax cut for payroll taxes paid, was a way to cut taxes that was quite progressive. If you did cuts to the income tax, they tended to go to high-income people. This was geared toward working people. It had been the biggest tax cut for working people probably in the history of the United States, and yet, in 2010, the polling showed that the majority of Americans believed that Obama had *raised* their taxes. In reality, no one's taxes had been raised.

GENE SPERLING

President Clinton came to the White House,[91] and this was a time when a lot of progressives and Democrats were split on whether to support the agreement, and if President Clinton had wanted to create division or draw supporters away, he easily could have. Instead, he came into the briefing room with President Obama and defended the agreement.

AUSTAN GOOLSBEE

I was thinking, *What is wrong with our messaging?* We could give hundreds of billions of dollars of tax cuts and nobody even *knew* it. They actually thought their taxes went up! So the fact that those tax cuts were in the stimulus—and Republicans had staked out a position that they hated everything about this stimulus—meant that they were going to let all those tax cuts expire for 98 percent of Americans. Economists certainly thought that the economy could not take a giant tax increase on 98 percent of workers. So we were pushing to extend the Making Work Pay tax credit and unemployment benefits. These were people who were literally hand-to-mouth. Whatever money they got they would go spend it, as opposed to tax cuts for the rich where, you know, one-third or more of the money, they're just gonna put in the bank.

JAMES KVAAL

The 2010 tax deal gave tax relief to almost every household. So by putting more money in the hands of American families, you were increasing consumer spending and propping up the economy.

AUSTAN GOOLSBEE

It was pretty well negotiated by Obama with nothing in his hand. He ended up getting two or three times more than what he had to give up, but he had to do it in a way that, you know, rather than saying, *Let's extend the stimulus*, he

---

91   December 10, 2010.

had to say, *Fine, we'll let all the stimulus go away, and we'll start a new payroll tax cut, unemployment benefits*, whatever. In reality it was the right decision. He was not going to be able to let the Republican tax cuts expire, though he wanted to, and made perfectly clear he wanted to. So he basically said, *We're gonna extend these for two years in exchange for getting all of these tax cuts for middle-income and working people, plus unemployment-insurance benefits and some other stuff, and we'll live to fight another day.*

MONA SUTPHEN

People were super-excited about the idea that we might be in the multilateral-treaty business again, so we were able to channel that enthusiasm even among people who didn't care about New START. They were just like, *If we get back into the treaty business, it means that Law of the Sea and other things that people want might come back onto the table, too.*[92]

BARNEY FRANK

I never thought much of the nuclear treaty anyway. They committed us to spending billions. It was a waste of money . . . Nancy Pelosi and I took the lead on the repeal of Don't Ask, Don't Tell . . . There was a point when a key question was in the Senate. Lindsey Graham, to his eternal shame, with some help from McCain, threatened to sink the nuclear treaty with the Russians if we pushed for the repeal of Don't Ask, Don't Tell. There were some in the administration that were kind of willing to give in to that.

---

92 In 1982, the United Nations adopted the Law of the Sea Treaty (formally the Third United Nations Convention on the Law of the Sea, or UNCLOS III), which outlined commercial responsibilities and environmental protections for the 140 million square miles of ocean and sea. (Prior to the treaty, the understanding was that each nation maintained sovereignties over its respective coastlines.) The US participated in the years-long negotiations for UNCLOS, but ultimately did not ratify the treaty. President Reagan believed "the underdeveloped nations who now control the General Assembly were looking for a free ride at our expense—again."

CHRISTOPHER KANG

Special Assistant to the President for Legislative Affairs, White House (2009–2011)
Senior Counsel and Special Assistant to the President, White House (2011–2014)
Deputy Counsel and Deputy Assistant to the President, White House (2014–2015)

I don't recall the idea that we would trade one priority for another. In that lame-duck session, the thought was that Don't Ask, Don't Tell repeal would be part of this broader Defense Authorization bill that's passed every year for the past fifty-some-odd years,[93] and that's how it would have gotten across the finish line. And then that bill was blocked, and after it was blocked, the White House, supporters of the bill, and leadership decided to move Don't Ask, Don't Tell [repeal] as a stand-alone bill, and really made the time and effort to push it through. That really made the difference.

JIM MESSINA

It was one of those issues that, when it [was signed into law] literally [three] days before Christmas, I was sitting on the Senate floor and just crying like a baby. It was one of the most difficult things I'd ever worked on, but in the end, history will judge us right.

MONA SUTPHEN

We ended up getting Don't Ask, Don't Tell [repeal] and New START over the finish line and not immigration.

---

93 The National Defense Authorization Act is annual legislation that has been passed by Congress since 1961 and specifies the budget and expenditures of the Department of Defense. In 2010, Representative Patrick Murphy (D-Florida) introduced an amendment to the 2011 Defense Authorization bill that would have repealed Don't Ask, Don't Tell. After several successful Republican filibusters against debate on the NDAA, Senators Joe Lieberman and Susan Collins introduced a bill focused solely on DADT's repeal, which passed both the House and Senate and was signed into law by President Obama on December 22, 2010.

CECILIA MUÑOZ

The DREAM Act went down by five votes [in the Senate] . . . The teams working on Don't Ask, Don't Tell and the DREAM Act all watched that vote in my office. That was right after the Don't Ask, Don't Tell vote—like, literally right after—and, you know, there were tears. Happy and sad tears.

TYLER MORAN

I was sitting up there in the [Senate] gallery with all the Don't Ask Don't Tell people and all the Dreamers for the vote . . . Not all the Dems voted for it.

CECILIA MUÑOZ

Valerie's office was in the same corner of the second floor as mine. She was my boss at the time, and she must have told the president that we were up there, because he came up and gave us a pep talk after it was over. He said, you know, "Remember that on the way to getting the Civil Rights Act and the Voting Rights Act passed, there were defeats on the way to those victories. And, for that matter, on the seventeen-year path it took to get Don't Ask, Don't Tell repealed, there were defeats before we got to that victory. And remember, this is one of those. Because the day will come when we're celebrating."

2011

John Boehner was met with loud cheers as he took the gavel from former Speaker Nancy Pelosi and held it up to his newly sworn-in 112th House of Representatives, dominated by 242 Republicans over 193 Democrats, still walking wounded from their losses two months prior. The famously quick to cry "proud son of Ohio," as Pelosi had characterized him in her introduction, had to wipe his nose from whatever sobbing he held back while giving his remarks to the opening session. "It's still just me," he admitted, trying to inject a little humor and modesty into what was likely the shining moment of his quarter century in Congress. After two minutes of expressing gratitude and niceties behind the podium, Speaker Boehner dove right in to his majority's new mission: "No longer can we kick the can down the road. The people voted to end business as usual, and today we begin to carry out their instructions."

The instructions to which Speaker Boehner referred were all enumerated in the Republicans' *Pledge to America*, a 2010 campaign-season manifesto. It included "permanently stopping job-killing tax hikes"; the repeal of the Affordable Care Act to prevent "more financial pain for seniors, families, and the federal government"; heavy spending cuts to set the budget back to "pre-stimulus, pre-bailout levels, saving us at least $100 billion in the first year alone" with a laser focus to "balance the budget and pay down the debt"; and the reduction of overwhelming regulations and government oversight that "prevents investors and entrepreneurs from putting capital at risk."

It was a celebration. The chamber's interior, one reporter noted, felt "sort of like the first day of high school." Chummy arm-grabs and handshakes ate up the afternoon. Eager to reverse the president's agenda, conservatives set about implementing the initiatives they had been fantasizing about for at least two years, but by the end of the week the mood had soured. Saturday, in northwest Tucson, a gunman opened fire at a Safeway where Representative Gabrielle Giffords held her annual "Congress on Your Corner" event for Arizona's Eighth District. An American flag was planted outside the grocery store's entrance where six were killed, including congressional staffer Gabe Zimmerman; US District Judge John Roll; and nine-year-old Christina-Taylor Green. Thirteen others were wounded; the congresswoman herself had suffered a head shot. Speaker Boehner ordered House flags flown at half-staff as funeral arrangements were made and surgeries were under way.

MICHAEL STEEL

She was talking with constituents. She was doing her job. She was meeting with the people she represented. The Speaker always believed—and I when I say "the Speaker," I mean Boehner; it's just always easier to refer to him that way—that our highest responsibility in some ways was protecting the institution of the House. So an attack on a member of the House was an attack on the institution, and it made absolutely no difference to him whether it was a Democratic or Republican member. The first responsibility was to make sure that the members and the staff were able to do their jobs safely.

JOSH LIPSKY

I was in Schenectady, New York, for an advance trip. We heard about the Gabby Giffords shooting. Everyone was emailing, very concerned. POTUS was supposed to go to GE up in Schenectady. So we heard that was going to be postponed, given the shooting, and were just on standby for what would happen next. We all rushed back to DC. I was out to dinner that night with my girlfriend, who's now my wife, and her parents. I got the call from the director of advance. "Can you get out to [Joint Base] Andrews first thing in the morning?" Of course, no one knew Gabby Giffords's status. It was up in the air whether she was going to make it or not.

CODY KEENAN

I was in the Situation Room already kind of freaking out. There were always those moments early in the presidency, whenever you got a first step up into something you felt like you're not supposed to be in. You had to constantly remind yourself to pay attention. *There is something happening here. Stop yourself from looking around. You're not on a tour. You're not watching history from the outside. You're an active participant.*

JOSH LIPSKY

This was going to be a twenty-four-hour advance. We usually had five or six days, but that was just the nature of this situation. You had these tragedies where you had to do your job—logistical arrangements, press arrangements, press releases—and in the meantime, you're wondering whether people were going to live or die. You're just trying to balance these two things and be respectful and get your job done.

CODY KEENAN

[Homeland Security advisor John] Brennan briefed everyone on what had happened—how many people were shot, how the congresswoman was doing, who the shooter was. There were questions at that point about, since a congresswoman was involved, whether there was a plot. Obviously it turned out that that wasn't true, but we didn't know that at the time . . . We did a quick statement for the president, and I think maybe it was Monday when we were asked to go speak at the memorial service, which was Wednesday.[94] So you had to start writing and researching really fast.

JOSH LIPSKY

[When] POTUS came . . . the plan was he was going to stop at the hospital first, before the speech and before the service. I waited with the press outside in the cars. It was the only time that I can remember that the [press] pool was quiet. Usually you're standing somewhere with them, and they're like, *Hey what's going on? How long is he gonna be in there? Do you know who he's with?* Everyone knew

---

94   January 12, 2011, at the McKale Center, University of Arizona.

exactly what was going on. There was nothing to say. Everyone was just quiet and reflecting on what this meant.

CODY KEENAN

When I met with the president to talk about what he wanted to say, with eulogies, obviously, the first thing you wanted to do was memorialize the departed and pay tribute to the heroes, and impart a couple lessons on what we're responsible for now that people were gone. What's incumbent upon us to do in their absence?

TERRY SZUPLAT

One of the things that we noticed was how divisive that event was, the vitriol and the nastiness that followed, politically. Rather than bringing people together, here was another instance, it seemed, where tragedy pushed us further apart.

JOSH LIPSKY

I don't remember how long he was at the hospital, but when we went to the event just across the street, and he met with the families backstage, I'm just not gonna talk about that. I just feel those are completely personal moments and it's not my place.

CODY KEENAN

The president leaned on that notion of civility, but not as a crutch. A lot of people used civility, especially on the Right when this happened, as an argument against doing anything about it. *Well, we just need to be more civil and this won't happen anymore.* Well, you know, it happened every single day. Shootings were not fueled by civility or incivility, but it's still something he wanted to talk about. It was his riff that he came up [with] that, "Did we tell [a spouse just how desperately] we loved them, not just once in a while, but every single day?"

TERRY SZUPLAT

So often [it] was the case he would go directly to the central issue or tension point, and I think it's one of the reasons why his speeches resonated so much. In that speech, of course, wanting, trying to fulfill that little girl's dreams, making "our democracy [to be] as good as Christina imagined it" became one of the most important lines.[95]

ARUN CHAUDHARY

With Rahm gone, one of the reasons he had Daley come in that was probably so attractive was that he fulfilled that same role: someone who was from outside the organization but still was a familiar face, especially one from Chicago.

BILL DALEY

The perception [was] that they had a big problem with the business community—that they weren't reaching out. Rahm got out just in time, and there was a sense that you had divided government back again [for the] first time since under Clinton. It was also, *Maybe we ought to get somebody who can hopefully reach out beyond the way we've reached out or not reached out.*

---

95 "Here was a young girl who was just becoming aware of our democracy; just beginning to understand the obligations of citizenship; just starting to glimpse the fact that some day she, too, might play a part in shaping her nation's future. She had been elected to her student council. She saw public service as something exciting and hopeful. She was off to meet her congresswoman, someone she was sure was good and important and might be a role model. She saw all this through the eyes of a child, undimmed by the cynicism or vitriol that we adults all too often just take for granted. I want to live up to her expectations. I want our democracy to be as good as Christina imagined it. I want America to be as good as she imagined it. All of us, we should do everything we can do to make sure this country lives up to our children's expectations." —President Barack Obama, University of Arizona, Tucson, Arizona, January 12, 2011.

ARUN CHAUDHARY

Rahm felt as much an outsider to our crew as did Daley. It wasn't until Denis [McDonough was appointed in 2013] that the Obama inner circle had been represented by a chief of staff, and I think that was a decision that was made by the president. To have his main point person not part of his traditional inner circle coming out of the campaign gave him perspective.

DAVID PLOUFFE

I obviously spent time in '09 and '10 thinking through the reelect and the things we needed to do and who would manage it. And so, yeah, when I came to the White House [in 2011] I basically had two jobs. My day job was just helping govern, and I then had a campaign to oversee. My recommendation to the president was that Messina would run it, and that I would oversee it from Washington. You know, somewhat what Karl Rove did in 2004 for Bush.

JIM MESSINA

When I left the White House in January to move to Chicago and start the campaign, our approval rating was under 40 percent . . . Every Friday, starting in February, we would have a discussion and rank the Republicans in terms of one to fifteen on who could be our opponent. We spent resources there, put staff based on those ratings, [and] every single week, Mitt Romney was number one on our list. We always assumed he was the only credible nominee for the Republicans, and we treated him like that for the entire two-year cycle.

DAVID PLOUFFE

That was all a very well organized, well thought out plan . . . Then Axe would go back to Chicago, rest up a bit, and put himself into the campaign.

DAVID AXELROD

It was an adjustment to leave the White House. When you're there, and you leave, it's like you're on a carousel that's going two hundred miles an hour and suddenly you're dumped on the side. And the carousel kept on going. It's an adjustment to return to the real world. But as a campaign consultant, I'm not sure I would have offered him as good advice if I had still been there, because I was back out and really sensing what was going on in the country.

BILL DALEY

I had known David for thirty years. He did just about every one of my brother Richard's elections. Anyway, then all of a sudden David was gone, and even though I knew Valerie and a few others, I wasn't that close with any of the people. Plouffe I didn't know at all. I mean, I met him but didn't pretend to know him.

DAVID AXELROD

I had a lot of other personal reasons for [leaving], but I always had a two-year commitment and I could not have worked beyond that. But, you know, like a lot of people who had worked in the White House, I would say it's the greatest experience of my life and I'd never do it again.

BILL DALEY

So the entire team was people who had been together from the very beginning, no doubt about it. That made it difficult, and all the slots were all filled. There was no full-scale sort of change beyond *We'll change the guy at the top—chief of staff role—and see if that makes a big difference.*

MATTHEW MILLER

That was the worst year of the Obama presidency, and that's after losing Congress in 2010. There was the debt-ceiling crisis in August, really the low point of his presidency, and there were a lot of low points.

JACK LEW

Director, Office of Management and Budget, White House (2010–2012)
White House Chief of Staff (2012–2013)
US Secretary of the Treasury (2013–2017)

The sequence of our engagements on budget issues actually started before the debt limit. It was on the continuing-resolution [bill for fiscal year 2011]—the funding of the government—where, in the spring, a potential shutdown was looming, and the question was, How do you engage? How would you deal with a new Republican majority with a vocal and often-dominant Freedom Caucus?[96] We made the judgment to try and work with Speaker Boehner and the majority to avoid a shutdown, to see if there was a way to navigate.

BRIAN DEESE

Consistent with how the president went about things, we were very focused on saying, *We got a real problem, we should try to do what we can to fix it, and we should assume the best of our opponents who are sitting across the table negotiating.*

GENE SPERLING

We were, from the start, trying to figure out how to negotiate, and we learned two things simultaneously. The positive thing was that John Boehner did believe in the type of Reagan–Tip O'Neill relationship where you were strong adversaries

---

96 The Tea Party–backed wing of the Republican House had not officially dubbed itself the Freedom Caucus until 2015, when Representative Jim Jordan of Ohio assumed chairmanship over a group of some thirty-six lawmakers, but their obstructionist practices and organization began in a less centralized manner at the outset of the 112th Congress.

but in the end figured how to move forward. The negative was realizing that he had so much division within his party that he could not deliver in the same way maybe Newt Gingrich had been able to—not because perhaps it was his fault, but simply because he just didn't quite have the authority. You saw that begin to play out in the fact that we couldn't even get past the appropriations negotiations, and this was a great frustration for the president.

BILL DALEY

It was obvious that the Tea Party people who had won and given the Speaker his majority had no loyalty to Boehner, Cantor, or any of the leadership. They had nothing to do with getting those people elected. They were outside the norm, and they didn't give a hoot. So the expectation that a Speaker could deliver his caucus, it didn't take long into the spring of '11 to see that that wasn't the case. You had a situation where Boehner and Cantor were having more problems with their own members than anything.

MICHAEL STEEL

At that point, filling that pledge for fiscal year 2011 would have meant a spending reduction of about $100 billion. And so when we got to that first spending fight, a substantial portion of the fiscal year was already over, and because a large part of the fiscal year was already over and for various other reasons, the spending cut, in dollar terms, wound up being much lower than $100 billion.

JACK LEW

We agreed, if I recall, to [$61 billion], and it was about half real reductions and half spending that was offset by other measures . . . [Boehner] may not have been able to sell the lower number [to his caucus].

GENE SPERLING

When you're on one side you never have total transparency into the deliberations [on] the other side, but we tended to expect a normal negotiation where sides moved closer together, where there were a few last-minute adjustments, where you each tried to be creative in finding ways to get the necessary votes, and I think what happened, from their point of view, was that Boehner didn't have a long rope to negotiate.

MICHAEL STEEL

That was the first time that a lot of—particularly the newly elected—members had to grapple with the complexities of the budget process, kind of how Washington spent money, which was a complicated and often seemingly irrational—and often actually irrational—process.

JACK LEW

He was criticized as not having a tough negotiator in the first round. I think that kind of came back to haunt him, that he was constantly being questioned.

MICHAEL STEEL

In that one, I didn't really recall the White House being terribly influential or important. Obviously in the debt-limit talks over the summer, the White House was very much involved, but this one—to the extent that they were exercising influence, it was with Senate Democrats, shaping what could get through the Senate after we passed it in the House.[97] I didn't remember dealing much with the White House. They had their priorities.

---

97 Budget negotiations ended in early April between House Republicans and Senate Democrats and the White House, with an agreement that would slash $38 billion in federal spending and fund the government through fiscal year 2011 (end of September).

JONATHAN FINER

Special Advisor for Middle East Affairs, Office of the Vice President (2011–2012)
Deputy Chief of Staff for Policy, Office of the Secretary of State (2013–2014)
Chief of Staff and Director of Policy Planning, Office of the Secretary of State (2015–2017)

The president's been very clear that his biggest regret, or one of them, was not doing more to follow up on Libya. There was a pretty rigorous debate about whether the administration should [have gone] ahead with that military intervention, and for those who were against it, it was not because they didn't believe in the validity of the mission—very much a human/civilian-protection goal of preventing a slaughter in Benghazi when [Muammar] Gaddafi's army was moving in. The reason people were concerned was because they were worried exactly about what would happen in the aftermath, how much of an investment would be required by the United States and our partners to put the country back on track.

DAN SHAPIRO

The decision there was connected to a much more limited and discrete event than what Syria would turn into. It was a civil war—sort of rebels against the Gaddafi regime—but the moment of truth was when Gaddafi's forces were advancing toward Benghazi and had declared that once they retook the city, they were gonna slaughter everybody in it. They seemed to be days or hours away from getting there, like an advancing army on an open desert road, so there was a different kind of initial imperative and decision to be made.

LEON PANETTA

Director, Central Intelligence Agency (2009–2011)
US Secretary of Defense (2011–2013)

I have used that as an example of NATO coming together in an effective way. I went to Naples, where we had an Allied Joint Force Command center located during the conflict. What they were doing was essentially identifying targets and assigning those targets to various members of NATO, who then conducted the operations pursuant to that.

DAN SHAPIRO

We made a decision that this was going to be an air campaign. It wouldn't involve a ground invasion, and beyond those early weeks I stepped out of it. That's about the time I came to Israel.

LEON PANETTA

I viewed it as something that was successful, in terms of the operation that we were involved with and what we were trying to achieve. The bigger problem became whether we had developed the kind of diplomatic follow-up that was necessary to keep Libya on the right track towards stability—helping them build institutions of governing, providing a support system.

DAN SHAPIRO

The mission was so well defined that you had the ability to prevent a humanitarian tragedy. We needed to do it. But in doing that, the president also set some lines, because he understood this could take us in deeper. He was not eager to have extended Middle East military engagements, for all the known reasons.

JONATHAN FINER

They'd seen what an enormous project that entailed in Iraq and Afghanistan and weren't sure the American people would be ready to take on another one.

LEON PANETTA

Every one of these countries was different. Every one had their own history, their own tribal divisions—it's not like you could do a cookie-cutter approach. Every one was unique. But at the same time, there were ways to work with these countries and the various factions within those countries to move them towards stability. Not every one was, obviously, going to turn into Jeffersonian democracy—we understood that—but at the very least, if we could have provided the support system to provide stability, we could have put them on the right track towards the future.

JONATHAN FINER

Not having engaged a massive nation-building effort, we probably erred too far on the other side and did not do enough to help Libya get back on its feet after taking the very justifiable step of protecting those civilians in Benghazi, which ultimately led to Gaddafi's ouster.

ROB ANDREWS

My criticism was less about the administration and its decision-making than the box we put ourselves in. The constitutional power for the Congress to declare war had been diluted to almost meaningless status.

BARBARA LEE

I opposed the first authorization to use force in 2001.[98] I knew it was going to set the stage for perpetual war.

LUIS GUTIÉRREZ

I thought it was a huge mistake, because what were the contingencies? Here was a tyrant who gave up any nuclear ambitions and sat down and negotiated with the West, and I didn't know what we were going to replace him with.

---

98   Three days after the attacks on September 11, 2001, a nearly unanimous 98 senators and 420 members of the House of Representatives sent Senate Joint Resolution 23, a.k.a. Authorization for Use of Military Force (AUMF), to President Bush's desk for his signature. The legislation granted the administration unprecedented war powers "under the Constitution to take action to deter and prevent acts of international terrorism." Two senators and ten House members abstained from the vote. Only Congresswoman Lee voted nay.

BILL DALEY

It was ironic, you know. The people who ended up defending Gaddafi were the same people who loved it when Reagan tried to kill him and a couple of his kids after the Pan Am flight thing.[99] Some people said, *Oh we shouldn't have gone after him because*—whatever reason. The reality was, he was nuts. That whole place was unraveling, and by the time we were faced with a decision of doing military action, Gaddafi's days were limited. The place was torn apart. It was divided, and the president ended up reacting to *Do you allow a slaughter in Benghazi of two hundred thousand to three hundred thousand—sort of an Assad situation?* Because Gaddafi was going to do that.

PETE HOEKSTRA

The French and the Brits hated Gaddafi, and I understood that. That's horrific, to find a plane with body parts all over your countryside. But Obama bought into the European NATO strategy to overthrow Gaddafi, from my perspective, with little evidence.

ROB ANDREWS

My concern about Libya and Syria was less about the specific policy choices that President Obama made, but its role in the continuing undermining of the separation-of-powers argument. And not to be "I told you so," but many of us would say, *Well, there may well come a day when someone will occupy the Oval Office in whom we don't have a lot of confidence.* A permanent state of war against an adjective—I mean, it's strange.

---

99   On December 21, 1988, Pan Am Flight 103 was flying over Lockerbie, Scotland, when a bomb exploded on board, killing all 243 passengers, 16 crew members, and 11 people on the ground. In 2003, the nation of Libya formally claimed responsibility for the bombing in a letter to the United Nations Security Council, and offered $2.7 billion to settle claims filed by victims' families. During the Libyan Civil War of 2011, Mustafa Abdul Jalil, former justice secretary of Libya, claimed Gaddafi had personally ordered the attack.

DR. HAROLD KOH

The Obama administration worked hard to say there was no "war on terror." We fought against particular terrorist networks that attacked the United States and had a continuing desire to do that. So al-Qaeda attacked the United States and killed three thousand people. That's different from attacking anyone anywhere who terrorizes someone. I didn't think I ever cleared a single document, of the thousands of documents I cleared, that used the term "war on terror." That's not a view. You couldn't battle "terror," but you could battle people who attacked us—but then, when you did that, you'd have to establish that those people were connected to the people that actually attacked us. They're not just "other people who hate America," because if you end up fighting against everyone who hated America, you'd be fighting for the rest of your life.

PETE HOEKSTRA

The problem was, in Libya and Egypt, Obama fundamentally changed our approach to the Muslim world by deciding that he would engage the radical jihadists of the Muslim Brotherhood. I'm talking about a whole series of speeches and actions that he took. The [2009] speech in Cairo was a part of it, but what he talked about with Mubarak and political change in Egypt. Then ultimately the political change took place in Libya . . . Gaddafi was an awful guy, but he had turned over his nuclear-weapons program. He had paid reparations to the families of Pan Am 103, and he was also cooperating with us in fighting radical jihadism. And the thank-you that Gaddafi got for doing that: five years later the Americans basically put out a death warrant.

LUIS GUTIÉRREZ

Republican colleagues of mine have said to me that they didn't understand how someone as stupid and dumb as Obama could ever be elected president. They actually believe he's stupid, and they actually saw themselves as smart in relation to him. Now, they wouldn't say he's stupid because he's black. They would not say that to me, but here's what I understood: "He's black *and* he's stupid." That was, for me, part of the difficulty in always challenging him, because I saw those forces at work, and I didn't want to contribute to those forces.

BEN LABOLT

That's what the birth-certificate stuff was about, too.

LUIS GUTIÉRREZ

It was all about lies and delegitimizing him. I had colleagues talk to me in the gym. We'd be talking, shaving, hanging out, and they'd be like, "Damn, Gutiérrez, that guy's so dumb. How do you do it?" They would never grant him who he was, whereas I believed most people in America, when they heard Obama speak? They heard a cultured, educated, worldly, sophisticated, complex man. The attempt to delegitimize him came with the birth certificate and everything he did and everything he said. Whether he was born in America or he was a Muslim or he wasn't a man of Christian faith, and did he really go to Harvard? And did he really get those grades?

CODY KEENAN

I know this sounds strange, but we didn't really think about it that often. We always knew it was there. How do I explain this? We never really acknowledged the birtherism as serious,[100] even when the polls would show that 60 percent of the Republican Party would believe it. Well, that's *their* problem.

---

100 The most notorious smear against Obama began in March 2008 and spread widely a month later, when supporters of Hillary Clinton's primary campaign pushed a baseless claim via email that "Obama's mother was living in Kenya with his Arab-African father late in her pregnancy. She was not allowed to travel by plane then, so Barack Obama was born there and his mother then took him to Hawaii to register his birth."

BARBARA LEE

They're totally complicit. He kept on, he fought hard, and he didn't let that deter him.

MICHAEL STRAUTMANIS

This navigation of race was something that, as an African American, I'd done all my life. And I guess I'd say that the trying to decide when to respond to the disgusting and insulting push that was the birth-certificate issue? Navigating that was something that I was used to. And so it was disheartening, in one respect, to see him have to deal with that, but in another sense, it was, you know, par for the course in a very sad way. And so just finding a way to deal with that, being able to swallow it and move on and to be able to push the agenda and really make an impact on the things that were really important, that's something African Americans had been doing in this country for a long time.

CODY KEENAN

We never sat around thinking about what we would write into a speech, like *Does this make him sound black? Does this make him sound Kenyan?* It wasn't something that crossed our minds. When it would bubble up, it would just make us angry. But it was never anything we talked about. Now, obviously, there were times where it became part of a speech, whether it's something as innocuous and positive as speaking at an HBCU commencement or when you get into community-policing stuff. Like, there you knew it's going to be closely viewed through a prism of race.

MICHAEL STRAUTMANIS

The thing that I remember most was not actually the day that he revealed his birth certificate. I just remember the constant drumbeat about it moving in the months leading up to that. I really had to bury my anger. I always felt like I had eyes on me, whether it was young staffers or interns who knew my relationship with the president. In some ways I was the closest thing they would ever get to him. Whether I had a message to deliver and focus on about a particular issue internally or externally, that anger I had to just bury deep to do my job.

ROB O'DONNELL
Press Assistant, Office of Public Affairs, US Department of Justice (2011)
Director of Broadcast Media, White House (2015–2017)

Birtherism was Donald Trump's calling card. He got famous in the Republican Party because of his attacks on President Obama, and the president had always been able to take that in stride.

DAVID PLOUFFE

There was strategy. Lifting up Trump as the identity of the Republican Party was super helpful to us. The president went out in the briefing room to present his long-form birth certificate,[101] [but] really to continue the dance with Trump. Our view was lifting Trump up at the White House Correspondents' Dinner, you know, as kind of the example of the Obama opposition. There was a strategy behind the material and the amount of time we spent on Trump. *Let's really lean into Trump here. That'll be good for us.*

CODY KEENAN

No, I didn't think it was deliberate to link him with Republicans. The way that came down was we would get a list of everyone who would be at the dinner, whether it's celebrities or reporters or whatnot, and we'd go through that list to see who was worth making fun of. And when we got the list, as soon as we saw Donald Trump we were like, *Oh my God. This is perfect.* But no, there was no real political strategy to it. We just decided to tee off on him for a little while, because, you know, it had been insulting on so many levels, what he was doing. Not just to our president but to our democracy and the people who were following this. The president of the United States having to take time out of his day to go out and show people proof that he was born in America was insane.

---

101   April 27, 2011.

BILL DALEY

He was the brunt of the jokes in '11. Some people thought it was so over the top, ·
the president's attack on him, and hilarious, that that's what motivated Trump
to double down. It was too late for him to run in '12, but no question he was
motivated after that to continue to be engaged on the birther thing and much
more aggressively anti-Obama and probably fed into his '16 run.

JON FAVREAU

I don't know what goes on in that addled mind of Donald Trump's. I heard the
same thing. Maggie Haberman of the *New York Times* said, she had sources that
said that that's what prodded him toward it for sure, but I don't know. When
you're thinking about it anyway, there probably would have been some triggering
event if not the dinner.

DAVID PLOUFFE

Well, who knows? There may be something to that. Trump had obviously played
around with running for president previously, as he did in '12, but Trump had a
deep motivation to prove himself, and I was sure he was mortified.

JON FAVREAU

I was sitting at the table right behind him, and he did not look happy. That's for
sure. I could see the back of his head, mostly, but a couple times he turned and
I could see he was not very pleased, which was funny.

DAVID PLOUFFE

I was in the room. The president was funny and good-natured and calm, and,
as close as an advisor as I was to him, he was particularly careful to keep me out
of any of the bin Laden stuff. Because having your chief political advisor being
aware of that was just not going to be a smart move. And so I didn't know that
night, at the Correspondents' Dinner, that the raid was happening.

LEON PANETTA

It was August of the year before that we'd been able to find the compound and began to conduct surveillance. We did it for all the way through until December-January, and we were piecing together bits of intelligence. We didn't have 100 percent information that bin Laden was there, but the president felt that, because this had gone on as long as it had, that he was becoming nervous that information might leak out and we might lose that opportunity. So that's when we took the next step, which was to develop the operations to go after bin Laden.

BILL DALEY

The first day I got there, Panetta was in the PDB.[102] And I thought, *This is nice of Leon, to come on my first day.* And he went through the possibility of bin Laden in this compound in Abbottabad. And they wanted to take it to the next level of putting on more resources, but I think I was the only non–national security White House person involved in every meeting.

LEON PANETTA

I think that's right. We were explaining to the president and to the National Security Council the first intelligence reports that indicated that we had located this compound in Abbottabad, what the nature of it was, and why it raised a very strong indication that it could be a hiding place. So that was a real breakthrough for the president, for the CIA, and for our whole effort to go after bin Laden.

FERIAL GOVASHIRI
Senior Advisor to the Deputy National Security Advisor, White House (2009–2014)
Personal Aide to the President of the United States, White House (2014–2017)

Do you know the setup of the National Security Council? I'll explain it from a physical perspective. You'd have all these agencies—the Department of

---

102 President's Daily Briefing.

Agriculture, State, CIA, whatever—and the heads of all these agencies make up an NSC meeting. One of the heads of these meetings was the national security advisor, who's based in the West Wing. Another person on the scene was the director of [the National] Counterterrorism [Center], and they'd meet in the Situation Room. Not all of [the cabinet members] were part of National Security Council meetings. If the president were hosting a meeting, that means he'd chair. But then, if the national security advisor was heading the meeting, it'd be called a "principals meeting."

BILL DALEY

We were having a lot of meetings with a lot of senior people. It got to a point where it was pretty hard. When the president went into the Situation Room, it's obvious he's in there. There was always a fear that at some point you'd have a call coming. "Oh, what's going on? He's there all the time" or "We hear that . . ." It was amazing that the government was able to keep quiet.

NICK SHAPIRO

I was at the intersection of press politics and policy for six years, and nothing was kept that secretive. Even the really secretive stuff, a lot more people knew about. It's amazing how many people outside of the White House did know about the stuff. It was kept in the White House so small, a handful or maybe two handfuls of people. Yet, at the same time, there were a lot of the people at the CIA, rightfully, because they were the ones looking for him. Everyone talked about how closely guarded the secret was, and it surely was, but the CIA had a good amount of folks who knew about it. They kept quiet, and that's a testament to the CIA.

LEON PANETTA

I briefed [Admiral] Bill McRaven of Special Operations on what we had found, and, to his credit, he came up with several approaches to deal with the compound. We discussed each of those, went over them with the White House and the NSC, and agreed, ultimately, to a commando raid. That became the principal operations discussion, as to how that would be conducted and how we would accomplish that.

BILL DALEY

McRaven came into the Situation Room with a total mock-up of the compound, and you had the most senior people meeting fairly regularly over those last couple weeks. As I said, to the point where we were getting a little nervous that the president was down in the Situation Room so much that *that*, in and of itself, was gonna raise some tremendous number of eyebrows.

LEON PANETTA

Even when we presented that final recommendation to the NSC, the president went around the room and people worried that it was very risky and did not think that it was something we should do. I told the president that, based on my own history in the Congress when they had a tough decision, I always pretended I was asking an ordinary citizen in my district, *If you knew what I knew, what would you do?* And I said, "If an ordinary citizen knew that we had the best evidence and location of bin Laden since Tora Bora,[103] I think that citizen would say that we have to conduct this operation."

CAROLYN MALONEY

Joe Biden told me that in the Situation Room, they talked about all the evidence that they had on the expected home of Osama bin Laden. They had circumstantial evidence, not concrete evidence that he was in that house. They

---

103 Months after the attacks on September 11, US forces intercepted radio communications of Osama bin Laden and pinpointed his location to the Tora Bora cave complex in a mountainous region of eastern Afghanistan. Along with allied forces, the US engaged Taliban fighters there between December 6, 2001, and December 17, 2001. However, requests to deploy eight hundred US Army Rangers as reinforcements were denied by General Tommy Franks, commander of US forces in Afghanistan. As a result, bin Laden, along with hundreds of al-Qaeda and Taliban fighters, was believed to have escaped into Pakistan during the campaign.

didn't know for sure, and the president went around the table and asked people if they would go in. Panetta said yes, but every other person at that table said no. Joe Biden told me that *he* said no, that we didn't have enough evidence. And we knew what happened with Jimmy Carter when he went in to free hostages and it didn't work out. It cost Jimmy Carter his reelection. Then the president said, "Well, let me think about it."

LEON PANETTA

He didn't make a decision, but the next morning he did. And we proceeded to implement the operation.

DAVID PLOUFFE

[On May 1] I got a call around noon from either Tom Donilon or Denis McDonough to come into the building. And the president then came into my office and said, "Hey, I couldn't tell you before, but here's what's going down."

PETE SOUZA

It was May 2 in Pakistan for the time change, but for us on the East Coast it was still May 1. It's certainly probably my most "famous" photo, but it's not my "favorite" photo of my career. There's not much action going on, but people were drawn to that photo because they can imagine what it must have been like—the tension, the anxiety, that must have been going on with everybody in that room.

Seated, from left: Vice President Biden; President Obama; Lt. General Marshall B. "Brad" Webb, Assistant Commanding General, Joint Special Operations Command; Deputy National Security Advisor Denis McDonough; Secretary of State Hillary Clinton; and Secretary of Defense Robert Gates. Standing, from left: Admiral Mike Mullen, Chairman of the Joint Chiefs of Staff; National Security Advisor Tom Donilon; White House Chief of Staff Bill Daley; National Security Advisor to the Vice President Tony Blinken; Director for Counterterrorism Audrey Tomason; Assistant to the President for Homeland Security and Counterterrorism John Brennan; and Director of National Intelligence James Clapper. Pete Souza, White House

PETE SOUZA

I mean, look, the decision had already been made. Right? It's not like anybody in that room could do anything about what was happening.

LEON PANETTA

It's a lot of emotions. But when you're close to it, when you're working with people and developing the planning on it, you had a certain comfort about the competence of the people that you're working with. [It] didn't give you the sense that you're simply rolling dice and you didn't know what may or may not happen. You had a higher confidence level that these were people that knew what the hell they're doing. You had trust in their ability to get the job done. I felt that way. Not to say I didn't say a hell of a lot of Hail Marys, but at the same time,

I also felt that this was a job that was being done by the best people on earth to do it. I just, deep down, felt that this was going to work.

DAVID PLOUFFE

Once it was clear that the mission was a success, we started working on his remarks that he would deliver to the nation that night.

ROB O'DONNELL

It was Sunday night. I was at the Justice Department then, and all of a sudden people came across the TV like, *The president's gonna give a prime-time address,* and I emailed my boss, Dean Boyd, who was the national-security spokesman. "Is there anything we should be aware of?" He emailed back, "I don't know. Let me check into it." Then half an hour or fifteen minutes before the president went on, Dean sent me an email, like, *Holy shit, we got bin Laden!* I was with my cousin and my sister, and we ended up going down to the White House that night to cheer on with everyone, and then I had to be at the Justice Department at five a.m. to send out the updated guidance for the day for the AG. That was just a wild night.

BILL DALEY

Starting the next day, Denis McDonough said there was a collective barf of information from the US government leaking and everybody telling their stories. Whether it was the CIA, the Pentagon, the White House, it was ridiculous how everybody just kind of threw up how important they were in the getting-bin-Laden story. Ridiculous.

LEON PANETTA

I've always looked on most of the jobs I had in Washington as not something I sought but I did because, when presidents ask you to do it, you do it. The same thing was true with the CIA. Frankly, when we were successful with the bin Laden raid, I thought, *This might be a great time to get the hell out of Washington,* because timing is everything. But then the president asked me to consider secretary of defense. I wanted to go home at some point, [and] didn't want to spend more time in Washington, but he kept coming back at me. And, as always when the president does that, I agreed to serve for the remainder of his first term.

YOHANNES ABRAHAM
Deputy National Political Director, Obama-Biden 2012
Chief of Staff, Office of Public Engagement and
Intergovernmental Affairs, White House (2013–2017)

Having been through the 2008 campaign, I knew what was coming up ahead. I moved out to Chicago—I forget the exact date—but I was one of the first few folks in the Chicago headquarters, before we even announced. I was extremely excited but also realized it was gonna be a long couple of years.

DAVID PLOUFFE

There's no doubt that anybody that's been through this will tell you—the Bush people, the Clinton people, the Reagan people—reelects were nowhere near as fun as the first one, because in the first one you're not an incumbent. You're an insurgent. And then basically in an incumbent race, the organization has taken on barnacles. So it's not as fun.

YOHANNES ABRAHAM

For a huge chunk of the first campaign, we were completely and totally unburdened by expectation. We were underdogs, and it's different when you're running as an incumbent. You're running on a record, and you're not running on a platform. Those are really different things.

DAVID PLOUFFE

But the core of '12 was Axe, Jim, and I, and Larry Grisolano. Depending on the issue, that was the real decision-making group. And we would do calls, and meetings when I could get to Chicago. So Axe was as involved in '12 as he was in '08. He wasn't overseeing the advertising. Larry was doing that, but he had David's proxy.

DAVID AXELROD

I missed my life in the White House to some degree, but I was happy to be freed of it to do the work that I had to do relative to the reelection. And quite frankly, I was exhausted, and I think I would not be here if I had tried to stay for eight years.

NATE LUBIN

I ended up going to Chicago in May. I was the first marketing person on the ground and was there all the way through. I ended up as the director of digital marketing—built that team from just me to twenty-some-odd people—but it was sort of a weird organizational thing. I was basically an internal consultant to the whole campaign. They gave a twenty-five-year-old $100 million to play with.

TEDDY GOFF

I became a member of the senior staff in the second campaign. The guiding premise of the campaign, from the day that I started—I remember in the first or second senior staff meeting, Jim Messina said, "Look, it's going to be a topsy-turvy year. These things are always unpredictable and I'm sure some stuff is going to go down, but we are preparing to run a campaign against Mitt Romney and we have to stay focused on that." That was always the prediction.

JEREMY BIRD

We felt, at the beginning, we were in an underdog situation because of what we inherited. A lot of Americans were feeling the lack of equality on the economic side and hadn't seen a change. We were in the position of having to convince them that we're on the right track forward, not back, that we'd seen progress but, at the same time, it's a really complicated thing to say to folks, because they hadn't seen it in their lives.

JON FAVREAU

You could tell people that it's going to take a long time, but that would only go so far. We're an impatient people, and if you're out of a job, having a president tell you, *Oh, no, no, no, it's just gonna take time. It'll eventually get better*, that doesn't help much. You're still gonna say, *No, buddy. I want you to fix this now.*

NATE LUBIN

The organization was better in '12 because we'd already come through once, and there was more prep time. We could get bigger faster, raise more money, and those of us who were there, working those hours, we were obviously super in the tank. It was an *If we don't win it's the end of the world* kind of thing.

JEREMY BIRD

On our [Democratic] base side, the challenge was we didn't have an opponent in the primary—although Senator Sanders flirted with running against us—and so we had to get people to actually pay attention. We had to get them active early to make sure we're not put in the position where we're behind after [Republicans] ran their primary and probably got stronger as an organization from it.

ROB ANDREWS

One thing you gotta remember, and this was true until the Iowa caucuses in 2016: Bernie was always a likable, interesting back-back-back bencher. At that stage of the game, anything he said was probably regarded as *Okay, he's an interesting fellow.* He wasn't nearly the figure in Democratic politics that he would become.

JIM MESSINA

We had to run a perfect campaign, and we surely didn't. But we had a couple theories of the case. One was, if this were a choice between Barack Obama and Mitt Romney, we would win that choice. If it were a choice between, were you happy with the economy, or did you want to vote for Democrats or Republicans, we would lose. We were still in the toughest economic situation, which we inherited.

STUART STEVENS

This idea that Mitt was going to run and roll right into '12 was just not accurate. He wanted to write that book, and I used to go down and visit him in La Jolla. He'd be sitting there in his shorts at the kitchen counter, happy as a clam, writing his book. The assumption was the economy would get better—this would have been February of 2009—and would improve at a normal historical rate. As it turned out, we had the slowest recovery in modern history. He probably thought that Obama would, given the rhetoric that he ran on—*There's not a liberal America and a conservative America*—make more effort to be bipartisan.

GENE SPERLING

Yes, one could have tried to get an even better Recovery Act, but had you missed the opportunity for a strong $800 billion plan signed into law twenty-seven days after inauguration, had you, in the effort to do a little more or a little better, ended up having to wait three or four more months, and the economy had spun down, it would have been a tragic mistake.

STUART STEVENS

My longtime partner, Russ Schriefer, and I had been doing all these [2010] races at my firm, and Mitt talked about getting together. "You're through on Election Day, right?" And I said yes. And he said, "Great, let's get together on Election Day." It was so Mitt. So we flew up to Boston, and he was pretty clear that he was on a track to run. Something changed. Just, personally, I had a bit of an issue about my involvement, because my longtime friend and client Haley Barbour was also talking about running. I didn't think Haley would run, but by the time around Thanksgiving, I think Mitt had pretty much decided to run.

JIM MESSINA

We would have to define Mitt Romney, but we also had to give our people a reason to believe and to vote. That wasn't ever going to come from negative campaigning. That's always going to come from having a vision. We had to build turnout. I spent four years of my life hearing everyone say, "Oh, the first campaign was so special. No one's excited about 2012."

JAMES KVAAL

You would at least be able to sleep at night with Mitt Romney in the Oval Office. There's no question that he's a highly qualified person and also fundamentally a decent person, a good man. To us, it felt like an important election if for no other reason than if Mitt Romney had been president, he would have unraveled universal health care, which was something that our country had been trying to accomplish for three or four generations. Also, his tax cuts for very wealthy people were wrongheaded, and it was disappointing that he was not willing to take action on climate change and move us off of fossil fuels. So there were big issues at stake. It's just they seemed more within the realm of conversation, in comparison to what Donald Trump would mean.

TEDDY GOFF

The absolutely most terrifying thing in politics that I'd ever seen until Donald Trump was the debt-ceiling debacle,[104] and that happened in the early days of the campaign.

---

104 The maximum amount of funds that the Treasury can borrow to pay for government appropriations (including interest payments on the nation's outstanding debt) had routinely been granted authorization with little to no dispute from Congress— until 1995, when the authorization was first held hostage by Speaker Gingrich and his "Republican Revolution" as a bargaining chip for budget negotiations. Insurgent Republicans resurfaced with the same tactic in 2011 after recapturing the House majority under Speaker Boehner.

CHRIS VAN HOLLEN

Republicans were threatening to default on the debt if they didn't get their way on [long-term deficit reductions], which was an incredibly reckless position to take. And so this was the height of sort of the budget wars, and the president appointed Biden to put together what became known as the Biden Group. That included House and Senate Republicans and Democrats. I served on that group.

JIM MESSINA

Anytime there was *really* a problem, the vice president would go up to the Hill and fix it. Thirty years, I mean, he just knew *everybody*. He was a legislator's legislator.

JASON FURMAN

We had the vice president lead discussions for about two months. Nothing leaked from them. A lot was done on paper. I had extensive discussions with Republicans where we would swap drafts and share things, and I thought that all worked quite well.

JACK LEW

I played the role in the room of briefing everybody on what the options were. I was actually proud that, at the end of it, [House majority leader] Eric Cantor had absolute faith that I was describing things fairly and looked at the options that he and Joe Biden were able to make political judgments based on understanding it, and it was not an insignificant piece of work. It formed a list of $200-ish billion of potential savings.

JASON FURMAN

Then those talks collapsed.

CHRIS VAN HOLLEN

I recall Cantor walking out of the negotiations, partly over disagreements, but also because he discovered that Boehner had opened up his own line of communication with the White House.

BILL DALEY

Cantor found out that Boehner and we had been talking and getting going towards a deal. He blew that up.

MICHAEL STEEL

It was always clear that there was going to be a next stage in the discussions. I think Mr. Cantor's explanation at the time was that he thought that the Democrats were going to end the talks on some pretext and blame him for being intransigent. He wanted to get out in front of that. I don't know why he had that indication or what the thinking was there, but Mr. Cantor is a very smart man and very sophisticated. He knew that we still had to increase the debt limit and that discussions with the White House were the only way to reach an agreement that would get that done in a responsible way.

AUSTAN GOOLSBEE

It's not really about who called what and whether Cantor was mad at Boehner. Fundamentally, the Republican Party was not willing to trade cuts for tax increases . . . but the fact that Obama would *entertain* the idea for sure showed he was willing to do things that the [Democratic] leadership in Congress was not keen on, because they were getting mad at him for even talking about it with them in private.

BILL DALEY

[One week later] Boehner and Cantor came back together. We were on a path, I firmly believed, that we could have gotten a deal, and it all unraveled rather quickly, partly because Democrats realized Obama was willing to deal on things that they didn't want him to deal on, i.e., Medicare and Social Security, and [Obama] was willing to go further than they really wanted him to.

JACK LEW

We would talk to Nancy Pelosi and Harry Reid about places we might have to go. We didn't tell them how every meeting went, what every meeting was, and all the minute back and forth. But the president was pretty comfortable that, if we had struck a deal, he could have sold it.

AUSTAN GOOLSBEE

The administration asked the Republicans, essentially, *You wanna cut entitlements. Here's a list of ten things. What would you wanna do first? Raise the retirement age on Social Security? Cap Medicare? What is your priority?* The fact that they even asked that question *really* irked the Democrats in Congress, who said, *You should not be offering anything for a grand bargain. You should be blasting them for proposing cuts to entitlements. Let's demonize them and we will defeat them based on that.*

JACK LEW

We came close a couple of times, and each time the Speaker would go back to the Republican caucus and they'd want more, or they'd say there was too much wiggle room, and there was a deep level of suspicion. It may have just been that what the Speaker might have been willing to agree to and what the majority of the Republican caucus was willing to agree to were not the same thing.

MICHAEL STEEL

Democrats never really accepted the legitimacy of the Bush tax cuts and were always obsessed with the revenue that they had lost. So they were willing to discuss reducing spending, but only in the context of also increasing taxes.

JASON FURMAN

We had a series of meetings in the Roosevelt Room and might as well have broadcast them on C-SPAN, because everyone would walk out of them and put their own spin on everything that had just happened.

GENE SPERLING

This was a frustrating period for the president, because he held back for the sake of getting a more significant fiscal agreement, only to see the Republicans mysteriously walk away from the table twice and then, even more mysteriously, try to blame him for their inability to stay at a table and finish a negotiation.

MICHAEL STEEL

Boehner's solution was that there [were] a number of increased government revenue [streams] that could be generated by tax reform. Our best calculation from outside sources was about $800 billion every ten years. That was really a hard line, from the moment the discussion started. *We can do this and no more on the tax front*, and the Speaker and the president had a handshake deal on a package of spending cuts with that level of increased revenue through tax reform, and for a variety of reasons, the president came back after that handshake and asked for an additional $400 billion in increased revenue.

AUSTAN GOOLSBEE

That's the Republican version. I'm not sure that's 100 percent accurate. We had a bit of the old Yasser-Arafat-in-the-negotiations-with-Bill-Clinton, in which he was making promises but couldn't deliver his own people. My impression of the $400 billion was, that was simply a counteroffer and they had been going back and forth. *I'll give you A. No, I won't take A. How about B? No, we won't take B. How about C?* They were just looking for some way to walk, because Boehner realized his people wouldn't accept anything. So they're like, *Oh, you changed the deal!*

JACK LEW

I know the story [has been] told from different perspectives with different heroes and different villains. I actually believed that everyone in the negotiation, meaning the Speaker, the president, the minority leader of the Senate, the Democratic leaders in the House and Senate, with everyone skeptical for different reasons, was approaching it looking to reach an agreement. I never thought that the negotiation was in bad faith. I think that there was a fundamental inability to go back and sell something fair and balanced in the House Republican caucus.

GENE SPERLING

They couldn't admit that they were walking away because they were so deeply divided. So they would then spend an enormous amount of energy and time trying to convince the media that somehow it was President Obama's fault.

AUSTAN GOOLSBEE

The way you knew that the grand-bargain discussion was doomed was that Republicans were unwilling to say anything that they actually wanted to cut, because they didn't want to cut. Their response to "Which of these is your priority? What are *you* demanding? We're gonna demand high-income tax increases. What are the entitlements that you're gonna cut?" was, "We want *you* to name things that *you* are going to cut." Because they wanted to condemn Democrats for cutting entitlements! So of course, in a world like that, it's never gonna work. That's why the grand bargain fell apart.

MICHAEL STEEL

So the Speaker began talking with Senator McConnell and Senator Reid about whether, if he ended discussions with the president, what *they* needed to pass a bill that would increase the debt limit. Senator Reid had been supportive for many years of this idea that if you put together a bipartisan group and forced a vote . . . you could pass a large bipartisan deficit-reduction package. So he was supportive of what came to be known as "the supercommittee," the Joint Select

Committee on Deficit Reduction.[105] And Boehner's priority was making sure that we hit the spending cuts and reforms equal to or greater than the debt-limit increase. So that was kind of his ask, and originally we put together the stuff that the Biden-Cantor talks had done—a cap on discretionary spending—and that got you about halfway to the debt-limit increase that the White House was seeking.

JACK LEW

One day, during one of the debt-limit battles, I walked into the Capitol and ran into Newt Gingrich. "Mr. Speaker, we lived through this together. Why do we have to go through it again? We know how it ends." He said, "That one is easy: because a lot of people in this building haven't lived through it." Now, he probably was right. They had to experience it, not just know the history of '95–'96. But if you repeat a play that was so potentially dangerous over and over again, and in an environment that becomes less and less attentive to history and, unfortunately, less and less attentive to fact, the chance of doing something really dangerous grows.

GENE SPERLING

To actually be at that moment where the Treasury Secretary was telling the president of the United States in the Oval Office the steps we would take in default, and knowing the risk to the economy and the incredible potential of hardship for average Americans, was a stomach-turning event.

---

105 From the Senate: Cochair Patty Murray (D-Washington), Max Baucus (D-Montana), John Kerry (D-Massachusetts), John Kyl (R-Arizona), Rob Portman (R-Ohio), Pat Toomey (R-Pennsylvania). From the House: Cochair Jeb Hensarling (R-Texas, Fifth District), Xavier Becerra (D-California, Thirty-First District), James Clyburn (D-South Carolina, Sixth District), Chris Van Hollen (D-Maryland, Eighth District), Dave Camp (R-Michigan, Fourth District), Fred Upton (R-Michigan, Sixth District).

JASON FURMAN

A decent amount of contingency planning was done for what would happen if we breached the debt limit. All of the options were terrible, and our main focus, of course, was making sure we never hit it. But, certainly the morning after, the Treasury would have been prepared to do the best that they possibly could.

JACK LEW

In 2011, we weren't even sure that it was physically possible to pick and choose to pay interest on the debt or not. So when the question was asked, "Would you prioritize debt payments," the system was designed to pay. Not to *not* pay. It took some work to figure out if there was even a mechanical pathway to pay the debt. Then, as a policy question, if you paid the debt, you're paying bondholders, whether they're mom-and-pop investors or sovereign governments owning US securities. So you're going to pay all those bills but you're not going to pay the veterans' hospitals? You're not going to pay, potentially, for Social Security?

GENE SPERLING

And then the potential threats of loss of confidence in the US financial system— it would have put a degree of risk to the economy and to ordinary people that was unthinkable, even when you had a couple of months to try to figure out how to do it in the most rational way.

JACK LEW

It's not as if our systems were set up to say, "Well, we'll pay for the lights, but we won't pay for the rent." The plumbing doesn't work to do that. The full faith and credit of the United States meant we pay all of our bills. We didn't pick and choose. And Congress had ultimately always agreed with that.

GENE SPERLING

When he actually saw them using the threat of defaulting the country as an actual budget tactic, he said to us, "We can't do this anymore." We were in the Oval when he said this to us. It was right before one of our discussions in the Cabinet Room with the Republican and the Democratic leadership. He literally looked at me, he looked at Jack, he looked at [Treasury Secretary] Tim [Geithner], he looked at Valerie, and he said, "And you better show that in your body language, because that's how I feel." He never backed down after that.

JACK LEW

The president made the right decision that we couldn't negotiate any longer over the debt limit, because it had gone from a kind of give-and-take with marginal leverage to an existential threat. And even if we could navigate in our window of time, if you let that continue, at some point this calculation or overreach would lead to default. And we just had to stop it. And obviously we did. It succeeded. We ended up extending the debt limit.

MICHAEL STEEL

The White House's number-one top priority was avoiding another debt-limit vote before his reelect. They wanted a number that would get them through the 2012 election. So we had enough cuts with the Biden-Cantor stuff and discretionary caps that we could get about halfway there . . . and then the Joint Select Committee on Deficit Reduction would have to come up with the other half, and originally, if they didn't, well, we would run out of debt-limit authority. But that would have put another debt-limit fight some time in 2012 if the supercommittee failed, and the White House found that unacceptable, so they came up with the idea for across-the-board spending cuts, called sequestration.[106]

GENE SPERLING

There was no high-fiving. There was relief.

DAVID PLOUFFE

Then we went on a bus tour of the Midwest. He would do town halls, and no one was happy with him. Republicans, Democrats, independents—it was an ugly period. And so in that case, it wasn't just like the chattering class in Washington. We were in Iowa, and he came back on the bus after the event and was like "No one's happy." And they weren't! It was a really poor reflection on our country.

JIM MESSINA

After the debt-limit stuff, one time David Plouffe called me and said, "Messina, I just need someone I trust. Do you think we can still win?" And it was the great advantage of being in Chicago and not in DC, because I started laughing at him. I was like, "Are you fucking kidding me? Of course we can still win." But it didn't seem like that for a while. It was tough times.

---

106 Debt-ceiling negotiations ended on August 2, 2011, when Obama signed the Budget Control Act, granting the president authorization to request, in increments, extensions on the debt ceiling, expected to last until the beginning of 2013. In exchange, the legislation cut $917 billion in discretionary spending for fiscal years 2012 through 2021, and tasked the Joint Select Committee on Deficit Reduction with seeking an additional minimum $1.5 trillion in savings over ten years. As a backup plan, the committee's failure to find such savings would automatically trigger a series of deep spending cuts—a.k.a. "sequestration"—across multiple government agencies.

DAVID PLOUFFE

I don't recall that, but if I did it, it would have been because you're in the middle of the bubble, it's really dark, and the president's leadership had been called into question. It was not a good moment for the Obama enterprise.

2011–2012

The proverbial clown car of Republican hopefuls puttered its way across the heartland. Minnesota congresswoman Michele Bachmann boasted in a TV interview about having God as a campaign surrogate, from whom she received "that calling" that prompted her to enter the primaries. Texas governor Rick Perry caved to pressure from evangelicals to reverse his position on a vaccine mandate, which he had previously supported in his state. Rick Santorum, an adamant opponent of LGBT equality, fell victim to the *Daily Show*'s lampooning his "Google problem," referring to the top search-engine result that associated the former senator's last name with the residual aftermath of anal sex. Mitt Romney battled protesters at the Iowa State Fair, where he famously defended beneficiaries of tax-code loopholes: "Corporations are people, my friend!"

Regardless of whether these rifts lost or gained support from the Republican base, the candidates succeeded in consuming network airtime, and may have incidentally permitted the incumbent's campaign to deal with its concerns relatively quietly.

For PACs such as the Obama Victory Fund, Michelle Obama was the saving grace, a donor-luncheon powerhouse who bagged $10 million in the first fundraising quarter, far more than her husband's efforts during that period. Operatives found themselves occupied with the more typical internal dysfunctions of a campaign, ranging from cracking down on press leaks to personnel shake-ups back in DC—including the departures of Axelrod and Press Secretary Robert Gibbs. A Gallup poll in August gave President Obama a devastating 26 percent approval rating regarding his handling of the economy. With an electorate still hobbling and corporate profits eating up larger proportions of the national income, the question loomed whether Americans would prefer a new president, one with a CEO background, rather than a constitutional-law professor.

The worries caused the campaign's nucleus to consider factors beyond the normal means. *Everything ought to be on the table* was a prevailing-enough sentiment, according to one senior official, that it prompted brief discussion about Secretary of State Hillary Clinton replacing Joe Biden on the ticket. A focus group was convened in the latter half of 2011 with the purpose of seeing if, somehow, a change in the roster might boost the numbers.

"It was never seriously considered," David Plouffe said. "It was really more of a way to measure a kind of energy." The result of the focus group was inconclusive, and the campaign moved on.

AUSTAN GOOLSBEE

It was extremely stressful to live through the financial crisis and then the economic crisis, and then kind of the political crisis. In a way, that was a pressing breakpoint, the end of the debt-ceiling fights. The government found itself in a new gridlock, not a lot of policy development . . . I didn't realize that, two hours after I left the government, that the government would be downgraded by the rating agencies.

DAVID PLOUFFE

We always knew a reelect was going to be hard. Everybody—Jim, the president, myself, David Axelrod—knew that, with the economy the way it was, we were gonna be up against it. And so, obviously the economy strengthened throughout '12, but right after the debt-ceiling crisis, the August jobs report came out and there were zero jobs. Zero.

JEREMY BIRD

I don't think I'll ever wake up with as much anticipation [as] on the first Friday of every month. To get the job numbers and see where we were, it would dictate a lot of what we were doing that month.

GENE SPERLING

Thursday evening was somewhat awkward because the [National Economic Council] director and the chairman of the [Council of] Economic Advisers knew this number and normally told it to the president, but then were not allowed to tell any of their peers. On this particular day, as we walked into the Oval, he said something like, "I don't think I like the look on your face." And I said, "It's zero. The job number was zero." He said, "What do you mean 'zero'?" I said, "It's zero." And he said, "You mean, exactly zero?" I said, "Yes." And he said, "You mean if I grab that piece of paper from your hand, I'm going to see a zero?" And I said, "Yes, sir." And he said, "Has this ever happened before?" I said, "Not to my knowledge."

AUSTAN GOOLSBEE

Just from a strictly statistical point of view, for the average-job-growth number the standard margin of error was plus or minus 100,000 or 150,000. There's a lot of fluctuation. You never wanted to take one month's number as meaning anything, so the fact that we had one month with zero didn't have to be a sign of a trend.

GENE SPERLING

President Obama was known for taking bad news pretty well, but we all knew that it was worse than being negative 20,000. That there was something political about "zero," and, sure enough, hours later on the House floor, they were handing out pins that said "President Zero." Of course the irony was that when [the Bureau of Labor Statistics] did the revisions, it turned out that over 100,000 jobs were created that month.

AUSTAN GOOLSBEE

It's not wrong to view the immediate aftermath as a result of the dysfunction in that debt-ceiling debate. It's not wrong to say that had a negative impact on the economy. Ultimately the kids really do not like to see Mom and Dad fighting.

The S&P downgrade of the government that happened right in the aftermath of the debt ceiling was based on political uncertainty.[107]

GENE SPERLING

A major retailer who had been in business for decades told us that it had hurt sales worse than any time since Pearl Harbor.

KAREEM DALE

No administration goes without criticism even from its own party, right? You certainly had progressives sometimes complaining that maybe the administration wasn't doing anything, from a progressive standpoint. I think we heard those things, but we always felt like we were headed in the right direction. I certainly think the American Jobs Act was a positive boost.

JARED BERNSTEIN

The American Jobs Act? I was just leaving when that was sort of getting under way. It looked like Congress really wasn't going to nibble.

GENE SPERLING

The president called me into the Oval Office. "We need to put forward our economic vision from our heart." And he said, "I want to know what we think is the best economic plan," and we could all edit together, but "for now," he said, "no editing—I want to know what you think is the best thing for us to do." We went through a monthlong period, working at a fast pace, and the president was deeply engaged in the details. And so the American Jobs Act had things that

---

107 Standard & Poor's downgraded the US creditworthiness to AA+ from AAA, a rating the nation had previously maintained for more than 70 years until S&P frowned upon 2011's "political brinkmanship" and a deficit agreement that "falls short" of the ability "to stabilize the government's medium-term debt dynamics." The downgrade immediately resulted in a dip in financial markets across the globe, including a staggering 634-point drop in the Dow Jones Industrial Average.

actually got passed—extension of the payroll tax cut, some small-business issues, veterans' tax credits, later the long-term-unemployment tax credits. But many of the things closest to his heart—the infrastructure investment, the investment in [reducing] blight in inner cities, funding for teachers and cops at state levels— didn't end up passing, but they staked out his vision.

BRAD JENKINS

Everyone was on board, from AFL unions to progressive groups like MoveOn and Greenpeace, and they were pushing each piece of that bill as a document, and hammering home to Republicans, *Vote on this. Vote for the payroll tax cuts. Vote for rebuilding public schools.* That was an opportunity to get everyone on the same page again.

GENE SPERLING

It was also him, as president, going from outside the negotiating table to the bully pulpit. It was critical for people to see a guide for things that he wanted to do, and even as he was a president who was still dealing with a tough economy and had to make some of the most unpopular but necessary decisions.

BRAD JENKINS

We were just trying to take it to Republicans and be on the offensive. It was a great thing to organize around, and, at the same time, [Jon] Carson went to Occupy. They were talking about the same things. Occupy was talking about more money for schools. The American Jobs Act had a *huge* funding for schoolteachers and rebuilding of public schools. We talked about raising the minimum wage. Occupy talked about that. We were 100 percent on the same wavelength on all these key things, so Carson wanted to meet these kids. He got on a train to New York and went to Zuccotti Park. In his head, he's thinking, *What are ways we can work with these guys? What are they gonna do next?* The world was watching, right? *Are they thinking about recruiting candidates? Voter registration? A list of policy initiatives?*

JON CARSON

Van Jones actually got me in touch with a gentleman there. I'll never forget. I called him and he called me back, got my voicemail, and the beginning of the voicemail, he said he wanted to make clear that he did not speak for Occupy Wall Street, "because nobody speaks for Occupy Wall Street," but he would be interested in meeting with me. But then we began to negotiate where. He did not want me anywhere near Zuccotti Park, so we met at this out-of-the-way Irish pub about five or six blocks from the main site.

BRAD JENKINS

Carson went to this Irish bar and spent two hours with them. And an hour and a half of it was all about, *How do we stay in the park?* That's all they wanted to talk about, because it was getting cold.

BARNEY FRANK

I was once in a debate with someone from Occupy on Bill Maher's show, and I confessed, as I did often, that I agreed more with Occupy than the Tea Party, obviously, but the Tea Party people got involved in politics. They registered. They voted. They lobbied Congress. People at Occupy smoked dope and had drum circles. I was very disappointed that I never saw a voter-registration table at any Occupy site, and this woman said, "Well, we weren't into that." Yeah, right, like influencing the way things happen? What help do you need to get people to register to vote? The unions would have been glad to help.

BRAD JENKINS

They had Jon Carson, the head of public engagement, who had an office in the West Wing right above the president, with a willing ear, wanting to organize and figure out how you use this huge moment in American history to organize. This was the guy who organized millions of volunteers, and that's all they wanted to talk about. And, again, he admitted, "That's important," but every time he asked a question on *What are you guys going to do next?* They were like, "No, we're not about being in the system. All we care about is staying here. We don't want it to end."

JON CARSON

My view of the whole thing changed over time. I think there's a new kind of organizing happening, and Occupy Wall Street was one of the first examples of it. There was a lot of criticism from old-time organizers that *They never created a list out of this* or *Never turned it into a permanent organization.* You might call it "idea based" versus "list based." It was this decentralized movement. People criticized them for not being able to clearly state what they wanted, but as far as what they were against, I thought they were pretty singularly focused on income inequality. It was really the beginning of the notion of that "1 percent" idea being used a lot.

BRAD JENKINS

They didn't want anything from us. They didn't want our help. We were not interesting or compelling at all to the fight.

Demonstrators gather for an Occupy Wall Street march in Zuccotti Park, Manhattan. September 30, 2011. John Lamparski, Getty

LEON PANETTA

The 9/11 attacks were something that hit us hard. The big problem we faced almost from the beginning was that this enemy disappeared into the mountains of Pakistan. We knew they were there because of intelligence, and we knew they were continuing to plan additional attacks on our country. And yet, in any other war, we would be able to use F-16s. We would be able to use B-2 bombers. We would put boots on the ground, and that was not the case, obviously, in Pakistan. So the question was, if we were going to confront an enemy that was continuing to plan to attack our country, how would we do that?

NICK SHAPIRO

The counterterrorism structure that President Obama built with the help of John Brennan was, I thought, one of the crowning achievements. I'd say a couple things to support that. Yes, ISIL had grown, but al-Qaeda was the one who could conduct those large-scale attacks—the 9/11s. They were very skilled. They had the ability to move people and cause significant damage. The counterterrorism operations that this president did—instead of invading countries like Afghanistan or Iraq—were dealt with surgically, using drones.[108] We dealt with it in a way that had the least civilian casualties and inflicted the most damage against the enemy, which was al-Qaeda in the AfPak region or in Yemen. Those were really the two areas we focused on the most.

LEON PANETTA

And when you consider the alternatives, if we had to go to full-scale war against al-Qaeda, I'd think history would say that it was an effective way to decimate our enemy in a way that resulted, really, in much less collateral damage than otherwise would have been the case.

---

108 The General Atomics MQ-1 Predator drone is a remotely piloted aircraft that was originally developed in the 1990s for reconnaissance and observation purposes, but has since been outfitted with Hellfire missiles and other ammunitions to serve in combat settings. Their offensive use by the US Armed Forces and Central Intelligence Agency is classified.

NICK SHAPIRO

So you had someone like Anwar al-Awlaki who, yes, was an American citizen.[109] At the same time, he had pledged allegiance to al-Qaeda and was trying to conduct lethal operations against American citizens. So this was not the same process that [we] went through with other terrorists that were removed from the battlefield. There was a higher [legal] standard that was met to do the operation against Awlaki.[110] So when you looked at the structure that the White House put in place, it was going after the most significant senior leaders, the folks who could afflict the most harm against Americans and who were plotting to kill Americans, but it was brought under the rule of law.

DR. HAROLD KOH

When you're fighting a terrorist network, you're invoking the laws of war. That meant that you're lawfully entitled to make decisions as long as you're hitting legitimate targets and doing it in accordance with the rules. I didn't go into the government to kill people. Nobody did. But the next time someone would say something like, "Let's get the lawyers off the backs of the generals," my answer

---

109 On September 30, 2011, a missile strike carried out by Predator drones killed al-Awlaki, US citizen and alleged operative of al-Qaeda in the Arabian Peninsula (AQAP), in Yemen's al-Jawf province. One year prior, Obama had authorized his killing by the CIA, citing the vast number of terrorist activities he was believed to be involved in or have inspired—including the attacks on September 11, the 2009 Fort Hood shooting, and the 2009 attempted bombing of Northwest Flight 253. Human-rights advocates have argued that the decision to kill al-Awlaki represented a violation of his due-process rights as an American citizen and amounted to an extrajudicial execution.

110 The justification for conducting a preemptive drone strike against an American national as an act of war—despite the target's not being recognized on any battlefield—centered around the argument that the US had the right to defend itself if facing a "continued and imminent threat," per a 2010 Office of Legal Counsel memo from the Department of Justice. The memo identified such a target as a "leader of an organization" (versus, say, an expendable foot soldier) who demonstrated efforts to attack the American people. Intelligence indicated al-Awlaki's connection to AQAP and multiple future plots, e.g., the poisoning of Western water supplies and explosives surgically implanted in humans, which would go undetected by airport security.

to that would be "Don't you dare." Generals need lawyers to help them make distinctions—whether something was a lawful act of war or murder. And so, as a lawyer, that's my job: to make sure that my client didn't break the law and commit murder.

NICK SHAPIRO

There was always a need to try and capture first, and if you can't capture, then you have to do something else.

BARBARA LEE

The Obama administration was very deliberative in how they approached this. They were always concerned about unintended consequences, collateral damage.

BILL DALEY

They thought about those things. They worried about them and tried to figure out whether you agreed or not that they should have done Awlaki, or whether or not you believed that we had the ability to go after people in other countries. But it was something the administration struggled with. I didn't think Cheney ever struggled with it. It didn't matter to him. I thought it *did* to Obama. And we may have ended up at the same place that they did, but I think there was a greater sense of concern around those issues than at least how you could seemingly read how the Bush administration approached these things.

DR. HAROLD KOH

Brennan and I had a great alliance. I barely knew him. He's not a lawyer, but he was extremely courageous on this point, I thought, and understood that the legitimacy of our actions followed from how clearly we specified and differentiated green-light zones from red-light zones. And how we carefully delineated rules in the yellow-light zones. There was a lot of public misunderstanding of the rules we articulated. Somebody like a Rand Paul said we could kill an American citizen sitting in a café in New York with a drone.[III] That's obviously false. He just didn't understand what the rules were.

LEON PANETTA

Like all weapons, it demanded that we thought about how to use it, when to use it, [and] to make sure that it's being used in a way that was in concurrence with our laws and our values.

TERRY SZUPLAT

Again, the technology was there. It's not going away. Other nations were increasingly, as we're seeing, developing these technologies. There're no international rules or norms governing these technologies yet, and so we, as the leader, had the opportunity—and, [Obama] would say, the responsibility—to, through our actions, set certain norms.

JONATHAN FINER

Secretary Clinton laid out what would accurately be described as the biggest strategic shift in foreign policy that the Obama administration made in the first term. That is, rebalancing our resources—militarily, economically, diplomatically—toward a region the president believed was going to play a larger role in all elements of our future: the Asia-Pacific. So Secretary Clinton laid out

---

III   "I rise today for the principle. That Americans could be killed in a café in San Francisco, or in a restaurant in Houston, or at their home in Bowling Green, Kentucky, is an abomination." —Rand Paul, participating in a March 7, 2013, Republican filibuster on the Senate floor to halt the nomination of John Brennan as CIA director.

this theory in a long article in *Foreign Policy*,[112] and the president gave a speech elaborating on this theme in the Australian Parliament in Canberra.

JEFFREY BLEICH

There were years of work that led up to the president's announcement in Canberra[113] of the [Asia] rebalance . . . We allocated our resources across the globe to reflect the rising economies and opportunities of the Indo-Pacific.

MICHAEL FROMAN

The goal there was to tie these countries more closely together. It started off with four relatively small countries, from Latin America to the Asia-Pacific, and the ultimate countries representing 40 percent of the global economy. A dozen economies [joined] the agreement over time. So that's what [the Trans-Pacific Partnership] would become. Defining high-standard rules of the road for the region, particularly in light of China moving ahead with its own state capitalist model and making sure that there was an alternative out there [to China] for trading partners and allies that reflected the values of an open rules basis.

---

112 "With Iraq and Afghanistan still in transition and serious economic challenges in our own country, there are those on the American political scene who are calling for us not to reposition, but to come home. They seek a downsizing of our foreign engagement in favor of our pressing domestic priorities. These impulses are understandable, but they are misguided. Those who say that we can no longer afford to engage with the world have it exactly backward—we cannot afford not to.

"Open markets in Asia provide the United States with unprecedented opportunities for investment, trade, and access to cutting-edge technology. Our economic recovery at home will depend on exports and the ability of American firms to tap into the vast and growing consumer base of Asia. Strategically, maintaining peace and security across the Asia-Pacific is increasingly crucial to global progress, whether through defending freedom of navigation in the South China Sea, countering the proliferation efforts of North Korea, or ensuring transparency in the military activities of the region's key players." —Secretary Clinton, "America's Pacific Century," *Foreign Policy*, October 11, 2011.

113 November 16, 2011.

MARK LIPPERT

Basically he felt that if you had treaty allies behind you, that you'd be in far better shape in the Asia-Pacific region. Then, add a few friends and partners with that to deal with China, with India, and with Indonesia—rising powers.

JONATHAN FINER

The other important thing happening at this time—and intimately tied to the president's thinking, I think, on the rebalance of Asia—was that we were drawing down our troops in Iraq. By the end of 2011, the last American combat forces had departed, which fulfilled a campaign promise the president had made to bring about a responsible end to that war.

LEON PANETTA

We had hoped to keep somewhere in between eight thousand to ten thousand of our troops, plus maintain our intelligence bases and diplomatic presence. We pretty much had designed a plan to do that. The biggest problem was the inability to develop the agreement.

JONATHAN FINER

What happened was, we decided that in order to keep ground forces in Iraq, we needed a sufficient degree of what were called "privileges and immunities"— protection for American forces from being subjected to the Iraqi legal system, which we, frankly, didn't have a ton of confidence in at that time while these American forces were deployed.

LEON PANETTA

There was an effort to try to work that out with Prime Minister [Nouri] al-Maliki. We always thought that, ultimately, Maliki would agree to provide that protection for our forces, and we just could not get there. We were kind of caught in a pressure point that ultimately resulted in the president saying, "If we want to do this more than the Iraqis want to do it, something's wrong."

JONATHAN FINER

The prime minister of Iraq decided that he did not want to take this agreement—and it's understandable, politically—because even though Maliki fundamentally believed that we were helpful to the stability of the country, for an Iraqi to say, *Not only do we need these American forces*, which were already controversial, *but we need to give them all this protection from Iraqi laws, almost no matter what they do*, I didn't think he could get parliamentary approval for that. So then he decided not to try, and so that prompted our decision about whether to keep forces in the country. The president decided to withdraw them.

KAREEM DALE

Leaving Iraq and ensuring that we didn't have more men and women coming home with disabilities was always something that was important to the president. It was a good thing, right? Fewer people fighting, fewer people coming home with fewer physical and mental disabilities. And you know, just in terms of the reelection, I did not work on the campaign in 2012. I was still in the White House, and we were just starting to pull ourselves out of that recession. People still were having difficulties and having a hard time seeing the progress being made, even though the unemployment rate was going down. People were rightfully concerned about getting jobs and feeding their families, but people were pleased that we were out of Iraq . . . I just don't think it was an either/or proposition.

JON FAVREAU

The Kansas speech . . . was the setup for the whole campaign. We talked about how economic inequality was the fundamental challenge of our time.[114] He wanted to stake that out early on in that race, and we knew that we wanted, no matter who the nominee was on the other side, to focus on the economy and to focus specifically on equality.

JAMES KVAAL

The Osawatomie speech showed how important it was to the president that we got back to this fundamental argument about reducing inequality by lifting people up in the middle and people trying to get into the middle. That speech sort of laid out his vision for the mistakes that had been made that got us to the point where economic growth was flowing almost exclusively to the top 1 percent, leaving ordinary Americans working harder and not seeing their incomes go up.

BILL DALEY

I left in '12, so the '12 election I was pretty much out of it.

---

114 "At the turn of the last century, when a nation of farmers was transitioning to become the world's industrial giant, we had to decide: Would we settle for a country where most of the new railroads and factories were being controlled by a few giant monopolies that kept prices high and wages low? Would we allow our citizens and even our children to work ungodly hours in conditions that were unsafe and unsanitary? Would we restrict education to the privileged few? Because there were people who thought massive inequality and exploitation of people was just the price you pay for progress.

"Theodore Roosevelt disagreed . . . And in 1910, Teddy Roosevelt came here to Osawatomie, and he laid out his vision for what he called a 'new nationalism.' 'Our country,' he said, 'means nothing unless it means the triumph of a real democracy . . . of an economic system under which each man shall be guaranteed the opportunity to show the best that there is in him.'" —President Obama at Osawatomie High School, Osawatomie, Kansas, December 6, 2011.

JACK LEW

The year I was chief of staff was obviously a uniquely challenging year, because the president was running for reelection. My responsibilities included far more than driving the fiscal-policy agenda. It was the full span of chief-of-staff responsibilities, which included everything foreign and domestic.

HEATHER FOSTER

Advisor, Office of Public Engagement, White House (2011–2015)

The Trayvon Martin case was always something that we were tracking, and it took people a while to understand. You know, everyone automatically jumped to *Oh, this kid got gunned down.* No. This was a young man who was in a gated community visiting his father over a holiday break. He was coming back from the store and was confronted by George Zimmerman and disappeared. No one contacted his parents. Charles Blow had written this column in the *New York Times*, and it just spiraled.[115]

ROY AUSTIN JR.

I was still in the Civil Rights Division when the Trayvon Martin incident happened, and when the president gave his remarks.

---

115   Charles Blow, "The Curious Case of Trayvon Martin," *New York Times*, March 16, 2012.

HEATHER FOSTER

When the reporter asked him the question, he said, "If I had a son, he'd look like Trayvon."[116] That was a moment since maybe the Beer Summit that had to have careful messaging. Regardless of what people say, people have a natural reaction when you mention race.

DANIELLE CRUTCHFIELD

A lot of times, as advisors, we'd come to decisions about the best way to respond as an administration, but one of the things that made the president special was that, with things like this, he had his own ideas about how to respond, about what he wanted to say.

CODY KEENAN

He was always more willing to push the boundaries. You know, I once had a different conversation about a different speech, and he told me, "Look, I wrote a book on race and identity. When you've been grappling with it for forty years, you have a better idea of what you want to say."

---

116 "Obviously this is a tragedy. I can only imagine what these parents are going through. And when I think about this boy, I think about my own kids, and I think every parent in America should be able to understand why it is absolutely imperative that we investigate every aspect of this and that everybody pulls together—federal, state, and local—to figure out exactly how this tragedy happened. So I'm glad that not only is the Justice Department looking into it, I understand now that the governor of the state of Florida has formed a task force to investigate what's taking place.

"I think all of us have to do some soul searching to figure out how does something like this happen. That means that we examine the laws and the context for what happened as well as the specifics of the incident. But my main message is to the parents of Trayvon Martin. You know, if I had a son, he'd look like Trayvon. And, you know, I think they are right to expect that all of us as Americans are going to take this with the seriousness it deserves, and that we're gonna get to the bottom of exactly what happened." —President Obama, press conference in the White House Rose Garden, March 23, 2012.

VALERIE JARRETT

Why is it that a child walking down the street with Skittles in their hand is instinctively scary? He said the same thing in his race speech about his grandmother who sometimes was "scared of [black men who passed her by on the street]." We should ask ourselves why that is, and we should see if we can do something about it.

HEATHER FOSTER

It was still a local issue, but all of the folks that I talked to in the communities desperately wanted him to provide, I don't know if the word is *reassurance*, but some validation. That's all they were looking for. They knew, courtswise, this might not turn out the way that we wanted, but they wanted this issue to be recognized. It's not right that a young black boy can get gunned down and that his parents had no idea where he was for twenty-four hours. That's unacceptable.

YOHANNES ABRAHAM

The killing of Trayvon Martin affected me deeply, personally. While I was on the campaign I wasn't involved in the deliberations around how or if the president would speak about him, and I imagine that decision was a tight circle in the White House. I would be surprised if anyone on the campaign had weigh-in on that. That's my guess, knowing how things would work. A lot of moments like that I experienced more as a private citizen than I did in my day-to-day work.

JAMES KVAAL

The president's goal was not just to get the economy growing again and create jobs but also to have a positive impact on middle-class incomes. Those were not necessarily the same thing. If you looked at the economic expansion we had in the 2000s, even over the course of that economic expansion you saw middle-class incomes fall, if you adjusted for inflation. So how did you have an economy that was growing based upon strong fundamentals—not a housing boom, not a tech boom—and, also, how did you make sure that economic growth was shared up and down the ladder?

JIM MESSINA

About every two or three weeks, at two o'clock in the morning, I'd get this call from this amazingly really brilliant political operative named Bill Clinton. "Jim, all presidential elections are always a referendum on the economic future. If you win that argument, you'll win the campaign." So it wasn't just about negative. It had to be about a positive vision. That's how "Forward" came about. We were able to put Romney in the box of defending the old policies of the past when we were for the future.

YOHANNES ABRAHAM

The communicators, I'm sure, spent a lot of time arguing about the ["Forward"] slogan and the design and all that. If you were an organizer and you were on the battleground-state team, getting those rallies off the ground was what you were tasked with, and that was your concern. I might be remembering this wrong, but the number-one thing you're afraid of in moments like that at a rally was a bad camera shot.

DAVID PLOUFFE

The president had an interview [scheduled] with Robin Roberts from ABC News and was going to discuss gay marriage, talk about his full evolution. If I recall, that was a Wednesday,[117] and Biden made his remarks the Friday before.

STUART STEVENS

The first time in history that anyone ever listened to Joe Biden—he came out for it, and clearly the reason Biden did it was because he was worried that [the campaign was] gonna back away from it. It wasn't a gaffe. He's not an idiot.

---

117   May 9, 2012.

DAVID PLOUFFE

I was really angry about this. Actually, I feel bad about this in retrospect.

BEN LABOLT

The president had said for a long time he wanted to make his position on it clear, and he previewed that answer over the years by saying he had evolved in his thinking. We knew the venue it was likely to come up in, so, you know, the VP jumping that by a few days was not part of the plan.

DAVID PLOUFFE

We were completely shocked—the president, myself, Jack Lew, others in the White House—when we got the transcript of the Biden interview. So it was not a trial balloon. We already had this laid out. We had strong words about it, because it made it look like the president was responding to the VP. And that was going to be an important moment for us. I wanted it to be the president's moment.

BEN LABOLT

At the same time it's like, when the history books note it, they both came out for same-sex marriage a week apart. To me, what's important was that they came out for it.

DAVID PLOUFFE

President Obama actually didn't really care. He said, "Well, listen, I'd been talking to Joe about this, so he probably thought he had the permission structure to do this." Which kind of infuriated me, because I wanted the president also to realize how this affected our best-laid plans.

HERBIE ZISKEND

Obama and Biden were extremely close colleagues. They genuinely loved each other. That's a real thing, whereas that's not always the case with previous presidents and vice presidents.

DAVID PLOUFFE

I was just maniacal about order and planning, and this was disrupted. Secondly, I thought it was historic, and I wanted the president to have that stage. It's a moment that would go through the decades and generations. Not surprisingly, a lot of the press commentary was, "Biden got ahead of Obama." None of that was true, and so at the end of the day the history books won't talk about that. It's a good lesson, but sometimes when you're in the middle of something it's hard to have that perspective.

HERBIE ZISKEND

Things like that happen when you're working at the White House. Early on in the administration there was a swine flu in the country. Biden made a comment about how he wouldn't advise families to use ["any system of public transportation where you're confined"].[118] It created a bit of a firestorm. It's hard to always be on message, but part of why people loved Biden was because he's a genuine, straightforward person and said what's on his mind, which was a virtue. But there were days when you'd be presented with challenging moments.

---

118 April 30, 2009.

TYLER MORAN

There had been a real pivot to the White House from the advocacy community to pressure the administration to grant legal status to Dreamers[119]—which, at that time, [the White House] was really pushing back and saying the president's office didn't have the authority to do it, [that] it was Congress's deal. There was a really ramped-up, intense pressure leading through '11 and then finally in '12.

LUIS GUTIÉRREZ

By this point, there's a broad movement. It's April of 2012, and he sent Cecilia Muñoz to speak to the Congressional Hispanic Caucus, because I had already met with Senator Rubio on a DREAM Act bill, which would give them status but wouldn't give them citizenship. And I had gone around telling everybody, "If Obama won't stop the deportations"—because his deportation numbers were going up—"we should all work with Rubio and get a bipartisan bill and at least set aside the Dreamers."

CECILIA MUÑOZ

I remember the meeting. While the press got really excited about a *Rubio puts Obama in a tough spot* narrative, the impetus for DACA . . . evolved from a bunch of policy shifts . . . Essentially, there're eleven million people who are deportable, and before the Obama administration, the [Homeland Security] strategy was to find as many of them as possible. So [DHS] Secretary Napolitano [began] modest steps toward establishing a system of priorities so that they went from *Let's find as many people as we can* to *Let's be strategic and go after people who are priorities because they pose some kind of harm or threat.* Everybody agreed the Dreamers should be low priority for enforcement, and lo and behold, Dreamers

---

119 In 2012, the Migration Policy Institute estimated some 114,000 undocumented immigrants, who would be protected under the 2010 DREAM Act, would instantly qualify to apply for permanent residence. (An estimated 96,000 were within the ages of 18–34.) Another 612,000 who qualified for conditional legal status would need to obtain a higher education or serve two years in the military to then apply for permanent residence.

kept ending up in the deportation pipeline because the policy was not airtight enough and the behavior at the agency was not changing enough. And Secretary Napolitano's barometer was *Are we still picking up Dreamers? Are we wasting enforcement resources on these folks?* Because that kept happening, she brought DACA to us.[120]

TYLER MORAN

On my first day at the White House I was told we were going to move on what became DACA and was in the Rose Garden on Friday for the announcement[121] . . . The president had basically approved giving deferred action to Dreamers. Then we had sixty days to stand up the program. So it was a pretty crazy summer, because on August 15, the first applications could be accepted.

---

120 On June 15, 2012, Secretary of Homeland Security Janet Napolitano instructed US Customs and Border Protection to defer enforcement on "certain young people who were brought to this country as children and know only this country as home"— specifically, those ages sixteen to thirty who have lived in the US for five years and with no criminal record, who are either enrolled in school or have served honorably in the Coast Guard or US military. Two months later, the administration initiated the Deferred Action for Childhood Arrivals (DACA) application program, which issued renewable two-year permits to qualifying individuals for work eligibility without fear of deportation.

121 "These are young people who study in our schools. They play in our neighborhoods. They're friends with our kids. They pledge allegiance to our flag. They are Americans in their heart, in their minds, in every single way but one—on paper. They were brought to this country by their parents, sometimes even as infants, and often have no idea that they're undocumented until they apply for a job or a driver's license, or a college scholarship.

   "Put yourself in their shoes. Imagine you've done everything right your entire life—studied hard, worked hard, maybe even graduated at the top of your class— only to suddenly face the threat of deportation to a country that you know nothing about, with a language that you may not even speak. That's what gave rise to the DREAM Act. It says that if your parents brought you here as a child, if you've been here for five years, and you're willing to go to college or serve in our military, you can one day earn your citizenship. And I have said time and time and time again to Congress that, send me the DREAM Act, put it on my desk, and I will sign it right away." —President Obama, White House Rose Garden, June 15, 2012.

PETE SOUZA

There's an interesting transition that took place in his presidency, and you could sort of see it best on the rope line. When the president finished making a speech and walked off the stage, he'd shake hands with people in the audience. And the first few years, there was a lot of excitement. People would shake his hand, and you'd see every fifth or sixth person with a little point-and-shoot camera. Then, somewhere along the way, I would guess probably around 2011—we certainly saw it in the campaign of 2012—everybody had a smartphone. Everybody was trying to get a selfie with him, and they were missing the moment of looking the president of the United States in the eye and shaking his hand.

KORI SCHULMAN
Deputy Chief Digital Officer, Office of Digital Strategy, White House (2009–2017)

You look at photos of East Room events early in the presidency in 2009. People were seated or standing, but they're looking at the president. A couple people had small handheld cameras, but then it's a total transition in the later years where it's just, like, a sea of iPhones.

PETE SOUZA

He did not like doing selfies. It got to the point where he would actually say to people on the rope line, "Put your camera down and shake my hand and look me in the eye." Now, he'd usually say that to the little kids, right? Kids that are twelve to fourteen, I mean—it's hard to say that to an adult. In terms of news cameras and stuff like that, it never bothered him. He didn't like to pose. He never liked to do a magazine cover shoot. He was very impatient. He wouldn't give people that much time. Even me.

Pete Souza: "I'd say 99 percent of what I did was documentary/candid photography . . . This was in the 1 percent category." Peter Souza, White House.

DANIELLE CRUTCHFIELD

Any president gets to a point where they're exhausted. We'd run very hard, and he'd get to the point, *I need a break.* At the same time, if we gave him that break, he'd be like, *I'm supposed to be out. There's something I could be doing. Shouldn't I be traveling? Shouldn't I be out?* Then, you gotta put him back out.

DAVID PLOUFFE

The number of people in the White House who interacted with the campaign in Chicago was minimal. We studied what the Bush people did pretty carefully, and Jack Lew and I had a great division of responsibility. So usually Dan Pfeiffer[122] and I were the only ones on the weekly call to Chicago. It's not like we had

---

122 Director of Communications, White House (2009–2013); Senior Advisor to the President, White House (2013–2015).

twenty-five different people in the White House offering opinions about what ads we should run in Ohio.

JOEL BENENSON

We ran a campaign in 2012 based on the idea that you build an economy from the middle out, not the top down. People had been feeling for more than a decade that corporate profits were staggeringly high and their wages were stagnant. There's disconnect there. I thought the Republicans totally misread that, and we were happy to engage that debate. We called for raising taxes on the very wealthy. President Obama ran in 2012 saying he was going to repeal the Bush tax cuts.

STUART STEVENS

There's no question that Barack Obama brought a different governing philosophy than the majority of the country. He'd always been seen as more ideologically left. Barack Obama was someone who had grown as well, because he's a smart and sane adult and, certainly in areas of foreign policy, he changed greatly, but he saw the world through a social-justice framework . . . When he said something like "You didn't build that," he's speaking from that worldview.[123] It's not just a gaffe. It was speak through a debate over the role of government in our society.

JOEL BENENSON

The American people at that point understood what President Obama was saying. Government *does* have a role to play in strengthening our economy. You could go back to Abraham Lincoln building the Transcontinental Railroad,

---

123 "If you were successful, somebody along the line gave you some help. There was a great teacher somewhere in your life. Somebody helped to create this unbelievable American system that we have that allowed you to thrive. Somebody invested in roads and bridges. If you've got a business—you didn't build that. Somebody else made that happen. The internet didn't get invented on its own. Government research created the internet so that all the companies could make money off the internet." —President Obama at a campaign stop in Roanoke, Virginia, July 13, 2012.

starting land-grant colleges and the National Academy of Sciences in the middle of the nineteenth century. The private sector didn't do those things. Dwight Eisenhower, a Republican, building the Interstate Highway System—what did it do? Opened markets across America to businesses big and small that could ship their products around the country. The notion that somehow, even in our capitalist society, that business alone created economic progress was just horseshit. Public universities educating Americans—business didn't do that. We had the most educated workforce in the world. Why?

TEDDY GOFF

Nobody really thought that he had this crypto-communist vision of America where anything you had was thanks to the government and there's no such thing as businesspeople having achievements. Obviously there were people who freakin' hated the guy and thought he wasn't even born in the United States or whatever, but the median voter in the United States basically liked the guy, trusted him, and believed he was doing his best. Instead, Romney overreached and made it out like Obama was a huge failure. Now, people didn't necessarily know the details of economic policy, they probably weren't satisfied with the pace of improvement, but nobody thought he made the economy worse.

STUART STEVENS

In that same press conference, he said the private sector's doing fine. One of the things I thought that's really important about the Obama years was, in our culture, the Center-Left had been much better about talking about those left behind and disadvantaged than the Center-Right. It's just not part of the Center-Right vocabulary. It's unfortunate, but it's the truth. During the Obama years, a lot of the voices that would speak to those who had been left behind, which were millions and millions of Americans, had been somewhat muted. They wanted to support the president, and they didn't want to help Republicans. So you had this phenomenon, and it's one of the contributing factors to Trump and Bernie Sanders, this sort of conspiracy of silence that things were better than they were.

2012–2013

The Romney campaign unveiled its running mate on a Saturday afternoon in Norfolk, Virginia. Paul Ryan, the baby-faced representative from Wisconsin's First Congressional District, had served since 1999, and to many conservatives, he was already mythologized as some mathlete who roamed the halls of the Longworth Building with copies of *The Path to Prosperity* under his arm. Ryan's *Prosperity* proposal, notorious for its aggressive measures to transform Medicare into a voucher system and abolish income tax for capital gains, mobilized voices within a growing Libertarian-bent wing of the Republican caucus and became the basis for the GOP's fiscal budget proposals. To Republicans with eyes on November 6, his cultivated, wonky persona smacked of a determination and intellect needed after Sarah Palin's provincial hokeyness.

Tens of thousands of operatives and state delegates descended upon south Florida in late August to witness Ryan take the stage at the Republican National Convention, not to mention booked performances around town by Journey, Kid Rock, and a pole-dancing Palin lookalike at Thee DollHouse. Also in store was a surprise celebrity appearance by Clint Eastwood, who, moments prior to his address on the final night of the RNC, made the spontaneous decision to improvise with an empty chair, where an imaginary President Obama sat for nearly eleven minutes as Eastwood criticized him on subjects ranging from unemployment numbers to his failure to close Gitmo. The invisible POTUS even talked back. "What do you mean, 'shut up'?" the eighty-two-year-old asked.

A few years later, Eastwood admitted he regretted his "silly" performance, but that night, while watching from backstage, the party's nominee did not appear to be in a state of panic. "Romney didn't really care," Stuart Stevens said of Eastwood's performance. "It was weird, it was freaky, but it's not where his head was. He was thinking about what he was gonna do."

JIM MESSINA

The entire world had been focused on his primary. We couldn't ever get our message out. We got through the debt-ceiling stuff, and the economic news was starting to turn around but [it still wasn't] great. It was just hard. But by the time he finally ground his way to the nomination, we were ready. I made these pins for the Chicago staff, and they said "DFA" on them. And I handed 'em out to like four hundred of our staff in our weekly meeting. Everyone was like, *What's DFA?* And I said, "We finally have an opponent. His name is Mitt Romney, and DFA stands for 'Done Fucking Around.' It is time to define this guy."

LUIS GUTIÉRREZ

David Axelrod and Senator Durbin both got me on a conference call and were really nice. "The president wants bygones to be bygones. He wants to set everything aside." Something like that. "We'd like to invite you to speak at the Democratic Convention in Charlotte." And you know what they did? They put me at *five* fuckin' o'clock! There were about fifteen people around, but to their credit, at prime time, they brought in undocumented Dreamers to speak who would have qualified for his executive action. So they did the old okeydoke with me again, but I went home feeling pretty good.

GENE SPERLING

When President Clinton gave his speech, you were dealing with a person who was 100 percent on board. Not just giving a great speech to be a statesman, but somebody at an emotional level that really wanted to defend him. He knew what it was like to make a good, fine economic decision for your country and have everybody against you. He knew what it was like to do two major fiscal deals that involved incredible amounts of negotiation and compromise, and he had to live with criticism about not accomplishing things he would have loved to do but just couldn't because of the political realities.

JOE LOCKHART

White House Press Secretary (1998–2000)

I was working for Facebook at the time. We did an event, I wanna say on the first day, and I had nothing else to do for the next three days. So I was there more for social purposes. I knew the president was giving a speech, but I wasn't really involved. I show up when asked and not without an invite.

GENE SPERLING

[Clinton] started writing almost two weeks in advance, calling [policy advisor] Bruce Reed and me for facts, for numbers, and so we're kind of helping to feed stuff, and so I was told when to meet President Clinton as he arrived at Charlotte. So, literally, I was there when his car came. We went up to the room and he pulled out just a ton of handwritten yellow pages. For the next two days, people typed his pages while you were sitting with him in that room.

JOE LOCKHART

I got a call from one of [President Clinton's] guys at like seven o'clock in the morning: "Would you mind coming by the suite? We're doing some speech prep, but he wants some fresh eyes and ears." I said, "When?" He said, "Now." I was fifteen minutes away, so I went over. So I probably got there seven thirty, eight o'clock in the morning, and we didn't leave the room till he gave the speech at nine or nine thirty [p.m.].

GENE SPERLING

Axelrod and Plouffe would keep texting us, [asking] could we feed the text. "It's kind of hard to fax over a hundred yellow pages of handwriting. You have to trust us. This is going well."

JOE LOCKHART

It was both a typical and atypical Clinton speech prep in this respect. One was, it was the morning of the speech and it wasn't done. That was typical. It was typical that he had in his mind what he wanted to say, but it wasn't put down. It was atypical that it got done before it had to get done. I mean, he clearly had a mental clock in his head, because he wanted it completed to make sure he could share it with Obama with enough time that Obama could have input. Which was interesting. That, I hadn't seen before. He was always open to ideas, but . . . I think he read it to David Axelrod and then sent it to Obama and they were okay with it.

GENE SPERLING

Little things came back. I didn't know how much was from [Obama] himself, but we were getting it from Favreau, Plouffe, and Axelrod—mostly small things, but [Clinton] really wanted to take everything, all the suggestions—so there was no tension. He wanted to make sure they were okay with things.

JON FAVREAU

Not me, I wasn't part of it. I remember getting the speech from whomever in Charlotte at the hotel a couple hours before, and then Axe and Plouffe and I all looked at it and made a few edits, and it was fine. It was great. We just made some cuts because it seemed unbelievably long.

GENE SPERLING

Again, you're around a table and discussing it, and President Clinton is x-ing out paragraphs and agreeing he's gotta keep it down. But you gotta remember, he's actually written this whole speech, and he's got an amazing memory. So even though you're cutting it out, he remembered every line.

JOE LOCKHART

The speech was probably an hour and a half. There was an obvious half hour that you could take out of it, which, that wasn't hard. He was willing. Taking the next half hour out of the speech took about eight hours. Gene and Bruce were there for a couple long blocks of time, but they had a meeting they had to go to. [Former Clinton advisor] Paul [Begala] was definitely there and he had to go do TV. So because I had no other commitment, because I'm a loser, I kind of was along with the president's staff and continually tried to push everybody. Because, you know, you get a group that's more than four or five people and you're trying to cut it down, but some people in the group were trying to put other stuff in.

GENE SPERLING

We had a little back room right where his hotel room was, with a podium. We did a practice or two, and we're all kind of crowded in there. I remember one time, me coming up to change something and somebody shouted, "Don't interrupt him!" And I was like, "No, that's from President Obama himself," and they're like, "Oh, okay, okay."

JOE LOCKHART

All through the day, we kept bringing up, "You could give the greatest speech since the Gettysburg Address, and if it goes too long, people will only focus on the atmospherics of it." So he stayed at it and stayed at it and cut it down.

GENE SPERLING

So we cut it down and he practiced it twice. We had it timed, and then he got out there and you know what happened.

JOE LOCKHART

He had a twenty-eight-minute speech on the teleprompter and proceeded to add in whatever it was, another fifteen or twenty minutes from memory, as if it was on the teleprompter. Whole sections had come out, which, by the way, if you watched the speech, it was a great speech. We had taken really good stuff out, and only he could answer this question about whether he knew all along he was gonna do it.

GENE SPERLING

He knew he was crushing it. He went back to things he had cut out and literally said them word for word. His memory was still so good. He had some ad-libs. When he said, "Ryan had to have brass balls" or something,[124] that was an ad-lib. But what people thought were ad-libs were really his just remembering things he had liked in his original speech.

JOE LOCKHART

I thought up until that, the campaign . . . they were doing okay. The country was in good shape. He had all the advantages of the incumbency, but it just hadn't crystallized into something yet.

---

124 "When Congressman Ryan looked into that TV camera and attacked President Obama's Medicare savings as, quote, 'the biggest, coldest power play,' I didn't know whether to laugh or cry . . . because that $716 billion is exactly, to the dollar, the same amount of Medicare savings that he had in his own budget. You got to get one thing. It takes some brass to attack a guy for doing what you did." —President Clinton at the Democratic National Convention, Time Warner Cable Arena, Charlotte, North Carolina, September 5, 2012.

DAVID PLOUFFE

The last sixty days, we had Benghazi. We had Hurricane Sandy. It's indescribably hard to run for reelection, much less win, when you've also got these serious events that intervene. You also had three presidential debates. I was probably working twenty-one, twenty-two hours a day, and you're trying to campaign with skill, energize people, and then you've got the governing piece.

NATE LUBIN

I was working fifteen, sixteen hours a day for a year straight. Gained a lot of weight. I was very pale. I went to the doctor at some point, and that wasn't super great. He was like, "You're healthy, you're okay right now, but you're not gonna be."

JAMES KVAAL

Voters were open to hearing Governor Romney's argument, and they knew him as a successful moderate governor of Massachusetts, as someone who had been successful in business before that, and they had an open mind [as] to whether he had the answers to the challenges in the economy.

TEDDY GOFF

It's worth noting that the country was heavily divided, and there were just not that many things that could change people's votes, but as these things go, the

"47 percent" video was a big deal.[125] It played into a thing that people really believed, and at that point you had like fifty days left.

DAVID PLOUFFE

We were in Columbus, Ohio, at an event, and I was backstage when the *Mother Jones* story broke.[126] So I looked at the video and got on the phone with Axelrod, Messina, and the campaign for a quick conference call. If I recall, our initial reaction was, *Don't do anything. This'll do its own damage*, then showed the president the video in the presidential limousine, and he couldn't believe it. He understood its significance, though his instinct was even stronger than ours. Which was, *Don't do anything with this right away.*

TEDDY GOFF

Unlike "You didn't build that," that *was* something people thought about Romney, whereas nobody really thought of Obama as having some sick vision for a government-run society. People *did* think that Romney was the kind of person who was a little bit disdainful of poor or working-class people and just not understanding of their lives. It was a lousy thing that was a perfect storm of

---

125 "There are 47 percent of the people who will vote for the president no matter what. All right? There are 47 percent who are with him, who are dependent upon government, who believe that they are victims, who believe that government has a responsibility to care for them, who believe that they are entitled to health care, to food, to housing, to you name it . . . These are people who pay no income tax. Forty-seven percent of Americans pay no income tax. So our message of low taxes doesn't connect, and he'll be out there talking about tax cuts for the rich. I mean, that's what they sell every four years. And so my job is not to worry about those people. I'll never convince them that they should take personal responsibility and care for their lives. What I have to do is convince the 5 to 10 percent in the center that are independents, that are thoughtful, that look at voting one way or the other depending upon, in some cases, emotion, whether they like the guy or not . . ."
     —Mitt Romney, at a May 17, 2012, fundraiser in Boca Raton, Florida. His remarks were recorded surreptitiously by a bartender who catered the $50,000-per-plate dinner.
126 David Corn's "SECRET VIDEO: Romney Tells Millionaire Donors What He REALLY Thinks of Obama Voters," *Mother Jones*, September 17, 2012.

kind of insulting the people he's talking about and also believable as a thing he might actually say.

YOHANNES ABRAHAM

At this point, you're mid-September. You're into the fall. You're post–Labor Day, and you're off and running. This is the point where campaigns would normally go to seven days a week.

TEDDY GOFF

If you think about the election in terms of news cycles, which is a little outdated, but there is such a thing as days, and there was only so much news a person could consume in a day. If three or four or five of those days were consumed in fighting over why you said something and what it meant, and then the second- or third-day stories of where the video came from and what's the deal, that's like 10 percent of the time you have left to prosecute your case.

JAMES KVAAL

He seemed to suggest that almost half the country was not important to him. It said something about him personally, but it was also true that his platform was not persuasive to those voters, that they weren't hearing the kinds of ideas from him that they felt would have had a changeable impact on their lives.

TEDDY GOFF

I remember the morning David Plouffe emailed Ben LaBolt, Larry Grisolano, Jim Messina, [Deputy Campaign Manager] Stephanie Cutter, myself—I forget who else—and basically instructed us to pounce. And I didn't hear from Plouffe often at all. So, you know, it's David Plouffe. It certainly was not an original email. He replied to an email somebody else wrote, but when Plouffe's instructing us to pounce, it's a big deal.

DAVID PLOUFFE

My email was like, *When the cloud lifts, let's figure out how to keep this in front of people.* One of the best ads we ran in that cycle was just the thirty seconds of him with the glasses clinking [and] talking. We didn't put any words around it. We didn't try and play it cute. We just wanted to keep that in front of people.

TEDDY GOFF

It knocked him off course. I remember talking to some Romney guys later who just seemed devastated by the whole thing and described crestfallen staff meetings where the campaign manager had to try and buck everybody up.

DAVID PLOUFFE

When you're given an opening, you have to relentlessly pursue it. You cannot let your opponent up off the mat, and that was obviously one of my most enjoyable two weeks in my American political history—between the "47 percent" tape and the first presidential debate. Romney just couldn't get out of his own way, and it began to open up. Everything we did during that period was smart, and, of course, you're reminded that those periods don't last long. Because basically everything we did in the first debate was not smart. The president didn't speak at all about that moment.

YOHANNES ABRAHAM

That first debate was scary.[127] I remember going home and my stomach was completely flipped. It was less any one moment than it was me realizing it was being received and spun. There was not like an "Oh my God" moment. I don't recall, "The answer on Portuguese imports was what turned the whole thing against him."

---

127 October 3, 2012 at the University of Denver, Colorado.

MICHAEL STEEL

My recollection was, we were prepping [for the vice-presidential debate] and watching Governor Romney's first debate, and man, he was good. He called Ryan afterward, and Ryan said something like, "Wow, you really raised the bar for me" or "increased the pressure on me."

JIM MESSINA

No one had ever lost a debate as badly as we lost that first debate. It just had been a slaughter. I remember right before we went into the spin room, we huddled on the phone with our pollster and heard the dire news on the focus groups. We discussed what we were going to say, and David Axelrod looked at me and said, "Jim, do you know the bad part about being the president's campaign manager?" And David opened the door to the spin room, pushed me through it, and said, "You first."

TEDDY GOFF

I thought it was probably worse for us than the "47 percent" was for Romney.

JIM MESSINA

I slid out there and all this press came over to me and I said, "We won this debate tonight!" That's all I could get out of my mouth before everyone started laughing.

TEDDY GOFF

It really almost reset the whole campaign. Because Obama was the incumbent, you're seeing him execute his duties as president, but you're not seeing him out on the campaign trail. As president, he's often subdued in press conferences or interviews. It's not the sort of screaming-fans rally environment you remembered from '08. So that was really the first glimpse that people got of him in that election as a candidate. It was a bummer, and we took a fairly significant hit in the polls.

JIM MESSINA

The polls said we had lost it 89 to 11 percent. Who knows who those 11 percent were? They had to be related to Barack Obama or me, and so we all got on the plane and flew back to Chicago to get ready for the spin the next morning. Then Pete Rouse called me from the White House and said, "You have to get on a plane. House and Senate Democrats are losing their minds. They want you to tell them it's going to be okay." I literally got on a plane, flew to Washington, appeared in front of the House and Senate caucuses, walked them through the tracking numbers from the night before, and explained why it was okay. I remember a senator, whom I love very much and could never bullshit, pulling me aside: "I have no idea if you're right, but I feel much better." I remember thinking to myself, *I hope I'm fuckin' right, too.*

YOHANNES ABRAHAM

It was really one of the first times where it was approximate enough to Election Day that I was really, truly scared that we would lose. That's what made the vice-presidential debate so energizing. I think I nearly dislocated my shoulder, like, pumping my fist after the vice-presidential debate. We were all so proud of the vice president, and obviously he did a really great job in a really key moment for us.

MICHAEL STEEL

The vice president clearly felt a mandate to get the ticket off the mat. So we expected him to be over the top, but he was borderline unhinged in his debate performance. He was clearly trying to show some fight, show the Obama-Biden ticket was back in the game, and I thought he was comically over the top at times. And a little factually challenged on some of his attacks.

TEDDY GOFF

But it's true that a gaffe that seems to confirm what people already think is the gaffe that does the most damage. In the second debate, a moment like "binders full of women," by the standards of Trump it's so quaint, right?[128] It's like, why do we even care? But in the context of that election, Romney had a women problem. He said all these sorts of lousy things—Planned Parenthood, he wanted to get rid of that. He did kind of cut a figure of this almost Eisenhower-era debonair patrician, which was nostalgic for some people but also representative of an era when women didn't have equal rights.

MICHAEL STEEL

At the time, Governor Romney said things that were mocked or belittled but turned out to be prescient. He's a smart, smart man who had done a great deal of preparation, not just to run for president but to *be* president. Part of that meant learning and thinking deeply about foreign policy, and I thought [his remarks on Russia in] the third debate were a good example of President Obama going for a cheap line or a cheap joke that, on thoughtful reflection, was very off base.[129]

STUART STEVENS

Yeah, it was bad. Obama, the *New York Times*, and others basically scolded Romney. They dismissed Romney's concerns about Russia, the same as Trump. They're both based upon an assumption that Russia was not a threat. Go back

---

128 "We took a concerted effort to go out and find women who had backgrounds that could be qualified to become members of our cabinet [in Massachusetts]. I went to a number of women's groups and said, 'Can you help us find folks?' and they brought us whole binders full of women . . . the University of New York in Albany did a survey of all fifty states, and concluded that mine had more women in senior leadership positions than any other state in America." —Governor Romney at Hofstra University, Hempstead, New York, October 16, 2012.

129 "Russia I indicated is a 'geopolitical foe' . . . Russia does continue to battle us in the UN time and time again. I have clear eyes on this. I'm not going to wear rose-colored glasses when it comes to Russia, or Mr. Putin." —Governor Romney at Lynn University, Boca Raton, Florida, October 22, 2012.

and read the *New York Times* editorial about this.[130] It's the same worldview as Trump: *Russia's our friend. We don't need to worry about Russia.* There was plenty of evidence in 2012, if you wanted to open your eyes.

BRANDON HURLBUT

We're days out from the election, and Hurricane Sandy hit DC pretty hard. The Metro wasn't running. There were no cabs. Luckily I didn't live too far from the DOE. I think I walked to work that day, and when I got in, it was pretty sparse. Of course, [Secretary Chu] arrived and we needed to get on a videoconference in the Situation Room with the president, and so all the senior staff was there. The president said, "The world is watching, and I'm gonna be judged by my response." He looked at us and said, "You guys gotta get that power back up." Another thing that he said that played out later was, "I have zero tolerance for red tape in this. If I hear of any red tape going on and bureaucratic snafus, there's gonna be a problem. So get this done and no red tape."

TEDDY GOFF

Romney made a big mistake. He made this charity drive [in Dayton, Ohio]. I didn't know how we got tipped off to it, but his own staff had bought stuff at a [Walmart] and put it in cardboard boxes with handwritten signs.[131] Then, by contrast, President Obama—who, arguably his best political skill was sort of his calmness under pressure, which was *not* stagecraft—did come through. That he

---

130 "Two decades after the end of the cold war, Mitt Romney still considers Russia to be America's 'No. 1 geopolitical foe.' His comments display either a shocking lack of knowledge about international affairs or just craven politics. Either way, they are reckless and unworthy of a major presidential contender . . . There are real threats out there: al-Qaeda and its imitators, Iran, North Korea, economic stresses. Mr. Romney owes Americans a discussion of the real challenges facing this country and his solutions to them." —"The Never-Ending Cold War," *New York Times*, March 28, 2012.

131 In an attempt to show sensitivity to those affected by Hurricane Sandy on the East Coast, at the last minute the Romney campaign transformed what was supposed to be a scheduled rally in Dayton into "a storm-relief event." Concerned that the charity drive might not prove successful, staff made the miscalculation of stocking a rental truck with $5,000 of goods before donors arrived.

was crisp, efficient, and decisive in that kind of situation. So, you know, you had Romney being clownish in his response and President Obama being perfectly pitched and poised in executing actual federal response.

STUART STEVENS

I never felt good about the race after Sandy. We were tracking a couple stats, like "Who do you think has momentum?" and "Who do you think's gonna win?" They're not always predictive, but they're always kind of interesting. And there was a forty-point shift in that during Sandy. Every time I've beaten an incumbent, you know, it's really like an NBA game. You really had to control the ball until the very end, and Sandy took away any ability to do that.

ARNE DUNCAN

Obviously you get better at being president by *being* president. His growth over time was pretty remarkable. Honestly, the thing that stood out for me the most was what *didn't* change. He and I obviously were friends. Our families were friends. And so we had a relationship going in, but his values and what his family meant to him, what his daughters meant to him, what his wife meant to him, the way he treated people and the way he treated staff—way beyond kind to my wife and kids, which he didn't need to be—it wasn't part of any contractual arrangement. What blew me away was how little those values changed.

DAVID AXELROD

That's, of course, why I loved working for him. He didn't run for office simply to hear "Hail to the Chief" or enjoy the trappings of it. He did it because he wanted to get important things done for the country, and was willing to risk his own political well-being to do it. So he was willing to do the hard things. That will be to his everlasting credit.

ARNE DUNCAN

On the day of the election, we played basketball in Chicago. We used to do that just to relax. It was looking good—probably 60–40 at that point, 55–35, against Romney—and I was in knots. I asked him how he was feeling, and he just sort of said, "I'm good. I got a wife who loves me and I got two great kids. Whatever happens, I'm gonna be fine." I never forgot that. Of course, he definitely wanted to win and it would have been devastating to lose, but he was telling the truth. He was really going to be fine, and I think of so many politicians who get consumed by the power and consumed by the role and the pageantry of it. That stuff's just not interesting to him. For me, the biggest lesson was, the presidency couldn't help but change you. But how little it changed his core values and what's really most important to him, it didn't change an inch.

STUART STEVENS

The race basically boiled down to one key factor: 1980, Ronald Reagan won 56 percent of the white vote and won a forty-four-state landslide. Mitt Romney won 59 percent of the white vote and lost. That's it, and that's really the whole race. That's the whole dynamic. So ask any question—could this have been different or could that have been different? Could Romney have done this or that? The essential question to ask would have been, "Would it have increased his share of nonwhite vote?" If the answer wasn't yes, then it wouldn't have had any impact on the race.

SCOTT BROWN

They spent a tremendous amount of money against me . . . and they wanted the Kennedy seat back. The president went all out, full steam, and Mayor Menino threw me under the bus. We had had a great relationship. I had worked with him as a state rep and a state senator, and I looked at him as a mentor. We invited him over the house for barbecues, and then, when he came back from the Democratic Convention, he wouldn't even look at me. I said to my wife, "It's over."

ROB ANDREWS

The Affordable Care Act was one of the main issues of the 2012 presidential race, and unemployment [had been at] five percent or five and a half, and the president won decisively. So the state of the economy was the major driver. Anyway, that's just my own view.

TYLER MORAN

Postelection, obviously the president's numbers with Latinos were, like, *huge*. Percentages in some of the states were impressive enough that people felt really confident about immigration. That's when the senior advisors decided that the White House would make a push on some kind of immigration reform, and it was in November that the president instructed us to have a bill ready for him, I think by the end of Christmas break. That was a delightful Christmas.

LUIS GUTIÉRREZ

After the election, they moved in the Senate and in the House; we were working with the Republicans.

TYLER MORAN

We saw a bipartisan effort there in the House, and we provided support to them, not as intensely as the Senate, because it was in the drafting stages. And the president did tons behind the scenes—phone calls that were not public, asking, "What can we do?" Boehner would say, "Well, back off. Give us some space." "Okay, we can do that." . . . Some Republicans sort of looked at the party's position on immigration and felt like, *We can't be the party that's going to stick with the old white men.* Like, *We're going to become dinosaurs, and if we don't start talking to people outside of ourselves, we're not gonna survive as a party.* That was kind of the postmortem that Priebus took the lead on after the election.[132]

JEREMY BIRD

After the election was over, I went to that thing they do at Harvard, where people from both sides spend a couple days talking through what it was like. It was really interesting, and they asked the Romney people, "How'd you get it so wrong?" He bought [$25,000] worth of fireworks for the Boston victory party. Basically, [Stuart Stevens] and Neil Newhouse said, "Well, we just got the composite of the electorate wrong." They thought it was going to look much more like '10 than '08.

ALLYSON SCHWARTZ

President Obama was pretty self-assured. After his reelection I said, "We really worked hard for you in Pennsylvania!" There was this moment at the end of the campaign where Paul Ryan came into Harrisburg to do a final rally. It was this sort of final push, and [Obama] said, "Well, we were never really too worried about Pennsylvania." Oh, that's good. We were all fighting to make sure that was true, but he was probably smart to know that it was really not in play.

SHOMIK DUTTA

The overconfidence was definitely on the Romney side. The Romney people were as surprised as the Hillary people [in 2016]. We had so much faith in our data. There was never a moment of real angst, other than the first debate. For me, at least, and my friends, we were enormously confident. And maybe we shouldn't have been, because the macro headwinds were daunting. There's never been a

---

132 Republican National Committee chair Reince Priebus, after spending months reviewing the Romney-Ryan loss, issued the *Growth & Opportunity Project*, a hundred-page report that detailed strategies for GOP victories in future presidential elections—e.g., the need for congressional Republicans to support comprehensive immigration reform. (The standout data point was the failure to attain more than 27 percent of the Latino vote in 2012.)

president elected with unemployment that high and with dissatisfaction that high. And yet we kind of threaded the needle, and our data guys were right.

PETE SOUZA

He was riding high. He'd just won reelection, and a month later, about a week away from his annual Christmas vacation, was the worst day of his presidency.

NICK SHAPIRO

I was the one who interrupted the Oval Office to first tell them about Sandy Hook. It was during the PDB. At first, we thought a small number of kids had been shot; only later did we learn the full extent. But it was a school. They were young, and this was actually out of the news for a really long time, and that's not normal. The early reporting, they really didn't know anything. And the FBI called for [Homeland Security Advisor John] Brennan. I said he was in the PDB. They said, "Well, Nick, you gotta know this" . . . and so I made the decision to go interrupt the PDB and hand Brennan a note about what had happened, even though he was already in the room with the president.

FERIAL GOVASHIRI

I actually sat next to Nick Shapiro in the NSC office when that was happening. He frantically ran up there, right as fast as he could, just bolting upstairs.

NICK SHAPIRO

I walked in and handed Brennan the note, and the president looked kind of shocked, because it was very abnormal to interrupt the PDB. And he kind of looked at me, and then Brennan looked at me and said, "Go ahead." Again, the scale of what had happened was not in the news yet, and I said out loud what had happened. And they said, "Okay." Then I left to let them discuss and told them I'd be back if there was more information.

ARNE DUNCAN

None of us ever anticipated a school shooting like that. No one ever anticipated twenty babies, five teachers, and a principal being killed. I had spoken to people who were not the first responders, but who were in the second wave that drove to the school: "Arne, this is bad. This is really, really bad."

CODY KEENAN

The president said that was his worst day in the White House. That was true for everybody. Favs and I shared an office in the West Wing, and we both found out at the same time. We had MSNBC on, and somebody had a news alert. We checked Twitter, and Alyssa Mastromonaco came down to the office. She was deputy chief of staff of operations at that point, so she'd been talking to the FBI and Brennan. She'd been getting updates. "Guys, this is worse than the news knows. The president's going to have to say something. All we know is that there are children who are dead. We don't know how many."

DANIELLE CRUTCHFIELD

I always dragged the bulk of my team to an outing at least one day every year, and we were planning a trip to go ice skating in Navy Yard. But I remember calling Alyssa, who was the deputy chief of staff. "Hey, you know, I heard . . ." It was early, when the first reports had happened. "Do we know anything more about it?" And she said, "I need you to come to my office."

NICK SHAPIRO

Shortly thereafter, Brennan came out and got on the phone with the FBI and started working through the details. There's an incredible picture of John Brennan in the Oval Office that day, talking to the president one-on-one about the shooting. That's when we heard the new report about just how many kids had been killed. It's the only picture you'll ever see of John Brennan in the Oval Office without his jacket on. The Oval Office was something everyone treated with respect, and John was someone who would never be without his jacket. But he went so quickly. That's when we learned the scale of it.

John Brennan briefs the president on Sandy Hook, Connecticut. December 14, 2012. Pete Souza, White House

PETE SOUZA

I think John had come up to the Oval like three different times, updating the president. I'm pretty sure this particular photo was when John confirmed to the president that twenty of the people killed were six or seven years old, first graders. Shit. I'm going to start crying as I think about this, because, you know, he's obviously being told this as a president, but I think he was reacting as a parent. He's putting himself in the shoes of every one of those parents. You send your kids off to school in the morning, and you never see them again because some madman just shot them to death.

CODY KEENAN

We started following the news and paying attention. Favs had been working on the second inaugural at the time, because that was coming up in a month. So I got to work on a statement, and Favs and I took it up to the Oval Office to show the president, and he said "This is right," except he took out one paragraph. I remember exactly what was in it. He just crossed out one paragraph and said, "I won't be able to get through this. It's too raw."

DANIELLE CRUTCHFIELD

I'd never seen the president look like that.

CODY KEENAN

He kept parts about "[We've endured too many of] these tragedies in the past few years, and each time I learn the news, I react not as a president but as anybody else would, as a parent. [And] that was especially true today." And I had a couple lines in there, him thinking about his own girls in their classrooms, what it would be like if he got that call, what it would take to stop him from running in that school as fast as he could, how he wouldn't be able to breathe until he knew his own children were safe. He took all that out and changed it to, "I know there is not a parent in America who doesn't feel the same overwhelming grief that I do." He modified a line I had in about the kids themselves and changed it to "beautiful little kids between [the ages of] five and ten years old" and that [was] where he stopped and paused.

PETE SOUZA

He started crying from the podium. He, like me, would always get emotional thinking about that.

CODY KEENAN

Everybody kept saying how remarkable it was that members of Congress would tear up, and I remember people mocking the president for crying that day. Gimme a break. I cried. Anyone in America who didn't should take a look at themselves.

DANIELLE CRUTCHFIELD

Eventually we got on the phone with the mayor of Newtown, and talked about what their plans were. They were initially going to have the memorial in a very small space, and it was one of those things where you couldn't push. This happened in their town. You had to figure out what worked for them, and what's the best way to help them so it's not chaos. So we had our teams jump in cars and drive there, and they got there early the next morning and snapped into action helping them plan the service.

CODY KEENAN

That was a Friday, and we moved quickly. The eulogy was on Sunday,[133] and that was extremely tough. How do you eulogize twenty little kids? Speechwriting is all about empathy. It's about being able to put yourself in your audience's shoes. But there are limits. If you don't have children, there's a limit to your empathy. You could do your best to imagine what a parent's going through. Terry Szuplat suggested that bit about being a father is like "having your heart outside your body [all the time], walking around." The president liked that and tweaked it a little bit. It was one of those speeches where he basically kept the first two pages intact and when he was in the car on the way to Newtown—it was a long drive from whatever airport we flew into—wrote a lot of it on yellow legal paper.

TERRY SZUPLAT

It's something that I mentioned to Cody. Obviously I didn't know if it was an actual quote that was attributed to anybody originally, but it's certainly one of those phrases that I had heard before and always held on to. As a parent myself, it really captured the daily tension in your life as you wanted these little beings to be safe and protected but you also wanted them to go out into the world and be independent, and what that's like, as a parent, to have to do that every day.

---

133 December 16, 2012.

CODY KEENAN

What I really loved was, "There's only one thing we can be sure of, and that's the love we have for our children, for our families, for each other. The warmth of a small child's embrace—that is true. The memories we have of them, the joy [that] they bring, the wonder we see through their eyes, that fierce and boundless love we feel for them, a love that takes us out of ourselves and binds us to something larger—we know that's what matters."

DANIELLE CRUTCHFIELD

He's actually phenomenal in those instances, because before anything, he's a parent. He spent hours with the families.

CODY KEENAN

We didn't have conversations around Tucson about gun legislation, but this was different. You had to. If you didn't, it would have been a catastrophic failure of leadership, and it happened just as he won reelection and we were coming up on a second term. I think our first thing, out of the gate, was going to be a push on immigration reform, but circumstances intervened. You had to do something about guns instead, even though we knew the odds were going to be really long.

BILL DAUSTER

It was a continuing frustration to us. Republicans were the problem. In contrast to the days of the assault-weapons ban decades before, Republican senators came to view, it seemed, the NRA as part of the wing of the Republican Party, an important-enough ally that they'd obtain greater cohesion with them than what was sensible for them.

CAROLYN MALONEY

After Sandy Hook, when we had twenty children murdered, I really thought that we would pass gun-safety laws. It's sort of like, how outrageous could it get before you did something?

ARNE DUNCAN

My wife's from Tasmania, and they had a massacre.[134] At that point, Australia changed a bunch of their gun laws, and there has not been a single mass shooting in twenty years. That's the gift that Australian political leaders gave to that generation of kids. They've never known a mass shooting. The prime minister paid a real price, politically, there, but he said it was worth it. Think about kids in Australia, the lack of fear they have, and think about how, for kids in America, it became normalized. We allowed our kids to grow up with that, and other nations didn't.

CODY KEENAN

There were moments where you believed we might have a chance, when polls came out showing that [91] percent of Americans favored background checks, including [87] percent of Republicans and [74] percent of NRA households. He traveled the country for a couple months making a push on that and the fact that we still couldn't get it done, when it was one of those things where you had fifty-four yes votes in the Senate but you needed sixty. The day that that vote

---

134 The Port Arthur massacre in Tasmania, Australia, was carried out by twenty-eight-year-old Martin Bryant on April 28–29 in 1996. Thirty-five people were killed and twenty-three wounded, the youngest victims aged three and six. As a result of the mass shooting, Prime Minister John Howard led an effort to convince the Australian states to adopt the National Firearms Agreement, which severely restricted the purchase and ownership of semiautomatic and fully automatic weapons, created a national gun registry, and instituted a temporary federal gun-buyback program. There have been no mass shootings of five or more people in Australia since the adoption of the NFA, and in 2015 gun homicide rates decreased by nearly 60 percent.

failed and he went out to do the statement in the Rose Garden was one of the two times I'd actually seen him angry, and cynical.[135]

ARNE DUNCAN

In terms of actually getting any basic legislation done to keep kids and keep parents safe? We got an F. We absolutely failed. There's no other way to put it. The fact that we, as a nation, allowed the sheer quantity of deaths each year, it's a choice we made. Other nations made other policy choices and they just didn't have the level of death we had.

BILL DAUSTER

The McConnell years were a study in ratcheting up dysfunction and obstruction from Republicans . . . It was remarkable to us that Senator McConnell was able to push his caucus to be even more obstructionist.

GENE SPERLING

Everybody always talked about that first debt limit, but what was staggering was how illogical it was that the Republicans walked away from negotiations with the president in the lame duck of 2012. When they did, the president was able to get the top [marginal tax] rate up to 39.6 percent without conceding to any of the entitlement cuts that they were for and that we didn't support.

135　On April 17, 2013, Democratic senator Joe Manchin of West Virginia and Senator Pat Toomey of Pennsylvania, a Republican, cosponsored a compromise amendment that would expand background checks to cover gun shows and internet sales. The bill was initially expected to pass, until five Democrats voted against it and only four Republicans voted in favor of the measure. President Obama called it "a pretty shameful day for Washington."

JACK LEW

Something that I never understood was why, when the fiscal-cliff[136] negotiation happened in 2012-2013—I was chief of staff at the time, it was obviously after the 2012 election—there was a pretty strong mandate for the extension of the tax reduction in the high end to be rolled back. It was a moment where Republicans could have gone back to the kind of bargain that the president was open to in 2011, but they didn't. They instead, I think, made the choice to just lose and to let the tax increase go through and not have their fingerprints on it in a meaningful way. And that would have been a moment where, if they wanted to put together some of the other pieces, they could have.

AUSTAN GOOLSBEE

It was because in 2012, Obama had just won the election and he had a mandate. So they were on the defensive.

GENE SPERLING

To me, it showed their degree of dysfunction. For progressives, it meant winning by getting the top rate back to 39.6 percent without having to make any concessions we opposed on Medicare or Medicaid, but with the significant downside of allowing the sequester to stay in place.

AUSTAN GOOLSBEE

To me, the Bush administration, plus the Fed, plus Obama really did several things right. They avoided what should have been another Great Depression. It's a great achievement, but it still drives me nuts that we did not have more

---

136 A term coined by Federal Reserve Chairman Ben Bernanke to describe the alarming combination of budgetary actions that would go into effect January 1, 2013: the expiration of Bush-era tax cuts coupled with the Budget Control Act's middle-class tax increases and slashing of defense and entitlement programs. If the tax increases and spending cuts weren't prevented with a substitute agreement before December 31, 2012, the economy was expected to fall back into a recession.

conditions on the money that the banks got in the fall of 2008. The banks acted with impunity precisely because they didn't have any conditions.

TED KAUFMAN

The inspector general at [the Department of] Justice studied that period and came out with a report—this was a few years later—and found out, of the six areas that Justice was working on, the whole fraud around the financial crisis was number six. It's in the report.[137] In addition to that, I'd interviewed one of the top people in the Eastern District of New York. He was going to be a Circuit Court of Appeals judge, and while he was talking about that, I asked, "By the way, what's your number-one priority?" And he said, "My number-one priority is cybercrime." Cybercrime. Not fraud enforcement.

BARNEY FRANK

You wouldn't go criminally against the institutions. You'd go against individuals. I still thought they could have and should have done more. I didn't think they would have gotten the CEOs or people at the top who were insulated, but I think it was a mistake.

TED KAUFMAN

If you read the prior testimonies, they all said, *We're gonna do it, don't worry.* Clearly they didn't. Then Lanny [Breuer], at his [New York City Bar Association]

---

137 "The FBI Criminal Investigative Division ranked complex financial crimes as the lowest of the six ranked criminal threats within its area of responsibility, and ranked mortgage fraud as the lowest subcategory threat within the complex financial crimes category. Additionally, we found mortgage fraud to be a low priority, or not listed as a priority, for FBI field offices in the locations we visited, including Baltimore, Los Angeles, Miami, and New York." —Audit of the Department of Justice's Efforts to Address Mortgage Fraud, US Department of Justice Office of the Inspector General, Audit Division, March 2014.

speech, said [if they indicted], "Innocent employees could lose their jobs."[138] Lanny never said that to me as a rationale for not prosecuting. Then Eric Holder gave the same kind of speech[139] . . . No one had mentioned to me that maybe we shouldn't prosecute people because it may cause an economic dislocation of the employees. So you mean to say if a guy could help the economy and he shot somebody, we shouldn't put him in jail?

MARGARET RICHARDSON

You had to have a credible belief that you would have a chance of succeeding at trial. I didn't think people who were looking at the way the financial cases unfolded, who were critical of the department, gave it a fair shake. It's not like they could point to some admission made by a CEO or general counsel of a bank. It's more just how could this have happened without people knowing or without criminal conspiracies happening. "There *must* have been evidence!"

TED KAUFMAN

You could question someone's judgment, but you couldn't question someone's motivation, because you just didn't know what it was. But let me say this: there's an incredible conflict of interest in the revolving door. When you looked at the

---

138 "To be clear, the decision of whether to indict a corporation, defer prosecution, or decline altogether is not one that I, or anyone in the Criminal Division, take lightly. We are frequently on the receiving end of presentations from defense counsel, CEOs, and economists who argue that the collateral consequences of an indictment would be devastating for their client. In my conference room, over the years, I have heard sober predictions that a company or bank might fail if we indict, that innocent employees could lose their jobs, that entire industries may be affected, and even that global markets will feel the effects." —Lanny Breuer, Assistant Attorney General for the Criminal Division, US Department of Justice, September 13, 2012.

139 "It does become difficult for us to prosecute them when we are hit with indications that if you do . . . bring a criminal charge, it will have a negative impact on the national economy, perhaps even the world economy . . . It has an inhibiting influence, impact on our ability to bring resolutions that I think would be more appropriate." —US Attorney General Eric Holder's testimony before the Senate Judiciary Committee, March 6, 2013.

revolving door on not just this issue but many issues, far too often people left the government to work for the very people they were supposed to prosecute or oversee. If I wanted to go back to Wall Street and had put somebody in jail, I'd have a difficult time going back to the firm I was with or starting with a new firm.

DAVID OGDEN

That's really cynical and unfair. Anybody in those jobs was looking to be successful at them. Nobody's trying to serve the clients that they someday hope to have. To the contrary, you're serving the United States. There's an energetic effort to make those cases if you can make 'em. I'm 100 percent with Lanny there.

MARGARET RICHARDSON

It's not like a bank would hire you if you were adverse to them and you rolled over. They would say, "I don't want that guy, because he's gonna blow it when he's defending us!" The reason that some of these institutions hire people with good reputations coming out of government was because they have good reputations coming out of government. This idea that someone would have caved in order to solicit favor from a future client just fundamentally misunderstands how those kinds of relationships evolve.

TED KAUFMAN

They felt the heat. Trust me. These were really smart guys. They weren't going to prosecute anybody? Nobody's going to jail?

BARNEY FRANK

As some of my liberal friends forget, we're the ones who believe in civil liberties and due process, and a key part of due process is, you should not be subjected to criminal sanctions unless you can be reasonably certain that your behavior would lead to that. The phrase "Ignorance of the law is no excuse" meant that, if the law was there and you didn't know it, that's your problem. But if the law was so ambiguous that nobody could know with any reasonable degree of assuredness, then you didn't go to jail. You don't send people to jail for vague stuff. The other part of it was, some of the stuff wasn't illegal. Having said all that, I think, yes, they should have prosecuted more. I am frustrated as to why they didn't.

MATTHEW MILLER

A lot of things that are corrupt are not illegal. There were a lot of cases we would have loved to make—I mean, it's true these were career-making cases. People tried as hard as they could, and they couldn't bring the cases. We had all these investigations going out of [the Southern District of New York]. It was assumed that those would bear fruit and would lead to criminal cases against various Wall Street entities—just because there were so many investigations going. I had always wondered, if you could rewind the clock to '09 and go, *Look, none of these open cases that we have are gonna bear fruit*, we probably would have thrown more resources at them.

MARGARET RICHARDSON

People wanted a perp walk—the same things that people were very grateful that the Obama administration had undone in the criminal-justice system with people with more street-type offenses. That's not how it worked.

MATTHEW MILLER

One of the stories about Eric Holder's time at DOJ was that in the first term, he was quietly doing a lot of things on criminal-justice reform. There was, of course, the crack-powder bill that passed in 2010, the Fair Sentencing Act.[140]

---

140 Previously, anyone convicted of possession of crack cocaine would be sentenced to prison one year for every five grams, and anyone convicted of possession of cocaine powder would be sentenced one year for every five hundred grams.

BARBARA LEE

It got rid of [five-year] mandatory minimums [for crack-cocaine possession], brought down the [sentencing ratio] on crack cocaine. It went from 100:1 to 18:1. There were a lot of issues members of the Black Caucus worked on day and night with the White House.

DAVID OGDEN

The racial-justice element in the crack-to-powder [ratio] was a pretty compelling storyline. Why were we putting these people in jail? Why were we putting nonviolent offenders in jail for their whole lives when the cost was so enormous and the toll, in terms of our sense of justice and in our communities, was so grave? Why didn't we have a more principled policy?

VALERIE JARRETT

We thought it was important to reduce those mandatory minimum sentences and take some of the savings to help people who were incarcerated have the skills and drug treatment that they needed. Or alcohol treatment, counseling. Whatever they needed so that when they were ultimately released from prison, they will be able to return to society as productive citizens.

MATTHEW MILLER

[Holder] was doing a lot of work that set the stage for 2013 and 2014, when he pushed through major reforms in the way DOJ treated people accused of crimes and people who've been convicted of crimes after they have been released from prison.

VALERIE JARRETT

[We worked on] reforming our bail systems so that people who were incarcerated were not there simply because they were poor. Because on average, our data showed that of the eleven million people who cycled through jails on an annual basis, they stayed on an average of twenty-three days. Yet only 5 [percent] were ultimately sentenced to prison. So ask yourself, was it worth keeping someone incarcerated for twenty-three days if ultimately we were going to release them? And were they there because they were dangerous, or were they there because they couldn't afford bail?

RON DAVIS

Police Chief, City of East Palo Alto (2005–2013)
Director, Community Oriented Policing Services (COPS),
US Department of Justice (2013–2017)
Executive Director, President's Task Force on 21st Century Policing (2014–2017)

She's right. Something like 65 percent of jail spaces was pretrial detainment, and we have a system that says, *If you have money, you get out. If you don't, you don't.* For a lot of these low-level crimes, people sit in jail because they don't have the bail. And that time in jail does more damage to the person who would be more likely to not recidivate again. In that time, they lose their job. They're disconnected from their family. There are tools now to assess somebody—whether they're likely to recidivate while they're on bail—and if you can reduce that population, get people alternatives to get out, they don't keep going to prison.

VALERIE JARRETT

The question was, what was society going to do to give them a second chance? Did they have the requisite skills to hit the ground running? Did they have the support system for housing, clothing, allowance, and job opportunities? We encouraged the private sector to hire people who had been incarcerated and not ask, on their applications, whether they had been incarcerated. The president signed an executive order for federal contractors to abide by "the ban on the box."[141]

---

141 In November 2015, President Obama ordered federal agencies to delay inquiries about job applicants' criminal history until later in the hiring process, while encouraging Congress to take up legislation to do the same for federal contractors, to "prevent candidates from being eliminated before they have a chance to demonstrate their qualifications."

HEATHER FOSTER

Two things happened that, to me, in 2013, really got President Obama thinking. A young woman named Hadiya Pendleton was killed a week after performing at the inauguration. She lived in Hyde Park, the same neighborhood the president [had] lived in, and was gunned down coming home from school . . . And in July, when you saw that George Zimmerman had been acquitted, people kind of lost their minds. I was here in DC. It was the same week as Delta Sigma Theta Incorporated, the largest African American female sorority out here, [was] having this centennial. And so I remember having dinner with friends in a restaurant, and the minute the verdict came across the television, people were screaming.

CODY KEENAN

He did have to acknowledge the very real anger out there about this. I didn't think it was anger that was limited to the black community, but we always had to be careful to do it in a way, and I'm not saying *he* knew he always had to be careful. I'm saying, just because the way the media environment worked, we would always have to be careful when talking about that. So you didn't alienate people along racial lines.

HEATHER FOSTER

That was when he first started talking about [how] we gotta do more things for boys and men of color, because they're faced with these ridiculous challenges that we still hadn't addressed in our society.

ROY AUSTIN JR.

In the Civil Rights Division we wrote a statement of interest in the *Floyd* case.[142] This was the New York City stop-and-frisk class-action lawsuit. We weighed in because the evidence was so stark that the vast majority of these searches had resulted in nothing—no contraband, no arrest. And then we sat there and watched when the New York City Police Department reduced the number of people [they were] stopping and frisking, violent crime in New York went *down*. So you didn't have to do this "broken windows" nonsense—there was another way that did not harm individuals and families primarily from minority and low-income communities.

RON DAVIS

Here's where the confusion set in. The broken-windows theory simply said that you fix things that were small before they led to bigger issues; that the small things led to bigger things, and if you didn't fix the broken windows, it would basically mean the community was apathetic. That many more broken windows would follow. Now, the problem had been that individual agencies started attaching zero tolerance to that theory. In other words, "broken windows" could work if you're saying, *Fix the small things*, which meant you fixed the window. You identified what the conditions were that caused a break-in and provided alternatives so that kids didn't break windows—education and mentoring programs, opportunities that the president always was fighting for. If it turned out that if you instead fought them or took them to jail for jaywalking and spitting on the sidewalk, then the collateral damage of that policy was devastating to communities, especially communities of color.

---

142 "If there is any identified constitutional violation within NYPD's stop-and-frisk practices, the Court's broad power to fashion injunctive relief is not at odds with robust efforts to protect the public. To the contrary, where there exists a systemic pattern of police misconduct, the entry of injunctive relief to correct that conduct inures to the benefit of safe and effective policing, not to its detriment. The City has argued that implementing Plaintiffs' requested relief will negatively impact NYPD's capacity to combat crime. In the experience of the United States, however, reform through a court-ordered process improves public confidence, makes officers' jobs safer, and increases the ability of the department to fight crime."

ROY AUSTIN JR.

This was, in many ways, the administration leaning in and saying, *This is a problem.* People who have never been stopped by the police don't get it. They think, *Oh, the police stop you. You didn't have anything on you. Your life is fine.* But in certain communities, people could hardly walk down the street without being accused of being a criminal or being stopped and searched. The psychological impact of that, even when you have nothing on you, is a significant burden to carry with you under this cloud of constant suspicion. People just didn't get that, and they didn't get it that a lot of these communities felt that it was because they were black or because they were Latino that this was happening to them.

RON DAVIS

As an enforcement strategy, it's terrible. It caused significant damage. It basically resulted in mass arrests, disparate treatment, and this was why you heard all the concern.

ROY AUSTIN JR.

Well, you attack the immigrant community, you attack poor people, and you attack black and brown individuals, they're not going to go to the local police department and say, "I know who did that." They don't trust the system, and without a community to trust the system, you couldn't fight the violent crime. You needed those people to talk to law enforcement, and if they didn't trust law enforcement, they're not going to answer their doors.

VALERIE JARRETT

Keeping young people out of the system to begin with has to do with everything from reducing the number of suspensions and expulsions to improving the level of education to ensuring we have after-school and summer-job programs.

RON DAVIS

Once a kid is suspended and/or arrested for the first time, then the likelihood of being rearrested grows exponentially. Imagine if you catch that kid with a spray can getting ready to mark that train or jump the turnstile, and you had a program for him—something to [fill] the idle time that he or she may have, something to even address the issues they may be having at home which is causing them to act out. Imagine those services and you have a likelihood that the kid will go in a different direction, never being entered into the criminal-justice system.

VALERIE JARRETT

We made a fair amount of progress, I think. The disappointment was really not being able to get meaningful legislation through that would give judges what they wanted, which was more discretion. Eric Holder directed prosecutors to use their discretion, but we wanted to give the judges the discretion as well.

CHRISTOPHER KANG

There's this myth that's been built up that the president and the White House didn't care about judicial nominations early on. In particular, in people's minds they have this May 2001 press conference that President Bush did with a number of his appellate nominees. He brought them [into the East Room] and did a big speech on judges and the importance of them. I don't think that those comparisons are fair, and I don't think that they really reflect where the president's priorities were, when you take into consideration the fact that he *did* have two Supreme Court vacancies to fill in his first two years.

BARBARA BOXER

It was really wonderful that he chose two women.[143] You know, he could have said, "I'm doing one." There's a lot of tokenism in the world today, and I thought that was a strong statement.

BILL DAUSTER

We had no problems with Sotomayor and Kagan. They were very good appointments, but that wasn't where the filibustering occurred. It was occurring in places like the DC Circuit [of Appeals], where Republicans just said, *There are enough judges there*, even though there were several vacancies. That is to say, they were going to try and maintain a political balance that was in the DC Circuit. That was early in the ramping up of obstruction.

CHRISTOPHER KANG

As early as 2009 and 2010, Republicans started to vote against and block lower-court, even district-court judges. They would require a cloture vote on noncontroversial circuit-court nominees, the idea being that *We're going to make the other side burn as much time as possible so they can't achieve anything legislatively.*

---

143 On May 26, 2009, President Obama nominated Sonia Sotomayor to the Supreme Court to replace Justice David Souter, a George H. W. Bush pick who had announced his retirement. Sotomayor, confirmed by the Senate three months later on a 68–31 vote, had served as a district judge for New York; President Clinton nominated her to the Second Circuit Court of Appeals in 1997.

On May 10, 2010, one month after Justice John Paul Stevens, a Gerald R. Ford nominee, announced his retirement, Obama nominated Solicitor General Elena Kagan to the bench. Kagan taught constitutional law at Harvard and had served in the Clinton administration. She was the first female SG for the Department of Justice. The Senate confirmed her nomination on a 63–37 vote on August 5, 2010.

SAXBY CHAMBLISS

R-Georgia, Eighth District, US House of Representatives (1995–2003)
R-Georgia, US Senate (2003–2015)

It was pretty obvious early on that one of the goals of the Obama administration was to put as many liberal judges as they could, particularly on circuit courts, and it's pretty obvious that, on the other side, McConnell wanted to make sure that didn't happen. So that's where the stalemate, the slowing down on the process, came from.

BILL DAUSTER

McConnell was slow-walking the confirmation process. He would dribble out district-court judges. Things that we used to do by unanimous consent, they'd have to force us to have roll-call votes on. And they caused us to have to file cloture on more district judges. Ninety percent of the district judges that had ever had cloture petitions were during McConnell's time.

CHRISTOPHER KANG

It's a little bit frustrating, the idea that he didn't care as much or that the numbers didn't show, because he didn't have as many confirmations or nominations as President Bush did early on . . . There probably was some sense of priorities about passing another piece of legislation over allowing Republicans to burn floor time. So at some point, there was a bit of give-and-take, but there's no question that in the second term, there's more that you could see visibly. In part that was because, having lost the House in 2011, there wasn't as much legislating being done. You could focus more on the Senate, where you didn't need the House to confirm anybody. So I think there was just more emphasis placed on confirmations generally, such that you had the most judges confirmed in that 113th Congress than you had had in decades.[144]

144 January 3, 2013 to January 3, 2015.

SAXBY CHAMBLISS

Mitch was a good minority leader, and he knew how to handle the process. He was successful in slowing it down, and that was one of the major reasons why Harry Reid changed the rules on us.[145] Once he changed that rule, then obviously you only had to have 51 votes. So the process was speeded up a little bit in the president's [second] term . . . I'd never seen anything like that done before. There had been conversation about it. Back during the Bush years, when we had to have sixty votes, we were in control and the Democrats were slow-walking President Bush's nominees. There was some conversation about changing the rule, but ultimately we didn't do it. The one really good thing that the Senate had always adhered to was the minority had certain rights. Those rights were guaranteed by the sixty-vote requirement. Once you eliminated that, you became more like the House. The changing of that rule, even though our Democratic friends voted for it, some of 'em were not happy about it.

CHRISTOPHER KANG

The judiciary is often the longest-lasting part of a president's legacy. I don't know, with all that President Obama accomplished, that that will necessarily be true for him, but oftentimes when people think about that, they think about the Supreme Court, and one reason there's a bit of a sour taste in people's mouths with respect to the judges was just how far Senate Republicans went to obstruct the nomination of Chief Judge Merrick Garland to the Supreme Court, to not even give him a hearing.

BRIAN DEESE

Not only would they not hold a hearing or a vote, but they wouldn't even meet with the guy.

145　In November 2013, Senate Majority Leader Reid updated parliamentary procedure so that the confirmation of federal judges and executive-office appointees no longer required the standard sixty-vote supermajority, but only a fifty-one-vote simple majority.

CHRISTOPHER KANG

But I also think about the district-court and the circuit-court judges . . . In terms of accomplishments, President Obama having four judges confirmed to the DC Circuit [of Appeals] was probably one of the biggest and most lasting that he will have had in terms of that court often being viewed as the second-highest court in the land. But then, I also think more broadly about the president's emphasis and success on trying to increase the diversity of the courts and making sure that the judiciary, as a democratic institution, really reflected the people that it served.

BILL DAUSTER

There is a story of accomplishment to tell there about African American, LGBT, women—people on the benches—and they can be proud of that accomplishment. People bring their experience to the court.

CHRISTOPHER KANG

The hope was that over time, you set these benchmarks for other presidents to meet. Having a more diverse judiciary will help instill greater public confidence in the institution, and also the role-modeling effect is incredibly important. There had only been one openly gay judge confirmed in history before President [Obama's appointments]. He appointed another [eleven]. Same with Asian Americans—there had only been eight to the bench serving when he took office. There are three times as many now. You start looking at those places where he made a difference, and people start thinking of themselves as becoming federal judges.

BEN LABOLT

Inclusivity and equality were some of the key themes that the Obama administration will be recognized for, and that's down at every level. Those were the small things, like appointing openly gay judges and ambassadors. They seem small individually, but they matter a lot collectively.

CHRISTOPHER KANG

I was always struck by the fact that the first federal judge to strike down a state constitution's ban on same-sex marriage was a district-court judge appointed by President Obama in Utah. That's not to say that another judge wouldn't have come to the same conclusion, but the fact of the matter was that Judge Robert Shelby was the first. That showed just how much influence and impact even a district-court judge could have on a conversation, on the direction of a law and on, really, the future of our country. That's an incredibly important part of the president's legacy that we won't really be able to measure for decades out but, looking back, will be just as important as all of the legislative accomplishments he had, or foreign-policy accomplishments he had, or regulations that he did.

ARNE DUNCAN

People understood what he stood for. I don't think it was an accident that you had such a cohesive cabinet. That you didn't have scandals and drama that you'd have in other places.

BRANDON HURLBUT

You look at all these different presidencies and they usually have some sort of scandal, and it didn't happen!

TREVOR TIMM

Executive Director, Freedom of the Press Foundation (2012–)

How do you define "scandal"? Certainly Barack Obama and the Obama family were role models in a personal capacity to millions of Americans, and rightly so. There were certainly no personal scandals. There were no corruption scandals, and no one accused Barack Obama of doing what, for example, Donald Trump does every day. He was looked at as a highly moral person and they were a highly moral family, at least on the personal side. But certainly the NSA revelation should constitute a major scandal. Here we had a constitutional-law professor who campaigned against the excesses of the NSA during the Bush administration[146]—literally talking about warrantless wiretapping, about how he would protect whistle-blowers who would come forward with information and be the most transparent administration ever—yet, from the start, he not only basically signed off on surveillance that had been occurring during the Bush years, but essentially doubled down on it.

TERRY SZUPLAT

So when I hear the word *scandal*, I always take that to mean, and I think most Americans understand that to mean, the misconduct or misbehavior of government officials. So Iran-Contra was a scandal because it was about the behavior and choices of the Reagan administration. Lewinsky was a scandal because it was about the personal misconduct and behavior of the president. So, by that definition, it's absolutely correct to say that the Obama White House was indeed scandal-free. Snowden, that was not a scandal in that sense.

TREVOR TIMM

Part of our mission was to encourage more whistle-blowers to come forward and advocate for journalists to be more aggressive on reporting on secret government programs, especially surveillance. You know, basically our wildest dreams came true when the most well-known whistle-blower of our generation came to two of our board members directly, and, June 6, all of a sudden you had a story in the *Guardian* where we found out that the NSA had been collecting every single American's phone-call records for years . . . and for the next five days there was

---

146 "I will provide our intelligence and law-enforcement agencies with the tools they need to track and take out the terrorists without undermining our Constitution and our freedom. That means no more illegal wiretapping of American citizens. No more national-security letters to spy on citizens who are not suspected of a crime. No more tracking citizens who do nothing more than protest a misguided war. No more ignoring the law when it is inconvenient. That is not who we are. And it is not what is necessary to defeat the terrorists. The FISA court works. The separation of powers works. Our Constitution works. We will again set an example for the world that the law is not subject to the whims of stubborn rulers, and that justice is not arbitrary." —Senator Obama, the Woodrow Wilson International Center for Scholars, Washington, DC, August 1, 2007.

a giant scoop each day, to the point where we were sitting in meetings figuring out how to react to the day-before scoop and the next one that would come after that.

SAXBY CHAMBLISS

I'd been in the intel world my last two years in the House, and all twelve years in the Senate I was on the Intel Committee. So by the time the Snowden event occurred, I was obviously well versed in the ways of the day-to-day practices of the seventeen intelligence agencies, but in this case particularly, what the NSA did relative to gathering information—how they did it, what they used it for, and all of those critical issues that they were required to deal with from a gathering standpoint—I knew that the NSA had limitations on what they could gather relative to US citizens. I knew that the people at NSA were professional. They were aware of sensitivities and the law relative to gathering information on US citizens.

TERRY SZUPLAT

Snowden was an individual in the bureaucracy choosing to leak massive amounts of classified information, and he wasn't the first leaker. He wasn't the last leaker. He was not an Obama-administration official. He was not an Obama-administration appointee. From my understanding, he would have done that no matter who the president was. And so I don't think that the fact that the disclosures occurred was "an Obama scandal." I'd be happy to have that discussion-debate with anybody, but scandals, the way we understand them, are about the misconduct and misbehavior of administration officials, and Snowden was not such a person.

TREVOR TIMM

Now, it wasn't personally Barack Obama who was doing all of this, but I certainly thought this was a scandal of the highest order that involved multiple intelligence agencies, the FBI, the Department of Justice. All of this was done in complete secrecy. The major program that everyone remembers—the one that I mentioned, about the NSA collecting all of our telephone records—was not actually written into law. They basically took a provision of the Patriot Act and worked it beyond recognition to the point where they were doing this when none of the American people knew about it, a lot of Congress members didn't know about it, and using a public law in which they created a radical interpretation which they kept completely secret.

SAXBY CHAMBLISS

So when all of this broke, some folks on our side—Senator [Rand] Paul wasn't maybe as outspoken as some on the [Democratic] side—but members of the Senate had a lot of things to say about what was going on who, frankly, didn't know what they were talking about. They didn't know that the folks at NSA *knew* that they were required to get a warrant. There were just these broad statements made, including by Snowden, that gave the impression to the American public and folks all around the world that NSA was listening in on phone conversations of average ordinary Americans, and that just simply was not the case.

TREVOR TIMM

The NSA surveillance revelations were certainly a black mark on the Obama administration, but then, separately, there was also this crackdown on whistle-blowers and leakers, which happened around the same time, actually, just before the Snowden revelations, where the Obama Justice Department started prosecuting more sources for journalists than all other administrations combined. They got the emails of Fox News reporter James Rosen and were engaged in leak prosecutions like none you [had] ever seen. They secretly got the records of twenty AP phone lines that affected over a hundred AP journalists.

MATTHEW MILLER

That was a huge mistake by the department. The way they handled that, it rightly blew up in their faces. And it partly blew up in their faces because it was a culmination of things. All of the cases that had been brought against leakers, I think, were conflated. You could make a strong argument that people who leaked classified information [and] didn't do it for a noble purpose—they did it not because they're trying to expose wrongdoing, but because either they wanted to ingratiate themselves with a reporter or they wanted to settle a score against an agency that they thought had done them wrong. [They] leaked information that served no whistle-blowing purpose. You could make a good case those people ought to be prosecuted. But all of those cases got wrapped together, and the AP case blew up because it wasn't just in isolation.

TREVOR TIMM

Everybody kind of forgets about [the AP case] because it was right before the Snowden revelations, but there was a huge backlash around this—not just from First Amendment scholars, but dozens of media organizations really worried that their entire profession was being undermined and threatened. Eric Holder, the attorney general, would later say that some of those incidents were some of his biggest regrets, but it doesn't mean that the damage wasn't already done. And if you took those events coupled with the Snowden revelations, you got a fairly damning picture of how the Obama administration expanded entrenched surveillance capabilities that could be very corrosive to a democracy.

TERRY SZUPLAT

That NSA program predated Obama, and my understanding of it was, not only did it predate Obama, but that when it came to the attention of the president and his most senior advisors, they worked diligently to put in limits to that program. So, again, this was one of the things where the programs that Snowden leaked and disclosed, I don't think those were "Obama programs." They were programs that had been conducted prior to Obama and under Obama, but I think the Obama administration brought more structure and rigor and standards and transparency to it.

SAXBY CHAMBLISS

He knew, like me, what the NSA was doing, and he was put in the same difficult box that myself and other members on the Senate Intelligence Committee were.

We knew what happened but couldn't give all the details of it. It's classified, yet we had to respond to and deal with colleagues and a media that thought all these horrible things were being done when, in fact, they really weren't being done.

TYLER MORAN

The White House effort [for immigration reform in 2013] was definitely a stealth operation . . . Behind the scenes, we gave a ton of bipartisan briefings. In the Senate, you had this Gang of Eight with Republicans who really believed they needed to reach out to Latinos and that they really had to push for [legislation].[147]

CECILIA MUÑOZ

In the administration, we had long since drafted a bill. We had a bill drafted in 2010. So we took that bill back out, revised it, [and] essentially fed pieces of that bill to the Gang of Eight in order to speed up the process. The 2013 bill was big and complex, obviously, and it was important to the president that we contribute in whatever way that was most useful . . . The Gang of Eight dynamic was such that it was important to be behind the scenes, so that's what we did.

TYLER MORAN

Lots of other Republicans were supportive, but they just felt nervous about any type of backlash—particularly if you looked at the composition of Republicans that ultimately came forward and voted for the bill, they didn't until there was this Corker-Hoeven Amendment, which basically put a shitload of resources on the southern border. So much so that Border Patrol could hold hands or something.[148] It was this unnecessary amount of resources, but it brought on

---

147 Michael Bennet (D-Colorado), Dick Durbin (D-Illinois), Jeff Flake (R-Arizona), Lindsey Graham (R-South Carolina), John McCain (R-Arizona), Bob Menendez (D-New Jersey), Marco Rubio (R-Florida), Chuck Schumer (D-New York).

148 The Border Security, Economic Opportunity, and Immigration Modernization Act of 2013, a.k.a. S.744, proposed a path to citizenship for millions of undocumented immigrants in exchange for funding line items such as posting US Border Patrol agents "every 1,000 feet along the southern border," an electronic exit-tracking system, and approximately seven hundred miles of fencing.

a ton more votes, and, if you think about the Senate, the fact that there were sixty-eight votes was insane. That doesn't happen on a huge, *huge, huge* piece of legislation . . . but there was also some naïveté about momentum that would be created for the House to then move.

BARBARA BOXER

We had a great bill, and that bill got so many votes. The comprehensive immigration reform was so good for the economy. It was fair to everybody, and it died because John Boehner would not bring it up.

TYLER MORAN

Boehner's a true believer on immigration, but, you know, it went from the Republican Study Committee to the Freedom Caucus, and . . . I can't speak for him, but I think he just had to make strategic decisions about rocking the boat. He'd already rolled them on the debt limit. I guess you had to pick and choose when to do that.

LUIS GUTIÉRREZ

We passed it in the Senate. We never got it done in the House. Then I went back to Obama because Janet Murguía, president of the National Council of La Raza, called him "deporter in chief," and that really stung Obama.

TYLER MORAN

The advocates started getting really restless. Instead of turning on the House as their focus for accountability, they turned on the White House . . . You know, trying to push for immigration reform, there was a feeling that [the White House] needed to show the American public that you believed in enforcement, and [that we weren't pushing for] open borders. But in hindsight, I was like, *What did we get for that?* We deported more people than ever before. All these families separated, and Republicans didn't give him one ounce of credit. There may as well have been open borders for five years.

2013–2014

Some foreign-policy critics pointed to Iraq's dilapidation as a direct result of the withdrawal of US military forces, a breakdown they claimed allowed al-Qaeda to resurface, and, in turn, ISIS to occupy various territories within the war-torn country. The State Department's Jonathan Finer considered this a common misconception. "A cataclysmic civil war erupted right next door in a country with a very fluid border region," he said. "It created both a climate that was conducive to the return of extremists and foreign fighters."

Stateside, the national-security community did not foresee the Syrian civil war as the last pair of American boots crossed the border out of Iraq and into Kuwait. Had Obama and al-Maliki signed a status-of-forces agreement, Finer explained, the intended minimal troop levels would not have provided enough of a presence to deter the neighboring conflict between the Syrian government and several rebel factions. And it wouldn't have prevented Syria's president of thirteen years, Bashar al-Assad, from attacking his own people with sarin gas.

At an August 24, 2013, intelligence meeting, President Obama had been told that al-Assad was responsible for the deaths of at least 1,429 innocent civilians three days prior in Ghouta, a suburb outside of Damascus; UN inspectors continued their investigation during a cease-fire while the White House readied strategies for a military strike, without the approval of Congress.

Four US Navy destroyers, stocked with hundreds of Tomahawk Land Attack Missiles, awaited orders in the eastern Mediterranean Sea from their commander in chief, who, some believed, might very well be pushing the limits of the president's war powers—an argument that was not dissimilar to candidate Obama's own criticisms of President Bush years prior. Speaker Boehner hinted a threat of impeachment. "It is essential you address on what basis any use of force would be legally justified," the Speaker wrote in an August 28 memo to the White House, "and how the justification comports with the exclusive authority of Congressional authorization under Article I of the Constitution." The House of Representatives, still in summer recess, would not return to Capitol Hill to deliberate on such matters until September, but the United States wasn't the only democracy considering strikes against the al-Assad regime.

The following day, British Parliament voted against military action, and Prime Minister David Cameron reassured the House of Commons that "the government will act accordingly." The UK's decision, likely combined with an NBC News poll that showed 80 percent of Americans wanting the president to seek congressional approval for war, must have given pause. On Friday, Obama spent forty-five minutes walking the South Lawn with Denis McDonough, a longtime national-security confidant who was seven months into his position as White House chief of staff. The contents of their discussion were not divulged to the public; it was only later that evening that the two would reconvene with advisors in the Oval. "I have a pretty big idea I want to test with you guys," Obama said.

PETE SOUZA

I photographed him walking along the south grounds. I photographed him with Rahm. I photographed him with Denis, and I don't remember exactly why I didn't photograph that particular walk, because I usually would. It may have been because it was already dark, but I was there when they came back into the Oval [on August 30] and he called in his national-security [team]. It was late, definitely after six thirty, which was usually about the time he went home. But I remember him walking in. I could tell by the look on his face that something was up.

Clockwise from Obama: White House Deputy Chief of Staff Rob Nabors; National Security Advisor Susan Rice; Deputy National Security Advisor Tony Blinken; Deputy White House Counsel Brian Egan; NSC Chief of Staff Brian McKeon; Communications Director Dan Pfeiffer; White House Chief of Staff Denis McDonough (standing); Deputy National Security Advisor Ben Rhodes. Pete Souza, White House

PETE SOUZA

The president had basically laid out what he and Denis had just talked about on their walk, that he was now gonna turn to Congress to authorize strikes.

DAN SHAPIRO

It became pretty apparent, first with the vote in the British Parliament and then as they began to whip the vote in Congress, that there was not much of an appetite for US military engagement. Polling also showed, widely, that there was not much support among the American people. So essentially, if you were to do the military strike, you'd be doing it without the political support one ideally wanted and needed, especially if it's going to be sustainable for military action, opening the possibility of a deeper and longer military involvement, as these things would often lead to. That's when he made the decision that there was a better option.

DENNIS ROSS
Senior Director for the Central Region, National Security
Council, White House (2009–2011)

I left the administration at the end of 2011. I was running a back channel between the Israelis and the Palestinians at that time . . . So my view on [the decision to not attack Assad] would be from the outside, not from the inside. I was up on the Hill, though, after the president made his decision, and what I heard mostly from Democrats was that they regretted that the president didn't act—that by throwing the ball to them, this was a way of not acting, and, had he acted, he would have actually had support. That came from some Senate Democrats.

BARBARA LEE

I remember organizing part of the opposition to not go in because, as awful as the use of chemical weapons by Assad was, the use of force would have made things worse . . . That's why I voted against the 2001 AUMF. I knew then, like I know now, that we'd set the stage for an endless war.

LUIS GUTIÉRREZ

In Syria, my issue was a little bit of a contradiction. He said there would be a red line. It was clear that this was a people's uprising, that this was clearly a continuation of the Arab Spring with broad-base support. We should have helped a lot more, a lot quicker to help those forces once we saw them using chemical weapons.

ROB ANDREWS

The articulation of the red line came as sort of an aside in a [2012] press conference the president gave.[149] It was not a formal declaration of policy made in a carefully calibrated speech or through the UN. I'm not saying, by the way, that every president's words aren't meaningful all the time. They are, but I suspect that's something they'd want to take back. The way that was formulated, and when, the problem then became *Assad clearly crossed the red line and nothing happened.*

JONATHAN FINER

Secretary Kerry was asked a question in London on September 9: *Is there anything that the Assad regime could do that would make you guys decide not to take military action?* This was while military action was being debated in Congress, because the president said he wanted them to authorize any use of force, and Secretary Kerry said, if they agreed to give up "[every single bit of his] chemical weapons" in the next week, that might be something we would consider.

---

149 "I have, at this point, not ordered military engagement in the situation, but the point that you made about chemical and biological weapons is critical. That's an issue that doesn't just concern Syria; it concerns our close allies in the region, including Israel. It concerns us. We cannot have a situation where chemical or biological weapons are falling into the hands of the wrong people.

"We have been very clear to the Assad regime, but also to other players on the ground, that a red line for us is we start seeing a whole bunch of chemical weapons moving around or being utilized. That would change my calculus. That would change my equation." —President Obama in the James S. Brady Press Briefing Room, August 20, 2012.

DAN SHAPIRO

That created a diplomatic opportunity.

JONATHAN FINER

Within a few hours, Secretary Kerry was on the flight home from London to Washington and the Russian foreign minister called—"Saw your comment, let's give this a try"—and, within forty-eight hours, he got back on a plane to Geneva, where we ended up negotiating this deal to remove the weapons. Secretary Kerry, and I thought the president would say the same, knew that there was a chance that this would appeal to the Russians, because the Russians had previously indicated that this might be something we could work on together.

DENNIS ROSS

It's also clear, from an Israeli standpoint, they felt that getting the removal was a significant accomplishment. The other side of it was, having articulated a red line and then not acting on it sent a message in the region, throughout the world, that you really couldn't count on American commitments.

DAN SHAPIRO

Israeli officials, military planners, and security professionals understood that we got a better result on chemical weapons than we would have had if we had gone ahead with the strikes. But they worried about the perception among others in the region. At a popular level, even among the Israeli public, you would hear this attitude. *Sure, maybe he got rid of the chemical weapons, but now will anybody ever believe he'll use force?* You know, *Will the Iranians ever believe it? Will other enemies?*

LEON PANETTA

I have to say, in the first four years, I thought the president was much more willing to engage in confronting terrorism, confronting al-Qaeda, dealing with the threats both in Iran and Afghanistan, as well as elsewhere. I had a sense that he knew that the United States had to provide leadership in dealing with those issues. I think his hope was that, ultimately, because of those efforts, we could withdraw not only from Iraq but ultimately from Afghanistan, and that we would not have to be tied down to another Middle East conflict. That was what I believed was his deepest hope. The problem was, the world did not cooperate. As always, what presidents find is that they have to respond to the world as it is, not as they would like it to be.

DAN SHAPIRO

It may be true that a decision not to be more present on the ground and not to make more of a commitment to help shape the end game was a factor in the chaos that followed. But one had to consider the counter scenario—which was the one [Obama] was intent on trying to avoid—that we would become an active participant in another unwinnable ground war, grinding on and on with us taking more losses, more responsibility, and more heat throughout the region.

JONATHAN FINER

It's important to focus on the outcome. What was being contemplated, had diplomacy not intervened, was a pretty limited military strike that by everybody's account would not have in any way destroyed Syria's chemical weapons. What diplomacy accomplished was the removal of 1,300 tons—actually, probably slightly more than 1,300 tons—of some of the most heinous weapons that existed anywhere on the planet.[150] We knew the risk, at the time, that Syria was not going to declare its entire supply but that it had declared the vast majority of it. That we were going to need to remain vigilant to be on the lookout for indications that they had kept some of this stuff.

---

150 Lethal at low concentrations, the nerve agent sarin gas typically causes death one to ten minutes after initial exposure, due to the inability to control the muscles related to breathing. Those that do not die typically have permanent neurological damage. Sarin was developed in Germany in 1938 by a group of scientists looking to create stronger pesticides. Its production and stockpiling were banned by the United Nations in 1993.

DAN SHAPIRO

In this part of the world, if you pull back your hand to throw a punch and then put your hand down without throwing a punch, the assumption is you're afraid to throw the punch and never will. It doesn't matter that you got a better result through a diplomatic alternative. We made pretty clear in the weeks and months that followed that the Iranians should take no comfort from this, and no conclusion should appropriately be drawn that, if necessary, [Obama] would not use military force in Iran to stop the nuclear program. He would have used it, had that been the only way to prevent an Iranian nuclear weapon. I was actually quite certain of that, having heard him discuss it many times. It may be the case that there were people in the region who did not believe that.

RICHARD NEPHEW

Director, National Security Council, White House (2011–2013)
Principal Deputy Coordinator for Sanctions Policy, US Department of State (2013–2015)

You gotta remember how this all was working on the Iranian side. [President Hassan] Rouhani had just been inaugurated in early August. I was part of the secret-talks team, and we met with the Iranians in Muscat the very last few days of August. Then we had an agreement, provisionally, that we were going to try and set up a P5+1 meeting.[151] We were basically saying, *We need to work with our partners. You need to hear from them, but we should also work out a little bit whether or not there's an agreement here before we get too far into that process.* You know, to avoid wasting time. We met with them, I wanna say the Thursday in New York before UNGA[152] started, and then a couple times during the weekend. And we were back and forth on the train to New York because it was convenient and easy to do that.

---

151 The five permanent members of the UN Security Council (United States, United Kingdom, France, China, and Russia), plus Germany.

152 Sixty-eighth session of the General Assembly of the United Nations, September 24–October 1, 2013.

WENDY SHERMAN

Under Secretary of State for Political Affairs, US Department of State (2011–2015)
Acting Deputy Secretary of State, US Department of State (2014–2015)

Quiet discussions went on before Rouhani's election and inauguration but did not really get much traction. When Rouhani was elected, President Obama believed there might be more of an opening, and had Deputy Secretary Bill Burns and Jake Sullivan and their small team continue talks in Muscat. The change that took place, besides Rouhani's election—that was noted not only in the secret channel but in the P5+1 negotiations. When Ahmadinejad was president and Saeed Jalili[153] ran the negotiations, everything was a set piece. The Iranians spoke in Farsi. The rest of us spoke in English. We traipsed around the world and didn't get much of anywhere. When Javad Zarif took over and became foreign minister, all of the negotiations were in English. There was clearly a shift in wanting to try to accomplish something. Rouhani had made that part of his election campaign.

DENNIS ROSS

After the Rouhani election, the talks got going in earnest and then led to the Joint Plan of Action, which was the interim agreement, as opposed to the Joint Comprehensive Plan of Action, which became the deal that was finalized. So there was an interim deal that was finalized at the end of November of 2013, and then it took until mid-July of 2015 to do the larger deal.

RICHARD NEPHEW

We entered those conversations with an extreme sense of realism. We weren't fooling ourselves in thinking that, you know, the outcome of walking away from the deal was good. It wasn't. Now, I was convinced that Obama would have walked away if he hadn't gotten something that was acceptable. But I was quite convinced that the Iranians would make the concessions we needed them

---

153 Secretary of the Supreme National Security Council, October 2007 to September 2013.

to make and that we would be able to package a sanctions release such that they could walk along with it. But I never really lost sight of the fact that, for the Iranians, this was an existential problem. I'm not saying they were on the verge of economic collapse within a day, but that we had established that our resolve in stopping them was pretty high. And they had to deal with that.

WENDY SHERMAN

President Obama gave Bill Burns and Jake Sullivan permission to float the possibility of a very limited civil, peaceful enrichment program if there was a quite severe monitoring and verification. That opened the door to a negotiation on an interim agreement where Iran froze and even rolled back parts of its program in return for some limited [economic] sanctions relief, in hopes that, in over six months, bringing this draft interim deal into the P5+1 process, we would be able to complete a final agreement.

DENNIS ROSS

One of the things that emerged during those talks was the Iranian side convinced our side that they were for real. There was a debate within the administration whether to take this interim step because, in effect, what we were doing was conceding the idea that they would have uranium enrichment.[154] We did it by saying *Here's this agreement that will effectively freeze the [nuclear] program that the Iranians have, will give us greater access to monitor what they're doing, and that the 20 percent enriched material that they have will rock back to basically zero.* They'd either convert it, or ship it out. And the debate was, *Okay, the biggest card we have to play is that in the end, they'll be able to enrich.* Now, the right to enrich wasn't acknowledged at this point, but by saying you're going to negotiate the limits of enrichment, you're conceding that they'd be allowed to enrich. So there was a concern that once you'd concede that, you had given up your greatest leverage.

---

154   Enriched uranium is uranium in which the percentage of the isotope uranium-235 has been increased beyond that found in nature, wherein uranium 235 represents 0.7204 percent of the total element's mass. Enriched uranium, capable of sustaining a nuclear-fission chain reaction, is a necessary component of both nuclear-power generation and nuclear weaponry.

RICHARD NEPHEW

Remember what our objective was then. Our objective was to get our initial Joint Plan of Action. That was the whole focus, something to get us started. And we didn't really bring in anybody else until after we had worked through a lot of—not all of, but a lot of the issues with the Iranians. And then, in early November, we presented to our [P5+1] partners the text that we had been working on with the Iranians. That wasn't finished, but we had made some progress, and so it had a lot of the blanks filled in, for lack of a better word.

WENDY SHERMAN

Iran always believed no deal was possible without a deal with the United States. Our partners understood that. They didn't always like it, but they understood it. That secret bilateral channel allowed us to get traction. Then, that draft interim agreement, with a handful of brackets still having to be resolved, came into the formal P5+1 process . . . We formally met in Geneva,[155] and Secretary Kerry joined, along with the other foreign ministers. This was the meeting where most publicly the French said it wasn't good enough. There were other concerns that ministers had. Secretary Kerry wanted to make sure that everybody was on board and comfortable with the Joint Plan of Action. So everybody went home for two weeks for further consultation, then came back to Geneva and got to a Joint Plan of Action.[156]

DENNIS ROSS

I think the administration was surprised by the Israeli opposition to it, because the administration succeeded in stopping the clock, and they got the rollback on the 20 percent. This was basically right on the threshold of highly enriched uranium, as opposed to low-enriched uranium. And so the idea that you were freezing what the Iranians would have *and* rolling back to 20 percent, I think they were under the presumption that the Israelis would have been supportive.

---

155 November 7-10, 2013.
156 November 24, 2013.

But there was also not the kind of briefing that the Israelis expected. They were blindsided when Kerry came to see Netanyahu on [November 6, 2013], and I know this well because I happened to be in Israel at the time.

RICHARD NEPHEW

They were upset. They may have known about it, so their sense of surprise in their being upset may have been a little bit feigned, but they were upset.

DENNIS ROSS

You ended up having a classic example of diplomacy, where surprises rarely work well unless they're far reaching and have changed the geopolitical circumstances. Fundamentally, most surprises in diplomacy don't go down well with the ones who are actually surprised, and so the Israelis didn't like this agreement at all. Netanyahu called it a "historic mistake."[157]

RICHARD NEPHEW

The longer comprehensive deal, we would start negotiating effectively in January. The way I had approached this was, after we had clearly established in the initial Muscat rounds that they wanted a deal, I thought that because we were serious about it and because they were serious about it, we would be able to work out some kind of framework.

---

157 At his weekly Sunday cabinet meeting, Netanyahu expressed opposition to the Joint Plan of Action. "What was achieved last night [in Geneva] is not a historic agreement, but a historic mistake," he said. "For years the international community has demanded that Iran cease all uranium enrichment. Now, for the first time, the international community has formally consented that Iran continue its enrichment of uranium . . . Israel is not bound by this agreement. We cannot and will not allow a regime that calls for the destruction of Israel to obtain the means to achieve this goal."

WENDY SHERMAN

Six months turned out to be *way* too little time to accomplish this complicated task, and it took us overall nearly eighteen months or so, depending on how you count when we began, to achieve a final agreement.

RICHARD NEPHEW

I couldn't have told you what I thought it was going to be, exactly, but I was convinced that, because Rouhani wanted it, and because Obama wanted it, we were gonna be able to work out some initial deal. And so long as politics in Washington and Tehran didn't screw it up, I thought we were going to get all the way to a comprehensive deal.

November 8, 2013: Obama, aboard Air Force One, *speaks with Prime Minister Netanyahu with the P5+1 talks for a Joint Plan of Action underway in Geneva.* Pete Souza, White House

BRIAN DEESE

At that point, I had moved from the White House over to [the Office of Management and Budget], and so I was actually dealing with all the furloughs and dealing with what happens when the government shut down.[158]

FERIAL GOVASHIRI

When the government shutdown happened, there was essential staff and nonessential staff out. But there were still people who worked, and because we aided the leadership, we would still have to come in and work when no one else did.

JAMES KVAAL

I remember the office being almost completely deserted. It was almost a ghost town.

TED CHIODO

I did everything. I ran the printers. I hole-punched the stuff. I didn't take a day off. You're working for free, and you had to work twice as hard. I had been used to that on the campaign, working around the clock in an office of one. So I felt, sometimes, when I got into a zone, I was sort of better. It was easier for me just to do everything.

FERIAL GOVASHIRI

People would still expect the same. You had to basically work double and triple as hard. So many people were excited—"Oh, we get the day off!"—and I was like, "Uh, someone else is doing your job for you." But it wasn't their fault.

---

158 Congress failed to pass a continuing resolution to fund the government after a
     Republican faction, led by Ted Cruz of Texas, demanded that the spending bill
     defund the Affordable Care Act. Democrats wouldn't budge for the freshman
     senator, whose gimmick lasted for sixteen days (October 1–17, 2013).

YOHANNES ABRAHAM

The shutdown was tough on everybody. If you were in this for the right reasons, there's something deeply heartbreaking about a government shutdown. Just physically, workload-wise, you're shrinking the staff down to a skeleton crew. That was a long set of days.

NATE LUBIN

So October 1, the day the shutdown happened, was the same day Healthcare. gov launched, and the launch broke and no one would pay attention for two and a half weeks because the government was shut down . . . [For] those of us who couldn't leave, it was a bizarre couple of weeks walking around the White House with nobody there and those of us trying to figure out what we could and couldn't do.

BRAD JENKINS

Doing the blocking and tackling of getting celebrities to get the word out [for Healthcare.gov] was going to be the way to go—that was my life for a year—but that all went to shit when the website wouldn't work for two months. We literally got seventy celebrities on the first day of enrollment to tweet out Healthcare.gov. We got Lady Gaga backstage at her concert, and all of her [forty-eight] million followers went to a website that didn't work. It was my worst nightmare.

NATE LUBIN

No one had heard anything but *This is broken and terrible and don't go there because it's not going to work.* The site was working by mid-December—not perfectly, but well enough.

BARNEY FRANK

We had expected the Republicans to get a lot of political pain from the shutdown and, in fact, the initial responses were bad. Then, the reason they never paid any price for the shutdown was that totally screwed-up rollout of the health-care bill. That was the unforgivable error of the Obama administration.

NATE LUBIN

Not enough people were signing up. The policy problem with that was, the people who were signing up early were people who needed health care. Which was good—we wanted those people to sign up. That's the point of the law. But if you only had six people willing to wait online for six hours, if you knew the basics of how health exchanges work, that's a recipe for a failing exchange. You needed to get young people, healthy people to sign up.

BRAD JENKINS

All of these celebrities were rip-shit pissed. Maybe they weren't angry, but their publicists and managers were emailing me: *What the fuck?* So we burned that bridge. It took two months to fix the website, and it's very hard to go back to Lady Gaga and ask her to tweet out Healthcare.gov again.

BARNEY FRANK

I would have been getting reports on it every other day. It was not just that the rollout was screwed up, but [Obama] and his top people appeared to be surprised by it. The negative publicity from that helped the health-care bill [lose] popularity and got Republicans off the hook for the shutdown. He's culpable for not having put everything possible into making sure that that administrative screwup didn't happen.

YOHANNES ABRAHAM

What we were then faced with was we still had the same number of people we needed to enroll by the deadline,[159] and it became, if not everybody's full-time

---

159 The deadline to apply for Obamacare coverage was March 31, 2014—a six-week extension from the initial date. On March 25, 2014, officials announced a second extension to mid-April.

job, then everybody's part-time job. I spent a significant chunk of my team's time on exactly that question. "You're my mayors' liaison. What mayors can you get to tweet out Healthcare.gov? What mayors can you get to hold events?" And you sort of went down the line with everybody's portfolios.

BRAD JENKINS

We had already been thinking of big ideas where we'd need break-emergency-glass moments for enrollment. We had flown Valerie out to LA, and she met with Zach [Galifianakis]. She met with screenwriters and producers. She met with will.i.am. Will was thinking about doing a health-care-type song similar to "Yes We Can," but apparently that never materialized. And, yeah, consumer experts were telling us, "This is going to be impossible. It's really hard to make health care sexy and cool."

NATE LUBIN

Between Two Ferns was a Valerie Jarrett–engineered thing. It wouldn't have happened without her. It had been an idea we'd talked about in the campaign at some point and had come back around.

KORI SCHULMAN

The digital team would have pie-in-the-sky brainstorms about tons of ideas that would never see the light of day. *Two Ferns* had been on this list for years, a dream project we would have loved to see happen.

BRAD JENKINS

Because the website was an epic disaster, it was hard for the president to come back and say, "Hey, go back to the website. It works now." So to come back with some humility and self-awareness, to completely make fun of himself, that was obviously the thing about that video. So when we first started talking to [Funny or Die], they made clear that it had to be like every other *Between Two Ferns*. It couldn't be watered down. It couldn't be some big Obamacare commercial.

NATE LUBIN

Partnerships like that were high risk, obviously. When you're the president of the United States, the upside and downside risks were not the same. The upside was, you'd get your message out a little bit, and it's hard to measure the value of some of those things. You know, you make a great case on health care, then some foreign-policy crisis happens and you gotta pivot to that. So the story would end up being that you screwed up.

YOHANNES ABRAHAM

We had to be as scrappy and creative as we could be, because we had a job we had to get done, and ended up getting done.

BRAD JENKINS

Valerie had told the president that this would be our breakthrough; tens of millions of people were going to watch it. That was the expectation, and so when we shot it[160] and it got thirty million views after we released it[161] in its first few days, Healthcare.gov saw a 40 percent uptick in traffic. Ninety percent of the people clicking Healthcare.gov from Funny or Die had never been to Healthcare.gov before. It was the exact healthy demographic who would never think to go to Healthcare.gov or who had never heard of it, and I got to brief the president about the success of the video.

YOHANNES ABRAHAM

You know, it's probably true that the urgency around enrollment did lead us to be creative in a way we might not have been otherwise.

---

160 February 24, 2014.
161 March 11, 2014.

BRAD JENKINS

Someone literally helped me clean baby-vomit stains off of my suit jacket before I went into the Oval, and I had maybe five minutes, way more time than we needed. But I walked him through it all. And not to sound hyperbolic, but no president ever went on a program like this—an internet-only, weird satirical show. It was the biggest video of the year, and I was thinking, *Wow, maybe he'll give me a fist bump.* It'd be this moment where Barack and I would become friends, and that did not happen. He smiled and congratulated me. Valerie was in the office as well, and he looked at her. "Val, I thought this was your idea?" And she was like, "No, no. This was Brad's." The biggest takeaway from all this was, he expected it. That decision was probably the least-important decision he had made in those twenty-four hours, whether to go on that stupid show. He's dealing with life-and-death matters on national security.

TERRY SZUPLAT

I wasn't in a policy position, so I wasn't running around meeting-to-meeting trying to figure out how to respond to any given situation, but just in the broadest general terms, it was an extremely challenging time, especially on the foreign-policy side. Russia's aggression towards Ukraine was one of the most consequential moments in Europe since the end of the Cold War. You actually had one nation essentially invading another nation and trying to rewrite the borders of post–World War II Europe. I mean, everyone in the White House and people around the world understood . . . how reckless this was on the part of Putin.

HEATHER FOSTER

We went through a year where there were a variety of crises. People don't talk about it anymore, but remember when Ebola was on the television screen twenty-four hours a day? People were massively concerned about catching Ebola, and, you know, here we are and people are almost laughing about it. Do you remember how they literally got rid of an entire airplane because one person had Ebola on the plane?

TERRY SZUPLAT

Ebola was certainly out of control in West Africa. Spring was sort of the rise of ISIS and its sweep across western Iraq. There may have been other issues here, but you had, as part of the rise of ISIS, a number of the kidnappings and beheadings in the spring/summer of '14. You had Ferguson. I mean, these were all happening at the same time. It was an incredibly challenging time.

TED CHIODO

2014 was tough. We were still basically making sure that the first two years after the reelect, that we were implementing that part of the president's agenda. There hadn't been a lot of easy decisions. We were still a ways away from the finish line, but I had always thought, aside from my shingles, it was a good time to get some new blood into the White House. I could only have done six poison-prevention proclamations. "The first thing about poison is, don't call 911. Try not to eat it. If you do, call the prevention hotline." There were only so many National Boating Week proclamations you could do without getting jaded.

ARUN CHAUDHARY

There was so much grind and so much hustle. You're doing the same things all the time, and it could be maddening. For me, doing the third Saint Patrick's Day celebration was one of the reasons why I was like, *You know what? I will have no problem leaving my job at the White House.* It was so much the same thing over and over again, but that's not to say it's not an honor to work there.

PETE SOUZA

The thing that I always admired about President Obama, as well as Michelle, was that, you know, maybe after the fifth or sixth time, you didn't really wanna do the Easter Egg Roll. And yet they always got up for the occasion. There was enthusiasm on their part for every Easter Egg Roll, and you could imagine having to do this every year. It's kinda like, at least, if it were *me*, I'd be like, *God, why do I have to do this again?* And those two, they rose to the occasion every single time. I thought they both realized that, Did this define the presidency? No. But it meant so much to the people that were involved, and as a result, they felt they were role models for all those kids to get people enthusiastic about reading, listening, participating in the whole Easter Egg Roll. Does that make any sense?

HEATHER FOSTER

You gotta remember: post-2009 was "postracial." It was all good. Everybody was holding hands. There's no more racism in our country. We had a black president, but there were a lot of disparity issues because of that 2008-2009 crash. You had unemployment in the double digits for African Americans. Things drastically impacted the African American community and other communities of color that weren't addressed at all. Nobody wanted to talk about it. Banks didn't loan to African Americans the way that they loaned to white Americans. To be honest, African Americans were holding on to a lot of issues, issues that had been issues since I'd been born.

RON DAVIS

Some people say that race relations got worse under President Obama, and I thought, as an African American, that's just completely false. It's like the old thing on "Men don't like to go to doctors." You go to the doctor, and the doctor says, "Hey, you got stage IV," and you come out saying, "I was okay until I saw the doctor." You were not even close to being okay. You just didn't know. So the president didn't create the tension. Circumstances and his leadership pulled the Band-Aid off of the wound that was not healing.

HEATHER FOSTER

These were issues that we continued to carry and were upset about, but people saw a window where this was actually going to get press attention.

MARGARET RICHARDSON

That early August there were a lot of conference calls trying to figure out what was happening on the ground in Ferguson.[162] There had also been a discussion about what to say, when to say it, when to go, and whether to go. We had obviously talked about what the goals were: trying to make sure that we were connecting with the relevant stakeholders, making sure [AG Holder] had time to talk to law enforcement as well as to the community activists—to young people, to people who were feeling like the protests weren't sparked by Michael Brown's death but the result of a simmering distrust and failure of community-police relations over a long period of time.

RON DAVIS

Law enforcement was forced to look in the mirror and acknowledge our own past, to recognize it'd take strong leadership to move forward. And some people resisted. But it was not a longstanding resistance, because the rank-and-file officers understood.

ROY AUSTIN JR.

I was a longtime prosecutor before I joined the administration. I was a civil-rights prosecutor and a street-crimes prosecutor in Washington, DC. And as a civil-rights prosecutor, part of our job was looking at excessive-force cases and prosecuting law enforcement, but in order to do that you would work closely with other law enforcement who'd help you. Whether it's the internal affairs of the local department, or the FBI civil-rights investigators, you're trying to make clear that you absolutely respect the profession, that we all needed law

---

162 On the weekend of August 9, 2014, protesters in Saint Louis County assembled outside the apartment complex of Michael Brown, an unarmed eighteen-year-old black man who had been shot and killed by Darren Wilson, a white police officer on duty. According to eyewitness accounts that were later corroborated by video footage, Brown's hands were raised during the encounter and he did not seem to pose a threat to Wilson. As hundreds more demonstrators took to the streets, the Saint Louis Police Department responded with militarized SWAT units in camouflage gear driving armored vehicles and carrying 5.56-mm rifles.

enforcement, while at the same time prosecuting those who were damaging the brand of good officers. So you were constantly in this kind of dichotomy of great officers helping you prosecute bad officers.

HEATHER FOSTER

Trayvon wasn't Michael Brown. Michael Brown was that guy that hung out in the neighborhood. Trayvon should have been more relatable to people in general, but the same kind of outcomes kept happening with these boys and men of color who kind of seemed to be on this track of, like, *How are you going to be successful in this society if all you're faced with is prejudice?*

VANITA GUPTA
Principal Deputy Assistant Attorney General, Civil Rights Division, US Department of Justice (2014–2017)

The cases were pretty different. [Michael Brown's] involved a shooting by a police officer, meaning a representative of government, in a certain sense, and Trayvon was killed by a private actor. So they were situated very differently that way. In Trayvon's case, the Justice Department announced an investigation but watched the state process unfold. In Michael Brown's case, the Justice Department opened a tandem federal investigation along with the state investigation. One very directly went to the broader systemic issues on race and policing, whereas Trayvon, I think, really forced people to ask themselves a lot of questions about race in America—about our own stereotypes, our own actions—and then ask a different set of questions about stand-your-ground laws.

HEATHER FOSTER

If you remember, the [Brown] shooting took place over the summer, when [Obama] had actually gone on vacation. Then, when he returned, Attorney General Holder went down to Ferguson. DOJ was doing this whole pattern-or-practice [investigation] with the police department, but everyone had been waiting on the district attorney to make the decision whether they were going to press charges [against Officer Darren Wilson]. And everyone who was in

Ferguson or was an activist in that area clearly told us if charges were not brought that they were going to protest, and that's what happened in November in multiple cities.

VANITA GUPTA

It certainly caught the attention of the Justice Department in important ways, and also caught the attention of the country to focus again on race and the criminal-justice system. You know, one of the things that Black Lives Matter did was really validate the experiences of Ferguson residents. And not just Ferguson residents, but also people of color in the region, around the ways in which the police and the courts interacted to harass and degrade people of color through fines and fees and policing practices. That discourse has continued, but those issues have not been resolved.

BRAD JENKINS

Black Lives Matter, as opposed to Occupy, had clear policy priorities as it related to use of force, community-police engagement, and all of these things.

JON CARSON

I mean, it's lasted longer right? BLM seemed to create local chapters with local goals. I think part of the problem for Occupy Wall Street was that the original idea was to just literally occupy Wall Street in New York. Then all these other cities sprung up and it wasn't exactly clear what they were going after, whether Oakland or Washington, DC, or Madison, Wisconsin, that had to do with that locality. Black Lives Matter had issues that could actually be concrete in the local area for most places.

HEATHER FOSTER

I found all of [the local leaders of BLM]. I called half of them while they were in the middle of protesting and introduced myself. "We'd like to have you come to the White House to talk more about what you've been doing and what makes you feel angry about these issues." The president had been clear with me in basically saying, *I want these young people to also understand what the government can and can't do*. Most people just didn't know what the power of the presidency was. There wasn't a magic wand he could have waved and everything would have been okay in Ferguson. It just didn't work like that. These were still local issues.

BRAD JENKINS

Simultaneously, while all of the BLM stuff was happening, the president had launched his My Brother's Keeper initiative. This was an initiative, interagency-wide, to study what we could do to provide more career pathways for young black boys.

VALERIE JARRETT

My Brother's Keeper was designed to help the lives of boys and young men of color and try to put their lives on a better trajectory, but at the same time, the broader community had to embrace them and realize that we're all Americans together.

BRAD JENKINS

Take a look at incarceration rates and dropout rates—there were clearly gaps in the system that they were falling through. And so while we were simultaneously releasing this, all of these atrocities were happening and being shot on iPhones. It was even more important for that team and for Heather to engage with BLM, and for the Department of Justice to be in touch with them.

HEATHER FOSTER

It was a difficult meeting to put together. Oval Office meetings usually had CEOs or members of Congress—people who were not kids that had been arrested forty-eight hours prior. These were people willing to push past laws to get what they wanted to get done, and so we didn't want people who were going to be upset and start flipping stuff over.

YOHANNES ABRAHAM

I've always thought folks were able to be more effective when they have a seat at the table, but yeah, it was probably not an uncomplicated decision for the folks who were invited.

HEATHER FOSTER

They were skeptical. Part of them was like, "This better not be a photo op. I could lose my credibility when I go back to my community." And, you know, I did my best. I met with all of them the night before. "Look, I'm the realest when it comes to being real. I'm not overly political. I'm not trying to run for office." And I told them, "This is a really important time in history. Everybody's looking at you. The best thing you can do for your communities is to communicate to the leader of the free world why you are protesting and why you are in the streets."

Obama meets with community leaders and law-enforcement officials in the wake of the events in Ferguson. From left to right: Milwaukee Mayor Tom Barrett, Ferguson activist and community organizer Rasheen Aldridge, New York Mayor Bill de Blasio, and Philadelphia Police Department Commissioner Charles Ramsey. Eisenhower Executive Office Building. December 1, 2014. Chip Somodevilla, Getty Images

2015–2016

For decades, China refused to engage in efforts to combat climate change. The US had already experienced its era of massive industrialization and growth, so China felt it had the license to pollute in order to grow, too. This was *their* time to develop, the government reasoned, but by the end of 2014, the country's domestic politics had changed.

The "airpocalypse" prompted schools in more than a dozen Chinese cities to keep windows shut. Field trips and sporting activities were often postponed or canceled. Participants in the 2014 Beijing Marathon dropped out toward the beginning of the race, after their face masks acquired an ash-like hue. "The most downloaded app was not some WhatsApp variety," Brian Deese said. "It's the AQI, the Air Quality Index. If you've ever been to any major Chinese city, you've probably used it yourself. You wake up in the morning, and the AQI answers the question whether or not you're going to go outside that day." The Xi administration acknowledged that, apart from economic incentives to invest in renewable energy, the government needed to commit to environmental concerns to maintain stability.

And so on November 12, 2014, the final day of the Asia-Pacific Economic Cooperation summit, President Xi Jinping and President Obama stood beside one another in the Great Hall of the People and announced a commitment to cut carbon emissions by 2030. Their joint decision was the culmination of a year and a half of quiet negotiations, a feat given the multiple conflicting issues between the two nations (e.g., China had long been irked by Obama's developing the Trans-Pacific Partnership, direct trade competition for the Central People's Government). "Over the past two days, I had a constructive and productive discussion with President Obama," Xi announced to the press. "We issued a joint statement on climate change, and we jointly announced our respective post-2020 targets. We agreed to make sure that international climate-change negotiations will reach an agreement as scheduled at the Paris conference in 2015, and we agreed to deepen practical cooperation on clean energy, environment protection, and other areas."

"As the world's two largest economies, energy consumers, and emitters of greenhouse gases," Obama added, "we have a special responsibility to lead the global effort against climate change . . . I commend President Xi, his team, and the Chinese government for the commitment they are making to slow, peak, and then reverse the course of China's carbon emissions."

The US-China climate deal was only the first step. After hashing out what was technically realistic for China to execute, the two nations then used their leverage to persuade the rest of the world to do the same.

TODD STERN

Kerry had in his mind, from the moment he got in [at State], that he wanted to ramp up the US-China cooperation. He wanted to do a joint statement with China expressing a joint US-China commitment on climate change. We drafted that. I negotiated that with my counterpart, Xie Zhenhua,[163] and then Kerry went off to China. The statement both made an expression of commitment and also established a new US-China climate-change working group, which became the new umbrella under which all of our China cooperation happened. So that was in April of 2013.

BRIAN DEESE

Kerry's engagement was important. I would point more fundamentally to the president's first meeting with President Xi, which was actually in Sunnylands in the United States. That was more than a year before we actually reached the public agreement with them, and in that meeting, the two of them had the first extended conversation about climate change.

TODD STERN

The first Xi-Obama meeting [was] at Sunnylands in June of 2013, where the most important deliverable, as it turned out, was a short but consequential agreement to start working together on the subject of an industrial gas called HFCs,[164] the

---

163 Vice chairman of the National Development and Reform Commission, 2007-2015.
164 Hydrofluorocarbons.

rapidly growing greenhouse gas used in refrigerants and air conditioners. That was a first important positive interaction between Obama and Xi.

JONATHAN PERSHING

For the Obama and Xi administrations, climate change turned out to be one of those areas where we thought we had enough that we could talk to each other about that it was worth elevating. It was a discussion that was had at the presidential level, and it counterbalanced the other areas where we had much less common ground. You have to find things that let you continue to talk to even countries you have hard times with, and you find whatever you can find to try and create some continued avenue of an opportunity. Human rights was one of the conflicts we had with them. They didn't like our interference, but we found climate change to be a place where we *could* play with them, and so it got moved *way* up the chain of command on both sides because it was a real opportunity to make progress. Obama cared about it, and Xi cared about it.

BRIAN DEESE

They weren't doing it for some diplomatic reason. They're doing it because, economically, they wanted to establish themselves as the global superpower on renewables. The cost of alternative sources of energy and more efficient ways of developing had been plummeting. In India, they're holding auctions for new electricity generation, where the solar bids were cheaper than the new coal bids. So we actually got toward a tipping point. Reducing emissions and increasing your growth were no longer at odds with each other. That's a market-driven thing, and . . . without that market transformation, it would have been extremely difficult to create a diplomatic construct that would have worked.

JONATHAN FINER

It was impossible for most of us to imagine how to successfully achieve an agreement in Paris without the groundwork that we laid with the Chinese years in advance. A meeting took place in the State Department soon after I got there in 2013, with Secretary Kerry. He was about to go to China[165] and said he really wanted to propose US and China work together on what might be possible in terms of setting an ambitious emissions target in advance of Paris. These so-called INDCs, every country had a target for how much they would reduce emissions.[166]

TODD STERN

I met with my team and came up with the idea of trying to do a joint statement between President Obama and President Xi announcing our targets for the Paris Agreement. We knew that they were going to be together in November [2014], because it was already on the calendar in Beijing, and so I talked to the White House about that. [Counselor to the President John] Podesta was there at that point, and I went with Kerry to China to lay this idea out, to try to work out this together . . . There was a sort of public-statement upshot of the Kerry trip that indicated we were going to collaborate in some way as we worked on our targets, but it didn't say anything about any presidential joint announcement, because of course we didn't actually know if we were going to succeed.

BRIAN DEESE

That set off a year of back-and-forth diplomacy, which culminated in the fall of 2014 when the president was at the UN General Assembly.[167] He had a set of private meetings with the Chinese delegation—basically that he wanted to negotiate an agreement. At the time, John Podesta was in the role that I ended up taking over, and the president designated John to say, *Okay, it's September.*

---

165 February 14-15, 2014.

166 Leading up to the 2015 Paris Agreement, countries participating in the United Nations Framework Convention on Climate Change published their post-2020 Intended Nationally Determined Contributions (INDCs), consisting of what actions they would take to achieve global emission-reduction goals in the context of their "national priorities, circumstances, and capabilities." Once the accord was finalized and a country formally joined the Paris Agreement, the "intended" was dropped from the moniker, and an INDC became a Nationally Determined Contribution.

167 September 24, 2014.

You've got a couple months to see if you can get an agreement with the Chinese.
Over the subsequent six weeks or so there was a lot of back and forth, but
that culminated in the announcement when the president went to Beijing in
November of 2014 for the US-China joint statement.

JONATHAN PERSHING

We [lobbied] other countries to themselves become a party, and while some
had executive-order structures, others had parliamentary-ratification provisions.
So I give Obama credit as well, because he just made calls. We all, at the State
Department, set up call-sheet stuff. We made our own calls. Kerry met with
foreign ministers. Obama met with heads of state. It would *never* have happened
without those calls.

BRIAN DEESE

We had about a year before the Paris conference, and that set off a frenetic year of
activity, including the president making decision after decision to prioritize this
issue, including, in early January of 2015, only eight weeks after he announced
the joint deal with China, getting on a plane to Delhi to be Prime Minister
Modi's guest at Republic Day. A big part of his decision to go on that trip was
to have an opportunity to talk in a very direct and personal way about what it
would take to get India to come on board.

JAKE LEVINE

When comparing the Paris Agreement to the Copenhagen Accord, the structure
of the two was radically different. The Paris Agreement was a voluntary
nonbinding agreement that asked every country to individually commit to
domestic policies, and it relied on some degree of competition and behavioral
nudging—the idea being if the US and China agreed to something aggressive,
then Mexico's gonna feel the pressure. And once Mexico announced, then
Brazil's gonna feel the pressure. That's exactly what happened and where Deese
was so critical in paving that path forward.

BRIAN DEESE

It was an all-out effort on all fronts to try to set the conditions so that we could have success in Paris at the end of 2015.

March 7, 2015: President Obama marches across Edmund Pettus Bridge while holding hands with Congressman John Lewis and 103-year-old Amelia Boynton Robinson—activists who were assaulted by state troopers and Klansmen in the "Bloody Sunday" demonstrations fifty years prior. Lawrence Jackson, White House

HEATHER FOSTER

Selma, you've seen the photo. That was my project, to figure out how to get President Obama to commemorate one of the most important marches in civil-rights history. For me, personally? Top five events. The day that motorcade came over that same bridge, that had all these people who were battered and beaten, was priceless.

CODY KEENAN

Valerie told us she agreed on the president's behalf to have him do Selma. I found out the day of the State of the Union address and was already exhausted by that. So we're sitting at the table going, *Oh, what the fuck!* It had just come up so fast. Obviously I was excited for the speech. I just couldn't handle it at the time.

HEATHER FOSTER

I had to introduce like eighty people to the president, and I was trying to get their names, and he was like, "I know who this is." I would be like, "Dr. *Lowry*." He would just look at me like, "I know who these people are. These are my *peeps*."

BARBARA LEE

There were moments during his presidency that [made me] realize he was a great president who had a very difficult time. In spite of the challenges from Mitch McConnell and the obstructionism by the Republican Congress, that he was going to do his job and he made me feel proud as an African American, the way he conducted himself.

YOHANNES ABRAHAM

I wasn't on the ground there, but speaking as an African American, it's funny. When you're a staffer you would have your head down, focused on execution and making sure that your piece of the thing happened well. In the run-up to Selma, you could get lost. *Okay, who's speaking? Who's gonna be in the greet beforehand? Okay, they're shutting down this road, so how can we . . .* It's a lot of work. I'm sort of specifically speaking about my experience as an African American with these moments that were heavy with history, but that's true across the board with the job. Just to take two minutes and reflect, every day—obviously, invariably something happened on any given day that was, for better or worse, worth internalizing and reflecting and putting in the context of history and life. Sorry to go down a philosophical rabbit hole.

CODY KEENAN

That was one of those speeches where you couldn't really screw it up. John Lewis said it best in his introduction: "If [someone] had told me . . . that one day I would be back here introducing the first African American president, I would have said . . . you're out of your mind." Symbolism would have been enough on its own, but we tried to think of something interesting to say beyond commemorating what happened. Of all people, Rudy Giuliani gave us that impetus. He was on Fox the week before, trotting out the same old racist dog-whistle bullshit that the president wasn't raised like us, doesn't love this country like "we" do.[168] He even began [a speech the night before] by saying, "I know this is a terrible thing to say," which we always laughed at, because it's like, "You could just stop yourself right there."

VANITA GUPTA

The president's speech came at a moment when there were heightened community-police tensions and a systematic assault on voting rights. He spoke to the moment with a sense of patriotism and kind of put it into a long arc of historical perspective—about the role people play in ensuring progress and change, that none of our institutions or our progress has been inevitable.

CODY KEENAN

Again, we were pissed off about it—by "we" I mean speechwriters and staff—but the president, everybody always talks about how he was calm or detached or whatever. He just didn't care about shit like that. He thought it was stupid. So I suggested it to him in the Oval. "It doesn't deserve a response," he said, "but it's an interesting idea. Who gets to decide what patriotism is? Who gets

---

168 "I very rarely hear him say the things that I used to hear Ronald Reagan say, the things I used to hear Bill Clinton say about how much he loves America. I do hear him criticize America much more often than other American presidents . . . It sounds like he's more of a critic than he is a supporter. You can be a patriotic American and be a critic, but then you're not expressing that kind of love that we're used to from a president." —Rudy Giuliani, *Fox & Friends*, February 19, 2015.

to define who is more American than somebody else?" It was one of those rare speech sessions where ideas flowed fast. When you think about the people who crossed that bridge, they weren't protected by law or custom. They were poor. They were powerless and willing to make incredible sacrifices, maybe even face death, to just win not special rights but equal rights that were promised in our Constitution. So we thought, *What could be more American than that?* Not blaming others or saying, "No, we're the *real* Americans here," but saying, "We're all Americans and we're going to put our lives on the line to prove it."

VANITA GUPTA

It was a call to action in a very hopeful way and reminded us of where we'd come from but also the work ahead we needed to do. I think, for a lot of us, it renewed our spirits in the fight for equality and justice.

CODY KEENAN

The speech itself was patriotism for grown-ups, and it's Barack Obama's core view of America, which was that our founding documents say, *We are imperfect.* The very language *to form a more perfect union* suggested that we were not perfect, that we'd been given the keys to this remarkable system of self-government that lets us make ourselves more perfect. He'd always said, before I'd ever worked for him, that the trajectory of American history is jagged. Sometimes you take two steps forward. Then you take a step back, even two steps back. But the trajectory is undeniably upwards, and that should give people hope.

RICHARD NEPHEW

You know, I was convinced from moment one that we would get a comprehensive deal with the Iranians. Obama was very public that he thought an agreement was fifty-fifty. He didn't shy away from that conclusion. Kerry may have been as optimistic as me. It's hard to judge, because he's just an upbeat kind of guy. I spent a lot of time with the guy and never saw him as anything but focused on getting it done.

CHRIS VAN HOLLEN

The president and his team were very engaged in the Iran nuclear deal. I mean, direct day-to-day involvement, negotiation and communication with members of Congress regarding the merits of the nuclear agreement. I believed strongly that it was the best way of preventing Iran from getting a nuclear weapon.

RICHARD NEPHEW

The number discussion—where we're all giving each other our confidence numbers—that was always at a staff level, where Wendy was the highest-ranking person. And she always refused to give us her number. We never got hers. It was only guys at the staff and expert level.

WENDY SHERMAN

It's binary. You either get there or you don't. Even if you get 99 percent of the way there, if you don't get the last 1 percent, you don't have a deal. That's why I would never give a percentage, because it doesn't matter if you get far. If it's not all the way, you don't have a deal. The symbol I used all the time was a Rubik's Cube. There were multiple moving pieces, and every time you moved a piece—the number of centrifuges, the level of enrichment, the level of the stockpile—it moved the other elements. And so you constantly had to recalibrate until all of the pieces fit snugly together and the last cube of the Rubik's Cube locked into place. That was what made this so staggeringly complex.

RICHARD NEPHEW

It'd been a year that we'd negotiated with the Iranians before Lausanne. And you know, during that process we were kind of working through what a comprehensive agreement could look like. So, you know, for Lausanne, it wasn't special for the date on the calendar.[169] We had simply agreed, in November [2013], that we needed to say by the end of March [2015] whether or not we

---

169 March 26 to April 2, 2015.

could actually hammer out an agreement in broad strokes, with the final coming by July. That was all laid out in the November agreement to extend the initial agreement, so that's why Lausanne got this special attention. It was less because of where we were in the process, which was kind of the same as what we had been doing, but more because we had established a deadline for ourselves that, if we weren't getting closer by the end of March, then maybe it's time to pack it in.

JONATHAN FINER

We knew we were close, because in Lausanne we had reached an understanding on most of the big outstanding issues and knew that it was a matter of whether we could get all of the details nailed down—and that that wasn't guaranteed, but that we were closer to getting a nuclear deal than certainly we had ever been before and that many people thought was possible. The challenge was that some things had happened that threw a lot of uncertainty into the process.

RICHARD NEPHEW

There was literally one moment where I hesitated. It was in March of 2015, when a lot of really bad leaks had come out of the process. They basically exposed all of the ideas and put them to test in Tehran and Washington before we were ready to present them as a package that made sense integrated. That was the only time I even went below 50 percent likelihood confidence number, but, even then, I was still like 49 percent.

WENDY SHERMAN

You really couldn't boil this down to one obstacle. There were many things along the way where one might have imagined we were at a dead end. I think there was unanimity among all of the P5+1 to try and get to the right outcome here, and the commitment to doing that was evident after [the] Ukraine [conflict] happened. We were sanctioning the Russians and, at the same time, they stayed focused in the room on ensuring Iran couldn't obtain a nuclear weapon because that was also in their national-security interest. So there were all kinds of things. The Cotton letter was signed with forty-seven senators essentially saying, "Never."[170] Bibi Netanyahu's speech in Congress,[171] and, obviously, many times that the Iranians balked at what was necessary, but the president of the United States was clear that we had to cut off all the pathways to fissile material for a nuclear weapon.

RICHARD NEPHEW

The Iranians just flat out asked, "How can we make sure this remains in effect throughout this entire longevity?" You know, they were basically saying, *We have to make a commitment to you that we're going to abide by it, but we have a Supreme Leader and he's going to be in place no matter what happens to politics.* He may die. You know, he's human. But they didn't have the same imminence of every four years the risk of switching over. So they had been asking us from moment one, "How do we get an agreement that will survive your presidential transitions?" And "How do we get an agreement that will survive your congressional transitions?"

JEFF WEAVER
Campaign Manager, Bernie Sanders for President, 2016

President Obama was not going to be on the ballot in 2016. Hillary Clinton had announced[172] and had basically cleared the field. It was really the beginning of the post-Obama era, right? Obama got the Democratic Party back on its historical trajectory as being a more inclusive party, which had been interrupted by the Reagan years and then the Clinton years and then the Bush years. A party more concerned about a working people was really a departure from the type of Democratic Party that had been built up by the Bill Clinton machine in the '90s. And so Bernie Sanders's candidacy was not a repudiation of Obama but, really, a continuation of the attempt to move the party back in the direction it had been moving since FDR—again, which had been interrupted by Reagan and then Bill Clinton's presidency and the Bush years.

---

170 March 9, 2015.
171 March 3, 2015.
172 April 12, 2015.

STUART STEVENS

I went to Middlebury College. I can remember Bernie Sanders running for mayor. I would ride my bicycle down Church Street in Burlington, and this guy's out there yelling about rent control.

DAVID PLOUFFE

I thought Trump had started running more as a lark, more to help build the brand . . . In 2015, the night before he [announced], it'd be interesting to know what he was thinking.[173] It probably was fair to assume *I'll show everybody that they're wrong about me*, but I don't know. I think we'll never know.

JEFF WEAVER

Bernie wanted to have a progressive candidate in the race. It appeared, by all accounts, Elizabeth Warren was not going to run, and Bernie Sanders had championed a core set of issues for his entire adult life. I thought he felt it was time for those issues to be brought on a national stage, on a presidential stage that would give them the attention that they needed and hopefully propel him into the White House so that those issues could be advanced.

TOM VILSACK

Change doesn't happen overnight. Our recognition of change may happen overnight, but the change itself happens incrementally, and you have to manage it. If you manage it properly, you can sustain it. If you don't manage it properly, then it's not going to last.

JON CARSON

The president truly believed he was just one part, the biggest part, but one part of a larger movement. The best example of that was when the Supreme Court

---

173 June 16, 2015.

made marriage equality the law of the land. The speech that the president gave in the Rose Garden talked about how this decision was the culmination of millions of Americans doing their parts over decades—every last member of the LGBT community who had the courage to come out to their own families, every ally who'd ever carried a sign, every city-council member that had passed a resolution barring discrimination back when most members of government weren't doing any of that.[174] Those humans that had worked over decades led to that.

BEN LABOLT

I'm not sure the court would have ruled the way that it did, had public opinion not so fully embraced marriage equality across demographics during Barack Obama's presidency. I thought part of the reason public opinion shifted was the president and the vice president, and other leaders, came out and not only endorsed marriage equality, but worked over the course of years to advance gay rights, to say that they were human rights, and that they were in the same category and on the same trajectory of civil rights as we know them.

VANITA GUPTA

There were loud cheers from the Civil Rights Division in the hallways of Main Justice. We were really exuberant. It was a really important moment, and again, the trajectory of change, even within the department, it fell around the litigating position of the United States in the last prior couple of years that it had evolved.

---

174 "Change for many of our LGBT brothers and sisters must have seemed so slow for so long. But compared to so many other issues, America's shift has been so quick. I know that Americans of goodwill continue to hold a wide range of views on this issue. Opposition in some cases has been based on sincere and deeply held beliefs. All of us who welcome today's news should be mindful of that fact, recognize different viewpoints, revere our deep commitment to religious freedom.

But today should also give us hope that on the many issues with which we grapple, often painfully, real change is possible. Shifts in hearts and minds is possible, and those who have come so far on their journey to equality have a responsibility to reach back and help others join them. Because for all our differences, we are one people, stronger together than we could ever be alone. That's always been our story." —President Obama, White House Rose Garden, June 26, 2015.

So to see that arc and have that outcome was historic. For the last prior couple of years, the administration had really been all-in on trying to advance and protect LGBT rights.

CODY KEENAN

As soon as he finished talking about marriage equality, we got on the helicopter to Charleston.[175]

HEATHER FOSTER

I just remember seeing Reverend Pinckney's widow that day and how people in that community compared it to the death of Martin Luther King, and how her own personal grief touched me in a different way. Vice President Biden and his wife had also just gone through their own personal loss.

CODY KEENAN

[Obama] had eulogized Beau Biden two weeks before, and that might have still been in his head. "What a good man. Sometimes I think that's the best thing to hope for when you're eulogized, after all the words and recitations and resumes are read, to just say somebody was a good man. You don't have to be of high station to be a good man." All of that was ad-libbed.

HEATHER FOSTER

I was running around, but another staffer texted me. "You need to come out here and hear this speech." I was like, "Yeah, yeah, yeah, yeah, yeah, I just gotta make sure that everything's good in the back when they're done." And she was like, "No, no, no. You gotta come hear this."

---

175 On June 17, 2015, at Mother Emanuel African Methodist Church in Charleston, South Carolina, white supremacist Dylann Roof entered Wednesday-night prayer meeting and shot and killed nine members of the congregation, including senior pastor and state senator Reverend Clementa Pinckney.

CODY KEENAN

When I was writing it, I didn't know he would sing. On the way to [Joint Base] Andrews, he mentioned on Marine One, "You know, if it feels right, I might sing it." That had never occurred to me. I was just like, "Hey, man, you do you." Within about thirty seconds, you saw the speech was in a black church and they've got someone on the organ while the president's speaking. I was like, *There is a 99.9 percent chance he sings.*

HEATHER FOSTER

When he started singing "Amazing Grace," I just bowled over. I was so tired afterwards that I just crawled into the back of another staffer's car: "I just need you to drive me to the hotel." When I turned my phone on, sixty-two messages from every walk of my life—people talking about how they were in their offices crying, and everybody said the same thing: *My president sees me. My president knows me.*

VANITA GUPTA

There really was an incredible sense of community and togetherness that I think everyone needed.

CODY KEENAN

And very quickly people forgot about Charleston, because there was a two-day stretch where the ACA was upheld and marriage equality became the law of the land. As we landed, and the sun was going down, the front of the White House was lit up in the colors of the rainbow.

JENNIFER PALMIERI

Director of Communications, White House (2013–2015)
Director of Communications, Hillary for America (2015–2016)

The memorable moments from when I was there? A couple shutdowns, Ebola, Healthcare.gov, ISIS beheadings, Ukraine, Bergdahl, the stupid GSA/Vegas trip—I left in 2015 just as things started getting better. As I came back to the White House just to visit with people, right after the greatest week ever, the president's like, "Yeah, man, you really should have stuck around."

CODY KEENAN

The Confederate flag came down,[176] and that was like the fourth-most-important thing of the week. We always joked how he passed trade-promotion-authority legislation through Congress,[177] which for a lot of presidents would have been like the biggest thing to happen to them all year. It was like the fifth-biggest thing of the week. It was exhausting and it was amazing. It was probably the week that might have summed up this White House and this country more than any other.

ROB O'DONNELL

Those ten days really set the tone for the last eighteen months. I was waiting to get my security clearance to go into the White House, and for the first time in a long time, we were like, *We're back out in front again. We're not going to be lame ducks.*

---

176 Following the Charleston shooting, calls increased for the removal of the Confederate flag from state government buildings. President Obama agreed, stating that the flag "belongs in a museum." On July 10, the flag was taken down from the South Carolina Capitol, where it had flown for fifty-four years.

177 Trade-promotion authority, also known as fast-track authority, is a temporary power granted to POTUS to negotiate trade agreements. In 2012, President Obama indicated interest in renewing the authority after it had expired in 2007, in order to conclude the Trans-Pacific Partnership. Legislation granting Obama fast-track authority narrowly passed the House by 218–208, and then passed the Senate on June 24, 2015, 60–38.

CODY KEENAN

It was a ten-day stretch that began with the worst of humanity and cruelty and malice, and it unfolded in ways nobody had expected. Nobody ever thought about the Confederate flag coming down and someone like Nikki Haley setting an incredible example.[178] Then, bang, the ACA was upheld again.[179] Bang, marriage equality. And then the president of the United States led the country in a eulogy on unearned grace. And again, that's where he hit things that you just couldn't reach as a speechwriter. It's not like I went to sit down and draft a eulogy and said, "Hey, I'm going to do a sermon on the concept of unearned grace." I mean, that's insane. It was his idea. He led the whole thing.

BARBARA LEE

It really was a watershed moment, not [just] for me personally but also the country and the world, when President Obama announced his vision for establishing relations with Cuba.[180] Since the mid-'70s I'd been trying to end this embargo. I'd taken delegations there. It just didn't make sense. It was a bad policy. When the president announced many of the policies that would shift

---

178 As governor of South Carolina, Haley called for the immediate removal of the Confederate flag from State House grounds on June 22, 2015, five days after the mass shooting in Charleston. "What I realize now more than ever," she said, "is people were driving by and they felt hurt and pain. No one should feel pain."

179 The 6–3 decision in *King v. Burwell* was the second Supreme Court case to have ruled in favor of the Affordable Care Act. In 2012's *National Federation of Independent Business et al. v. Sebelius, Secretary of Health and Human Services, et al.*, several businesses (joined by attorneys general from twenty-six states) argued that Health and Human Services Secretary Kathleen Sebelius violated the Constitution by enforcing the "individual mandate," which required most Americans to either purchase health insurance coverage or pay a "penalty." In a 5–4 decision, SCOTUS determined "that the mandate may be upheld as within Congress's power to 'lay and collect taxes.'"

180 July 1, 2015: Following fifty-four years of strained diplomatic relations, President Obama announced that Cuba and the United States would reopen their respective embassies, which had been shuttered under the Eisenhower administration. Both embassies began officially operating on July 20, and Secretary of State John Kerry presided over a reopening ceremony at the US embassy in Havana on August 14, the first time the US's top diplomat had visited the country since 1945.

towards normalizing, you know, any way I could have helped move the ball forward.

CHRIS VAN HOLLEN

I'd always raise the case of Alan Gross, my constituent who was held prisoner in Cuba for over [five] years, and a number of members of Congress also engaged in trying to change our bankrupt policy. And the president was focused on the need to change our approach, but the fact that Alan Gross was being held prisoner made it difficult to move forward. So we had to resolve the Alan Gross situation in a way that would be advantageous to the United States. That ultimately involved identifying some prisoners the Cubans were holding. Some of our intelligence assets had been discovered and imprisoned by the Cubans, and they were released. That person was released about the same time that [three] of the [remaining] Cuban Five were released.

BARBARA LEE

I was part of the work that led to Alan Gross's release. It was just really quite dynamic. Also, I went with Secretary Kerry when he reopened the embassy, and the Marines who actually took down the flag when we left Cuba? They were there. They were in their eighties.

JONATHAN FINER

Summer of 2015, yeah, so a few things about that: One was that, just a week before we got to Vienna, the Supreme Leader Ayatollah Khamenei of Iran put out a series of statements that said, *The following are red lines.* There were seven main ones. Each of these seemed, on its face, to contradict a fundamental aspect of the agreement that we thought we had reached in Lausanne.

RICHARD NEPHEW

I was still convinced, from the start, that the interest of both countries and the leaderships of both countries were gonna get it done.

JONATHAN FINER

Some people had said, "We'll never get a deal. They're going back on what they had already said." Our sense at that point was, we will not treat that as the official Iranian position. We need to see what they say in the room with the negotiators. We need to go and test this. It's too important for abandonment.

DENNIS ROSS

There were those who felt it was so significant to get the deal done because it made sure that the Iranians wouldn't be able to have a nuclear weapon anytime soon, and it would create the possibility of more-enduring channels that maybe offered the prospect of moderating their behavior—because maybe you could integrate them into the international financial system in a way that would also build their states into doing less troublemaking. That was one side of the debate. There was another side that said people who were against the deal were overstating its weaknesses and the people who were for it were overstating its strengths.

JONATHAN FINER

The other thing that happened was that one month before we were supposed to get to Vienna, Secretary Kerry was riding his bike and ended up hitting a curb, falling, and fracturing his femur, which was a very serious injury. It required him to have surgery and be medevaced from [France] to recuperate for a bit. So there was some question initially as to whether, physically, he'd be up to both the intense many hours of negotiations and also even traveling back to Europe to conduct them. Because we'd always done [the negotiations] in Europe, so that no one would be able to claim some sort of unfair home-country advantage. In the end, Secretary Kerry recovered extraordinarily well but remained in a high level of pain throughout a lot of that negotiating period.

DENNIS ROSS

The natural instinct, before you close a deal, is to satisfy yourself that you couldn't do better, that you couldn't get more. It works in many high-stakes negotiations that way. My view was there was going to be a deal. Now, I'm sure if you're in the middle of negotiations, you ride a roller coaster of emotions where one day you think, *Okay, we got it*, and then the next day you think, *We're gonna lose it*. And I'm sure that's what the mood was there. I'm sure of it.

RICHARD NEPHEW

You couldn't sustain, year on year, 45 percent inflation. That would be unsustainable in our system and in our economic experience. Now, that doesn't necessarily mean much, because for the Iranian experience that kind of inflation was normal. So for their own psyche, it was a little bit of a different impact than it would be for the US, but this was, to me, one of the key points of the whole thing. We were in a position where we desperately didn't want the Iranian nuclear program going any further than it was, and the Iranians desperately didn't want the sanctions to go any further than they were. So our interests synchronized, and to me, that overcame a lot in terms of pens being thrown and all that. That's all kind of a sideshow compared to the fact that the national interests on both sides were so strong.

JONATHAN FINER

We stayed for almost three weeks, the longest any secretary of state had ever remained in any single city outside the United States in the history of the country. At moments during that period it looked like things would fall apart. There were some intense negotiating sessions and instances of people storming out or shouting at each other, and by the end—late the evening of July 13, early in the morning of July 14—we nailed down the final substantive details such that we had an agreement. And we were able to announce that agreement in front of the world on July 14.

DENNIS ROSS

But after 15 years, the Iranians will have a large nuclear infrastructure that is legitimate and puts them in a position where the path to Obama's block is simply deferred for that period of time. So the challenge becomes, you couldn't say it's blocked all the paths. You could say you blocked fifteen years and you now have time, and you need to do something with that time to make it even less likely. And I think there was a not-insignificant part of the national-security community that looked at it that way.

WENDY SHERMAN

When people would say they didn't like the deal, I'd ask, "What's your alternative?" The two alternatives most people talk about were: That we should have bombed their facilities, but you cannot bomb away knowledge. They have mastered the entire nuclear fuel cycle. So you could have bombed their buildings, but within two or three years, they would have recreated them, and probably underground, in secret. The second that people talked about was that you should have continued to sanction them and tighten the noose. The only reason we got countries around the world to enforce the sanctions was because we said we would be committed to giving diplomacy a try. So if you blew up the diplomacy, you're not going to have the cooperation of countries around the world to impose sanctions, because they all took an economic hit to enforce those sanctions.

JONATHAN FINER

I think for many of us, this stood as the foremost example of what a combination of willingness to use military force, if necessary—because the president had always said that—economic sanctions, diplomatic engagements through negotiations, what all of those tools that we had at our disposal could accomplish if used in a concerted, coordinated strategy toward the goal that we set. Which was preventing Iran from getting a nuclear weapon, and we accomplished that.

CHRIS VAN HOLLEN

That's why you had the Israeli intelligence services insisting that Netanyahu stick with the deal.

YOHANNES ABRAHAM

That time period generally felt good. It felt like we had turned the corner, and 2014 had been a tough year for a lot of reasons, but by that point, we had been executing well. Things felt good. That summer, as a general matter, felt like things were moving in our direction writ large in terms of our priorities.

JEN PSAKI

I would say 2014 was not his favorite year of his presidency. It was probably not the best year of his presidency, and not on the communications front either. He was ready to do things differently and was open to different approaches, and so in 2015, we really had this clean slate. I mean, I'd been there before, but it'd been a while. I think a big part of it was, we focused on *What is the president good at and how can we utilize that to use his time? Let's focus those conversations on things he cares deeply about. Let's do some different platforms like podcasts and more digital options*, because, honestly, they'd reach a lot more people. It was a waste of time for him to go fly to a factory, get a tour, and give ten minutes of remarks. No one covers it. No one cares. It's not getting his message out. Obviously, a lot of this he was up for and game for, and so part of our process was presenting things to him, seeing what he liked and what worked.

FERIAL GOVASHIRI

The First Lady was having an event for these young women, a pop-up concert,[181] and the president wanted to support her and do a surprise drop-in. "Get the logistics real quick so we know what we're walking into." Quickly, I was trying

---

181 On July 23, 2015, the First Lady and Education Secretary Arne Duncan hosted 140 college-bound students at the "Beating the Odds" summit, part of FLOTUS's Reach Higher initiative to complete education past high school.

to get anyone on her staff to get me the details. "Who is performing? Where is it? And where is the First Lady going to be speaking?" No one could hear their phones in there, but this one person finally wrote back. All I got in response was, *East Room. W-A-L-E.* So the president was like, "Okay, where am I going?" I was like, "You're going to the East Room." He just bolted. I had to quickly tell Secret Service, and so I caught up to him down the colonnade and he yelled out, "Who's performing again?" And I was like, *"WHALE!"* He stopped, half turned, and looked me in the eye. "You mean Wale."

BRAD JENKINS

Look. We all make mistakes.

FERIAL GOVASHIRI

My jaw was down. He just shook his head and took off. All the things ran through my brain—him meeting the singer and announcing the wrong thing to all these young girls, who probably knew exactly who he was, and losing cool points. Or being in front of the media and saying, "Whale," and that would have been my fault. I was seriously on the verge of *Should I resign?* Thank God he was the coolest person, because otherwise I would have made him look like such a nerd because I'm such a nerd. He hugged me and was like, "It's okay, but you really need to get up on your music."

Govashiri and President Obama in the Green Room. July 23, 2015. Pete Souza, White House

PETE SOUZA

I remember the occasion, but not the photo. Not to diminish how meaningful this was to Ferial; to me it was one of a million things that happened in eight years.

FERIAL GOVASHIRI

I went back and did a deep dive about the singer, and I saw that he has a song about how people call him "whale" even though his name is Wale, and I just thought, *Dude, put an accent on your name!*

ROB O'DONNELL

All of the talk that if only President Obama had spent more time schmoozing with lobbyists and members on Capitol Hill and doing the DC parlor games, then he would have gotten stuff done? Boehner basically being forced out as leader of his own caucus justified the fact that some of that talk wasn't based in reality or merit.

MICHAEL STEEL

Remember, when it came to Boehner leaving, and when he did, he never wanted to do the job that long. He probably would have left at least maybe after the 2014 midterms or something like that. I mean, he was clearly aiming to leave and turn over the House majority to Mr. Cantor, and then, when Mr. Cantor lost his primary, it meant Boehner had to stick around a little longer than he planned.

ROB O'DONNELL

Boehner was the consummate person who had his glass of red wine, he had his cigarette, he was well liked by the entire Republican caucus. He couldn't even get the intransigent Republicans on board. And, like, that's how I think some people felt about Boehner leaving. It was like a vindication.

MICHAEL STEEL

I was actually gone by then. I left in May of 2015 to go work for Governor Bush's presidential campaign . . . I think the Speaker was an underappreciated figure in terms of changes he often forced by sheer personal will—whether that's on school choice, ending earmarks in Congress, or staring down the president to force trillions of dollars in spending cuts . . . There were obviously substantial areas of difference, but they both believed that free trade made America more prosperous. When it came to the wars in Iraq and Afghanistan, candidate Obama was more naive than President Obama. And so once he got into office and grappled with the reality of what we were facing, he came around to policies that were similar to the Bush administration in a lot of ways.

BRIAN DEESE

When people talked about Obama's foreign policy, people wouldn't usually go to climate. But it's a good example of the sort of slow, persistent, patient diplomacy, recognizing that to engineer that kind of change actually did take multiple years and a chessboard approach. It took six-plus years to push that kind of change.

JONATHAN FINER

There was just an incredible momentum in Paris. Once people got in the room and started negotiating, things really did, for the most part, proceed in a pretty linear and direct way.

BRIAN DEESE

The thing that's interesting about the actual Paris Agreement was that these were two weeklong negotiating sessions. And because of how much of a disaster Copenhagen was, in 2009, France—who hosted the Paris conference, obviously—was dead set against having heads of state come at the end of the conference. They were worried about Copenhagen. Everyone had PTSD.

JAKE LEVINE

It's interesting, because in the second term, Copenhagen was panned as this awful disaster, and a meaningless result. But that's not really true. Ultimately, we did bring all of these countries to the table to sit down, negotiate, and focus, at least to sort of get to a commitment. You had to be an incrementalist here to appreciate it, but it was a bit of a sea change from where the negotiations had been, in terms of these so-called developing nations versus the so-called developed nations.

BRIAN DEESE

So they said, "Look, we shouldn't have the heads of state come at the end. It will be a disaster. Instead, the heads of state should come at the beginning." But that created its own problem because you had Obama, Xi, Modi, and all of these folks come right at the beginning of the conference and then leave. Once they left, they'd leave their negotiators to pull things together.

JONATHAN FINER

Brian, Secretary Kerry, and I were all there for that.

BRIAN DEESE

We knew that the United States and China being willing to exert pressure on their respective counterparts was key. So what the president decided was, rather than get into all of the particulars, he had a direct conversation with President Xi. At the beginning of the conference they sat across the table from each other, looked at each other eye to eye, and basically said, *We've developed trust, but this is still going to be difficult. There's going to be a moment over the next two weeks where the United States and China are going to have to respectively make good on the commitment, and we need to be prepared to direct our teams at that moment to get things done, to bring this to a close.* President Xi agreed to that.

JONATHAN PERSHING

You're always trying to assess, to triage. You are thinking about where you need that highest, most senior input, where you need them to come in and make calls with their counterparts. This may often be to people in a different place, and in a different time zone—but still needs to be timely enough to affect the outcome.

BRIAN DEESE

As these conferences would go, there was a huge amount of bickering and fighting. Things looked like they could go either way. With seventy-two hours left, when Kerry, Todd Stern, and I were in the trenches on a day-to-day basis, every night President Obama called heads of state from back in the United States just to touch base.

TODD STERN

We were on the opposite sides of some tough issues for a long time, all the way up until maybe two days before the end, and there was a point then, late in the day, when I got together with [Chinese negotiator] Xie and we were still looking at a number of sticking points. Xie said to me, "Now we have to get together and figure out how to resolve this." He's not talking about just big-picture issues in general, but . . . issues that we needed to resolve and use our influence to do that.

BRIAN DEESE

On [Thursday] night, very late US time, superlate—like four in the morning— French time, the president called President Xi just before the conference was intended to end.[182] *Things are stuck. Now is the moment to bring things to a close. I'm going to direct my team that we can no longer allow each side to bicker.* President Xi agreed to do the same. That produced a meaningful change in the posture of the Chinese negotiating team, and created an environment where it was still quite frenetic over the last forty-eight hours . . . Then there was the hiccup with the "should/shall" at the very end.

TODD STERN

There was a meeting of the whole plenary on Saturday. Fabius, the French foreign minister, made a speech to everybody,[183] and here we are just about at the final moment, on the brink of achieving this big thing and the final draft was going to be circulating within an hour or two. We went back to our various delegation rooms to wait for the thing to come over the wire, and when it did we started to print copies. I grabbed the first one and sat down to read it and, "4.4—wait a minute, what was that?"

JONATHAN FINER

Our position was to not have it be a legally binding agreement—that every country's political commitment to do its part should be enough. So everybody knew that inserting the word "shall" would have been a deal breaker. The word "shall" hadn't been in a draft of the agreement for many months, and so when

---

182 December 10–11, 2015.
183 Laurent Fabius, Minister of Foreign Affairs and International Development, 2012–2016.

we saw this in the final version that had been printed, Secretary Kerry called Foreign Minister Fabius, who had control of the document. "I hope that this is a mistake. This is a huge problem for us."

TODD STERN

We sat down with our lawyers and immediately realized this was not a word we could accept. It was actually a highly threatening moment for the entire negotiation. That language was *not* in the penultimate draft, and it wasn't what had been agreed to. I'd actually discussed that with Xie, and I had discussed it with Fabius—this is Article 4, Paragraph 4—"shall" is a word that connoted a legally binding undertaking and "should" is a word that does *not* connote a legally binding undertaking.[184] It's just black and white.

JONATHAN FINER

Fabius seemed surprised that this word had appeared, and within forty-five minutes had called us back and said yes, this was a mistake.

TODD STERN

Fabius didn't know that had happened, but they had already sent what was supposed to be the final for everybody. So we had to actually go in the plenary room, and the danger was that if a few countries would say, *We're not going to allow it. If Fabius wants this changed, we want to make five other changes.* And you might say, "Well, no, just tell them it was an accident." Why would they believe *that?*

---

184 "Developed country Parties should continue taking the lead by undertaking economywide absolute emission reduction targets. Developing country Parties should continue enhancing their mitigation efforts, and are encouraged to move over time towards economy-wide emission reduction or limitation targets in the light of different national circumstances."

JONATHAN FINER

We had to go around to other delegations and explain that this was not a change. We were seeing to something that had already been negotiated but had been mistakenly transcribed.

TODD STERN

It's perfectly plausible to think this was a last-minute special favor to the United States. Not that it was a mistake, but that "shall" was what it was *supposed* to be. In any event, that was a huge risk, a huge danger. If five countries felt abused by the agreement in one way or another because some pet thing of their own hadn't gotten in and thought we were getting special treatment, the whole thing could have fallen apart.

JONATHAN FINER

In the end, everybody backed off.

TODD STERN

In the actual public meeting, once it resumed, Fabius was masterful. He never announced to the whole group what had happened. He just read through a number of errata-type changes—"There's a comma here, there's a word there"— and right before part four, he just read what it was supposed to say. He didn't say, "It says 'shall' and now it's gonna say 'should.'" He just read, "For part four, we need to *blah-dah-bump*." And he slammed the gavel down and it was done.[185]

---

185 Fabius's banging of the gavel the evening of Saturday, December 12, 2015, confirmed the political commitments of 190-plus countries to lower greenhouse-gas emissions. United Nations Secretary General Ban Ki-moon: "This is truly a historic moment. For the first time, we have a truly universal agreement on climate change, one of the most crucial problems on Earth."

JONATHAN FINER

Everybody had this sense of seizing the moment and, to some extent, the uncertainty of the subsequent election infused our side with the greater sense of urgency. But the rest of the world was not conforming itself to our political calendar. That, in and of itself, would not have been enough to move anybody other than the United States.

JOEL BENENSON

In a campaign, you know when you have it clinched. Clinched in the sense of, if you have two viable candidates, the ability of one to catch the other in delegates. The math is the math. You can't change the math unless you dramatically change the trajectory, and if you pile up enough wins, at some point it is very hard to catch up. March 15, 2016, was the night at which [the Clinton campaign] basically had a delegate lead that we were never going to relinquish again.

JEFF WEAVER

We won four states on Super Tuesday, and we came within an inch of winning Massachusetts. And certainly after New Hampshire, the second contest, when Bernie Sanders won by [twenty-two] points, you know, there was a tremendous amount of concern among certain establishment forces.

CODY KEENAN

People forget how contentious 2008 was. There was the whole [pro–Hillary Clinton] PUMA movement that said they would never vote for Barack Obama no matter what,[186] and, obviously, that never materialized. It might have been even more contentious this time around.

---

186 People United Means Action, aka Party Unity, My Ass!

JEREMY BIRD

Sanders was done after she won Missouri. That day when she won all five of those states?[187] There's no way he was winning.

JEFF WEAVER

He came within 1,500 votes of winning Missouri. He won Michigan. He came within half a percentage point of winning Illinois. Many of Secretary Clinton's weaknesses had been exposed in the primary, and that's not a criticism of her. I mean, clearly she had a problem with young people. She had a problem with people of color who were under forty-five, which, you know, Bernie Sanders consistently won African Americans under forty-five. He was winning young Latinos even before that. So she clearly had problems with young people, with working-class people, with rural people, and independents. Those were all laid on the table during the primary process, and I didn't think that there was an effort to deal with it.

JOEL BENENSON

That's nonsense. He lost Ohio. He lost North Carolina to us. He lost Illinois to us. In reality, what the long campaign did was both suck up resources, and Senator Sanders's message became the foundational message of the attack on Hillary Clinton from the Republicans. So basically, from March through June, they didn't have to attack her. He did, and he made the argument that they were going to make across the country.

---

187 March 15, 2016: After clinching primary victories in North Carolina, Florida, Illinois, and Ohio, Secretary Clinton beat out Sanders by 1,531 votes in Missouri. The Vermont senator's spokesman reassured the press that the candidate would not request a recount in the interest of saving "taxpayers of Missouri some money." Instead, his focus would remain on "taking the contest all the way to the Democratic National Convention in Philadelphia."

BARBARA BOXER

I thought Bernie had a very good populist message, but it was narrow. He didn't really talk about women's health, equality, diversity, and immigration. Her campaign was more focused on broader issues than that. I certainly always got along with Bernie, but I was very strong for Hillary.

LUIS GUTIÉRREZ

Sanders literally sat next to me for years on the Financial Services Committee,[188] but he never once talked to me, even though I was, you know, very much a leader on immigration. He never addressed those issues to me, and with Hillary, it was different. I knew her from when her husband was president, and I met with her like September of '91 for the first time. We campaigned together. So we were good, and I endorsed her in New York with thousands of people cheering on. It was a much more open, easier relationship with her.

JEFF WEAVER

I would describe Bernie Sanders as a movement politician, right? He believed in governing with a strong grassroots movement. I thought in many ways Barack Obama ran as a movement politician. It's an admittedly difficult thing to maintain once you get into office, but Bernie Sanders wanted to transform the country. That's not just passing a few laws. He wanted to fundamentally change the way the government and economic actors related to regular people.

STUART STEVENS

One of the truisms of the conservative Republican world had been that the country was actually more center-right than Barack Obama, but because of Bush fatigue, his incredible charisma as a candidate, and the economic crash, the country accepted and embraced Barack Obama even though he was more

---

188 Sanders served on the committee during his years in the House of Representatives (1991-2007).

left than the country. There's a lot of data to suggest that's true. However, you looked at Bernie Sanders, and the idea that an obscure democratic socialist from this tiny state could become the most popular politician in America? You had to ask the question, "Is the country more center-left than it used to be?"

JOEL BENENSON

I got criticized roundly by all the Bernie bros and the trolls on Twitter when going into the New York primary in late April. I thought he was running a negative campaign and should tone it down. They all went crazy: *Tone it down?!* I said, "Go read his speeches." He was attacking her every day, but you're going to have to overcome difficult things to win the general election.

TAD DEVINE

Chief Strategist, Bernie Sanders for President, 2016

She had to win that nomination on her own right. We can debate the merits of whether or not the deck was stacked. I mean, a lot of what came out afterward vindicated our view that the process was not as fair and balanced as it should have been.

ROB O'DONNELL

There's no question the DNC was culpable, and Bernie supporters had every right to be upset. I didn't even know how the DNC set their debate schedule, but the process from an outsider's perspective felt like most of the DNC folks were Clinton supporters or had ties there. They should have—similar to what the president would do, particularly around the Russian-hack stuff—gone out of their way to make the entire process look like it was a big tent and that Bernie's team felt like they had a say. They just didn't do that, and there's no question that it felt to Bernie supporters, and even to an objective person, that the scales had been tipped a bit.

JOEL BENENSON

His diagnosis of a rigged political and economic system for working people was spot on. He just tried to make her more of the cause of that than she deserved or that was necessary or productive, when it was clear he wasn't going to get the nomination.

MICHAEL FROMAN

Given the politics around this election, it was understandable that she took the position she did with [opposing the Trans-Pacific Partnership]. I didn't think it was fundamentally about what was in the agreement, which itself was sound, but the politics became unmanageable. It was difficult to push back against a fact-free debate, or a postfact debate, with the complexities of international trade.

JONATHAN FINER

Senator Sanders never supported it. Secretary Clinton did write in her book very positive things about TPP, but in the end their positions were not all that different. The sort of pro–free trade community in the United States had for a long time underestimated some of the dislocations and disaffections related to trade, and I think that, plus a series of other factors, led to a shift in our politics that was not very well foreseen. It caught a lot of people by surprise . . . What it cost us, strategically, was our partners and allies in Asia [who began] to question whether this new commitment encapsulated in the rebalance was real.

JENNIFER GRANHOLM

It was all about jobs and uncertainty, and we were in this era of accelerations, accelerations related to technology displacing workers in addition to globalization. The combination, for Michigan, had been so powerful. Each technology platform was moving so fast that the training for people to keep up wasn't as adequate as one would have hoped.

JEFF WEAVER

The president certainly came to us through back channels many times, on how he was under a tremendous amount of pressure to endorse Secretary Clinton and to be supportive of her much earlier in the process. It's never a positive when the sitting Democratic president was going to endorse your opponent, but we did obviously know it was coming.

TAD DEVINE

We all knew where the campaign was at that juncture. It was obvious that Hillary was going to be the nominee of the party. The question was, how was that all going to be accomplished? What was the choreography behind it? You know, I think Bernie had spoken to the president and the vice president several times during the course of the campaign. They were always constructive meetings and conversations, and I expected the same would be true when he met with the president at the White House.

CODY KEENAN

I was walking out of West Exec on the day Bernie had come to a meeting in the EOB, and a bunch of young staffers on the top of the steps were just trying to get a glimpse of Bernie Sanders showing up. My first thought was, *This is not viewing hours. Fall in line. Get back to work.*

ROB O'DONNELL

It was important for the president to sit down with Senator Sanders, hear his views, and make sure that, moving forward, we would incorporate them. He had defied expectations beyond anyone's imagination, and it was really important that we showed him the respect as he wound down his campaign.

GENE SPERLING

I wasn't in every conversation, but I didn't think there was anything that transactional. I really did not believe in any way that there was some agreement about 2016. This was a president who had a bit of loyalty toward his secretary of state and thought that she was the best hope to be elected and protect his legacy. I didn't think it was more complicated than that. If Biden had run, he would have been in a difficult position. My guess is he would have stayed out of it. Who could have even imagined the circumstances that would lead to that?

TAD DEVINE

I thought Obama, and Biden in particular, were very much in sync with Bernie's message. I think if Biden had run, he would have delivered the same message that Bernie was delivering about the economy and about ideas like tuition-free public colleges. I think Biden was very much on board, and he made that clear in the Rose Garden when he spoke about not running and also the agenda that he thought the country should follow.

JEFF WEAVER

I did think that the president, and the vice president as well, frankly, did a commendable job of trying, despite tremendous internal pressure, to stay out of it and let the voters decide.

DANIELLE CRUTCHFIELD

Going out stumping for HRC took him back to the campaign trail, the old days when the bubble was smaller. That's genuine. He legitimately loved it and he fed off the crowd, too.

ROB O'DONNELL

The president would make the case for Secretary Clinton in interviews, speeches, and videos. We were doing prep for one of these interviews right before the

DNC. It was [White House Press Secretary] Josh Earnest, Jen Psaki, myself, and maybe Ben Rhodes, and he really made the case for how strongly he felt about her candidacy. Everything he said was really true about Secretary Clinton. For me, as someone who had been an Obama guy since 2008, I was always skeptical and hesitant, but that was what really turned me around. That day forward I was like, *Okay, I'm fully on board with the Clinton campaign.*

LUIS GUTIÉRREZ

Nobody ever remembers me speaking at the conventions, except you know which convention people remember me speaking at? This last one, they put me at eight o'clock on Monday[189]—Hillary Clinton. Maybe I should have endorsed *her* in 2008!

JOEL BENENSON

And, you know, Bernie endorsed her. He campaigned for her. He did all those things, but with two third-party candidates on the ballot, there was a comfortable place for disaffected Bernie Sanders voters to go, based on a message he drove for thirteen months. And for some other voters, when that message was reinforced in the Republican campaign, it added another brick to the load you're carrying.

---

189 July 25, 2016.

2016–2017

The month of October delivered no shortage of favorable news for President Obama's presumed successor. The media crowned Hillary Clinton the victor of all three presidential debates against Donald Trump. When the Department of Homeland Security and the Director of National Intelligence issued a joint statement fingering the Kremlin as the perpetrator behind the Democratic National Committee's email hack, the Clinton camp expected headlines sympathetic to its cause. But the same afternoon, the news cycle became consumed by a video in which the leader of the Republican Party bragged on a hot mic about groping women. "When you're a star," Trump said, "they let you do it. You can do anything."

One White House aide felt at the time that the jaw-dropping footage, recorded in 2005, was "a deal breaker for a lot of undecided voters and maybe decided voters." Not so. The true October surprise of the election didn't come from either campaign's opposition-research teams, but from the director of the FBI. On October 28, James Comey, months after closing his investigation into Clinton's handling of classified information, alerted Congress to possible new findings related to Email-gate. "Of course, we don't ordinarily tell Congress about ongoing investigations," Comey wrote, "but here I feel an obligation to do so, given that I testified repeatedly in recent months that our investigation was completed."

The Democratic Party nominee's lead narrowed, and caution pervaded the West Wing. "The polls are right until they're not," suggested Brian Deese during one meeting on the Friday before Election Day. Communications staffer Rob O'Donnell interpreted the quip to mean that "if the American public decided over the weekend that they liked Hillary Clinton but they were gonna vote for

Trump, then that could happen. The polls were only as good as Snapchat, in that they captured that moment." The world watched with trepidation. "It tended to be with many, if not most, countries the sort of first topic that everybody asked about," Jonathan Finer recalled. "'Is it true that Mr. Trump might win?'"

KORI SCHULMAN

The evening before the election, I was there late, until midnight or so. I was the last person in my office and had been watching the Philly rally on TV. It was really quiet. I walked out of the EEOB, and the lights were on in the White House. I remember thinking, *Tomorrow when I leave, we'll know.* I felt some calm in that.

ROB O'DONNELL

I had spoken to Clinton-campaign folks even up until the afternoon on Election Day, and they were pretty much, *You know, it's going to be a normal day. We feel pretty confident.* [At the White House] we were all talking through Hillary Clinton coming to visit on Thursday, how we would manage that, and what people were doing for election-night celebrations. I was at a victory party for Senator [-elect] Van Hollen because my brother worked on the campaign, and, unlike the 2012 Election Day, where you're sitting on pins and needles all day long, we pretty much took it for granted.

DAVID CUSACK

We had become very tightly knit crews, family-like, and so we decided, since it was such a historic occasion, that we would watch it together in our offices. So we had a whole pizza-and-beer-and-wine party to watch, and I was there with my brother, who was actually Al Gore's body person from '96 to 2000. Everyone else there was under the age of thirty, and by nine thirty or so, we started to get an inkling that something was amiss.

JEN PSAKI

No one thought he was going to win—no one in the White House that I talked to in the days leading up to it. The president was out there the whole day on Monday. He did a bunch of stuff Tuesday. It was the overnight, from Tuesday to Wednesday, when everybody was in a complete state of shock.

VALERIE JARRETT

It was brutal. I didn't see it coming.

CODY KEENAN

I'd been awake all night, watching returns with Ben Rhodes, Dan Pfeiffer, and my wife, Kristen. The president called at two a.m. "We're going to have to rework tomorrow's remarks a little bit." He suggested a few things he wanted to say. Then I sobered up and got to work.

DAVID CUSACK

We were there until about one thirty in the morning. There was already a team with POTUS setting up all the phone calls, but we had to think about protesters on Pennsylvania Avenue, making sure to tell the Secret Service how we were planning to handle all that stuff. So I was watching all these young people put aside the personal feelings about how the election turned, and just be able to flip a switch and think about everything that we needed to do around campus.

KORI SCHULMAN

I woke up every hour to check my phone to see where things stood—if more ballots were going to be counted. I tried to convince myself that there was some kind of path.

JOHN DINGELL

She had that damned election won. I voted for her, and the end result was Trump, who everybody thought couldn't win and wouldn't win. They thought he was crazy. By golly, he wasn't a majority winner, but he did get a majority of the votes in the electoral college.

DAVID PLOUFFE

My strong suspicion on election night was he probably had mixed reactions to winning. I'm sure he was seething that night.

JENNIFER PALMIERI

It felt like a reckoning to me. Tensions had been simmering under the radar, and we'd gone through twenty years of incredible disruption. People don't express frustration when you're in the middle of a crisis. They wait until it's passed. The Great Recession, when you're going through that, everybody was still just getting by, and then things started getting better but not for everyone, and that's when this all came crashing down. Even if Hillary had won, that reckoning would still have been there.

JENNIFER GRANHOLM

Obama would have been elected in a heartbeat. Voters responded to Trump because he was angry and was talking about NAFTA and jobs. You know, Bernie Sanders would have been elected in Michigan, too. He was so clear about that message.

JEFF WEAVER

Hindsight is twenty-twenty, as they say.

ROB O'DONNELL

I got no sleep. I remember the morning being a Wednesday, so typically we'd have our senior-communication-team huddle. And I was like, *Do we still have that? What's the protocol now that Donald Trump has been elected president?*

JEN PSAKI

I didn't know what the president anticipated in terms of people's reactions to the fact that the country just elected this misogynist, and how we all felt about that as humans. Because we all worked for somebody who was entirely different, and what did that say about the country?

ROB O'DONNELL

I got in at maybe eight fifteen and grabbed a water from the mess in the West Wing. I ran into Denis McDonough. "Good morning, Rob." He looked like he had spent most of the night up following the elections and, obviously, being chief of staff to the president, had to think through all the different mechanisms of governing and regulations that maybe would come undone. He had the weight of the entire government to think about.

CODY KEENAN

I went in early and the first thing that struck me was that my assistant couldn't stop crying. "I know you're upset and everybody's upset, but you gotta stop crying. We're at work." And it struck me that there were so many young people who got their start not just in politics, but postcollege—like Rob O'Donnell, who dropped out of college to join the campaign. Barack Obama was all they knew. Winning elections was all they knew. We lost in the midterms, but they didn't know defeat at this scale.

KORI SCHULMAN

It was like a funeral. My eyes were full of tears.

ROB O'DONNELL

Everyone just wanted to get through their mornings before having any real conversations with anyone. Then, sometime later, they held a meeting with the entire comms team in Josh Earnest's office. Josh and Psaki led it off, and then they opened the floor for people to talk.

FERIAL GOVASHIRI

The president walked in the Oval. We looked at each other, didn't need to say anything. He knew he was going to have to make a statement that day. So he's like, "Can you go get Cody?"

CODY KEENAN

Josh talked about the campaigns he'd lost. Psaki talked about the campaigns she'd lost. She'd been on Kerry. I hadn't been on a losing campaign, only because I had started working for Ted Kennedy out of college—Obama was my first actual campaign—but Kennedy was a big Kerry surrogate in 2004. We lost that pretty hard, and on Inauguration Day in 2005 most people got the day off just because they wanted the Mall cleared. But in the Senate we had to confirm a bunch of President Bush's nominees. So I had to go to work, and I took the Metro surrounded by people in cowboy boots and fur coats all headed to the ball. That was my hell.

ROB O'DONNELL

Cody had begun speaking about what the president was going to say. "It's going to be the type of remarks that no one will be excited about." It wasn't a call to arms for Democrats. It was very gracious, and exactly the message the president wanted to send.

FERIAL GOVASHIRI

I peeked my head in Josh Earnest's office. Pretty much all of the communications team was in there, along with some other staffers. Normally I would never barge in on a meeting, but anytime the president was looking for someone, I would walk into anything and demand answers. So I cut through, and Cody was in the center. Our staff at that time was younger than when we had started, and Cody was a senior staffer and was trying to talk everyone down. I needed to grab him, but everyone was listening and crying—not just one tear or two tears, like *crying*—and I decided I wasn't going to interrupt. I knew the president had a couple extra minutes.

CODY KEENAN

I was sharing how, if you wanted to stay in politics and keep making a difference, you were going to lose all the time. "What defines you is how you get back up and move forward. We're still in this office for another two and a half months, and there're still a lot of things to get done. The country's watching us today to see how we carry ourselves."

ROB O'DONNELL

Some people were just stone silent.

FERIAL GOVASHIRI

The president was like, "Where is he?" Then I said, "I think it's gonna be a couple minutes. He's in the middle of something." I would never say that. I would always say something like, "He's coming" or "He's on his way." And the president knew something was up, so I told him the story. "I don't want to interrupt him. He's helping all these other staffers feel better." And he's like, "What?" I told him how, like, they're very upset and crying. He's like, "I'm going to go in there," and I was like, "No, no. You're not going to fit in there. It's gonna be mayhem. More people are gonna come if they know you're in there." And he was like, "You know what? Send them all in here."

ROB O'DONNELL

Two minutes later, Ferial came back. "The president would like to see all of you in the Oval." I didn't think the president had any clue how many people actually worked in the communications office. There were like thirty of us. He'd worked with most of them but had never seen all of them at once.

FERIAL GOVASHIRI

No one ever really heard that before. They kind of looked at each other. "No, I'm serious. Please. This is not a joke. Everyone just go to the Oval right now." I ran out of another door through the Roosevelt Room to get in front of everybody, and I got to the president first. "Sir, they're all coming in. There's a lot of them." And he said, "Okay, bring them in."

ROB O'DONNELL

At first, fifteen people streamed in. He was like, "How many more people are there?" And if you look at the Pete Souza photo, it's a lot. Half of them are crying. And then he made a joke: "Well, I would have let you guys continue on your communications meeting, but that didn't look like it was going particularly well."

*Pete Souza: "They filed in and essentially formed a semicircle almost around the whole Oval Office. I think the president had to change what he had planned to say, because he was just going to have this conversation with [Cody]." * Peter Souza, White House.

CODY KEENAN

He gave a pep talk and went around the room shaking everybody's hands. Most of those staffers barely ever interacted with the president. Some had never even met him. That turned things around for a lot of people.

PETE SOUZA

These were young kids in their twenties, and here's the president of the United States trying to take the high road and say, "The people have spoken," and as much as we're disappointed in what happened, we had to go forward with the transition of power.

ROB O'DONNELL

The president's press statement was initially planned to be delivered from the Cabinet Room, but it ended up being a nice day. It wasn't raining, and the president felt that, having it in the Cabinet Room, which wasn't particularly well lit and wasn't a huge space, sent the wrong message. The Rose Garden would send a more uplifting message. We went out there an hour later.

CODY KEENAN

That one photo of everyone looking despondent on the colonnade has always bothered me. I wished we had set a better example out there.

ROB O'DONNELL

I didn't think anyone on the colonnade knew that they were going to be on TV or part of the pictures. You had your whole bank of photographers, and 95 percent of them were facing the president. Every once in a while you'd see a photographer turn around and snap a shot. My assumption was they wanted to see Valerie or Jen. Had I known I was going to be on camera, I would have shaved. I probably would have worn a different shirt. Then people started creating memes of my face and talked about how much I looked like Macaulay Culkin.

Ferial Govashiri: "I think everyone was in shock and scared of the unknown, and scared of the things that Donald Trump had talked about." Susan Walsh, Associated Press

CODY KEENAN

I mean, I'm glad we weren't all smiling or anything, but we should have looked more resolute.

KORI SCHULMAN

I was at my desk in the EEOB and was torn about where I wanted to see it. I didn't end up going out in the Rose Garden, and I watched it on TV in the digital office with my team. It was helpful to have that distance.

DAVID CUSACK

Everyone had a shared grief and did not want to be alone in their own offices, so we just moved in chairs and tables and stuff like that. I moved ten people into my office, and that's where everyone worked for two days. Granted, we probably started drinking around one or two o'clock each day.

JEN PSAKI

There were points where you felt dishonest, because publicly it's like, *We're carrying out a graceful transition*, but privately you're thinking, *Are you serious?*

ROB O'DONNELL

People felt a certain way and wanted to know that he felt the same. You'd been elected to two terms. Your approval rating's at 60 percent. The American people were clearly happy with what you've done. There were no scandals. Then, having Hillary Clinton, who ran on a platform that's much similar to ours and lost, must have been extremely difficult.

PETE SOUZA

He's got thicker skin than I'll ever have.

JEN PSAKI

Basically we'd given ourselves until about Thanksgiving to mourn and get it out of our systems, but Donald Trump came two days after the election to the White House for the meeting. So we all had to pull ourselves together for that.

KORI SCHULMAN

I broke down. There was the live stream of the president next to Trump in the Oval, and you saw the MLK bust in the background. That made it more real to me, seeing that contrast in that office.

DAVID CUSACK

For most people, the reset of going back home for Thanksgiving helped. I needed them to refocus, and they did. Again, we were doing operations and logistics. For us, it was all about the whole peaceful transition of power. No one ever said anything inappropriate about the incoming administration. We were gonna hand over to them the best-possible-working buildings, and do all that we could so that they could hopefully find the right path.

BRIAN DEESE

We made ourselves available and tried to be supportive, and the thing that was challenging was that it was hard to figure out who we were interfacing with. It took their transition a long time to have folks in place. In a lot of areas that just never happened because there wasn't anybody on the other side.

KORI SCHULMAN

I interacted with our incoming counterparts. We met Dan Scavino, Gerrit Lansing, and Ory Rinat with the Heritage Foundation, but the meetings and the conversations that we had were very much oriented around the handoff of assets like WhiteHouse.gov and social-media channels. Those meetings were obviously challenging.

ROB O'DONNELL

The Clinton administration would have carried on our stuff on the economy, on how we regulated Wall Street, on how we did climate change, and all of a sudden, the president had to think about how the absolute inverse was going to happen. How do we ensure what we've done stays done? To make sure we race to the finish on some key priorities that we hope will then *not* become undone?

BRIAN DEESE

Postelection, it operated at two levels. We were—and this came directly from the president—very committed, even in the wake of the election, after we all absorbed what had happened and the implications, that we were going to run the transition in the same by-the-book way that the Bush administration ran it with us. And we had an operating strategy where we had to focus on the set of things that we thought were important before the election and the things that we intended to drive through.

YOHANNES ABRAHAM

On both a personal and a professional level, I think Brian's right. You're immediately going down the list of things that were potentially at risk come January. In some ways that manifested itself personally, meaning that you thought about how you spent a lot of 2013 trying to get policy *x* done. Then you thought about the birthdays or weddings you missed in the course of that. And, you know, just on a personal level you couldn't help but kind of do that math. It was sad.

BRIAN DEESE

Whether it was around health care or the environment, we knew the things we needed to get done—rule makings or decisions—and tried to get them done in a workmanlike way and not draw tons of unneeded attention.

VAN JONES

Merrick Garland should [have gone] on the Supreme Court. He should have recess-appointed a bunch of judges. He should [have] also let Leonard Peltier out of prison. I mean, screw it.

BRIAN DEESE

We were clear eyed from the get-go that the Garland nomination was an uphill fight and that it could well be the case that we wouldn't end up even with a hearing . . . There was an ongoing debate that played out across issue areas. On one hand, people argued that if we took aggressive executive action, it would draw even more attention to the issue and make it more likely that the incoming administration would seek to unravel the good that we'd done. Therefore, that line of argument led you to say, *Keep your head down. As important as it may seem, to do this big thing could actually backfire.* The other argument was obvious. *This is the last chance to lock in gains. You might as well make this as difficult as possible. It's not like you can poke the bear any more than the bear has already been poked.*

VAN JONES

You have an authoritarian, kleptocratic regime, and we had a lot at stake. Who cared at this point? You should just [have done] what's right. Let them figure it out.

BRIAN DEESE

Frankly, the way that we approached it—this sounds corny but it's actually true—was largely *What are we prepared to do? What did we actually work to actually be able to get done in a responsible way? All those things we should do, and things that we aren't prepared to do and would be scattershot and thrown together at the last minute, we shouldn't do.*

JOSH LIPSKY

There was a lot of work to be done between then and January 20 no matter who was coming in next. There were priorities for us, and that didn't change. The election just put a very finite time in front of us.

BRIAN DEESE

A good example's the announcement we made jointly with Canada to indefinitely withdraw the Arctic from offshore oil and gas drilling.[190] That was something that we had been working on for over a year with the Trudeau administration, and the agency had done a huge amount of technical work to understand the legal and factual reasons for doing a withdrawal. So the view was that they would do what they're gonna do with respect to oil and gas, and in December, we did what we thought was the right thing. But at the same time, there were arguments that said, like, *You should take the entire Pacific Ocean off the table for oil and gas drilling. Go ahead and do that, because who knows where the future's gonna lie?*

JASON FURMAN

We certainly implemented executive orders that we had, in effect, been working on for a couple of years. We tried to get most of our executive orders done early, and done in a way that wouldn't be subject to a Congressional Review Act [resolution].[191] There's always the idea that—and we crossed our t's and dotted our i's—when you do a better notice-and-comment process for regulation,[192] not only do you get a better-quality regulation that's better designed, but you also get something more likely to withstand attempts to change it.

---

190 One month before his successor was to take the oath of office, President Obama cited a 1953 law to ban new offshore oil and gas drilling in more than one hundred million acres of US Arctic waters, which allowed "the president of the United States . . . from time to time [to] withdraw from disposition any of the unleased lands of the outer Continental Shelf." The statute included no provision for rescinding the order, meaning any attempt by a subsequent administration to reverse it could be stymied by court challenges for years.

191 The Congressional Review Act, signed into law by President Clinton in 1996, allows Congress sixty legislative days to review and overrule any regulation issued by government agencies by a simple majority.

192 A common rule-making procedure for proposed regulations, which are posted and open to comment by the public for input.

BRIAN DEESE

If we hadn't done the work, then we weren't going to do it well. We wanted to do things the way we had been doing them and be able to seriously justify them if they were going to be associated with our administration. That's not just quaint. It's practically important, too. As all of these legal defenses get geared up, being able to justify that these regulatory actions were actually based in a record of strong fact, that's what would carry the day in court.

DAN SHAPIRO

Something else happened during that period. The Israeli right wing got very excited about Trump's victory and started to say and do things that they felt demonstrated there were no more restrictions on settlement building. Eventually the UN resolution was presented,[193] and ultimately, the president decided—but really very late, only after the resolution was coming up on a vote—that there wasn't a good hook to hang a veto on. It included language about violence incitements and terror, which made it more balanced. It was consistent with many previous resolutions that the United States had allowed to pass in previous administrations and in that sense reflected the longstanding and known disagreement between the United States and Israel.

---

193 On December 23, 2016, the United Nations Security Council presented Resolution 2334, which asserted "the inadmissibility of the acquisition of territory by force." Fourteen members voted for "condemning all measures aimed at altering . . . the Palestinian Territory occupied since 1967, including East Jerusalem."

"Expressing grave concern," the resolution went on, "that continuing Israeli settlement activities are dangerously [imperiling] the viability of the two-State solution based on the 1967 lines." No nations voted against the resolution. The US abstained from the vote.

JONATHAN FINER

Secretary Kerry's concern about the future viability of the two-state solution's very much rooted in his love for and concern about the future of Israel.[194] He had personally known Prime Minister Netanyahu since both of them lived in Boston as young men. He made an early series of visits to Israel as part of his work on the Foreign Relations Committee in the Senate, and this was something that he felt was of fundamental importance to the world and the United States. It was that core of beliefs, both intellectual and emotional, that led to his deep concern about steps that both the Israelis and the Palestinians were taking that made the prospects of a two-state solution even more remote than they'd ever been. Some concluded that it may well be too late.

DAN SHAPIRO

[The UN vote] was definitely not, as the prime minister alleged, a US-planned and -initiated and -advocated event. It was something we knew we might have to deal with. We had to make the call when we saw it, and the president did that.

---

194 "Regrettably, some seem to believe that the US friendship means the US must accept any policy, regardless of our own interests, our own positions, our own words, our own principles—even after urging again and again that the policy must change. Friends need to tell each other the hard truths, and friendships require mutual respect . . .

"They fail to recognize that this friend, the United States of America, that has done more to support Israel than any other country, this friend that has blocked countless efforts to delegitimize Israel, cannot be true to our own values—or even the stated democratic values of Israel—and we cannot properly defend and protect Israel if we allow a viable two-state solution to be destroyed before our own eyes. And that's the bottom line. The vote in the United Nations was about preserving the two-state solution. That's what we were standing up for. Israel's future as a Jewish and democratic state, living side by side in peace and security with its neighbors . . .

"The truth is that trends on the ground—violence, terrorism, incitement, settlement expansion, and the seemingly endless occupation—they are combining to destroy hopes for peace on both sides and increasingly cementing an irreversible one-state reality that most people do not actually want." —Secretary Kerry, in the Dean Acheson Auditorium at the Department of State, December 28, 2016.

CODY KEENAN

I don't have a whole lot about what was going on behind the scenes with Russia stuff. Hillary people blamed us for not speaking up about it during the campaign, but my thinking there was, if Barack Obama got involved and started saying during the campaign that Russia's trying to swing the election, that suddenly would make it very political.

JONATHAN FINER

There was a consensus among almost everybody that this was an incredibly serious thing that needed to be investigated by both law enforcement and intelligence professionals so that we could determine exactly what had happened and remove as much doubt as possible as to who was responsible or what had taken place.

TERRY SZUPLAT

They actively meddled in our election in an attempt to influence the outcome. This was not an ally. This was an adversary. I didn't think NATO's expansion east caused this. I didn't think anything that Hillary Clinton or Barack Obama did caused this. This was all rooted in a fundamentally different worldview that Putin and those around him have had.

JONATHAN FINER

What had happened was so egregious and so unprecedented—at least in terms of the fact we were entering a new age of cyber-espionage used for political purposes—that we could not just let this pass. So what we ended up doing was a series of statements as we developed a clearer understanding of what had happened, that laid out publicly, in October and then again in January, what we knew.

CODY KEENAN

Had we spoken out during the election it would have just hardened people's stances. The voters on the right would have said, *He's making all this up, the fix is in, it's bullshit*, and he was always averse to politicizing foreign policy. And you know, there had been a lot of those discussions, but that had to be a hard decision to make.

JONATHAN FINER

In October, seventeen intelligence agencies came together to say that Russia had done this, but did not really wade into the question of why or with what intent, and then in January, a similar declaration that the intent was actually to help one candidate, Mr. Trump, and at the expense of the other, Secretary Clinton. We also expelled dozens of Russian officials who were under diplomatic cover but who we believed were related to the intelligence activity. We imposed sanctions on Russian intelligence entities and closed two Russian diplomatic facilities that we thought were used, to some extent, for intelligence purposes: one in Maryland and one in New York State.

TERRY SZUPLAT

Vladimir Putin and those around him saw their interests threatened by the United States, or they perceived them to be threatened, and they perceived that their path toward status and influence regionally and around the world was to oppose and challenge the United States, and to create a buffer of weak or pro-Russian countries around their periphery.

JONATHAN FINER

People argued that we should have gone further. That maybe the president himself should have spoken to this; that maybe we should have called for the establishment of some independent commission, but this was an incredibly complicated issue at an incredibly complicated time and that was the way we chose to handle it.

JOSH LIPSKY

Obviously, you look back and see things could have been done differently. I think most decisions that were made, at the time, made sense. It didn't mean the right decisions were made, but I understood the logic behind them.

JEN PSAKI

But the last couple of days, there was a realization. We were cleaning out our offices. Most of our staff had left by the last week, and the president was, I thought, pretty tired and wistful about leaving. We didn't spend a ton of time talking about that. We just all kind of tried to enjoy the moments we were there.

YOHANNES ABRAHAM

Think about any moment in your life. High school, college, a graduation-type moment where you were saying bye to a set of people who had helped you grow, who had worked side by side with you, that you cared about deeply. High school for most people is four years. College for most people is four years. For a lot of us, this was ten years, this general cast of friends and colleagues. The emotion heightened just by duration, by time, and then by the scale and scope of what we did together, and then it's further heightened because we're all disappointed in the election outcome. I remember, those couple days, feeling really grateful for the people, a deep amount of affection for the people I was saying goodbye to.

DAVID CUSACK

On the nineteenth, I actually had pneumonia, but we made sure we wanted to transfer the building and everything over to the next administration the same way that Bush 43 did to us. My team spent the night going through each office space making sure nothing was damaged or broken, because by that point we had off-boarded about 430 out of the 450 employees. And so they went around— obviously they had drinks in hand—and made sure everything was copacetic.

PETE SOUZA

The rest of my staff was already gone. The way they off-boarded people, you did it over the last two weeks. I was the only one left in my office.

YOHANNES ABRAHAM

Valerie and I did, like, four laps around the grounds on the nineteenth. And I don't remember if it was the nineteenth or the eighteenth, but I had just come from some goodbye and was rushing from the second floor of the West Wing and was cutting through the lobby. I was going to the East Wing for something, or maybe I was going to the Roosevelt Room, I forget. But I ran into Lieutenant General Flynn. You know, it just made real the transition that was about to happen.

JOSH LIPSKY

The night of the nineteenth, I remember walking to the Metro with my box of stuff and there was a sea of people in MAGA hats coming towards us because they were going to the Mall. There was a concert at the Lincoln the night of the nineteenth, and it was such a strange scene. This was the physical manifestation of the transition of power.

KORI SCHULMAN

For the inauguration, people said how you wouldn't be able to walk or take a cab—that there'd be no way you'd get to the White House complex, which, in both cases, turned out to be utterly false. We were down to a real skeleton crew, and I was the only person left on my team. So I was there superlate on the nineteenth and came back on the twentieth when it was still dark. I was paranoid about not being able to get onto the complex or into the building, which, again, was no problem.

JOSH LIPSKY

They told us we didn't need to go into work, so I just stayed home and watched.

DAVID CUSACK

Most of my team slept overnight in their offices—either on the couches or on couch cushions—and I walked in at like seven o'clock in the morning. They were just getting up, so I had gone and bought them donuts and orange juice. They were brewing coffee. So from there, it was like seven to nine or so finishing all the work. A little bit after nine, I went up to the Navy steps so that I could watch Trump arrive from the church to the tea. So I watched that, and then walked over to the West Wing to do a sweep through each floor, to make sure everything was copacetic, and then I sat down in the Roosevelt Room where Anita [Breckenridge] was and Ben [Rhodes] and some of the other folks, because the bus for Andrews was leaving at eleven thirty.

KORI SCHULMAN

The few people there on January 20 had to turn over whatever remaining pieces of technology they had in the Roosevelt Room. And so I went into the Roosevelt Room, and there were the two doors—there's obviously the one from the hallway to the West Wing lobby and then the one that the president would use from the Oval, and that door was propped open. And through the door, you could just see them, with the couch on its side, changing over the Oval. That's a visual I'll never be able to unsee.

DAVID CUSACK

They all left right around eleven thirty to get on the buses to [Joint Base Andrews], and so I was the last remaining Obama staffer. I went into the Outer Oval and sat at Brian Mosteller's desk for about twenty minutes or so, and it was pretty mellow . . . and at 11:54 a.m., four people walked in. One was an [Office of Administration] person. The other three were Trumpers. I stood up and said, "We're still president for five more minutes. Please leave." And the OA person looked at me, and I was like, "I'm serious." So he turned around and brought them back out. I know that might sound petty, but we were still president until 11:59 a.m. So I went and sat back down at Brian's desk, and exactly at 11:59 I stood up and walked out to the colonnade.

YOHANNES ABRAHAM

I don't remember seeing Marine One take off.

PETE SOUZA

I planted myself on a bench seat right across from him. I wanted to make sure that I was on that helicopter. I couldn't make that picture unless I was on the helicopter.

President Obama aboard Marine One. January 20, 2017. Pete Souza, White House

PETE SOUZA

If you go back in history with the last five presidents, everyone had a similar picture. But every picture was of the Capitol, and so I did not have a conversation with the pilot. I just assumed that they would circle the Capitol, and for whatever reason, they didn't. Then I still kind of took pictures of him and Michelle, and the pilot finally flew over the White House. It came into view through the window, and then I got my shot. But I never even thought about trying to get a picture of him looking at the White House. In my mind I was thinking about a picture of him looking at the Capitol. That's what I had seen by previous White House photographers with previous presidents.

DAVID CUSACK

When I left, I crossed West Exec. I took a photo, like a selfie, because right over my shoulder were all the new Trump employees taking a group photo outside the West Wing, and the time stamp was exactly noon. And that was a really long walk home.

PETE SOUZA

For the most part he kept his emotions pretty in check. Whatever he was feeling would be conjecture on my part. Certainly any president, after eight years of enormous responsibility and hard work, would look forward to, *Okay, I did what I did. I did what I could. And now it's time to turn it over to somebody else.* I think that's what he'd say.

AUTHOR'S NOTE

The interviews for this oral history were conducted and recorded in person or by phone from May 2016 to October 2017. A handful of quotes came via email follow-ups, and, in some cases, merged with previous transcripts (ellipses noted).

I personally transcribed every audio file save one brief call. (Nothing personal, Reggie Love—I just didn't find that masochistic impulse to do them all myself until after I sent your interview to an online service.) I have also taken the liberty of inserting bracketed text for accuracy and editing quotes for the sake of brevity and clarity, while mindful not to alter the substance of the transcript. The most common instances include grammar usage (except where colloquial use better serves the flow); verb tenses; gratuitous usage of adjectives/adverbs ("really," "very," "kinda," "sorta"); expletive constructions ("there are," "here are," "there is"); clichés ("at the end of the day"); and, for lack of a better term, verbal tics ("I mean," "um," "ah"—again, except where it's occasionally useful to signal reluctance or clearly distinguish a statement as opinion or speculation—e.g., "I think").

A few interview subjects requested that I overhaul their transcripts if I came across excessive verbiage or their prattling on. Ellipses are used throughout to indicate breaks in transcripts—i.e., fusing sentences in conversation that were not spoken one immediately after the other—and all quotes are applied within the context of their respective conversational threads. So you won't find a White House aide saying, "This is why Republicans are bad!" in a passage about health-care legislation if the interviewee said it with regard to, say, blocking judicial nominations or birtherism.

Lastly, this oral history was unauthorized. Dozens of participants had already spoken to me over a span of several months before I connected with and received cooperation from the Obama White House, the Obama Foundation, and the postpresidency Office of Barack and Michelle Obama.

ACKNOWLEDGMENTS

First, to my editors: David Blum, who took a chance on this project before I had cultivated a single source in Obamaworld, I'm not sure where I'd be today if it had not been for your faith in me; and Laura Van der Veer, for your patience with my neuroses and your steady hand throughout. To my accomplices and colleagues: Meredith Jacobson, for copyediting your guts out; Drew Salisbury, for pitching in on footnotes; Sarah Rackoff, for help on all the financial stuff; Tosten Burks and Jay Ruttenberg, for the extra sets of eyes on those chapter intros; Roni Greenwood, your fact-checking kept me on my toes; and for the generosity of the staff at Tavern on Jane in Manhattan, where I spent hours poring over the MS with red pens, and for the compassion from friends at 68 Jay Street Bar in Brooklyn, where I convalesced too often.

And to the hundreds of DC alums who answered my calls and emails, on and off the record: thanks again for making the time.

APPENDIX

Parentheses indicate years served up to January 20, 2017.

Executive Office of the President of the United States

Office of the Chief of Staff

White House Chief of Staff

- Rahm Emanuel (2009–2010)
- Bill Daley (2011–2012)
- Jack Lew (2012–2013)
- Denis McDonough (2013–2017)

White House Deputy Chief of Staff

- Jim Messina (2009–2011)
- Mona Sutphen (2009–2011)
- Nancy-Ann DeParle (2011–2013)
- Alyssa Mastromonaco (2011–2014)
- Mark B. Childress (2012–2014)
- Rob Nabors (2013–2015)
- Anita Breckenridge (2014–2017)
- Kristie Canegallo (2014–2017)

Counselor to the President
- Pete Rouse (2011–2014)
- John Podesta (2014–2015)

Senior Advisor to the President
- Valerie Jarrett (2009–2017)
- Pete Rouse (2009–2010)
- David Axelrod (2009–2011)
- David Plouffe (2011–2013)
- Dan Pfeiffer (2013–2015)
- Brian Deese (2015–2017)
- Shailagh Murray (2015–2017)

Office of the National Security Advisor

Assistant to the President for National Security Affairs
- James L. Jones (2009–2010)
- Tom Donilon (2010–2013)
- Susan Rice (2013–2017)

Deputy Assistant to the President for National Security Affairs
- Ben Rhodes, Deputy National Security Advisor for Strategic Communications (2009–2017)
- Tom Donilon (2009–2010)
- Denis McDonough (2010–2013)
- Tony Blinken (2013–2015)
- Avril Haines (2015–2017)

Assistant to the President for Homeland Security and Counterterrorism
- John Brennan (2009–2013)
- Lisa Monaco (2013–2017)

Director, Domestic Policy Council

- Melody Barnes (2009–2012)
- Cecilia Muñoz (2012–2017)

Director, National Economic Council

- Larry Summers (2009–2010)
- Gene Sperling (2011–2014)
- Jeffrey Zients (2014–2017)

Office of Cabinet Affairs

- Chris Lu, White House Cabinet Secretary (2009–2013)
- Danielle C. Gray, White House Cabinet Secretary (2013–2014)
- Broderick D. Johnson, White House Cabinet Secretary (2014–2017)

Chair, Council of Economic Advisers

- Christina Romer (2009–2010)
- Austan Goolsbee (2010–2011)
- Alan Krueger (2011–2013)
- Jason Furman (2013–2017)

Chair, Council on Environmental Quality

- Nancy Sutley (2009–2014)
- Michael Boots (2014–2015)
- Christy Goldfuss (2015–2017)

Office of Communications

Director of Communications
- Ellen Moran (2009)
- Anita Dunn (2009)
- Dan Pfeiffer (2009–2013)
- Jennifer Palmieri (2013–2015)
- Jen Psaki (2015–2017)

White House Press Secretary
- Robert Gibbs (2009–2011)
- Jay Carney (2011–2014)
- Josh Earnest (2014–2017)

Director of Speechwriting
- Jon Favreau (2009–2013)
- Cody Keenan (2013–2017)

Office of Digital Strategy

- Macon Phillips, Director (2009–2013)
- Nate Lubin, Director (2013–2015)
- Jason Goldman, Chief Digital Officer (2015–2017)

Office of the First Lady

Chief of Staff to the First Lady
- Jackie Norris (2009)
- Susan Sher (2009–2011)
- Tina Tchen (2011–2017)

Press Secretary for the First Lady
- Katie McCormick Lelyveld (2009–2011)
- Hannah August (2011–2014)
- Joanna Rosholm (2014–2017)

White House Social Secretary
- Desirée Rogers (2009–2010)
- Julianna Smoot (2010–2011)
- Jeremy Bernard (2011–2015)
- Deesha Dyer (2015–2017)

Office of Legislative Affairs

- Phil Schiliro, Director (2009–2011)
- Rob Nabors, Director (2011–2013)

- Miguel Rodriguez, Director (2013)
- Katie Beirne Fallon, Director (2013–2016)
- Amy Rosenbaum, Director (2016–2017)

Office of Management and Administration

- Cameron Moody, Director (2009–2011)
- Beth Jones, Director (2011–2015)
- Cathy Solomon, Director (2015–2017)

Office of Management and Budget

- Peter Orszag, Director (2009–2010)
- Jack Lew, Director (2010–2012)
- Sylvia Burwell, Director (2013–2014)
- Shaun Donovan, Director (2014–2017)

Office of National Drug Control Policy

- Gil Kerlikowske, Director (2009–2014)
- Michael Botticelli, Director (2014–2017)

Office of Political Affairs

- Patrick Gaspard, Director (2009–2011)

Office of Political Strategy and Outreach

- David Simas, Director (2014–2017)

Office of Public Engagement and Intergovernmental Affairs

- Valerie Jarrett, Director (2009–2017)
- Jon Carson, Director (2011–2013)

Office of Scheduling and Advance

- Alyssa Mastromonaco, Director (2009–2011)
- Danielle Crutchfield, Director (2011–2014)
- Chase Cushman, Director (2014–2017)

Office of Science and Technology Policy

- John Holdren, Chair (2009–2017)

Office of the Staff Secretary

- Lisa Brown, Staff Secretary (2009–2011)
- Rajesh De, Staff Secretary (2011–2012)
- Douglas Kramer, Staff Secretary (2012–2013)
- Joani Walsh, Staff Secretary (2014–2017)

Oval Office Operations

- Brian Mosteller, Director (2009–2017)

US Trade Representative

- Ron Kirk (2009–2013)
- Michael Froman (2013–2017)

Office of the Vice President

- Ronald A. Klain, Chief of Staff (2009–2011)
- Bruce Reed, Chief of Staff (2011–2013)
- Steve Ricchetti, Chief of Staff (2013–2017)

White House Chief Usher

- Stephen W. Rochon (2007–2011)
- Angella Reid (2011–2017)

White House Counsel

- Greg Craig (2009–2010)
- Bob Bauer (2010–2011)
- Kathryn Ruemmler (2011–2014)
- Neil Eggleston (2014–2017)

CABINET OF THE UNITED STATES

US Department of State

US Secretary of State
- Hillary Clinton (2009–2013)
- John Kerry (2013–2017)

US Ambassador to the United Nations
- Susan Rice (2009–2013)
- Samantha Power (2013–2017)

US Deputy Secretary of State
- Jim Steinberg (2009–2011)
- Bill Burns (2011–2014)
- Wendy Sherman (2014–2015, acting)
- Tony Blinken (2015–2017)

US Department of the Treasury

US Secretary of the Treasury
- Tim Geithner (2009–2013)
- Jack Lew (2013–2017)

US Deputy Secretary of the Treasury
- Neal S. Wolin (2009–2013)
- Sarah Bloom Raskin (2014–2017)

Commissioner, Internal Revenue Service
- Douglas H. Shulman (2008–2012)
- Steven T. Miller (2012–2013)
- Daniel Werfel (2013)
- John Koskinen (2013–)

US Department of Defense

US Secretary of Defense
- Robert Gates (2006–2011)
- Leon Panetta (2011–2013)
- Chuck Hagel (2013–2015)
- Ash Carter (2015–2017)

Chair, Joint Chiefs of Staff
- Admiral Michael Mullen, US Navy (2007–2011)
- General Martin E. Dempsey, US Army (2011–2015)
- General Joseph Dunford, US Marine Corps (2015–)

US Department of Justice

US Attorney General
- Eric Holder (2009–2015)
- Loretta Lynch (2015–2017)

US Deputy Attorney General
- David Ogden (2009–2010)
- Gary Grindler (2010–2011)
- James M. Cole (2011–2015)
- Sally Yates (2015–)

US Solicitor General
- Edwin Kneedler (2009)
- Elena Kagan (2009–2010)
- Neal Katyal (2010–2011)
- Don Verrilli (2011–2016)
- Ian Gershengorn (2016–2017)

Director, Federal Bureau of Investigation
- Robert Mueller (2001–2013)
- James Comey (2013–)

US Secretary of the Interior

- Ken Salazar (2009–2013)
- Sally Jewell (2013–2017)

US Secretary of Agriculture

- Tom Vilsack (2009–2017)
- Michael Scuse (2017)

US Secretary of Commerce

- Otto J. Wolff (2009)
- Gary F. Locke (2009–2011)
- Rebecca M. Blank (2011)
- John E. Bryson (2011–2012)
- Rebecca M. Blank (2012–2013)
- Cameron Kerry (2013)
- Penny Pritzker (2013–2017)

US Secretary of Labor

- Hilda Solis (2009–2013)
- Seth Harris (2013, acting)
- Tom Perez (2013–2017)

US Secretary of Health and Human Services

- Kathleen Sebelius (2009–2014)
- Sylvia Burwell (2014–2017)

US Secretary of Housing and Urban Development

- Shaun Donovan (2009–2014)
- Julian Castro (2014–2017)

US Secretary of Transportation

- Ray LaHood (2009–2013)
- Anthony Foxx (2013–2017)

US Secretary of Energy

- Steven Chu (2009–2013)
- Ernest Moniz (2013–2017)

US Secretary of Education

- Arne Duncan (2009–2015)
- John King (2016–2017)

US Secretary of Veterans Affairs

- Eric Shinseki (2009–2014)
- Bob McDonald (2014–2017)

US Secretary of Homeland Security

- Janet Napolitano (2009–2013)
- Jeh Johnson (2013–2017)

Director of National Intelligence

- Dennis C. Blair (2009–2010)
- David C. Gompert (2010)
- James R. Clapper (2010–2017)

Director, Central Intelligence Agency

- Leon Panetta (2009–2011)
- Michael Morell (2011)
- David Petraeus (2011–2012)
- Michael Morell (2012–2013)
- John Brennan (2013–2017)

Administrator, US Environmental Protection Agency

- Lisa Jackson (2009–2013)
- Gina McCarthy (2013–2017)

Administrator, US Small Business Administration

- Karen Mills (2009–2013)
- Maria Contreras-Sweet (2014–2017)

Chair, Board of Governors of the Federal Reserve

- Ben Bernanke (2006–2014)
- Janet Yellen (2014–)

UNITED STATES SENATE

President

- Vice President Joe Biden (2009–2017)

President Pro Tempore

- D-Robert Byrd, West Virginia (2009–2010)
- D-Dan Inouye, Hawaii (2010–2012)

- D-Patrick Leahy, Vermont (2012–2015)
- R-Orrin Hatch, Utah (2015–)

Democratic Leadership

Leader

- Harry Reid, Nevada (2005–2015)
- Chuck Schumer, New York (2017–)

Whip

- Dick Durbin, Illinois (2005–)

Republican Leadership

Leader

- Mitch McConnell, Kentucky (2007–)

Whip

- Jon Kyl, Arizona (2007–2013)
- John Cornyn, Texas (2013–)

United States House of Representatives

Speaker of the House

- D-Nancy Pelosi, California (2007–2011)
- R-John Boehner, Ohio (2011–2015)
- R-Paul Ryan, Wisconsin (2015–)

Democratic Leadership

Leader

- Steny Hoyer, Maryland (2007–2011)
- Nancy Pelosi, California (2011–)

Whip
- Jim Clyburn, South Carolina (2007–2011)
- Steny Hoyer, Maryland (2011–)

Republican Leadership

Leader
- John Boehner, Ohio (2007–2011)
- Eric Cantor, Virginia (2011–2014)
- Kevin McCarthy, California (2014–)

Whip
- Eric Cantor, Virginia (2009–2011)
- Kevin McCarthy, California (2011–2014)
- Steve Scalise, Louisiana (2014–)

Dean of the House

- D-John Dingell, Michigan (1995–2015)
- D-John Conyers, Michigan (2015–)

SUPREME COURT OF THE UNITED STATES

Chief Justice

- John Roberts (2005– ; nominated by George W. Bush)

Associate Justices

- John Paul Stevens (1975–2010; nominated by Gerald R. Ford)
- Anthony Kennedy (1988– ; nominated by Ronald Reagan)
- David Souter (1990–2009; nominated by George H. W. Bush)
- Clarence Thomas (1991– ; nominated by George H. W. Bush)

- Ruth Bader Ginsburg (1993– ; nominated by Bill Clinton)
- Stephen Breyer (1994– ; nominated by Bill Clinton)
- Samuel Alito (2006– ; nominated by George W. Bush)
- Sonia Sotomayor (2009– ; nominated by Barack Obama)
- Elena Kagan (2010– ; nominated by Barack Obama)

APPOINTMENTS ON THE FEDERAL JUDICIARY

US COURT OF APPEALS

District of Columbia Circuit, Washington

- Sri Srinivasan (2013–)
- Patricia Ann Millett (2013–)
- Nina Pillard (2013–)
- Robert L. Wilkins (2014–)

First Circuit, Boston

- Ojetta Rogeriee Thompson (2010–)
- William J. Kayatta Jr. (2013–)
- David Jeremiah Barron (2014–)

Second Circuit, New York City

- Denny Chin (2010–)
- Raymond Lohier (2010–)
- Susan L. Carney (2011–)
- Christopher F. Droney (2011–)
- Gerard E. Lynch (2009–)

Third Circuit, Philadelphia

- Joseph A. Greenaway Jr. (2010–)
- Thomas I. Vanaskie (2010–)
- Patty Shwartz (2013–)
- Cheryl Ann Krause (2014–)
- Luis Felipe Restrepo (2016–)

Fourth Circuit, Richmond

- Barbara Milano Keenan (2010–)
- James A. Wynn Jr. (2010–)
- Albert Diaz (2010–)
- Henry Franklin Floyd (2011–)
- Stephanie D. Thacker (2012–)
- Pamela Harris (2014–)
- Andre M. Davis (2009–)

Fifth Circuit, New Orleans

- James E. Graves Jr. (2011–)
- Stephen A. Higginson (2011–)
- Gregg Costa (2014–)

Sixth Circuit, Cincinnati

- Jane Branstetter Stranch (2010–)
- Bernice B. Donald (2011–)

Seventh Circuit, Chicago

- David F. Hamilton (2009–)

Eighth Circuit, St. Louis

- Jane L. Kelly (2013–)

Ninth Circuit, San Francisco

- Mary H. Murguia (2011–)
- Morgan Christen (2012–)
- Jacqueline Nguyen (2012–)
- Paul J. Watford (2012–)
- Andrew D. Hurwitz (2012–)
- John B. Owens (2014–)
- Michelle Friedland (2014–)

Tenth Circuit, Denver

- Scott Matheson Jr. (2010–)
- Robert E. Bacharach (2013–)
- Gregory A. Phillips (2013–)
- Carolyn B. McHugh (2014–)
- Nancy Moritz (2014–)

Eleventh Circuit, Atlanta

- Beverly B. Martin (2010–)
- Adalberto Jordan (2012–)
- Robin S. Rosenbaum (2014–)
- Julie E. Carnes (2014–)
- Jill A. Pryor (2014–)

Federal Circuit, Washington

US Court of Appeals for Veterans Claims
- Coral Wong Pietsch (2012–)
- Margaret Bartley (2012–)
- William S. Greenberg (2012–)

US Court of Federal Claims
- Elaine D. Kaplan (2013–)
- Lydia Kay Griggsby (2015–)

US Court of International Trade

- Mark A. Barnett (2013–)
- Claire R. Kelly (2013–)
- Jennifer Choe-Groves (2016–)
- Gary Stephen Katzmann (2016–)

District Courts

US District Court for the District of Columbia

- Beryl A. Howell (2010–)
- Robert L. Wilkins (2010–2014)
- James E. Boasberg (2011–)
- Amy Berman Jackson (2011–)
- Rudolph Contreras (2012–)
- Ketanji Brown Jackson (2013–)
- Christopher Reid Cooper (2014–)
- Tanya S. Chutkan (2014–)
- Randolph D. Moss (2014–)
- Amit Priyavadan Mehta (2014–)

First Circuit

District of Maine

- Nancy Torresen (2011–)
- Jon D. Levy (2014–)

District of Massachusetts

- Denise J. Casper (2010–)
- Timothy S. Hillman (2012–)
- Indira Talwani (2014–)
- Mark G. Mastroianni (2014–)
- Leo T. Sorokin (2014–)
- Allison Dale Burroughs (2014–)

District of New Hampshire
- Landya B. McCafferty (2013–)

District of Puerto Rico
- Pedro Delgado Hernández (2014–)

District of Rhode Island
- John J. McConnell Jr. (2011–)

Second Circuit

District of Connecticut
- Michael P. Shea (2012–)
- Jeffrey A. Meyer (2014–)
- Victor Allen Bolden (2015–)

Eastern District of New York
- William Francis Kuntz (2011–)
- Margo Kitsy Brodie (2012–)
- Pamela K. Chen (2013–)
- Joan Azrack (2014–)
- Ann Donnelly (2015–)
- LaShann Moutique DeArcy Hall (2015–)

Northern District of New York
- Mae D'Agostino (2011–)
- Brenda K. Sannes (2014–)

Southern District of New York
- Vincent L. Briccetti (2011–)
- J. Paul Oetken (2011–)
- Paul A. Engelmayer (2011–)
- Alison J. Nathan (2011–)
- Katherine B. Forrest (2011–)
- Edgardo Ramos (2011–)
- Andrew L. Carter Jr. (2011–)
- Jesse M. Furman (2012–)
- Ronnie Abrams (2012–)
- Lorna G. Schofield (2012–)

- Katherine Polk Failla (2013–)
- Analisa Torres (2013–)
- Nelson S. Roman (2013–)
- Valerie E. Caproni (2013–)
- Vernon S. Broderick (2013–)
- Gregory Howard Woods (2013–)

Western District of New York

- Elizabeth A. Wolford (2013–)
- Frank Paul Geraci Jr. (2013–)
- Lawrence J. Vilardo (2015–)

District of Vermont

- Christina Reiss (2009–)
- Geoffrey W. Crawford (2014–)

Third Circuit

District of Delaware

- Leonard P. Stark (2010–)
- Richard G. Andrews (2011–)

District of New Jersey

- Claire C. Cecchi (2011–)
- Esther Salas (2011–)
- Kevin McNulty (2012–)
- Michael A. Shipp (2012–)
- Madeline Cox Arleo (2014–)
- John Michael Vazquez (2016–)
- Brian R. Martinotti (2016–)

Eastern District of Pennsylvania

- Nitza I. Quiñones Alejandro (2013–)
- Jeffrey L. Schmehl (2013–)
- Luis Felipe Restrepo (2013–2016)
- Gerald Austin McHugh Jr. (2014–)
- Edward G. Smith (2014–)
- Wendy Beetlestone (2014–)

- Mark A. Kearney (2014–)
- Jerry Pappert (2014–)
- Joseph F. Leeson Jr. (2014–)

Middle District of Pennsylvania
- Robert D. Mariani (2011–)
- Matthew W. Brann (2012–)
- Malachy E. Mannion (2012–)

Western District of Pennsylvania
- Cathy Bissoon (2011–)
- Mark R. Hornak (2011–)

Fourth Circuit

District of Maryland
- James K. Bredar (2010–)
- Ellen Lipton Hollander (2010–)
- George Levi Russell III (2012–)
- Paul W. Grimm (2012–)
- Theodore D. Chuang (2014–)
- George J. Hazel (2014–)
- Paula Xinis (2016–)

Middle District of North Carolina
- Catherine Eagles (2010–)
- Loretta Copeland Biggs (2014–)

Western District of North Carolina
- Max O. Cogburn Jr. (2011–)

District of South Carolina
- J. Michelle Childs (2010–)
- Richard Mark Gergel (2010–)
- Timothy M. Cain (2011–)
- Mary Geiger Lewis (2012–)
- Bruce Howe Hendricks (2014–)

Eastern District of Virginia
- John A. Gibney Jr. (2010–)
- Arenda L. Wright Allen (2011–)
- M. Hannah Lauck (2014–)

Western District of Virginia
- Michael F. Urbanski (2011–)
- Elizabeth K. Dillon (2014–)

Northern District of West Virginia
- Gina Marie Groh (2012–)

Southern District of West Virginia
- Irene C. Berger (2009–)

Fifth Circuit

Eastern District of Louisiana
- Nannette Jolivette Brown (2011–)
- Jane Margaret Triche Milazzo (2011–)
- Susie Morgan (2012–)

Middle District of Louisiana
- Brian Anthony Jackson (2010–)
- Shelly Deckert Dick (2013–)
- John W. deGravelles (2014–)

Western District of Louisiana
- Elizabeth Erny Foote (2010–)

Northern District of Mississippi
- Debra M. Brown (2013–)

Southern District of Mississippi
- Carlton W. Reeves (2010–)

Eastern District of Texas
- James Rodney Gilstrap (2011–)
- Amos L. Mazzant III (2014–)
- Robert W. Schroeder III (2014–)

Southern District of Texas
- Marina Marmolejo (2011–)
- Nelva Gonzales Ramos (2011–)
- Diana Saldaña (2011–)
- Gregg Costa (2012–2014)
- Alfred H. Bennett (2015–)
- George C. Hanks Jr. (2015–)
- Jose Rolando Olvera Jr. (2015–)

Western District of Texas
- David Campos Guaderrama (2012–)
- Robert L. Pitman (2014–)

Sixth Circuit

Western District of Kentucky
- David J. Hale (2014–)
- Gregory N. Stivers (2014–)

Eastern District of Michigan
- Mark A. Goldsmith (2010–)
- Gershwin A. Drain (2012–)
- Terrence G. Berg (2012–)
- Matthew Frederick Leitman (2014–)
- Judith Ellen Levy (2014–)
- Laurie J. Michelson (2014–)
- Linda Vivienne Parker (2014–)

Northern District of Ohio
- Benita Y. Pearson (2010–)
- Jeffrey J. Helmick (2012–)

Southern District of Ohio
- Timothy Black (2010–)

Eastern District of Tennessee
- Pamela L. Reeves (2014–)
- Travis Randall McDonough (2015–)

Middle District of Tennessee

- Kevin H. Sharp (2011–)
- Waverly D. Crenshaw Jr. (2016–)

Western District of Tennessee

- John Thomas Fowlkes Jr. (2012–)
- Sheryl H. Lipman (2014–)

Seventh Circuit

Central District of Illinois

- Sue E. Myerscough (2011–)
- James E. Shadid (2011–)
- Sara Lynn Darrow (2011–)
- Colin S. Bruce (2013–)

Northern District of Illinois

- Gary Feinerman (2010–)
- Sharon Johnson Coleman (2010–)
- Edmond E. Chang (2010–)
- John Z. Lee (2012–)
- John J. Tharp Jr. (2012–)
- Thomas M. Durkin (2012–)
- Sara L. Ellis (2013–)
- Andrea R. Wood (2013–)
- Manish S. Shah (2014–)
- Jorge Luis Alonso (2014–)
- John Robert Blakey (2014–)

Southern District of Illinois

- Staci Michelle Yandle (2014–)
- Nancy J. Rosenstengel (2014–)

Northern District of Indiana

- Jon DeGuilio (2010–)

Southern District of Indiana

- Jane Magnus-Stinson (2010–)
- Tanya Walton Pratt (2010–)

Eastern District of Wisconsin

- Pamela Pepper (2014–)

Western District of Wisconsin

- William M. Conley (2010–)
- James D. Peterson (2014–)

Eighth Circuit

Eastern District of Arkansas

- D. Price Marshall Jr. (2010–)
- Kristine G. Baker (2012–)
- James Maxwell Moody Jr. (2014–)

Western District of Arkansas

- Susan Owens Hickey (2011–)
- Paul K. Holmes III (2011–)
- Timothy L. Brooks (2014–)

Northern District of Iowa

- Leonard Terry Strand (2016–)

Southern District of Iowa

- Stephanie Marie Rose (2012–)
- Rebecca Goodgame Ebinger (2016–)

District of Minnesota

- Susan Richard Nelson (2010–)
- Wilhelmina Wright (2016–)

Eastern District of Missouri

- Audrey G. Fleissig (2010–)
- John Andrew Ross (2011–)
- Ronnie L. White (2014–)

Western District of Missouri

- Mary Elizabeth Phillips (2012–)
- Brian C. Wimes (2012–)
- Stephen R. Bough (2014–)

- M. Douglas Harpool (2014–)
- Roseann A. Ketchmark (2015–)

Eastern and Western District of Missouri
- Brian C. Wimes (2012–)

District of Nebraska
- John M. Gerrard (2012–)
- Robert F. Rossiter Jr. (2016–)

District of South Dakota
- Jeffrey L. Viken (2009–)
- Roberto A. Lange (2009–)

Ninth Circuit

District of Alaska
- Sharon L. Gleason (2012–)

District of Arizona
- Jennifer Guerin Zipps (2011–)
- Steven Paul Logan (2014–)
- John Joseph Tuchi (2014–)
- Diane Humetewa (2014–)
- Rosemary Márquez (2014–)
- Douglas L. Rayes (2014–)
- James Alan Soto (2014–)

Central District of California
- Jacqueline H. Nguyen (2009–2012)
- Dolly M. Gee (2010–)
- Josephine L. Staton (2010–)
- John A. Kronstadt (2011–)
- Michael W. Fitzgerald (2012–)
- Jesus G. Bernal (2012–)
- Fernando M. Olguin (2013–)
- Beverly Reid O'Connell (2013–)
- André Birotte Jr. (2014–)

Eastern District of California
- Kimberly J. Mueller (2010–)
- Troy L. Nunley (2013–)
- Dale A. Drozd (2015–)

Northern District of California
- Richard G. Seeborg (2010–)
- Lucy H. Koh (2010–)
- Edward J. Davila (2011–)
- Edward M. Chen (2011–)
- Yvonne Gonzalez Rogers (2011–)
- Jon S. Tigar (2013–)
- William H. Orrick III (2013–)
- James Donato (2014–)
- Beth Labson Freeman (2014–)
- Vince Girdhari Chhabria (2014–)
- Haywood Stirling Gilliam Jr. (2014–)

Southern District of California
- Anthony J. Battaglia (2011–)
- Cathy Ann Bencivengo (2012–)
- Gonzalo P. Curiel (2012–)
- Cynthia Ann Bashant (2014–)

District of Hawaii
- Leslie E. Kobayashi (2010–)
- Derrick Kahala Watson (2013–)

District of Montana
- Dana L. Christensen (2011–)
- Brian Morris (2013–)
- Susan P. Watters (2013–)

District of Nevada
- Gloria Navarro (2010–)
- Miranda Du (2012–)
- Andrew Patrick Gordon (2013–)
- Jennifer A. Dorsey (2013–)
- Richard Franklin Boulware II (2014–)

District of Oregon
- Marco A. Hernandez (2011–)
- Michael H. Simon (2011–)
- Michael J. McShane (2013–)

Eastern District of Washington
- Rosanna M. Peterson (2010–)
- Thomas O. Rice (2012–)
- Stanley Allen Bastian (2014–)
- Salvador Mendoza Jr. (2014–)

Tenth Circuit

District of Colorado
- William J. Martínez (2010–)
- R. Brooke Jackson (2011–)
- Raymond P. Moore (2013–)

District of Kansas
- Daniel D. Crabtree (2014–)

District of New Mexico
- Kenneth John Gonzales (2013–)

Northern District of Oklahoma
- John E. Dowdell (2012–)

District of Utah
- Robert J. Shelby (2012–)
- David Nuffer (2012–)
- Jill Parrish (2015–)

District of Wyoming
- Nancy D. Freudenthal (2010–)
- Scott W. Skavdahl (2011–)

Eleventh Circuit

Northern District of Alabama
- Abdul K. Kallon (2010–)
- Madeline Hughes Haikala (2013–)

Middle District of Florida
- Charlene Honeywell (2009–)
- Roy B. Dalton Jr. (2011–)
- Sheri Polster Chappell (2013–)
- Brian J. Davis (2013–)
- Paul G. Byron (2014–)
- Carlos Eduardo Mendoza (2014–)

Northern District of Florida
- Mark E. Walker (2012–)

Southern District of Florida
- Robert N. Scola, Jr. (2011–)
- Kathleen M. Williams (2011–)
- Robin S. Rosenbaum (2012–2014)
- Darrin P. Gayles (2014–)
- Beth Bloom (2014–)
- Robin L. Rosenberg (2014–)

Middle District of Georgia
- Marc Thomas Treadwell (2010–)
- Leslie Joyce Abrams (2014–)

Northern District of Georgia
- Amy Totenberg (2011–)
- Steve C. Jones (2011–)
- Leigh Martin May (2014–)
- Mark Howard Cohen (2014–)
- Eleanor Louise Ross (2014–)

SOURCES

Abrahamson, Zachary, and James Hohmann. "The Crime Scene: Safeway."
Politico, January 9, 2011. https://www.politico.com/story/2011/01
/the-crime-scene-safeway-047295.

Adler, Michael. "Iran Foreign Minister Confident Nuclear Deal Wrapped Up
Soon." Breaking Defense, November 8, 2013. https://breakingdefense.
com/2013/11/exclusive-iran-foreign-minister-confident-nuke-agreement
-wrapped-up-soon-iran-leaders-likely-to-approve.

"After New Hampshire: Updates, Analysis and Results." Election 2016.
New York Times, February 9, 2016. https://www.nytimes.com/live
/new-hampshire-primary-2016-election.

Agence France-Presse. "Under Fire Palestinian Leader Gets Obama's First
Call." ABS-CBN News, January 22, 2009. http://news.abs-cbn.com
/world/01/21/09/under-fire-palestinian-leader-gets-obamas-first-call.

Agnew, Phillip. "What President Obama Told Me about Ferguson's
Movement: Think Big, but Go Gradual." *Guardian*, December 5,
2014. https://www.theguardian.com/commentisfree/2014/dec/05
/obama-ferguson-movement-oval-office-meeting.

Al-Khalidi, Suleiman. "Syria Moves Chemical Weapons before Wider
Offensive: Defector." Reuters, July 21, 2012. https://www.reuters.com
/article/us-syria-defector-chemical/syria-moves-chemical-weapons-before
-wider-offensive-defector-idUSBRE86K09F20120721.

Allen, Jared, and Roxana Tiron. "GOP to Defend 'Don't Ask, Don't Tell.'" *The Hill*, May 25, 2010.

Allen, Mike, and David Rogers. "Bush Announces $17.4 Billion Auto Bailout." *Politico*, December 19, 2008. https://www.politico.com/story/2008/12 /bush-announces-174-billion-auto-bailout-016740.

Almond, Roncevert Ganan. "US Ratification of the Law of the Sea Convention." Diplomat, May 24, 2017. https://thediplomat .com/2017/05/u-s-ratification-of-the-law-of-the-sea-convention.

Amadeo, Kimberly. "AIG Bailout: Cost, Timeline, Bonuses, Causes, Effects." Balance, September 30, 2017. https://www.thebalance.com /aig-bailout-cost-timeline-bonuses-causes-effects-3305693.

Amadeo, Kimberly. "TARP Bailout Program." Balance, April 24, 2017. https://www.thebalance.com/tarp-bailout-program-3305895.

American Benefits Council. "Comparison of the Coverage and Revenue Provisions in America's Healthy Future Act (as Approved by the Senate Finance Committee), the Affordable Health Choices Act (S. 1679, as Approved by the Senate HELP Committee), and the America's Affordable Health Choices Act (H.R. 3200, the House 'Tri-Committee' Bill)." American Benefits Council, October 16, 2009. https://www.americanbenefitscouncil.org /pub/?id=e60a979b-b26c-d96f-c982-a912492b3dfd.

American Nurses Association. "Top Five Myths About H.R. 3200." American Nurses Association. Last accessed February 9, 2018. http://www .nursingworld.org/healthcarereformmyths.

Americans with Disabilities Act of 1990. 42 USC § 12101, July 26, 1990. https://www.govtrack.us/congress/bills/101/s933.

America's Affordable Health Choices Act of 2009, H.R. 3200. 111th Congress,
    introduced July 14, 2009. https://www.congress.gov/bill/111th-congress
    /house-bill/3200.

Anderson, Elisha. "Underwear Bomber Umar Farouk Abdulmutallab
    Sues over Treatment in Prison." *Detroit Free Press*, October 23, 2017.
    https://www.freep.com/story/news/local/michigan/detroit/2017/10/22
    /underwear-bomber-suing-over-prison-treatment/788781001.

Andrews, Edmund L., and Peter Baker. "A.I.G. Planning Huge Bonuses After
    $170 Billion Bailout." *New York Times*, March 14, 2009. http://www
    .nytimes.com/2009/03/15/business/15AIG.html.

Andrews, Travis M. "Clint Eastwood Explains—and Regrets—His Speech
    to an Empty Chair." *Washington Post*, August 4, 2016. https://www
    .washingtonpost.com/news/morning-mix/wp/2016/08/04/clint
    -eastwood-explains-and-regrets-his-speech-to-an-empty-chair.

Ariosto, David, and Deborah Feyerick. "Christmas Day Bomber Sentenced to
    Life in Prison." CNN, February 17, 2012. http://www.cnn
    .com/2012/02/16/justice/michigan-underwear-bomber-sentencing
    /index.html.

Associated Press. "After Long Wait, Franken Sworn in as Senator." NBC
    News, July 7, 2009. http://www.nbcnews.com/id/31778598/ns
    /politics-capitol_hill/t/after-long-wait-franken-sworn-senator.

Associated Press. "Barack Obama's Grandmother Dies." CBS News,
    November 3, 2008. https://www.cbsnews.com/news
    /barack-obamas-grandmother-dies/.

Associated Press. "BP Comment about 'Small People' Causes Anger." *San
    Diego Union-Tribune*, June 16, 2010. http://www.sandiegouniontribune
    .com/sdut-bp-comment-about-small-people-causes-anger-2010jun16
    -story.html.

Associated Press. "Global Markets Follow Wall Street's Plunge."
    CBS News, August 9, 2011. https://www.cbsnews.com/news
    /global-markets-follow-wall-streets-plunge.

Associated Press. "New 39.6 Percent Tax Bracket for Wealthiest People."
    Politico, January 22, 2014. https://www.politico.com/story/2014/01
    /income-taxes-2014-tax-brackets-102466.

"Australian Parliament Speech by President Obama." C-SPAN video
    (30:54), November 16, 2011. https://www.c-span.org/video/?302734-1
    /australian-parliament-speech-president-obama.

Axelrod, David. *Believer: My Forty Years in Politics*. New York: Penguin
    Books, 2015.

Bacon, Perry, Jr. "Can Obama Count on the Black Vote?" *Time*, January 23,
    2007. http://content.time.com/time/nation/article/0,8599,1581666,00
    .html.

Bai, Matt. "Newt. Again." *New York Times Magazine*, February 25, 2009.
    http://www.nytimes.com/2009/03/01/magazine/01republicans-t.html.

Baker, Al. "Bloomberg Wants Terror Trial Moved." *New York
    Times*, January 27, 2010. https://cityroom.blogs.nytimes
    .com/2010/01/27/a-growing-cry-to-move-a-terror-trial.

Baker, Jackson. "Rep. Tanner Makes Stunning Announcement: He
    Won't Run for Reelection." *Memphis Flyer*, December 1, 2009.
    https://www.memphisflyer.com/JacksonBaker/archives/2009/12/01
    /rep-tanner-makes-stunning-announcement-he-wont-run-for-reelection.

Baker, Peter, Jim Rutenberg, and Bill Vlasic. "Early Resolve: Obama Stand in
    Auto Crisis." *New York Times*, April 28, 2009. http://www.nytimes
    .com/2009/04/29/us/politics/29decide.html.

Balz, Dan, and Chris Cillizza. "Sen. Arlen Specter Loses Pennsylvania Primary; Rand Paul Wins in Kentucky." *Washington Post*, May 19, 2010. http://www.washingtonpost.com/wp-dyn/content/article/2010/05/18/AR2010051805561.html.

Balz, Dan, and Shalaigh Murray. "Lieberman Defeated in Democratic Primary." *Washington Post*, August 9, 2006. http://www.washingtonpost.com/wp-dyn/content/article/2006/08/08/AR2006080800596.html.

"Barack Obama: 'A More Perfect Union' (Full Speech)." YouTube video (37:09), posted by Obama for America, March 18, 2008. https://www.youtube.com/watch?v=zrp-v2tHaDo.

"Barack Obama Rally in Wilmington, Delaware—Part 1." YouTube video (5:01), posted by "chrisbarrett," February 3, 2008. https://www.youtube.com/watch?v=e4Cyuw_EUlc.

Barr, Andy. "2008 Turnout Shatters All Records." *Politico*, November 5, 2008. https://www.politico.com/story/2008/11/2008-turnout-shatters-all-records-015306.

Barrett, Ted, and Dana Bash. "Senate Halts 'Don't Ask, Don't Tell' Repeal." CNN Politics, September 22, 2010. http://www.cnn.com/2010/POLITICS/09/21/senate.defense.bill/index.html.

Barzilai, Yaniv. "How bin Laden Escaped in 2001—the Lessons of Tora Bora." Daily Beast, December 15, 2013. https://www.thedailybeast.com/how-bin-laden-escaped-in-2001the-lessons-of-tora-bora.

Bash, Dana, and Ed Hornick. "Kennedy Returns to Washington as Health Care Talk Heats Up." CNN Politics, March 5, 2009. http://www.cnn.com/2009/POLITICS/03/05/kennedy.health.care/index.html.

"BASIC Group Wants Global Deal on Climate Change by 2011." *Hindu*, April 26, 2010. http://www.thehindu.com/news

/BASIC-group-wants-global-deal-on-climate-change-by-2011
/article16372558.ece.

Batalova, Jeanne, and Margie McHugh. "DREAM vs. Reality: An Analysis of
Potential DREAM Act Beneficiaries." Policy Briefs, July 2010. Migration
Policy Institute. https://www.migrationpolicy.org/research
/dream-vs-reality-analysis-potential-dream-act-beneficiaries.

Bazelon, Emily. "A Legacy Litigated." Slate, May 29, 2013. http://www.slate
.com/articles/news_and_politics/jurisprudence/2013/05/barack_obama_s
_legacy_the_president_s_signature_achievements_must_survive.html.

Bazelon, Emily. "Obama's Fight Song (Finally)." Slate, June 4, 2013.
http://www.slate.com/articles/news_and_politics/jurisprudence/2013/06
/barack_obama_judicial_nominees_the_president_named_three_people
_to_the_u.html.

"Ben Bernanke Refers to Fiscal Cliff." C-SPAN video (1:10), February 29,
2012. https://www.c-span.org/video/?c4274061
/ben-bernanke-refers-fiscal-cliff.

Bendery, Jennifer. "Obama Leaving His Mark on Judiciary as Senate Confirms
Gay, Black Judges." Huffington Post, June 17, 2014. https://www
.huffingtonpost.com/2014/06/17/obama-judges_n_5503075.html.

Bengali, Shashank, David S. Cloud, and Paul Richter. "President Obama's
U-turn on Syria Is a Gamble." Los Angeles Times, August 31, 2013. http://
articles.latimes.com/2013/aug/31/world/la-fg-obama-assess-20130901.

"Benjamin Netanyahu Speech to Congress 2015." YouTube video (43:24),
posted by New York Times, March 3, 2015. https://www.youtube.com
/watch?v=wRf1cdw4IAY.

Bigg, Matthew, and Nick Carey. "Protesters Disrupt Town-Hall Healthcare
Talks." Reuters, August 7, 2009. https://www.reuters.com/article

/us-usa-healthcare-townhalls/protesters-disrupt-town-hall-healthcare
-talks-idUSTRE5765QH20090808.

Bloomberg News. "Company News; Daimler-Benz and Chrysler Revise Ratio for Stock Swap." *New York Times*, June 9, 1998. http://www.nytimes .com/1998/06/09/business/company-news-daimler-benz-and-chrysler -revise-ratio-for-stock-swap.html.

Blow, Charles. "The Curious Case of Trayvon Martin." *New York Times*, March 16, 2012. http://www.nytimes.com/2012/03/17/opinion/blow-the -curious-case-of-trayvon-martin.html.

Boehner, John. "Boehner Seeks Answers from President Obama on Syria." Office of the Speaker of the House, August 28, 2013. https://www.speaker .gov/press-release/boehner-seeks-answers-president-obama-syria.

Booth, William. "Israel's Netanyahu Calls Iran Deal 'Historic Mistake.'" *Washington Post*, November 24, 2013. https://www.washingtonpost.com /world/israel-says-iran-deal-makes-world-more-dangerous/2013/11/24 /e0e347de-54f9-11e3-bdbf-097ab2a3dc2b_story.html.

Borofsky, Yael, Jesse Jenkins, and Devon Swezey. "Obama Announces Climate Deal, UNFCCC Crumbles?" Breakthrough Institute, December 18, 2009. https://thebreakthrough.org/archive/obama_announces_climate_deal_u.

Bosman, Julie. "Provoking Palin's Inner Bear." *New York Times*, October 19, 2008. https://thecaucus.blogs.nytimes.com/2008/10/19 /provoking-palins-inner-bear/.

Boyer, Dave. "Obama Finalizes Regulation to 'Ban the Box' on Hiring Job Applicants with Criminal Records." *Washington Times*, November 30, 2016. https://www.washingtontimes.com/news/2016/nov/30 /obama-finalizes-regulation-ban-box-job-applicants.

"BP Oil Spill Timeline." *Guardian*, July 22, 2010. https://www.theguardian
    .com/environment/2010/jun/29/bp-oil-spill-timeline-deepwater-horizon.

Bradner, Eric. "Clinton Wins Missouri Democratic Primary as Sanders
    Concedes." CNN Politics, March 18, 2006. http://www.cnn
    .com/2016/03/17/politics/sanders-concedes-missouri-to-clinton/index
    .html.

Breslow, Jason M. "Dennis Ross: Obama, Netanyahu Have a 'Backdrop
    of Distrust.'" *Frontline*, January 6, 2016. https://www.pbs.org/wgbh
    /frontline/article/dennis-ross-obama-netanyahu-have-a
    -backdrop-of-distrust/.

Brown, Carrie Budoff. "Kennedy Reemerges on Health Reform." *Politico*,
    May 29, 2009. https://www.politico.com/story/2009/05
    /kennedy-reemerges-on-health-reform-023111.

Brown, Carrie Budoff. "Senate Gang of 8 Immigration Reform Bill (Full
    Text)." *Politico*, April 17, 2013. https://www.politico.com/story/2013/04
    /senate-gang-of-8-immigration-reform-bill-full-text-090192.

Brundage, Amy. "Extending Middle Class Tax Cuts for 98% of Americans and
    97% of Small Businesses." President Obama White House Archives, July
    9, 2012. https://obamawhitehouse.archives.gov/blog/2012/07/09
    /extending-middle-class-tax-cuts-98-americans-and-97-small-businesses.

Buck Research. "Senate Finance Committee Approves Health Care Reform
    Proposal," FYI 32, no. 68 (October 19, 2009): 1. http://analysis.hrservices
    .conduent.com/wp-content/uploads/sites/2/2009/10/FYI-10-19-09-Senate
    -Finance-Committee-Approves-Health-Care-Reform-Proposal.pdf.

Byers, Dylan. "Obama Campaign Tried to Plug Leaks." *Politico*,
    July 17, 2013. https://www.politico.com/story/2013/07
    /obama-campaign-tried-to-plug-leaks-094355.

Calderone, Michael. "Who's Andy Martin?" *Politico*, October 13, 2008. https://www.politico.com/blogs/michaelcalderone/1008/Whos_Andy _Martin.html.

Calmes, Jackie, and Jeff Zeleny. "Obama Vows Swift Action on Vast Economic Stimulus Plan." *New York Times*, November 22, 2008. http://www .nytimes.com/2007/04/05/us/politics/05obama.html.

Cameron, Carl, and Associated Press. "Democrats Back Lamont; Lieberman Files for Independent Run." Fox News, August 9, 2006. http://www .foxnews.com/story/2006/08/09/democrats-back-lamont-lieberman -files-for-independent-run.html.

"Candidate Barack Obama in 2002." YouTube video (0:17), posted by Peoples Party, October 2, 2014. https://www.youtube.com/watch?v=6MjSzxVkI-c.

CBS News and Associated Press. "Dodd: Show Me the Bailout Money." CBS News, January 12, 2009. https://www.cbsnews.com/news /dodd-show-me-the-bailout-money.

CBS News and Associated Press. "Kerry Warns Important Issues in Iran Nuclear Talks 'Unresolved.'" CBS News, November 8, 2013. https://www.cbsnews.com/news /kerry-warns-important-issues-in-iran-nuclear-talks-unresolved.

CBS News and Associated Press. "Man Who Secretly Videotaped Mitt Romney's '47 Percent' Remarks Comes Forward." CBS News, March 14, 2013. https://www.cbsnews.com/news/man-who-secretly-videotaped -mitt-romneys-47-percent-remarks-comes-forward.

Center for Climate and Energy Solutions. "15th Session of the Conference of the Parties to the United Nations Framework Convention on Climate Change." Center for Climate and Energy Solutions, December 22, 2009. https://www.c2es.org/content/cop-15-copenhagen.

Centers for Disease Control and Prevention. "Facts About Sarin." Centers for Disease Control and Prevention, November 18, 2015. https://emergency .cdc.gov/agent/sarin/basics/facts.asp.

Centers for Medicare & Medicaid Services. "Medical Loss Ratio." Healthcare. gov. Last accessed February 9, 2018. https://www.healthcare.gov/glossary /medical-loss-ratio-mlr.

Cherkis, Jason, and Sam Stein. "The Inside Story of Why Clint Eastwood Talked to an Empty Chair at the GOP Convention." Huffington Post, January 26, 2016. https://www.huffingtonpost.com/entry/the-inside -story-of-why-clint-eastwood-talked-to-an-empty-chair-at-the -gop-convention_us_56a289e2e4b0d8cc109a047b.

"Chicago: Jesse Jackson." Bartcop Entertainment, October 3, 2002. http:// www.suprmchaos.com/bcEnt-Thu-100302.index.html. [Author verified photo via email with AP photographer Sue Ogrocki.]

"China's President Xi and Obama Discuss Climate Change by Phone." Reuters, December 11, 2015. https://www.reuters.com/news/picture /chinas-president-xi-and-obama-discuss-cl-idUSKBN0TU0FI20151211.

"Chrysler Announces Major Downsizing." Road & Track, February 14, 2007. http://www.roadandtrack.com/car-culture/a12995 /chrysler-announces-major-downsizing/.

Cillizza, Chris. "How Ted Kennedy Helped Change the Course of the 2008 Election." Washington Post, March 30, 2015. https://www .washingtonpost.com/news/the-fix/wp/2015/03/30 /how-ted-kennedy-helped-change-the-course-of-the-2008-election.

Clark, William P. "Reagan and the Law of the Sea." The Heritage Foundation, October 9, 2007. https://www.heritage.org/global-politics/commentary /reagan-and-the-law-the-sea.

Clinton, Bill. "Transcript of Bill Clinton's Speech to the Democratic National Convention." *New York Times*, September 5, 2012. http://www.nytimes .com/2012/09/05/us/politics/transcript-of-bill-clintons-speech-to-the -democratic-national-convention.html.

Clinton, Hillary. "America's Pacific Century." *Foreign Policy*, October 11, 2011. http://foreignpolicy.com/2011/10/11/americas-pacific-century.

"CNBC's Rick Santelli's Chicago Tea Party." YouTube video (4:36), posted by the Heritage Foundation, February 19, 2009. https://www.youtube.com /watch?v=zp-Jw-5Kx8k.

"CNN Debunks False Report about Obama." CNN, January 23, 2007. www .cnn.com/2007/POLITICS/01/22/obama.madrassa.

Cohen, Andy. "The Myth of the Filibuster-Proof Democratic Senate." *San Diego Free Press*, September 11, 2012. https://sandiegofreepress .org/2012/09/the-myth-of-the-filibuster-proof-democratic-senate.

Cohn, Jonathan. "From Boston, a Lesson about Obamacare." *New Republic*, October 31, 2013.

"Colonel Gaddafi 'Ordered Lockerbie Bombing.'" BBC News, February 23, 2011. http://www.bbc.com/news/uk-scotland-south-scotland-12552587.

Commission on Presidential Debates. "October 22, 2012 Debate Transcript." Debate between President Barack Obama and former Governor Mitt Romney, Lynn University, Boca Raton, Florida, October 22, 2012. http://www.debates.org/index .php?page=october-22-2012-the-third-obama-romney-presidential-debate.

Condon, Stephanie. "Bill Clinton to Senators: Health Reform 'Imperative.'" CBS News, November 10, 2009. https://www.cbsnews.com/news /bill-clinton-to-senators-health-reform-imperative.

"Congresswoman Giffords Shot by Gunman in Arizona, Judge Killed." *PBS NewsHour*, January 8, 2011. https://www.pbs.org/newshour/politics /congresswoman-shot-by-gunman-in-arizona.

Cook, John. "Ted Kennedy Brain Cancer Is in Remission." Gawker, May 19, 2009. http://gawker.com/5261619 /ted-kennedy-brain-cancer-is-in-remission.

Coppins, McKay. "The Making of Romney's Storm Relief Event." BuzzFeed News, October 31, 2012. https://www.buzzfeed.com/mckaycoppins /the-making-of-romneys-storm-relief-event.

Corn, David. "SECRET VIDEO: Romney Tells Millionaire Donors What He REALLY Thinks of Obama Voters." *Mother Jones*, September 17, 2012. http://www.motherjones.com/politics/2012/09 /secret-video-romney-private-fundraiser/.

Cote, Owen R., Jr. "Appendix B: A Primer on Fissile Materials and Nuclear Weapon Design." *Avoiding Nuclear Anarchy: Containing the Threat of Loose Russian Nuclear Weapons and Fissile Material.* CSIA Studies in International Security, John F. Kennedy School of Government, Harvard University, 1996.

"Cotton and 46 Fellow Senators to Send Open Letter to the Leaders of the Islamic Republic of Iran." Office of Senator Tom Cotton, March 9, 2015. https://www.cotton.senate.gov/?p=press_release&id=120.

Crowley, Michael. "What Worries Ben Rhodes about Trump." *Politico Magazine*, January/February 2017. https://www.politico .com/magazine/story/2017/01/obama-foreign-policy-legacy-ben-rhodes -donald-trump-china-iran-214642.

"DaimlerChrysler Dawns." CNN Money, May 7, 1998. http://money.cnn .com/1998/05/07/deals/benz.

Dauster, William G. "The Senate in Transition, or How I Learned to Stop Worrying and Love the Nuclear Option." *NYU Journal of Legislation & Public Policy* 19, no. 4 (December 2016): 632–83. http://www.nyujlpp .org/wp-content/uploads/2016/12/The-Senate-in-Transition-or-How-I -Learned-to-Stop-Worrying-and-Love-the-Nuclear-Option-19nyujlpp631 .pdf.

Davenport, Coral. "Nations Approve Landmark Climate Accord in Paris." *New York Times*, December 12, 2015. https://www.nytimes.com/2015/12/13 /world/europe/climate-change-accord-paris.html.

Davenport, Kelsey. "Timeline of Nuclear Diplomacy with Iran." Arms Control Association, November 2017. https://www.armscontrol.org /factsheet/Timeline-of-Nuclear-Diplomacy-With-Iran.

Davey, Monica. "Celebrating Obama in Grant Park." *New York Times*, November 5, 2008. https://thecaucus.blogs.nytimes.com/2008/11/05 /waiting-for-obama-in-grant-park/.

Davis, Julie Hirschfeld, and Michael D. Shear. "Unrest over Race Is Testing Obama's Legacy." *New York Times*, December 8, 2014. https://www .nytimes.com/2014/12/09/us/politics/unrest-over-race-is-testing-obamas -legacy-.html.

Dawes, Daniel E. *150 Years of Obamacare*. Baltimore: Johns Hopkins University Press, 2016.

"Debt Ceiling: Timeline of Deal's Development." CNN Politics, August 2, 2011. www.cnn.com/2011/POLITICS/07/25/debt.talks.timeline/index .html.

de la Merced, Michael J. "Appeals Court Refuses to Block Chrysler's Sale." *New York Times*, June 5, 2009. https://dealbook.nytimes.com/2009/06/05 /appeals-court-refuses-to-block-chryslers-sale-to-fiat.

"Delaware Primary Results." Election 2008. *New York Times*, February 5, 2008. https://www.nytimes.com/elections/2008/primaries/results/states /DE.html.

Dennis, Steven T. "Barack Obama Takes Executive Action on DREAM Act." *Roll Call*, June 15, 2012. https://www.rollcall.com/news/Obama-issues -DREAM-order-215406-1.html.

Dermer, Ron. "What Was Concluded in Geneva Last Night Is Not a Historic Agreement, It's a Historic Mistake." Facebook, November 24, 2013. https://www.facebook.com/ambdermer/photos /a.1451178395107 841.1073741826.1450 515471840800/1477205249171822.

Deshishku, Stacia. "President Obama Statement on Trayvon Martin Case." CNN Politics, March 23, 2012. http://whitehouse.blogs.cnn .com/2012/03/23/president-obama-statement-on-trayvon-martin-case.

DeSilver, Drew. "What Is the House Freedom Caucus, and Who's in It?" Pew Research Center, October 20, 2015. http://www.pewresearch.org /fact-tank/2015/10/20/house-freedom-caucus-what-is-it-and-whos-in-it.

Dewan, Shaila. "Zero Job Growth Latest Bleak Sign for US Economy." *New York Times*, September 2, 2011. http://www.nytimes.com/2011/09/03 /business/economy/united-states-showed-no-job-growth-in-august.html.

DeYoung, Karen. "Kerry Hurt in Bike Accident; Rest of Europe Visit Canceled." *Washington Post*, May 31, 2015. https://www.washingtonpost .com/world/kerry-suffers-leg-injury-in-bicycle-accident-transported-to -hospital/2015/05/31/24bd2630-077a-11e5-a7ad-b430fc1d3f5c_story.html.

"Disclosure of Classified Information." 18 USC 798, United States law in effect as of January 3, 2012. https://www.gpo.gov/fdsys/granule /USCODE-2011-title18/USCODE-2011-title18-partI-chap37-sec798.

"Doesn't 'Love' America? Giuliani Clarifies Obama Patriotism Comments." Fox News Politics, February 19, 2015. http://www.foxnews.com /politics/2015/02/19/giuliani-clarifies-obama-patriotism-comments -wasserman-schultz-weighs-in.html.

Donohue, Kelsey. "The First Lady Hosts the 'Beating the Odds' Summit." President Obama White House Archives, July 24, 2015. https:// obamawhitehouse.archives.gov/blog/2015/07/24 /first-lady-hosts-beating-odds-summit.

Doty, Cate. "Former SC Governor Endorses Obama." *New York Times*, January 2, 2008. https://thecaucus.blogs.nytimes.com/2008/01/02 /former-sc-governor-endorses-obama.

Douglas, Alexandra. "Obama and Hispanic Dems Will Meet Today to Talk Immigration." It's Our Community (blog), March 18, 2009. http:// itsourcommunity.blogspot.com/2009/03/obama-and-hispanic-democrats -will-meet.html.

Douglas, Danielle. "Holder Concerned Megabanks Too Big to Jail." *Washington Post*, March 6, 2013. https://www.washingtonpost .com/business/economy/holder-concerned-megabanks-too-big-to -jail/2013/03/06/6fa2b07a-869e-11e2-999e-5f8e0410cb9d_story.html.

Dove, James T., Douglas Weaver, and Jack Lewin. "Health Care Delivery System Reform: Accountable Care Organizations." *Journal of the American College of Cardiology* 54, no. 11 (September 8, 2009): 985–8. https://doi .org/10.1016/j.jacc.2009.07.014.

Draper, Robert. *Do Not Ask What Good We Do: Inside the US House of Representatives*. New York: Free Press, 2012.

Draper, Robert. "The Ultimate Obama Insider." *New York Times Magazine*, July 21, 2009. http://www.nytimes.com/2009/07/26/magazine/26jarrett-t .html.

Drexhage, John, and Deborah Murphy. *Copenhagen: A Memorable Time For All the Wrong Reasons?* International Institute for Sustainable Development, December 2009. https://www.iisd.org/pdf/2009/cop _memorable_time_wrong_reasons.pdf.

Duggan, Jennifer. "Beijing's Smog Clouds City's Marathon." *Guardian*, October 20, 2014. https://www.theguardian.com/environment /chinas-choice/2014/oct/20/beijings-smog-clouds-citys-marathon.

Eastwood, Clint. "Transcript: Clint Eastwood's Convention Remarks." National Public Radio, August 30, 2012. https://www.npr .org/2012/08/30/160358091/transcript-clint-eastwoods-convention-remarks.

Eggen, Dan. "Rick Perry Reverses Himself, Calls HPV Vaccine Mandate a 'Mistake.'" *Washington Post*, September 13, 2011. https://www .washingtonpost.com/politics/rick-perry-reverses-himself-calls-hpv -vaccine-mandate-a-mistake/2011/08/16/gIQAM2azJJ_story.html.

"Election 2010: House Map." *New York Times*, November 2, 2010. https:// www.nytimes.com/elections/2010/results/house.html.

Ellis, David. "US Seizes Fannie and Freddie." CNN Money, September 7, 2008. http://money.cnn.com/2008/09/07/news/companies/fannie _freddie/index.htm.

Emery, David. "After Birth." Snopes, September 18, 2016. https://www.snopes .com/hillary-clinton-started-birther-movement.

Estes, Adam Clark, Dashiell Bennett, and Philip Bump. "The Tale of Rand Paul's Drone Filibuster." *Atlantic*, March 6, 2013. https://www.theatlantic .com/politics/archive/2013/03/rand-paul-filibuster/317660.

Everts, Sarah. "The Nazi Origins of Deadly Nerve Gases." *Chemical & Engineering News* 94, no. 41 (October 17, 2016): 26–28. https://cen.acs .org/articles/94/i41/Nazi-origins-deadly-nerve-gases.html.

Fahrenthold, David A. "Trump Recorded Having Extremely Lewd Conversation about Women in 2005." *Washington Post*, October 8, 2016. https://www.washingtonpost.com/politics/trump -recorded-having-extremely-lewd-conversation-about-women-in -2005/2016/10/07/3b9ce776-8cb4-11e6-bf8a-3d26847eeed4_story.html.

Fahrenthold, David A., and Katie Zezima. "For Ted Cruz, the 2013 Shutdown Was a Defining Moment." *Washington Post*, February 16, 2016. https:// www.washingtonpost.com/politics/how-cruzs-plan-to-defund-obamacare -failed--and-what-it-achieved/2016/02/16/4e2ce116-c6cb-11e5-8965 -0607e0e265ce_story.html.

Fain, Thom. "TBT: Remember When Newt Gingrich Led the Republican Revival of '94?" *Providence Journal*, December 1, 2016. http://www .providencejournal.com/zz/elections/20161201 /tbt-remember-when-newt-gingrich-led-republican-revival-of-94.

Farley, Robert. "One of Obama's First Calls Was to Palestinian Leader, and Israeli Leader." Politifact, May 8, 2009. http://www.politifact .com/truth-o-meter/statements/2009/may/08/chain-email /one-obamas-first-calls-was-palestinian-leader-and-.

Felsenthal, Carol. "How Obama Pushed Axelrod Out of the White House." *Chicago*, September 24, 2013. http://www.chicagomag.com /Chicago-Magazine/Felsenthal-Files/September-2013/Obama-Axelrod.

Ferguson Action. "Breaking: Ferguson Activists Meet with President Obama to Demand an End to Police Brutality Nationwide." Ferguson Action, December 1, 2014. http://fergusonaction.com/white-house-meeting/.

Fieldhouse, Andrew. "President Obama's Policies Revived the Economy." *US News & World Report*, March 13, 2012. https://www.usnews .com/debate-club/is-obama-turning-the-economy-around /president-obamas-policies-revived-the-economy.

"Former President Bill Clinton at the 2012 Democratic National Convention."
C-SPAN video (49:34), September 5, 2012. https://www.c-span.org
/video/?c3779974/former-president-bill-clinton-2012-democratic
-national-convention.

Franke-Ruta, Garance. "Democratic Rep. Gabrielle Giffords, Others Shot at
Arizona Safeway." *Atlantic*, January 8, 2011. https://www.theatlantic.com
/politics/archive/2011/01/democratic-rep-gabrielle-giffords
-others-shot-at-arizona-safeway/69138.

Fraud Enforcement and Recovery Act of 2009. Pub. L. 111–21, S. 386, 123 Stat.
1617, May 20, 2009. https://www.govtrack.us/congress/bills/111/s386.

Fuller, Matt. "Boehner Won't Bring Up Senate Immigration Bill."
Roll Call, June 26, 2013. https://www.rollcall.com/news
/boehner-wont-bring-up-senate-immigration-bill.

"Full Text: Biden's Announcement That He Won't Run for President."
Washington Post, October 21, 2015. https://www
.washingtonpost.com/news/post-politics/wp/2015/10/21
/full-text-bidens-announcement-that-he-wont-run-for-president.

Gallup News. "Presidential Approval Ratings—Barack Obama." Last accessed
February 9, 2018. http://news.gallup.com/poll/116479/barack-obama
-presidential-job-approval.aspx.

Garrow, David. *Rising Star: The Making of Barack Obama*. New York: William
Morrow, 2017.

Geithner, Timothy F. *Stress Test: Reflections on Financial Crises*. New York:
Broadway Books, 2014.

"Getting Frank on Dodd-Frank." Transcript, interview with former
representative Barney Frank. Third Way, July 27, 2015. www.thirdway.org
/transcript/getting-frank-on-dodd-frank.

Gilsinan, Kathy. "Five Years in a Cuban Prison." *Atlantic*, November 30, 2016. https://www.theatlantic.com/international/archive/2016/11 /alan-gross-castro/509075.

Gilson, Dave. "The Venn-Diagram That Explains How the Ryan-Murray Budget Deal Happened." *Mother Jones*, December 13, 2013. https://www .motherjones.com/politics/2013/12/chart-ryan-murray -budget-defense-pentagon.

Glauber, Bill, and Don Walker. "Romney Names Ryan as His VP Pick on USS Wisconsin." *Milwaukee Journal Sentinel*, August 11, 2012. http:// archive.jsonline.com/news/statepolitics/romneyryan-ticket-launches -from-uss-wisconsin-d36f609-165839386.html.

General Motors Corporation. "2009–2014 Restructuring Plan." General Motors Corporation, February 17, 2009. https://static01.nyt.com /packages/pdf/business/20090217GMRestructuringPlan.pdf.

Goldfarb, Zachary A. "S&P Downgrades US Credit Rating for First Time." *Washington Post*, August 6, 2011. https://www.washingtonpost.com /business/economy/sandp-considering-first-downgrade-of-us-credit -rating/2011/08/05/gIQAqKeIxI_story.html.

Goldman, David. "Senate Vote Fails, Obama Gets $350B." CNN Money, January 15, 2009. http://money.cnn.com/2009/01/15/news/economy /senate_tarp_vote/index.htm.

Goldstein, Amy. "Obama Administration Will Allow More Time to Enroll in Health Care on Federal Marketplace." *Washington Post*, March 25, 2014. https://www.washingtonpost.com/national/health-science /obama-administration-will-allow-more-time-to-enroll-in-health-care-on -federal-marketplace/2014/03/25/d0458338-b449-11e3-8cb6-284052554d74 _story.html.

Good, Chris. "John Boehner's First Day." *Atlantic*, January 5,
    2011. https://www.theatlantic.com/politics/archive/2011/01
    /john-boehners-first-day/68924/.

Gottlieb, Stuart. "Blame the Obama Doctrine For Iraq." Daily Beast, June 29,
    2014. https://www.thedailybeast.com/blame-the-obama-doctrine-for-iraq.

Granville, Kevin. "What Is TPP? Behind the Trade Deal That Died." *New York
    Times*, January 23, 2017. https://www.nytimes.com/interactive/2016
    /business/tpp-explained-what-is-trans-pacific-partnership.html.

Gray, Louise and Alastair Jamieson. "Copenhagen Climate Summit: Deal
    Agreed amid Chaos." *Telegraph*, December 19, 2009. http://www
    .telegraph.co.uk/news/earth/copenhagen-climate-change-confe/6843304
    /Copenhagen-climate-summit-deal-agreed-amid-chaos.html.

Greene, Brian. "How 'Occupy Wall Street' Started and Spread." *US News &
    World Report*, October 17, 2011. https://www
    .usnews.com/news/washington-whispers/articles/2011/10/17
    /how-occupy-wall-street-started-and-spread.

Greenwald, Glenn. "NSA Collecting Phone Records of Millions of Verizon
    Customers Daily." *Guardian*, June 6, 2013. https://www.theguardian.com
    /world/2013/jun/06/nsa-phone-records-verizon-court-order.

Grunwald, Michael. "Did Obama Win the Judicial Wars?" *Politico*,
    August 8, 2016. https://www.politico.com/story/2016/08
    /obama-courts-judicial-legacy-226741.

Grunwald, Michael. *The New New Deal: The Hidden Story of Change in the
    Obama Era*. New York: Simon & Schuster, 2012.

Grynbaum, Michael M., and Jeff Zeleny. "Obama Wins South Carolina
    Primary." *New York Times*, January 26, 2008. http://www.nytimes
    .com/2008/01/26/us/politics/26cnd-carolina.html.

Guevara, Meghan. "Pretrial Populations: Who Is in Jail, Who Is Out, and
    Who Is Deciding?" Crime and Justice Institute, March 4, 2015. http://
    www.courts.ca.gov/documents/PretrialSummit2015
    -7IdentifyingJailPopulation.pdf.

Gunpolicy.org. "Australia: Total Number of Gun Deaths." Last accessed
    February 9, 2018. http://www.gunpolicy.org/firearms/compareyears/10
    /total_number_of_gun_deaths.

Hainey, Michael. "Clint and Scott Eastwood: No Holds Barred in Their First
    Interview Together." *Esquire*, August 3, 2016. http://www.esquire.com
    /entertainment/a46893/double-trouble-clint-and-scott-eastwood.

Halliday, Jean. "Car Execs, Agency Defrauded DaimlerChrysler, Lawsuit
    Says." *Advertising Age*, February 28, 2005. http://adage.com/article/news
    /car-execs-agency-defrauded-daimlerchrysler-lawsuit/102251.

Halloran, Liz. "Gang Of 8 Champion Plan, Declare 'Year Of Immigration
    Reform.'" NPR Politics, April 18, 2013. https://www.npr.org/sections
    /itsallpolitics/2013/04/18/177780665
    /bipartisan-senate-gang-prepares-to-sell-immigration-plan.

Halperin, Mark, and John Heilemann. *Double Down: Game Change 2012*.
    New York: Penguin Books, 2013.

Harris, John F. "Farewell to an Original Clinton Warrior." *Washington Post*,
    October 16, 1998. http://www.washingtonpost.com/wp-srv/politics
    /special/clinton/stories/rahm101698.htm.

Health Equity and Access Reform Today Act of 1993, S. 1770. 103rd Congress,
    introduced November 22, 1993. https://www.congress.gov
    /bill/103rd-congress/senate-bill/1770/cosponsors.

Healy, Jack. "Utah Judge Unexpected as a Hero to Gay People." *New York Times*, December 29, 2013. http://www.nytimes.com/2013/12/30/us/utah -ruling-on-marriage-puts-judge-in-spotlight.html.

Healy, Patrick. "To Avoid Conflicts, Clintons Liquidate Holdings." *New York Times*, June 15, 2007. http://www.nytimes.com/2007/06/15/us /politics/15clintons.html.

Hechtkopf, Kevin. "Rally Interrupts Dem Rep.'s Health Care Town Hall." CBS News, August 3, 2009. https://www.cbsnews.com/news /rally-interrupts-dem-reps-health-care-town-hall.

Henig, Jess. "False Euthanasia Claims." FactCheck.org, July 29, 2009. https:// www.factcheck.org/2009/07/false-euthanasia-claims.

Herszenhorn, David M. "At Obama's Urging, Bush to Seek Rest of Bailout Funds." *New York Times*. January 12, 2009. http://www.nytimes .com/2009/01/13/washington/13cong.html.

Herszenhorn, David M. "Parts of Health Bill May Pass Separately, Pelosi Says." *New York Times*, January 28, 2010. https://prescriptions.blogs.nytimes .com/2010/01/28/parts-of-health-bill-may-pass-separately-pelosi-says.

Herszenhorn, David M. "Senate Committee Approves Health Care Bill." *New York Times*, July 15, 2009. https://thecaucus.blogs.nytimes .com/2009/07/15/senate-committee-approves-health-care-bill.

Horwitz, Sari. "Read the Letter Comey Sent to FBI Employees Explaining His Controversial Decision on the Clinton Email Investigation." *Washington Post*, October 28, 2016. https://www.washingtonpost.com/news/post -nation/wp/2016/10/28/read-the-letter-comey-sent-to-fbi-employees -explaining-his-controversial-decision-on-the-clinton-email-investigation.

"House Passes Health Care Reform Bill." CNN Politics, November 8, 2009. http://www.cnn.com/2009/POLITICS/11/07/health.care.

House Republican Conference. *A Pledge to America*. House Republicans, September 23, 2010. https://www.gop.gov/resources/library/documents /solutions/a-pledge-to-america.pdf.

Hulse, Carl. "Taking Control, GOP Overhauls Rules in House." *New York Times*, January 5, 2011. http://www.nytimes.com/2011/01/06/us /politics/06cong.html.

Hulse, Carl, and Adam Nagourney. "Specter Switches Parties; More Heft for Democrats." *New York Times*, April 28, 2009. http://www.nytimes .com/2009/04/29/us/politics/29specter.html.

Human Rights First. "Facts about the Transfer of Guantanamo Detainees." Human Rights First, March 7, 2017. https://www.humanrightsfirst.org /resource/facts-about-transfer-guantanamo-detainees.

Human Rights First. "Guantánamo by the Numbers." Human Rights First, December 12, 2017. https://www.humanrightsfirst.org/sites/default/files /gtmo-by-the-numbers.pdf.

Internal Revenue Service. "The Making Work Pay Tax Credit." Internal Revenue Service, September 23, 2016. https://www.irs.gov/newsroom /the-making-work-pay-tax-credit.

"Interview With South Carolina Governor Nikki Haley." Transcript. CNN, July 10, 2015. http://www.cnn.com/TRANSCRIPTS/1507/10/cnr.07.html.

"Iowa Jefferson Jackson Dinner." C-SPAN video (4:01:12), November 10, 2007. https://www.c-span.org/video/?202117-1/iowa-jefferson-jackson -dinner. [Approximate speaking times: Senator Obama (20 minutes), Senator Clinton (19 minutes), former senator Edwards (18 minutes), Senator Dodd (17 minutes), Senator Biden (17 minutes), Governor Richardson (12 minutes).]

"Iranian Inflation Accelerates, Posing Headache for New President." Reuters, July 25, 2013. https://www.reuters.com/article/iran-inflation /iranian-inflation-accelerates-posing-headache-for-new-president -idUSL6N0FV1Y120130725.

"Iran's Khamenei Threatens to 'Set Fire' to Nuclear Deal If West Violates." Reuters, June 14, 2016. https://www.reuters.com/article/us-iran-nuclear -khamenei/irans-khamenei-threatens-to-set-fire-to-nuclear-deal-if-west -violates-idUSKCN0Z02MA.

Isenstadt, Alex. "Town Halls Gone Wild." *Politico*, July 31, 2009. https://www .politico.com/story/2009/07/town-halls-gone-wild-025646.

Isidore, Chris. "Auto Sales Worst in 26 Years." CNN Money, February 3, 2009. http://money.cnn.com/2009/02/03/news/companies/auto_sales.

Isidore, Chris. "Daimler Pays to Dump Chrysler." CNN Money, May 14, 2007. http://money.cnn.com/2007/05/14/news/companies/chrysler_sale.

Janega, James. "Your Guide to the Obama Grant Park Rally." *Chicago Tribune*, November 4, 2008. http://www.chicagotribune.com/chi-obama-rally -qanov02-story.html.

Johnson, Glen. "Mitt Romney Planned Boston Harbor Fireworks Show That Was Scotched by Election Loss." Boston.com, November 8, 2012. https:// www.boston.com/uncategorized/noprimarytagmatch/2012/11/08/mitt -romney-planned-boston-harbor-fireworks-show-that-was-scotched-by -election-loss.

Johnson, Simon. "What Did TARP Accomplish?" *New York Times*, November 19, 2009. https://economix.blogs.nytimes.com/2009/11/19 /what-did-tarp-accomplish.

Johnson, Ted. "How Funny or Die Got President Obama on Zach Galifianakis' 'Between Two Ferns.'" *Variety*, March 11, 2014. http://variety

.com/2014/digital/news/president-obama-on-zach-galifianakis-between
-two-ferns-watch-1201129329.

"Jon Stewart Makes Rick Santorum One of Google's Most-Searched Terms."
Hollywood Reporter, May 10, 2011. https://www.hollywoodreporter.com
/news/jon-stewart-makes-rick-santorum-187219.

Justia. "Notice and Comment." Justia. Last accessed February
9, 2018. https://www.justia.com/administrative-law
/rulemaking-writing-agency-regulations/notice-and-comment.

"Justice Department Follows Bush Administration in Invoking 'State Secrets'
Privilege in Rendition Lawsuit." Fox News, February 9, 2009. http://
www.foxnews.com/politics/2009/02/09/justice-department-follows-bush
-administration-invoking-state-secrets-privilege.html.

"Justice Department Oversight." Testimony from Attorney General Eric
Holder. C-SPAN video (2:29:42), March 6, 2013. https://www.c-span
.org/video/?311311-1/justice-department-oversight&start=8388. [Relevant
segment at 2:19:28.]

Kaiman, Jonathan. "China Strengthens Environmental Laws." *Guardian*,
April 25, 2014. https://www.theguardian.com/environment/2014/apr/25
/china-strengthens-environmental-laws-polluting-factories.

Kane, Paul. "Reid, Democrats Trigger 'Nuclear' Option; Eliminate Most
Filibusters on Nominees." *Washington Post*, November 21, 2013. https://
www.washingtonpost.com/politics/senate-poised-to-limit-filibusters
-in-party-line-vote-that-would-alter-centuries-of-precedent/2013/11/21
/d065cfe8-52b6-11e3-9fe0-fd2ca728e67c_story.html.

Kantor, Jodi. *The Obamas*. New York: Little, Brown and Company, 2012.

Kaufman, Leslie, and Charlie Savage. "Phone Records of Journalists Seized by US." *New York Times*, May 13, 2013. http://www.nytimes.com/2013/05/14/us/phone-records-of-journalists-of-the-associated-press-seized-by-us.html.

Kennedy, Caroline. "A President Like My Father." *New York Times*, January 27, 2008. http://www.nytimes.com/2008/01/27/opinion/27kennedy.html.

Kennedy, Edward. "A Letter to the President from Senator Ted Kennedy." *Health Care in America*. President Obama White House archives, May 12, 2009. https://obamawhitehouse.archives.gov/health-care-in-america.

Kephart, Janice. "Amnesty by Any Means." Center for Immigration Studies, October 18, 2011. https://cis.org/Amnesty-Any-Means.

Kershner, Isabel. "Emboldened by Trump, Israel Approves a Wave of West Bank Settlement Expansion." *New York Times*, January 24, 2017. https://www.nytimes.com/2017/01/24/world/middleeast/israel-settlement-expansion-west-bank.html.

Khan, Huma. "President Obama Hails Senate Health Care Bill as Ben Nelson Jumps on Board." ABC News, December 19, 2009. https://abcnews.go.com/Politics/HealthCare/senator-ben-nelson-approves-health-care-bill-obama/story?id=9381054.

Khimm, Suzy. "The Sequester, Explained." *Washington Post*, September 14, 2012. https://www.washingtonpost.com/news/wonk/wp/2012/09/14/the-sequester-explained.

Kimball, Zack. "Obama Trip to Schenectady Postponed." *Shen Pen*, January 10, 2011. https://theshenpen.wordpress.com/2011/01/10/obama-trip-to-schenectady-postponed.

Kirkpatrick, David D., Mike McIntire, and Jeff Zeleny. "Obama's Camp Cultivates Crop in Small Donors." *New York Times*, July 17, 2007. http://www.nytimes.com/2007/07/17/us/politics/17obama.html.

Klaidman, Daniel. *Kill or Capture: The War on Terror and the Soul of the Obama Presidency.* New York: Houghton Mifflin Harcourt, 2012.

Klein, Rick, and Ed O'Keefe. "Ted Kennedy Diagnosed With Malignant Brain Tumor." ABC News, May 20, 2008. http://abcnews.go.com/Politics /Health/story?id=4894479.

Kliff, Sarah. "The Obamacare Provision That Terrifies Insurers." *Washington Post*, July 18, 2013. https://www.washingtonpost.com/news/wonk /wp/2013/07/18/the-obamacare-provision-that-terrifies-insurers.

Klinkner, Philip. "The Causes and Consequences of 'Birtherism.'" Paper presented at the 2014 Annual Meeting of the Western Political Science Association, Seattle, WA, April 2014. https://wpsa.research.pdx.edu /papers/docs/Birthers.pdf.

Klußmann, Uwe, Matthias Schepp, and Klaus Wiegrefe. "Did the West Break Its Promise to Moscow?" Spiegel Online, November 26, 2009. http:// www.spiegel.de/international/world/nato-s-eastward-expansion-did-the -west-break-its-promise-to-moscow-a-663315.html.

Knowlton, Brian. "Obama Meets with McCain in Chicago." *New York Times*, November 17, 2008. http://www.nytimes.com/2008/11/18/us /politics/18transition.html.

Kornblut, Anne E., and Matthew Mosk. "Clinton Owes Lead in Poll to Support from Women." *Washington Post*, June 12, 2007. http://www .washingtonpost.com/wp-dyn/content/article/2007/06/11 /AR2007061102216.html.

Kraushaar, Josh, and Manu Raju. "Coleman Concedes Race to Franken." *Politico*, June 30, 2009. https://www.politico.com/story/2009/06 /coleman-concedes-race-to-franken-024383.

Kurtz, Judy. "Journey, Kid Rock Bring the Beat to Tampa." *The Hill*, August 27, 2012. http://thehill.com/conventions-2012/gop-convention -tampa/245307-journey-kid-rock-bring-the-beat-to-tampa-.

Landler, Mark. "Obama Tries to Reclaim Momentum With Midwest Bus Tour." *New York Times*, August 15, 2011. http://www.nytimes .com/2011/08/16/us/politics/16obama.html.

Landler, Mark. "Photos Tell a Tale of Anguished Deliberations." *New York Times*, September 6, 2013. http://www.nytimes.com/2013/09/07/world /middleeast/photos-tell-a-tale-of-anguished-deliberations.html.

Lee, Carol E., and Amie Parnes. "Biden Would Avoid Subways, Planes after Swine Flu Outbreak." *Politico*, April 30, 2009. https://www.politico.com/story/2009/04 /biden-says-avoid-planes-subways-puts-out-clarifying-statement-021925.

Lee, Jolie. "Healthcare.gov Gets Traffic Boost after Obama's 'Funny or Die' Video." *USA Today*, March 12, 2014. https:// www.usatoday.com/story/news/nation-now/2014/03/12 /healthcare-obama-between-two-ferns/6319483.

Lee, Kristen A. "Tampa Bay Strip Clubs Prepare for Republican Convention with Sarah Palin Stripper, Online Chat Rooms." *New York Daily News*, July 23, 2012. http://www.nydailynews.com/news/election-2012/tampa -bay-strip-clubs-prepare-republican-convention-sarah-palin-stripper -online-chat-rooms-article-1.1120079.

Libit, Daniel. "Won't You Be My Mentor?" *Politico*, March 30, 2009. https:// www.politico.com/story/2009/03/wont-you-be-my-mentor-020639.

Linthicum, Kate, and Richard Verrier. "Michelle Obama Makes Fundraising Swing through Southern California." *Los Angeles Times*, June 14, 2011. http://articles.latimes.com/2011/jun/14/nation /la-na-michelle-obama-20110614.

Lizza, Ryan. "The Obama Memos." *New Yorker*, January 30, 2012. https://
www.newyorker.com/magazine/2012/01/30/the-obama-memos.

Koul, Shuvait. "Low Auction Bid Prices Show Solar Cheaper
Than Coal In India." The Climate Group. November
11, 2014. https://www.theclimategroup.org/news
/low-auction-bid-prices-show-solar-cheaper-coal-india.

Lowrey, Annie. "How Osama bin Laden Escaped." *Foreign Policy*, December
11, 2009. http://foreignpolicy.com/2009/12/11
/how-osama-bin-laden-escaped-2/.

"Luis Gutierrez: Luis at DNC: Democratic National Convention, Day 1."
C-SPAN video (7:11), July 26, 2016. https://www.c-span.org
/video/?c4615251/luis-gutierrez.

"Luis Gutierrez Remarks at 2012 Democratic National Convention." YouTube
video (6:04), posted by DNCConvention2012, September 6, 2012.
https://www.youtube.com/watch?v=XVOO_TVJ51A.

MacAskill, Ewen. "Phenomenon Obama Draws Crowds of Thousands."
Guardian, January 5, 2008. https://www.theguardian.com/world/2008
/jan/05/barackobama.usa.

Mak, Tim. "Inside the CIA's Sadistic Dungeon." Daily Beast, December 9,
2014. https://www.thedailybeast.com/inside-the-cias-sadistic-dungeon.

Mangan, Dan. "Ticktock: Obamacare Deadlines You Need to Know." CNBC,
October 1, 2013. https://www.cnbc.com/2013/09/30/ticktock-obamacare
-deadlines-you-need-to-know.html.

"March 2013 *Post*-ABC Poll: Obama and Politics, the Catholic Church, Gun
Control." *Washington Post*, April 12, 2013. https://www.washingtonpost
.com/politics/polling/march-2013-postabc-poll-obama-politics/2013/04/12
/b1a4a4bc-8a8e-11e2-a88e-461ffa2e34e4_page.html.

Marimow, Ann E. "Justice Department's Scrutiny of Fox News Reporter
    James Rosen in Leak Case Draws Fire." *Washington Post*, May 20, 2013.
    https://www.washingtonpost.com/local/justice-departments-scrutiny
    -of-fox-news-reporter-james-rosen-in-leak-case-draws-fire/2013/05/20
    /c6289eba-c162-11e2-8bd8-2788030e6b44_story.html.

Martin, Roland S. "The Full Story behind Wright's 'God Damn America'
    Sermon." CNN, March 21, 2008. http://ac360.blogs.cnn.com/2008/03/21
    /the-full-story-behind-wright%E2%80%99s-%E2%80%9Cgod-damn
    -america%E2%80%9D-sermon.

Mateja, Jim. "How Chrysler Marriage Failed." *Chicago Tribune*, May 15, 2007.
    http://articles.chicagotribune.com/2007-05-15/news/0705141000_1
    _daimler-benz-cerberus-capital-management-carmakers.

Mayer, Jane. "The Trial." *New Yorker*, February 15, 2010. https://www
    .newyorker.com/magazine/2010/02/15/the-trial-2.

McKinney, Rick. "Dodd-Frank Wall Street Reform and Consumer Financial
    Protection Act: A Brief Legislative History with Links, Reports and
    Summaries." Law Librarians' Society of Washington, DC, December 10,
    2010. http://www.llsdc.org/dodd-frank-legislative-history.

McMorris-Santoro, Evan. "The Obama Campaign Remembers 2012 Very
    Differently Than Bernie Sanders." BuzzFeed News, November 8, 2015.
    https://www.buzzfeed.com/evanmcsan
    /the-obama-campaign-remembers-2012-very-differently-from-bern.

Melby, Todd. "Franken Declared Senate Winner, Coleman Concedes."
    Reuters, June 30, 2009. https://www.reuters.com/article/us-usa
    -senate-minnesota/franken-declared-senate-winner-coleman-concedes
    -idUSTRE55T5Y420090630.

"Memorial Service for Shooting Victims in Tucson." C-SPAN video (1:38:14),
    January 12, 2011. https://www.c-span.org/video/?297455-1

/memorial-service-shooting-victims-tucson&start=3913. [Relevant segments at 1:05:50 and 1:14:00.]

Mendick, Robert. "Colonel Gaddafi Warned Tony Blair of Islamist Attacks on Europe, Phone Conversations Reveal." *Telegraph*, January 7, 2016. http://www.telegraph.co.uk/news/politics/tony-blair/12086505/Tony-Blairs-phone-conversations-with-Colonel-Gaddafi-revealed.html.

Merica, Dan. "Top Latino Congressman Endorses Hillary Clinton." CNN Politics, December 14, 2015. https://www.cnn.com/2015/12/14/politics/hillary-clinton-immigration-endorsement-luis-gutierrez/index.html.

"Michigan Primary Results," Election 2016. *New York Times*, March 8, 2016. https://www.nytimes.com/elections/2016/results/primaries/michigan.

"Mitt Romney Says 'I Had Binders Full of Women' During US Presidential Debate." YouTube video (2:37), posted by ODN, October 16, 2012. https://www.youtube.com/watch?v=OX_AN4w3da8.

Mohammed, Arshad, and Andrew Osborn. "Kerry: Syrian Surrender of Chemical Arms Could Stop US attack." Reuters, September 9, 2013. https://www.reuters.com/article/us-syria-crisis-kerry/kerry-syrian-surrender-of-chemical-arms-could-stop-u-s-attack-idUSBRE9880BV20130909.

Morgan, David, and Lewis Krauskopf. "US Government Scrambles to Provide Access to Obamacare Sites." Reuters, October 1, 2013. https://www.reuters.com/article/us-usa-healthcare/u-s-government-scrambles-to-provide-access-to-obamacare-sites-idUSBRE98T14R20131002.

"Mr. Obama Mrs. Hillary Crashes a Secret China India Meeting Unprecented." YouTube video (1:43), posted by Giulia Ozyesilpinar, December 26, 2016. https://www.youtube.com/watch?v=fs8YznVSqE8. [Relevant segment at 0:45: "Are you ready for me or do you guys need to

talk some more? . . . It's up to you . . . Come on, what do you think? . . .
Premier, are you ready for me or do you want to wait?"]

Mukoro, Jay. "Partying with Obama in Chicago." *Guardian*, November 5,
  2008. https://www.theguardian.com/commentisfree/cifamerica/2008
  /nov/05/uselections2008-barackobama.

Murray, Mark. "NBC Poll: Nearly 80 Percent Want Congressional Approval
  on Syria." NBC News, August 30, 2013. https://www.nbcnews.com/news
  /other/nbc-poll-nearly-80-percent-want-congressional-approval-syria
  -f8C11038428.

Nagourney, Adam. "Obama Takes Iowa in a Big Turnout as Clinton Falters;
  Huckabee Victor." *New York Times*, January 4, 2008. http://www.nytimes
  .com/2008/01/04/us/politics/04elect.html.

Nagourney, Adam. "Obama Wins Election." *New York Times*, November 4,
  2008. www.nytimes.com/2008/11/05/us/politics/05campaign.html.

Nakamura, David. "White House Chief of Staff William Daley Quits; Budget
  Chief Jacob Lew Fills Post." *Washington Post*, January 9, 2012. https://
  www.washingtonpost.com/politics/white-house-chief-of-staff-william
  -daley-will-quit-his-post/2012/01/09/gIQAz15xlP_story.html.

"Nancy Pelosi—What She Is Willing to Do to Pass Healthcare." YouTube
  video (0:14), posted by SomePoliticalClips, January 31, 2010. https://www
  .youtube.com/watch?v=imUyBlc7NHQ.

National Intelligence Council. "Assessing Russian Activities and Intentions in
  Recent US Elections." Office of the United States Director of National
  Intelligence, January 6, 2017. https://www.dni.gov/files/documents
  /ICA_2017_01.pdf.

Nelson, Libby. "Watch Obama and Seth Meyers Viciously Mock Donald
  Trump to His Face in 2011." Vox, May 4, 2016. https://www.vox

.com/2016/5/4/11591114/donald-trump-obama-seth-meyers
-white-house-correspondents-dinner.

"Netanyahu: Nuclear Deal with Iran a 'Historic Mistake.'" YouTube video
(2:43), posted by Joseph Wouk, November 24, 2013. https://www.youtube
.com/watch?v=ytbXQ-iTIms.

"The Never-Ending Cold War." Editorial. *New York Times*, March 28, 2012.
http://www.nytimes.com/2012/03/29/opinion/the-never-ending-cold
-war.html.

Norris, Floyd. "As Corporate Profits Rise, Workers' Income Declines." *New
York Times*, August 5, 2011. http://www.nytimes.com/2011/08/06/business
/workers-wages-chasing-corporate-profits-off-the-charts.html.

"NY Fed to Provide $29 Billion in Bear Stearns Financing." Reuters, March
24, 2008. https://www.reuters.com/article/us-bearstearns-fed/ny-fed-to
-provide-29-billion-in-bear-stearns-financing-idUSWAT00917720080324.

Obama, Barack. "A Just and Lasting Peace." Nobel Lecture, Oslo, Norway,
December 10, 2009. https://www.nobelprize.org/nobel_prizes/peace
/laureates/2009/obama-lecture.html.

Obama, Barack. "Remarks in Washington, DC: 'The War We Need to Win.'"
Transcript. The American Presidency Project, August 1, 2007. http://www
.presidency.ucsb.edu/ws/?pid=77040.

Obama, Barack. "Review of Detention Policy Options." Executive Order No.
13493, 74 Federal Register 16 (January 27, 2009). https://www.hsdl
.org/?abstract&did=232168.

Obama, Barack. "Text of Obama's Statement on the Economy." NBC News,
November 7, 2008. http://www.nbcnews.com/id/27597283/ns/politics
-decision_08/t/text-obamas-statement-economy/#.WoFEsJPwbXE.

Obama, Barack. "Text of President Obama's Address to Congress." ABC
    News, September 9, 2009. http://abcnews.go.com/Politics/HealthCare
    /transcript-president-obama-address-joint-congress-health-care
    /story?id=8527252.

Obama, Barack. "Transcript: 'This Is Your Victory,' Says Obama." CNN
    Politics, November 4, 2008. http://edition.cnn.com/2008
    /POLITICS/11/04/obama.transcript.

"Obama for America: New Obama Ad Attacks Mitt Romney's '47%' Speech."
    YouTube video (0:33), posted by "NewsStew," September 27, 2012. https://
    www.youtube.com/watch?v=2znAdnTLmFw.

"Obama Foreign Policy Speech." C-SPAN video (40:39), August 1, 2007.
    https://www.c-span.org/video/?200258-1/obama-foreign-policy-speech.

"Obama Gets Personal in Health Care Town Hall Meeting." CNN Politics,
    August 15, 2009. http://www.cnn.com/2009/POLITICS/08/15/obama
    .health.care/index.html.

"Obama: If I Had a Son He'd Look Like Trayvon Martin." YouTube video
    (1:38), posted by CBS News, March 23, 2012. https://www.youtube.com
    /watch?v=Yt_g5JPdP8Y.

"Obama Iowa Victory." C-SPAN video (15:18), January 3, 2008. https://
    www.c-span.org/video/?203210-1/obama-iowa-victory.

"Obama Launches 'My Brother's Keeper' to Help Young Minority Men."
    Yahoo News, February 27, 2014. https://www.yahoo.com/news/obama
    -launches--my-brother-s-keeper--to-help-young-minority-men
    -025659695.html.

"Obama Leaving the Hilton Chicago." YouTube video (2:11), posted by
    "dancingstripes11," November 7, 2008. https://www.youtube.com
    /watch?v=GoYrK2qWvE4.

"Obama Transition Team Comes To Downtown DC." *Penn Quarter Living*, November 7, 2008. http://pqliving.com/obama-transition-team-hq-in-pq.

"Obama Victory Speech." C-SPAN video (18:17), November 2, 2004. https://www.c-span.org/video/?184268-14/obama-victory-speech.

Office of Senator John Hoeven. "Senate Passes Hoeven-Corker Amendment with Overwhelming Support." Office of Senator John Hoeven, June 26, 2013. https://www.hoeven.senate.gov/news/news-releases /senate-passes-hoeven-corker-amendment-with-overwhelming-support.

Office of Senator Sherrod Brown. "Brown, Kaufman File Amendment On Too Big To Fail Legislation." Office of Senator Sherrod Brown, April 29, 2010. https://www.brown.senate.gov/newsroom/press/release /brown-kaufman-file-amendment-on-too-big-to-fail-legislation.

Office of Senator Sherrod Brown "Sens. Brown, Kaufman Announce New Bill to Prevent Mega-Banks from Placing Our Economy at Risk." Office of Senator Sherrod Brown, April 21, 2010. https://www.brown.senate .gov/newsroom/press/release/sens-brown-kaufman-announce-new-bill -to-prevent-mega-banks-from-placing-our-economy-at-risk.

Office of the Speaker of the House. "Full Text: Boehner's Speech to the Opening Session of the 112th Congress." Speaker Ryan's Press Office, January 5, 2011. https://www.speaker.gov/speech /full-text-boehners-speech-opening-session-112th-congress.

O'Keefe, Ed, and Craig Whitlock. "New Bill Introduced to End 'Don't Ask, Don't Tell.'" *Washington Post*, December 11, 2010. http://www .washingtonpost.com/wp-dyn/content/article/2010/12/10 /AR2010121007163.html.

Olson, Scott, and Getty Images. "President-Elect Obama Meets with the Transition Economic Advisory Boar[d]." Zimbio, November 7, 2008.

http://www.zimbio.com/pictures/MGXGxJxKxwT/President+Elect
+Obama+Meets+Transition+Economic/oViiN5UvTEF.

Osborn, Kris. "Syria Draws Tomahawk Missiles Back into Spotlight." Military.
    com, August 29, 2013. https://www.military.com/daily-news/2013/08/29
    /syria-draws-tomahawk-missiles-back-into-spotlight.html.

"Over 300 in Winterset for Grassley 'Town Hall.'" RadioIowa,
    August 12, 2009. https://www.radioiowa.com/2009/08/12
    /over-300-in-winterset-for-grassley-town-hall.

Paletta, Damian, and Matt Phillips. "S&P Strips US of Top Credit Rating."
    Wall Street Journal, August 6, 2011. https://www.wsj.com/articles
    /SB10001424053111903366504576490841235575386.

Palmer, Karen S. "A Brief History: Universal Health Care Efforts in the US."
    Physicians for a National Health Program, spring 1999. http://www.pnhp
    .org/facts/a-brief-history-universal-health-care-efforts-in-the-us.

Parker, Ashley. "'Corporations Are People,' Romney Tells Iowa Hecklers
    Angry over His Tax Policy." *New York Times*, August 11, 2011. http://www
    .nytimes.com/2011/08/12/us/politics/12romney.html.

Parker, Steve. "Even After $14 Billion in TARP Money, Detroit's on
    Life-Support." Huffington Post, February 7, 2009. https://www
    .huffingtonpost.com/steve-parker/even-after-14-billion-in_b_156158.html.

Parsons, Christi, and Andrew Zajac. "Senate Committee Scraps Healthcare
    Provision That Gave Rise to 'Death Panel' Claims." *Los Angeles Times*,
    August 14, 2009. http://articles.latimes.com/2009/aug/14/nation
    /na-health-end-of-life14.

Pear, Robert. "Obama to Ask for $1.2 Trillion Increase in Debt Limit." *New
    York Times*, December 27, 2011. http://www.nytimes.com/2011/12/28/us
    /politics/obama-to-ask-for-1-2-trillion-increase-in-debt-limit.html.

Pew Research Center. "Why Own a Gun? Protection Is Now Top Reason: Perspectives of Gun Owners, Non-Owners." Pew Research Center, March 12, 2013. http://www.people-press.org/2013/03/12 /why-own-a-gun-protection-is-now-top-reason.

Pickler, Nedra. "Fallon Named Obama Legislative Affairs Director." *San Diego Union-Tribune*, December 13, 2013. http://www.sandiegouniontribune .com/sdut-fallon-named-obama-legislative-affairs-director-2013dec13-story .html.

"PM Netanyahu Meets US Sec of State John Kerry." YouTube video (7:57), posted by Prime Minister of Israel, November 6, 2013. https://www .youtube.com/watch?v=O8oilc_qAok.

Porter, Henry. "Witnessing History in Chicago's Grant Park." *Vanity Fair*, November 2008. https://www.vanityfair.com/news/2008/11 /witnessing-history-in-chicagos-grant-park.

"President-Elect Barack Obama Holds First Press Conference." YouTube video (18:53), posted by C-SPAN, November 7, 2008. https://www.youtube .com/watch?v=R9VcS-EF7To.

"Presidential Health Care Address." C-SPAN video (52:02), September 9, 2009. https://www.c-span.org/video/?288799-1 /presidential-health-care-address.

"Presidential Health Care Town Hall Meeting." C-SPAN video (1:10:30), August 15, 2009. https://www.c-span.org/video/?288390-1/presidential -health-care-town-hall-meeting&start=1609. [Relevant segment at 25:47.]

"Presidential News Conference." C-SPAN video (56:24), July 22, 2009. https://www.c-span.org/video/?287910-2/presidential-news-conference.

"Presidential Remarks on Jobs and the Economy." C-SPAN video (27:53), July
    15, 2010. https://www.c-span.org/video/?294569-1/presidential-remarks
    -jobs-economy. [Relevant segment at 22:11.]

"Presidential Remarks on the Economy." C-SPAN video (1:02:51), December
    6, 2011. https://www.c-span.org/video/?303034-1/presidential-remarks
    -economy&start=726. [Relevant segment at 12:11.]

"Presidential Remarks on the US Automotive Industry." C-SPAN video
    (19:11), March 30, 2009. https://www.c-span.org/video/?284971-2
    /presidential-remarks-us-automotive-industry.

"President Obama ABC News Interview on Same-Sex Marriage." C-SPAN
    video (1:12), May 9, 2012. https://www.c-span.org/video/?305933-1
    /president-obama-abc-news-interview-marriage.

"President Obama Campaign Rally in Roanoke." C-SPAN video (2:11), July
    13, 2012. https://www.c-span.org/video/?c3840411/obama-july-13-2012.

"President Obama Eulogy at Clementa Pinckney Funeral Service." C-SPAN
    video (37:57), June 26, 2015. https://www.c-span.org/video/?c4542228
    /president-obama-eulogy-clementa-pinckney-funeral-service. [Relevant
    segment at 8:32.]

"President Obama Holds a News Conference." YouTube video (21:59), posted
    by the Obama White House, August 20, 2012. https://youtu.be
    /PBRqRl6RbDM. [Relevant segment at 20:16.]

"President Obama Makes a Statement on the Shooting in Newtown,
    Connecticut." YouTube video (3:57), posted by the Obama White House,
    December 14, 2012. https://www.youtube.com/watch?v=mIAoW69U2_Y.

"President Obama on Death of Osama bin Laden." YouTube video (9:27),
    posted by the Obama White House, May 1, 2011. https://youtu.be
    /ZNYmK19-doU.

"President Obama on Fiscal Cliff Negotiations." C-SPAN video (10:48), December 31, 2012. https://www.c-span.org/video/?310137-1/president-obama-fiscal-cliff-negotiations.

"President Obama on His Birth Certificate & the Real Issues Facing America." YouTube video (5:21), posted by the Obama White House, April 27, 2011. https://www.youtube.com/watch?feature=player_embedded&v=bnYJI4QTpXs.

"President Obama Speaks at Newtown High School." YouTube video (18:04), posted by the Obama White House, December 17, 2012. https://www.youtube.com/watch?v=gfaYUrgcCrY.

"President Obama Speech to Muslim World in Cairo." YouTube video (58:40), posted by C-SPAN, June 4, 2009. https://www.youtube.com/watch?v=B_8890BKkNU.

"President Obama Statement on Immigration Policy." C-SPAN video (9:08), June 15, 2012. https://www.c-span.org/video/?306620-2/president-obama-statement-immigration-policy.

"The President Speaks on the Supreme Court's Decision on Marriage Equality." YouTube video (9:04), posted by the Obama White House, June 26, 2015. https://www.youtube.com/watch?v=b715GKJNWXA.

Preston, Julia. "House Backs Legal Status for Many Young Immigrants." *New York Times*, December 8, 2010. http://www.nytimes.com/2010/12/09/us/politics/09immig.html.

"Profile: Umar Farouk Abdulmutallab." BBC News, October 12, 2011. http://www.bbc.com/news/world-us-canada-11545509.

Public Broadcasting Service. "The Card Game." *Frontline,* November 24, 2009. https://www.pbs.org/wgbh/pages/frontline/creditcards.

Raju, Manu. "Death Leaves Committee Vacancy." *Politico*, August
26, 2009. https://www.politico.com/story/2009/08
/death-leaves-committee-vacancy-026454.

Ramirez, Eddy. "How to Spend $100 Billion on Education." *US News & World
Report*, February 18, 2009. https://web.archive.org/web/20090307092555
/https://www.usnews.com/blogs/on-education/2009/2/18
/how-to-spend-100-billion-on-education.

Rampton, Roberta, and Jeff Mason. "Obama's Syria Decision: A Walk, a
Debate, and a New Approach." Reuters, August 31, 2013. https://www
.reuters.com/article/us-syria-crisis-obama
-decision-idUSBRE98001520130901.

Rattner, Steven. *Overhaul: An Insider's Account of the Obama Administration's
Emergency Rescue of the Auto Industry.* New York: Houghton Mifflin
Harcourt, 2010.

"Reactions from Around the World." *New York Times*, November
5, 2008. https://thecaucus.blogs.nytimes.com/2008/11/05
/reactions-from-around-the-world/.

Real Time with Bill Maher, Season 11, episode 292. Panel: Josh Barro, Barney
Frank, Alexis Goldstein (OWS), Jay-Z, Larry Miller. Aired August 2, 2013.
http://www.imdb.com/title/tt3071528/fullcredits.

"'Rectal Hydration': Inside the CIA's Interrogation of Khalid Sheikh
Mohammed." NBC News, December 9, 2014. https://www.nbcnews.com
/storyline/cia-torture-report/rectal-hydration-inside-cias-interrogation
-khalid-sheikh-mohammed-n265016.

Republican National Committee. "Growth & Opportunity Project." The
Growth & Opportunity Project, March 18, 2013. https://www
.washingtonpost.com/news/post-politics/wp/2013/03/18
/the-full-rnc-growth-and-opportunity-project-report.

Reuters. "Lockerbie Settlement." *New York Times*, August 14, 2003. http://
www.nytimes.com/2003/08/14/world/lockerbie-settlement.html.

"Rev. Jeremiah Wright 'Confusing God and Government' April 13, 2003."
Vimeo audio (38:50), posted by David A. Morse, April 13, 2003. https://
vimeo.com/42601818. [Relevant segment at 34:19.]

Richter, Paul. "Key, Secret Concessions Opened the Way for Iran Nuclear
Deal." *Los Angeles Times*, July 14, 2015. http://www.latimes.com/world
/middleeast/la-fg-iran-saga-20150713-story.html.

Riley, Charles. "Obama's Census Form—Signed, Sealed, Delivered." CNN
Politics, April 3, 2010. http://politicalticker.blogs.cnn.com/2010/04/03
/obamas-census-form-signed-sealed-delivered.

Riley, Charles. "Super Committee: Who Are These Guys?" CNN Money,
August 11, 2011. http://money.cnn.com/2011/08/11/news/economy
/debt_committee_members/index.htm.

Roberts, Christine. "Michele Bachmann, GOP Congresswoman, on 2012
Presidential Race: 'I've Had That Calling.'" *New York Daily News,* May 31,
2011. http://www.nydailynews.com/news/politics/michele-bachmann
-gop-congresswoman-2012-presidential-race-calling-article-1.142302.

Roberts, Michael. "Budget Control Act of 2011." Balance, March 10, 2017.
https://www.thebalance.com/budget-control-act-of-2011-1669442.

Robles, Frances, and Julie Hirschfeld Davis. "US Frees Last of the 'Cuban
Five,' Part of a 1990s Spy Ring." *New York Times*, December 17, 2014.
https://www.nytimes.com/2014/12/18/world/americas/us-frees-last-of-the
-cuban-five-part-of-a-1990s-spy-ring-.html.

Romer, Christina, and Jared Bernstein. *The Job Impact of the American Recovery
and Reinvestment Plan.* January 2, 2009. https://web.archive

.org/web/20090121095209/https://otrans.3cdn.net/45593e8ecbd339d074
_l3m6btite.pdf.

"Romney: 'I'm Not Going to Wear Rose-Colored Glasses When it Comes to
Russia.'" YouTube video (0:28), posted by ABC News, October 22, 2012.
https://www.youtube.com/watch?v=01A2N5aWA6E.

Rosenthal, Jack. "A Terrible Thing to Waste." *New York Times Magazine,*
July 31, 2009. http://www.nytimes.com/2009/08/02/magazine/02FOB
-onlanguage-t.html.

Rovner, Julie. "Abortion Funding Ban Has Evolved Over the Years." *Morning
Edition*, National Public Radio, December 14, 2009. https://www.npr.org
/templates/story/story.php?storyId=121402281.

Roy, Avik. "The Tortuous History of Conservatives and the Individual
Mandate." *Forbes*, February 7, 2012. https://www.forbes.com/sites
/theapothecary/2012/02/07/the-tortuous-conservative-history-of-the
-individual-mandate/#3bd4759655fe.

Ruger, Todd, John Council, and John Pacenti. "Obama Names Record
Number of Gay Federal Judges." *National Law Journal*, July 21, 2014.
https://www.law.com/nationallawjournal/almID/1202663836700.

Saad, Lydia. "New Low of 26% Approve of Obama on the Economy." Gallup
News, August 17, 2011. http://news.gallup.com/poll/149042/new-low
-approve-obama-economy.aspx.

"Samantha Power '99 to Join National Security Council." *Harvard
Law Today*, January 30, 2009. https://today.law.harvard.edu
/samantha-power-99-to-join-national-security-council.

Samuelsohn, Darren. "Giuliani: Obama Doesn't Love America." *Politico*,
February 18, 2015. https://www.politico.com/story/2015/02
/rudy-giuliani-president-obama-doesnt-love-america-115309.

"Sandy Hook Shooting: What Happened?" CNN.com, December 14, 2012. http://www.cnn.com/interactive/2012/12/us/sandy-hook-timeline/index .html.

Sanger, David E. "Gingrich Threatens US Default If Clinton Won't Bend on Budget." *New York Times*, September 22, 1995. http://www.nytimes .com/1995/09/22/business/gingrich-threatens-us-default-if-clinton-won -t-bend-on-budget.html.

Sanger, David E., and Charlie Savage. "US Says Russia Directed Hacks to Influence Elections." *New York Times*, October 7, 2016. https://www .nytimes.com/2016/10/08/us/politics/us-formally-accuses-russia-of -stealing-dnc-emails.html.

Sargent, Greg. "The Odds of an Iran Nuclear Deal Just Got Better." *Washington Post*, May 7, 2015. https://www.washingtonpost.com/blogs /plum-line/wp/2015/05/07/the-odds-of-an-iran-nuclear-deal-just -got-higher.

Savage, Charlie. "Accused 9/11 Mastermind to Face Civilian Trial in NY." *New York Times*, November 13, 2009. http://www.nytimes.com/2009/11/14 /us/14terror.html.

Scarborough, Rowan. "US Troop Withdrawal Let Islamic State Enter Iraq, Military Leaders Say." *Washington Times*, July 26, 2015. https://www .washingtontimes.com/news/2015/jul/26 /us-troop-withdrawal-let-islamic-state-enter-iraq-m.

Scheiber, Noam. "Exclusive: The Memo that Larry Summers Didn't Want Obama to See." *New Republic*, February 21, 2012. https://newrepublic .com/article/100961/memo-larry-summers-obama.

Schelzig, Erik. "Democratic US Rep. John Tanner Says He's Retiring." *San Diego Union-Tribune*, December 1, 2009. http://www.sandiegouniontribune

.com/sdut-democratic-us-rep-john-tanner-says-hes-retiring-2009dec01
-story.html.

Schmidle, Nicholas. "Getting bin Laden." *New Yorker*, August 8, 2011. https://
www.newyorker.com/magazine/2011/08/08/getting-bin-laden.

Schmitt, Eric. "Obama Issues Order for More Troops in Afghanistan." *New
York Times*, November 30, 2009. http://www.nytimes.com/2009/12/01
/world/asia/01orders.html.

Schor, Elana. "Barack Obama's Economic Advisers." *Guardian*, November 24,
2008. https://www.theguardian.com/world/2008/nov/24
/obama-white-house-economy.

Schor, Elana. "Mark Penn's Campaign Blunders." *Guardian*, April 7, 2008.
https://www.theguardian.com/world/2008/apr/07/hillaryclinton
.uselections20081.

Scott, Eugene. "Nikki Haley: Confederate Flag 'Should Have Never Been
There.'" CNN Politics, July 10, 2015. https://www.cnn.com/2015/07/10
/politics/nikki-haley-confederate-flag-removal/index.html.

"Secretary Kerry Remarks on Middle East Peace." C-SPAN video (1:14:24),
December 28, 2016. https://www.c-span.org/video/?420776-1
/secretary-state-kerry-state-solution-path-middle-east-peace.

"Senate Report Finds CIA Interrogation Tactics Were Ineffective." NBC News,
December 9, 2014. https://www.nbcnews.com/storyline/cia-torture-report
/senate-report-finds-cia-interrogation-tactics-were-ineffective-n264621.

Seselja, Edwina, and Jessica Haynes. "Barack Obama's Most Noteworthy
Speeches." Australian Broadcasting Corporation, January 10, 2017. http://
www.abc.net.au/news/2017-01-11/barack-obamas-best-speeches/8172738.

Sfondeles, Tina. "Emanuel Shrugs Off Criticism after Being Mentioned in DNC Video." *Chicago Sun-Times*, July 28, 2016. https://chicago.suntimes .com/news/rahm-shrugs-off-criticism-after-featured-in-dnc-video.

Silverleib, Alan, and Tom Cohen. "Obama Signs Debt Ceiling Bill, Ends Crisis." CNN Politics, August 2, 2011. http://www.cnn.com/2011 /POLITICS/08/02/debt.talks/index.html.

Sisk, Richard. "New President Barack Obama Jumps in on Mideast and Stirs a Phone Flap." *New York Daily News*, January 21, 2009. http://www .nydailynews.com/news/politics/new-president-barack-obama-jumps -mideast-stirs-phone-flap-article-1.422639.

Slajda, Rachel. "Teabaggers Try to Shout Down Health Care Reform at Town Halls." Talking Points Memo, August 3, 2009. https://talkingpointsmemo .com/dc/teabaggers-try-to-shout-down-health-care-reform-at-town-halls.

Smith, Ben, and Byron Tau. "Birtherism: Where It All Began." *Politico*, April 22, 2011. https://www.politico.com/story/2011/04 /birtherism-where-it-all-began-053563.

Smith, Emily. "Timeline of the Health Care Law." CNN Politics, June 28, 2012. http://www.cnn.com/2012/06/28/politics/supreme-court-health -timeline/index.html.

Smith, Helena. "Greek Socialists Achieve Resounding Win in Snap Election." *Guardian*, October 5, 2009. https://www.theguardian.com/world/2009 /oct/05/pasok-wins-snap-greek-poll.

Sonmez, Felicia. "Senate Republican Filibuster Blocks Obama DC Circuit Nominee Caitlin Halligan." *Washington Post*, December 6, 2011. https:// www.washingtonpost.com/blogs/2chambers/post/senate-republican -filibuster-blocks-obama-dc-circuit-nominee-caitlin-halligan/2011/12/06 /gIQAtp6nZO_blog.html.

"Speaker Boehner's Remarks to the Opening Session of the 112th Congress."
    YouTube video (12:41), posted by Speaker John Boehner, January 5, 2011.
    https://www.youtube.com/watch?v=N3LggDTCTUE.

Stanglin, Doug. "Frontier to Remove Carpet, Seat Covers in Ebola Plane."
    USA Today, October 16, 2014. https://www.usatoday.com/story/news
    /nation/2014/10/16/frontier-airlines-ebola-amber-vinson/17366797.

Starr, Terrell Jermaine. "The Air Force Is Retiring the
    Predator Drone for the More Deadly Reaper." Jalopnik,
    February 28, 2017. https://foxtrotalpha.jalopnik.com
    /the-air-force-is-retiring-the-predator-drone-for-the-mo-1792832541.

Stelter, Brian. "The Facebooker Who Friended Obama." *New York Times*, July
    7, 2008. http://www.nytimes.com/2008/07/07/technology/07hughes
    .html.

Stolberg, Sheryl Gay, Carl Hulse, and Jeff Zeleny. "Health Vote Caps a
    Journey Back From the Brink." *New York Times*, March 20, 2010. http://
    www.nytimes.com/2010/03/21/health/policy/21reconstruct.html.

Stratford, Michael. "Obamas' Own Student Debt Topped $40,000 Each."
    Inside Higher Ed, August 27, 2013. https://www.insidehighered.com
    /quicktakes/2013/08/27/obamas-own-student-debt-topped-40000-each.

Strauss, Valerie. "Education Activists Seek to Collaborate with Occupy Wall
    Street." *Washington Post*, October 15, 2011. https://www.washingtonpost
    .com/blogs/answer-sheet/post/education-activists-seek-to-collaborate
    -with-occupy-wall-street/2011/10/15/gIQAbrDZmL_blog.html.

Subramanian, Ram, Ruth Delaney, Stephen Roberts, Nancy Fishman, and
    Peggy McGarry. *Incarceration's Front Door: The Misuse of Jails in America*.
    Center on Sentencing and Corrections, VERA Institute of Justice,
    February 2015. http://www.safetyandjusticechallenge.org/wp-content
    /uploads/2015/01/incarcerations-front-door-report.pdf.

Supreme Court of the United States. "Syllabus: *National Federation of Independent Business et al. v. Sebelius, Secretary of Health and Human Services, et al.* Certiorari to the United States Court of Appeals for the Eleventh Circuit." Supreme Court of the United States, June 28, 2012. https://www.supremecourt.gov/opinions/11pdf/11-393c3a2.pdf.

Supreme Court Review. "The Justices of the United States Supreme Court." Supreme Court Review. Last accessed February 9, 2018. http://supremecourtreview.com/default/justice.

Tapper, Jake. "Leaker of Stimulus Memo Uncovered?" ABC News, February 23, 2012. https://web.archive.org/web/20120225173615/http://abcnews.go.com/blogs/politics/2012/02/leaker-of-stimulus-memo-uncovered.

TeachingAmericanHistory.org. "Progressive Party Platform of 1912." TeachingAmericanHistory.org. Last accessed February 9, 2018. http://teachingamericanhistory.org/library/document/progressive-platform-of-1912.

"Timeline: Auto Industry in Crisis." Reuters, May 1, 2009. https://www.reuters.com/article/us-autos-crisis-sb/timeline-auto-industry-in-crisis-idUSTRE5402PG20090501.

"Timeline of Retiring D-Sen. Max Baucus." *Montana Standard*, February 9, 2014. http://mtstandard.com/timeline-of-retiring-d-sen-max-baucus/article_9fad48c0-912e-11e3-b130-0019bb2963f4.html.

Todd, Chuck. "The White House Walk-and-Talk That Changed Obama's Mind on Syria." NBC News, August 31, 2013. https://www.nbcnews.com/news/other/white-house-walk-talk-changed-obamas-mind-syria-f8C11051182.

Toppo, Greg. "American Jailed for 5 years in Cuba Made Little Attempt to Disguise His Work." *USA Today*, November 29, 2015. https://www

.usatoday.com/story/news/2015/11/29/alan-gross-cuba-prison-60
-minutes/76536660.

"TPP: What Is It and Why Does It Matter?" BBC News, January 23, 2017.
http://www.bbc.com/news/business-32498715.

Twin, Alexandra. "Stocks Crushed." CNN Money, September 29, 2008.
http://money.cnn.com/2008/09/29/markets/markets_newyork.

"UK Says 'No' to Syria Strikes as Cameron Loses Vote in Parliament."
YouTube video (1:30), posted by Euronews, August 29, 2013. https://www
.youtube.com/watch?v=LJoOiDoosjM.

"'Underwear Bomber' Sues Feds over Prison Treatment." CBS News, October
20, 2017. https://www.cbsnews.com/news/umar-farouk-abdulmutallab
-underwear-bomber-sues-feds-over-prison-treatment.

United Nations. *Paris Agreement*. United Nations Framework Convention on
Climate Change, December 12, 2015. http://unfccc.int/files/essential
_background/convention/application/pdf/english_paris_agreement.pdf.

United Nations. "Oceans and the Law of the Sea." United Nations. Last
accessed February 9, 2018. http://www.un.org/en/sections/issues-depth
/oceans-and-law-sea/.

United Nations Security Council. "Israel's Settlements Have No Legal
Validity, Constitute Flagrant Violation of International Law, Security
Council Reaffirms." United Nations, December 23, 2016. https://www
.un.org/press/en/2016/sc12657.doc.htm.

United Nations. "Status of Ratification of the Convention." United Nations
Framework Convention on Climate Change, May 9, 1992. http://unfccc
.int/essential_background/convention/status_of_ratification/items/2631
.php.

United States Census Bureau. "2010 Overview." United States Census Bureau. Last accessed February 9, 2018. https://www.census.gov/history/www /through_the_decades/overview/2010_overview_1.html.

United States Congress. "SA 3733." Senate Amendment. *Congressional Record*, April 28, 2010. https://www.congress.gov/crec/2010/04/28/CREC-2010 -04-28-pt1-PgS2765.pdf.

United States Department of Energy. "Revolution Now: The Future Arrives for Five Clean Energy Technologies—2016 Update." United States Department of Energy, September 2016. https://www.energy.gov/sites /prod/files/2016/09/f33/Revolutiona%CC%82%E2%82%ACNow%20 2016%20Report_2.pdf.

United States Department of Health and Human Services. "CMS Roadmaps Overview." Centers for Medicare & Medicaid Services. Last accessed February 9, 2018. https://www.cms.gov/Medicare/Quality-Initiatives -Patient-Assessment-Instruments/QualityInitiativesGenInfo/Downloads /RoadmapOverview_OEA_1-16.pdf.

United States Department of Homeland Security. "Exercising Prosecutorial Discretion with Respect to Individuals Who Came to the United States as Children." Memorandum from Secretary of Homeland Security Janet Napolitano to David V. Aguilar (Acting Commissioner, US Customs and Border Protection), Alejandro Mayorkas (Director, US Citizenship and Immigration Services), and John Morton (Director, US Immigration and Customs Enforcement), June 15, 2012. https://www.dhs.gov/xlibrary /assets/s1-exercising-prosecutorial-discretion-individuals-who-came-to-us -as-children.pdf.

United States Department of Homeland Security. "Joint Statement from the Department Of Homeland Security and Office of the Director of National Intelligence on Election Security." United States Department of Homeland Security Archives, October 7, 2016. https://www.dhs.gov

/news/2016/10/07/joint-statement-department
-homeland-security-and-office-director-national.

United States Department of Justice. "Assistant Attorney General Lanny A.
Breuer Speaks at the New York City Bar Association." Office of Public
Affairs, September 13, 2012. https://www.justice.gov/opa/speech/assistant
-attorney-general-lanny-breuer-speaks-new-york-city-bar-association.

United States Department of Justice. "Attorney General
Appoints Gary G. Grindler Chief of Staff." Office of Public
Affairs, January 3, 2011. https://www.justice.gov/opa/pr
/attorney-general-appoints-gary-g-grindler-chief-staff.

United States Department of Justice. *Audit of the Department of Justice's
Efforts to Address Mortgage Fraud.* Audit Division, Office of the Inspector
General, March 2014. https://oig.justice.gov/reports/2014/a1412.pdf.

United States Department of Justice. "The Fair Sentencing Act of 2010."
Memo from Acting Deputy Attorney General Gary G. Grindler to all
federal prosecutors, August 5, 2010. https://www.justice.gov/sites/default
/files/oip/legacy/2014/07/23/fair-sentencing-act-memo.pdf.

United States Department of Justice. "Former Deputy Attorney General
James Cole." United States Department of Justice Archives. Updated
February 14, 2017. https://www.justice.gov/archives/dag/staff-profile
/former-deputy-attorney-general-james-cole.

United States Department of Justice. "Memorandum for the Attorney
General Re: Applicability of Federal Criminal Laws and the Constitution
to Contemplated Lethal Operations Against Shaykh Anwar al-Aulaqi."
Office of Legal Counsel, July 16, 2010. https://fas.org/irp/agency/doj/olc
/aulaqi.pdf.

United States Department of Justice. "Statement of Interest of the United
States: *David Floyd, et al. v. The City Of New York, et al.*" United States

District Court, Southern District Of New York, June 12, 2013. https://
www.justice.gov/sites/default/files/crt/legacy/2013/06/13/floyd_soi_6-12-13
.pdf.

United States Department of Labor. "The Employment Situation: February
2009." Bureau of Labor Statistics, March 6, 2009. https://www.bls.gov
/news.release/archives/empsit_03062009.pdf.

United States Department of Labor. "The Employment Situation—September
2011." Bureau of Labor Statistics, October 7, 2011. https://www.bls.gov
/news.release/archives/empsit_10072011.pdf.

United States Department of Labor. "Local Area Unemployment Statistics:
Michigan." Bureau of Labor Statistics. Data last extracted February 9,
2018. https://data.bls.gov/timeseries/LASST26000000000003.

United States Department of State. "Travel to Seoul, Beijing, Jakarta, Abu
Dhabi, Tunis, and Paris, February 13–20, 2014." United States Department
of State Archives. Last accessed February 9, 2018. https://2009-2017.state
.gov/secretary/travel/2014/t5/index.htm.

United States Environmental Protection Agency. "Reducing
Hydrofluorocarbon (HFC) Use and Emissions in the Federal Sector
through SNAP." United States Environmental Protection Agency. Last
accessed February 9, 2018. https://www.epa.gov/snap/reducing
-hydrofluorocarbon-hfc-use-and-emissions-federal-sector-through-snap.

United States House of Representatives. "Final Vote Results for Roll Call 342."
Office of the Clerk, September 14, 2001. http://clerk.house.gov/evs/2001
/roll342.xml#N.

United States Institute of Peace. "Iran by the Numbers: Economy." The Iran
Primer, May 25, 2016. http://iranprimer.usip.org/blog/2016/may/25
/iran-numbers-economy.

United States Institute of Peace. "Khamenei: Red Lines on Nuclear Deal." The
    Iran Primer, June 23, 2015. http://iranprimer.usip.org/blog/2015/jun/23
    /khamenei-red-lines-nuclear-deal.

United States Nuclear Regulatory Commission. "Uranium Enrichment."
    United States Nuclear Regulatory Commission, August 2, 2017. https://
    www.nrc.gov/materials/fuel-cycle-fac/ur-enrichment.html.

University of New Hampshire Survey Center. "CNN/WMUR Poll." CNN,
    June 15, 2007. http://i.a.cnn.net/cnn/2007/images/06/15/june.poll.pdf.
    [Primary voters were asked, "Which Democratic candidate do you think
    is the strongest leader?" Answers: Clinton 48 percent, Obama 12 percent.]

Urbina, Ian. "Beyond Beltway, Health Debate Turns Hostile." *New York
    Times*, August 7, 2009. http://www.nytimes.com/2009/08/08/us
    /politics/08townhall.html.

Valdes-Dapena, Peter. "Cars That Wrecked Chrysler." CNN Money, June 10,
    2009. http://money.cnn.com/galleries/2009/autos/0904/gallery.chrysler
    _trouble/index.html.

Wallsten, Peter, Lori Montgomery, and Scott Wilson. "Obama's Evolution:
    Behind the Failed 'Grand Bargain' on the Debt." *Washington Post*, March
    17, 2012. https://www.washingtonpost.com/politics/obamas-evolution
    -behind-the-failed-grand-bargain-on-the-debt/2012/03/15/gIQAHyyfJS
    _story.html.

"Walter Cronkite Memorial Service." C-SPAN video (2:21:18),
    September 9, 2009. https://www.c-span.org/video/?288808-1
    /walter-cronkite-memorial-service.

"*Washington Post*–ABC News Poll." *Washington Post*, June 4, 2007. http://
    www.washingtonpost.com/wp-srv/politics/polls/postpoll_060307.html.

Watt, Nicholas, and Nick Hopkins. "Cameron Forced to Rule Out British Attack on Syria after MPs Reject Motion." *Guardian*, August 29, 2013. https://www.theguardian.com/world/2013/aug/29 /cameron-british-attack-syria-mps.

Weisman, Jonathan. "GOP Doubts, Fears 'Post-Partisan' Obama." *Washington Post*, January 7, 2008. http://www.washingtonpost.com/wp-dyn/content /article/2008/01/06/AR2008010602402.html.

White House. *2009 Annual Report to Congress on White House Staff*. Washington, DC: President Obama White House Archives, 2009. https://obamawhitehouse.archives.gov/briefing-room/disclosures /annual-records/2009.

White House. *2010 Annual Report to Congress on White House Staff*. Washington, DC: President Obama White House Archives, 2010. https:// obamawhitehouse.archives.gov/briefing-room/disclosures /annual-records/2010.

White House. *2011 Annual Report to Congress on White House Staff*. Washington, DC: President Obama White House Archives, 2011. https:// obamawhitehouse.archives.gov/briefing-room/disclosures /annual-records/2011.

White House. *2012 Annual Report to Congress on White House Staff*. Washington, DC: President Obama White House Archives, 2012. https:// obamawhitehouse.archives.gov/briefing-room/disclosures /annual-records/2012.

White House. *2013 Annual Report to Congress on White House Staff*. Washington, DC: President Obama White House Archives, 2013. https:// obamawhitehouse.archives.gov/briefing-room/disclosures /annual-records/2013.

White House. *2014 Annual Report to Congress on White House Staff.*
     Washington, DC: President Obama White House Archives, 2014. https://
     obamawhitehouse.archives.gov/briefing-room/disclosures
     /annual-records/2014.

White House. *2015 Annual Report to Congress on White House Staff.*
     Washington, DC: President Obama White House Archives, 2015. https://
     obamawhitehouse.archives.gov/briefing-room/disclosures
     /annual-records/2015.

White House. *2016 Annual Report to Congress on White House Staff.*
     Washington, DC: President Obama White House Archives, 2016. https://
     obamawhitehouse.archives.gov/briefing-room/disclosures
     /annual-records/2016.

White House. "Administration Announces Nearly $8 Billion in
     Weatherization Funding and Energy Efficiency Grants." President Obama
     White House Archives, March 12, 2009. https://obamawhitehouse
     .archives.gov/the-press-office/administration-announces-nearly-8-billion
     -weatherization-funding-and-energy-efficie.

White House. "Chief of Staff Denis McDonough." President Obama White
     House Archives. Last accessed February 9, 2018. https://obamawhitehouse
     .archives.gov/administration/senior-leadership/denis-mcdonough.

White House. "Read Out of President's Call with Greece's George
     Papandreou." President Obama White House Archives, October 4, 2009.
     https://obamawhitehouse.archives.gov/the-press-office
     /read-out-presidents-call-with-greeces-george-papandreou.

White House. "Remarks by the President during Federal Judicial Appointees
     Announcement, the East Room." President George W. Bush White House
     Archives, May 9, 2001. https://georgewbush-whitehouse.archives.gov
     /news/releases/2001/05/20010509-3.html.

White House. "Remarks by the President on the Economy in Osawatomie, Kansas." President Obama White House Archives, December 6, 2011. https://obamawhitehouse.archives.gov/the-press-office/2011/12/06 /remarks-president-economy-osawatomie-kansas.

White House. "Remarks by the President on Trayvon Martin." President Obama White House Archives, July 19, 2013. https:// obamawhitehouse.archives.gov/the-press-office/2013/07/19 /remarks-president-trayvon-martin.

White House. "Remarks by the President to the White House Press Corps." President Obama White House Archives, August 20, 2012. https://obamawhitehouse.archives.gov/the-press-office/2012/08/20 /remarks-president-white-house-press-corps.

White House. "United States–Canada Joint Arctic Leaders' Statement." President Obama White House Archives, December 20, 2016. https:// obamawhitehouse.archives.gov/the-press-office/2016/12/20 /united-states-canada-joint-arctic-leaders-statement.

White House. "US-China Joint Presidential Statement on Climate Change." President Obama White House Archives, September 25, 2015. https:// obamawhitehouse.archives.gov/the-press-office/2015/09/25 /us-china-joint-presidential-statement-climate-change.

Williams, Roberton C., Leonard E. Burman, Surachai Khitatrakun, Jeff Rohaly, and Eric Toder. "An Updated Analysis of the 2008 Presidential Candidates' Tax Plans." Tax Policy Center, September 12, 2008. http:// www.taxpolicycenter.org/publications/updated-analysis-2008-presidential -candidates-tax-plans-updated-september-12-2008.

Wilson, Scott. "James Jones to Step Down as National Security Advisor." *Washington Post*, October 8, 2010. http://www.washingtonpost.com /wp-dyn/content/article/2010/10/08/AR2010100802953.html.

Wong, Scott, and Shira Toeplitz. "DREAM Act Dies in Senate." *Politico*, December 18, 2010. https://www.politico.com/story/2010/12 /dream-act-dies-in-senate-046573.

Woods, Jeff. "Bredesen Criticizes Obama's Health Care Plan." (Nashville) *City Paper*, September 16, 2009. http://nashvillecitypaper.com/content /city-news/bredesen-criticizes-obamas-health-care-plan.

"YouTube Debate: Would You Meet with Iran/Syria/North Korea?" YouTube video (3:24), posted by PoliticsTV, July 23, 2007. https://www.youtube .com/watch?v=x1dSPrb5w_k.

Zeleny, Jeff, and Patrick Healy. "Obama Shows His Strength in a Fund-Raising Feat on Par With Clinton." *New York Times*, April 5, 2007. http:// www.nytimes.com/2007/04/05/us/politics/05obama.html.

Zeleny, Jeff, and Carl Hulse. "Kennedy Chooses Obama, Spurning Plea by Clintons." *New York Times*, January 28, 2008. http://www.nytimes .com/2008/01/28/us/politics/28kennedy.html.

Zeleny, Jeff, and Jennifer Steinhauer. "Clinton Defeats Obama in Nevada." *New York Times*, January 19, 2008. http://www.nytimes.com/2008/01/19 /us/politics/19cnd-dems.html.

INDEX

Page numbers in *italics* refer to photos. Page numbers followed by "n" refer to notes.

ABOUT THE AUTHOR

Brian Abrams is the author of three bestselling Kindle Singles oral histories: *And NOW . . . An Oral History of Late Night with David Letterman, 1982–1993*; *Gawker: An Oral History*; and *Die Hard: An Oral History*. Abrams has written for the *Washington Post Magazine*, *Time*, and *The Lowbrow Reader*. He lives in New York City. You can visit www.brianlabrams.com for more information and follow the author on Twitter @BrianAbrams.